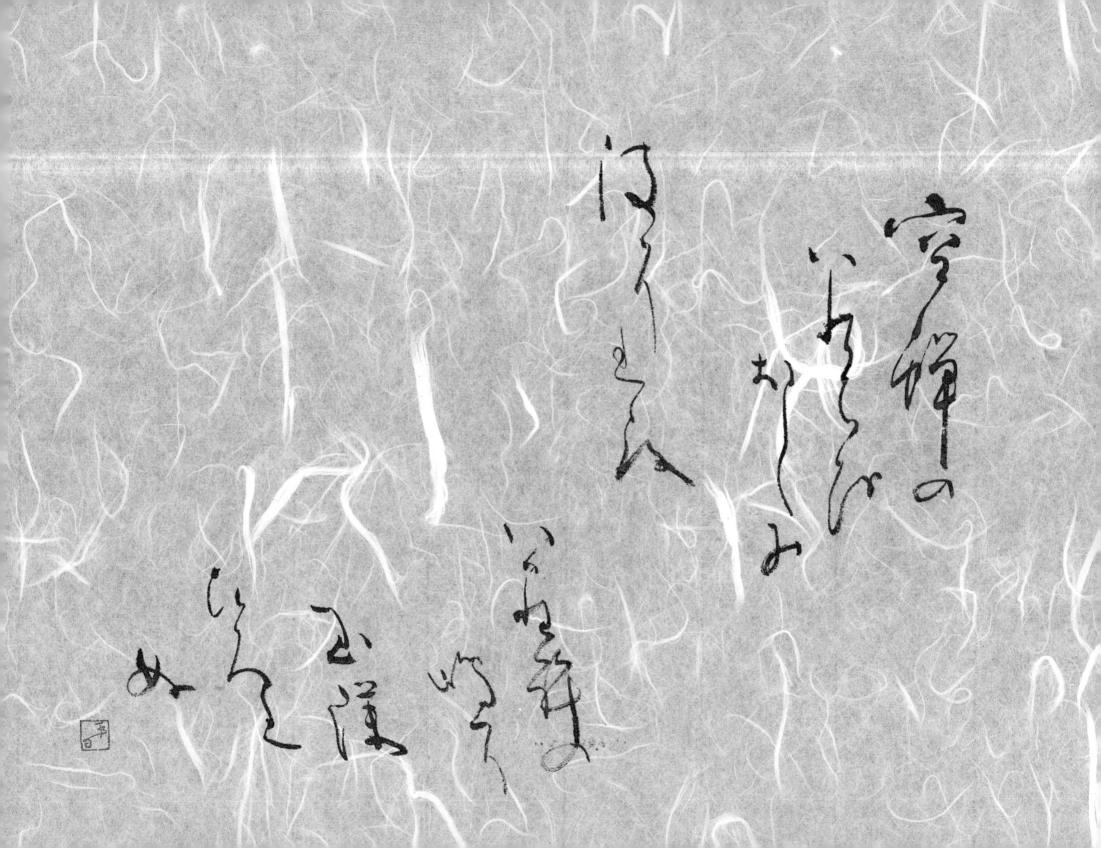

DIAGRAPHICS

JAPAN CREATORS' ASSOCIATION
PRESENTS
THE MOST COMPLETE COLLECTION
OF CREATIVE DIAGRAMS EVER ASSEMBLED

DIAGRAPHICS, a bold, new collection of graphs, charts, tables and other visual renderings, thoroughly explores the highly imaginative world of diagramatic graphics. This unique resource book is designed to be the most complete accumulation of creative diagrams ever assembled. It features some of the world's finest artists and designers and their interpretations of conveying information visually in clear and concise terms, using a minimal amount of words.

The information-laden images featured within DIAGRAPHICS cover a wide spectrum of subject matter, crossing social and intellectual barriers, without being restricted to any geographical area. This diversity of graphs, diagrams and charts reveals the inventive skill and uninhibited imagination utilized by the participating creators. Working with dull and indifferent data, regardless of the subject matter, these innovative designers and artists are able to transform this mundane information into vibrant and attention-getting forms of communication.

As with all other JCA publications, DIAGRAPHICS' two main objectives are to present its featured artists to clients on an international level, and hopefully to spark the imagination of fellow creators. Through these publications and our art agency activities, JCA is striving to unite the millions of creative energies dispersed throughout the world into one power, and then make this power easily accessible to anyone.

CONTENTS

DIAGRAMS IN FOCUS.

Nigel Holmes
Executive Art Director
TIME Magazine, New York City
USA

Holmes on Charts

There is a multitude of numbers flying around our lives. They need to be captured, pinned down, explained, attached to meanings; in short, to be made into <u>information</u>. Unexplained numbers are not information. We mistakenly refer to the "Information Explosion" in the world today, There is no information explosion — it's a numbers explosion, and it falls to designers to turn the numbers into useful information. Unfortunately too few are doing it.

It is fashionable to dress up statistics in order to make them more palatable, more acceptable to a non-specialist audience. This is both desirable and dangerous at the same time.

It is <u>desirable</u> to help readers who may be baffled or bored by a mass of facts. If you can attract them, make them smile perhaps, and get them to <u>see</u> the facts, then you have gone a long way to help-

図表についてのホームズ氏の意見

今、我々の生活の場をめぐって、多くの数字が飛び交っている。これらの数字はつかまえ、固定し、説明し、意味を与えなくてはならない。つまり、情報化しなくてはならないのである。説明されない数字は情報ではない。我々は今日世界における「情報爆発」を誤って説明している。実は情報爆発というものは存在しない。そこにあるのは数字の爆発である。そして、その数字を役に立つ情報に転換するのはデザイナーの責任である。しかし、不幸なことに、それを実行している人は殆どいない。

統計数字を粉飾し、専門家でない一般大衆の気に入られ、受け入れられるようにすることは時代の流れである。だが、それは望ましいことであると同時に危険を伴うことでもある。

DIAGRAMS IN FOCUS.

Nigel Holmes
Executive Art Director
TIME Magazine, New York City
USA

ing them understand the information.

It is <u>dangerous</u> when the method of "attraction" in fact <u>detracts</u> from the data. If the attracting illustration gets in the way of the facts that it is supposed to clarify, it is much worse than no illustration at all. It would be preferable then to present the data in an unadorned way, and to run the risk of being boring. Sometimes chartmakers betray the trust of their readers, and get carried away with a drawing, thus losing sight of their primary role: that of making charts, communicating data.

The best results occur when a perfect marriage of image and statistics shows both partners off equally well. The illustration leads the reader into the numbers by indicating the subject matter. Then it "illustrates" the numbers, either as an abstract idea made concrete (for example: the unemployment rate <u>rockets</u> up; interest rates <u>crash</u> down — accompanied by appropriate images), or it literally is a picture of the subject (baseball statistics with the shape and color of a baseball field as a background).

There are two distinct schools of thought when it comes to the presentation of statistics by any method other than the purely straightforward. A factor that is often omitted by those who side with the unadorned statistic is the medium in which the chart or diagram is displayed. Part of the chartmaker's art is to choose a form for a specific job that correctly corresponds in tone with its surroundings. A highly illustrated chart seems out of place in a learned journal. A plain line drawn on graph paper may be too dry for the fast read expected by newspaper buyers. The only common ground between the two is that both must be <u>correct.</u> As long as <u>accuracy</u> is not forfeited for <u>artistic</u> <u>appearance</u>, then I'm on the side of the illustrated chart, diagram or map.

Having fun with statistics doesn't necessarily mean that the end result has to look "funny". But it certainly shows when the designer has enjoyed doing the work; when care and attention has been taken with the <u>whole</u> job. That means attracting, entertaining, educating, informing, explaining — accurately.

ぼう大な量の事実を前にしてまごついたり、あるいはあきあきしている読者を助けるのは望ましいことだ。もし、読者を引きつけ、彼等の微笑をさそい、事実を知らせることができるならば、それは彼等に情報を理解させる手助けをしたことになる。

注意を引きつける方法が、実際はデータから注意をそらすことになれば危険である。もしも注意を引きつけるためのイラストが、明確にされるべき事実を邪魔するのであれば、それはイラストが全然ないよりはるかに悪い。

その場合は、データを飾らずに提示し、人々にそっぽを向かれる危険を冒す方がまだましである。時として、図表制作者は読者の信頼を欺き、飾ることに熱中するあまり、図表を作成しデータを伝えるという第一の役割を見失いがちである。

イメージと統計数字が完全に結合することによって、双方が同じようにうまく表現される場合に最も良い結果が得られる。イラストで主題となる事柄を示すことによって、読者を数字へと導くことができる。それは、抽象的アイディアを具体化したもの（例えば急上昇する失業率、急低下する利率などと、それに伴う適当なイメージ）または、文字通り主題の絵（野球場の形と色を背景にした野球の統計数字）でもよいだろう。

純粋に直接的な方法によらない統計数字の提示について、二つのはっきり異なる考えがある。紛飾しない統計数字を好む人々がしばしば見落とすのは、図表が示される媒体である。まわりの調子に正しく対応するような特定の仕事のためのフォルムを選択することは図表制作者の技術の一部である。高度にイラスト化された図表は、知的な新聞、雑誌には場違いなように見える。また、グラフ用紙に描かれた単純な線は、新聞購読者の速読にとっては、余りにも味気ないものであろう。これら二つの間の唯一の共通の場は、双方とも正確でなければならないことである。正確さが芸術的な見せかけによってゆがめられない限り、私は表であれ地図であれ、イラストの図表に賛成である。

統計数字を楽しむことは、必ずしも、最終的結果として面白く見えなければならないということを意味しない。しかし、デザイナーが仕事を楽しんでやった時、また仕事全体に気配りと注意が払われた時、確かにそのような結果が現れる。それは、正確さをもって読者を引きつけ、楽しませ、教え、報わせ、説明してくれることを意味する。

ナイジェル・ホームズ
タイムマガジン・NY
エグゼクティブアートディレクター

DIAGRAMS IN FOCUS.

Yukio Kanise
President
Kanise Design Office
Member of Japan Typography Association
Japan

DIAGRAMS AS AESTHETIC COMPOSITIONS—HIGH EXPECTATIONS FOR THE FUTURE

The task of graphic design often seems glamorous, but when we examine the actual production process, we discover there are many tedious aspects.

There are many cases when a designer is asked to accurately express and simplify a company's data report through a method of visual communication, and in such cases, a high degree of ability is required.

Diagrams are the most typical of this type of assignment, and diagrams are often just an accumulation of tedious work.

Thinking back on the past, I can still remember very clearly that around 1960 there were not many good diagrams in Japan, and I was dazzled by the sophisticated beauty of the diagrams in the American magazine "Fortune."

The numbers and statistics which were supposed to be explained to the readers were clearly and attractively expressed. As I remember, I was quite surprised to see a glimpse of hope for the field of diagrammatic communication.

Since that time, many excellent diagrams have surfaced, mainly through annual report publications, and these have consistently been organized, attractive, and clear.

On one hand, graphic design in Japan has progressed with the development of industry, and in recent years we have found an increase in the number of high-quality diagrams included in publications such as encyclopedias. However, most of the diagrams in annual reports (which are often known as sales/business reports in Japan) have become un-original and carelessly produced. I do not understand this turn of events. It is unfortunate, because Japanese graphic design has reached a certain level of world-wide notoriety for its excellence.
From what I have heard, companies in the USA pay close attention to annual reports sent to stockholders, and the effort is made to express the achievements of a company's business as attractively and clearly as possible. It seems that they are truly aware that such efforts meet with the stockholders' approval and attract business to their companies.

We often find boring bar/line diagrams or pie graphs used by Japanese companies, and coloring is often monotonous. Among these, there are some which are inaccurate because the numerical values have been misunderstood or exaggerated.

美しい結晶体としてのダイアグラム
いま期待をこめて……

グラフィック・デザインの仕事は一見華やかに見えるが、その制作過程を見ると実に地味な仕事が多い。

感性のみでは解決のつかない問題をテーマとしている場合も多々あり、特に企業が抱えている問題をビジュアルな処理で適確に解決し、表現しようとする場合、デザイナーには高度な力量が求められる。

ダイアグラムの場合はその最たるもので、地味な仕事の集積のようだ。

少し古い話になるが、日本ではまだまだダイアグラムに良いものが見当らなかった1960年頃、アメリカのFORTUNE誌で見かけたダイアグラムのソフィスティケートされた美しさに眼を奪われたのを、今でも鮮明に覚えている。

それらは、読者に伝達したい数値の推移が、わかりやすく表現されていて、しかもそれぞれに工夫が凝らしてあった。ダイアグラムの表現の可能性を垣間見た思いがして、ハッとした記憶がある。

その後は主としてアメリカの年次報告書（Annual Report）にすぐれたダイアグラムを多く見かけるようになったが、それらは一段と洗練されていて美しく明解であった。

一方日本では産業の発展に伴いグラフィックデザインも進展を遂げ、ダイアグラムも近年では百科事典など一部の出版物では、ずいぶん良い仕事を見かけるようになった。

しかし多くの企業で出している年次報告書類——日本では多くの場合営業報告書となっているが——のダイアグラムは、ほとんどが類型的でイージーに制作されたものになっているのはどうしたことだろうか。これ程日本のグラフィックデザインのレベルが高くなり、海外からも注目されるようになってきたのに残念なことだ。

聞くところによると、アメリカの企業では株主に対して発送する年次報告書には細心の注意を払い、会社の業績をできる限り美しく、わかりやすく、将来の展望も含めて感動的にアピールできるよう配慮がなされているようだ。そのことが株主の理解と賛同を得、企業の発展につながることを彼等は充分に心得ているように思える。

日本の大多数の企業が採用しているダイアグラムは、退屈な棒グラフか折線グラフ、円周の分割によるパーセントの表示くらいしか見かけなく、色彩も単調なものがほとんどだ。なかに

DIAGRAMS IN FOCUS.

Yukio Kanise
President
Kanise Design Office
Member of Japan Typography Association
Japan

An extreme example might be a sales-profit graph. Suppose the graph shows an increase of one hundred million yen exaggerated by one hundred million yen and one thousand, one hundred million yen increased to one thousand two hundred million yen per year. This could be read incorrectly if the amount of one hundred million yen were omitted. Read in this way, the graph would show a one hundred million yen increase the first year and two hundred million yen the second year, which would appear as a steep increase in the graph. Like this example, when a graph is unclear, it may produce a loss in a company's credit.

は数値の意味をとり違えて、また誇大に表現しようとするあまり、不自然なものもある。

極端な例として、営業利益のグラフの場合で1年毎に11億円が12億円にというように1億円ずつ増えていく場合、10億円を省略して図示することが考えられる。この方法をとると、最初の年は1（億円）で次の年は2（億円）となり、グラフにすると急激な増加を表すことになる。この様に間違った受け取り方をされるグラフを作成することは企業の信用の失墜につながることになる。

DIAGRAMS IN FOCUS.

Certain basic elements are essential in diagrams. Strong visual expression, clarity, accuracy, elegance, a style of impression — these must come from a complete understanding of the data combined with a high grade of talent and effort. These elements are the way to transmit accurate data in an attractive format.

From a graphic designer's standpoint, this is a difficult task requiring intellect and sensibility. It comes under the category of tasks taking a great deal of time but giving little reward.

Good diagrams can be created with a solid understanding of the company's position and a strong sense of design.

In the future, methods used now for graphic expression will be produced through computer graphics, but a positive attitude and the trust of clients will be essential even then.

I hope that diagrams will continue to project the future with accurate information, attractive formats, and in an intellectually stimulating style.

ダイアグラムには、グラフィック・デザインのベーシックな要素が濃縮されているように思える。ビジュアル表現の強さ、明解さ、伝達の確かさ、優美さ、ある種の感動——それらはテーマの正しい理解と、誠意を込めて制作された完性度の高さからくるものに違いない。それらは知的な美しさを伴ない乍ら真実を伝える手立てである。

グラフィック・デザイナーの立場から考えれば、これはもうストイックで、知性と感性が平等に要求される難しい仕事である。まず時間がかかるわりに報われることの少ない仕事の部類に入る。

良いダイアグラムは、企業側の理解とすぐれたデザイナーの良識があってはじめて作り得るものである。

今後はコンピューター、グラフィックスの利用などでダイアグラムにも今までとは違った表現が可能になるものと思われるが、それにも結局は依頼者と制作者の積極的な姿勢と信頼関係が不可欠であろう。

ダイアグラムは、美しく知的な楽しさをもち、確かな情報で未来を暗示するものであってほしい。

蟹瀬行雄
蟹瀬デザインオフィス
代表取締役社長
日本タイポグラフィー協会会員

DIAGRAMS IN FOCUS.

Bill Brown
Professor
University of California Los Angeles
ICO America/Art Consultant
USA

DIAGRAPHICS 1986

I have always been fascinated with the process of representing ideas or information that are not visible to the human eye. Diagrams, x-rays, organization charts, family trees, architectural plans have all amazed me with the clarity with which they speak to us in a special language of symbols and form. Since childhood I have been particularly intrigued with maps, whether of my own block, a new city or of the world. This is a distillation of information that is unique; the most successful representations of the spaces in which we live can capture my interest and inspection time and time again, because my fascination is not so much with the map itself, but with the process of transforming the information into a special visual vocabulary. Often the sheer beauty and imagination of the transformation create works that are themselves pieces of art with a special quality of simplicity and elegance.

ダイヤグラフィックス　1986年

　私は常に、人間の目には見えない考えや情報を表現する過程に魅惑されてきました。ダイアグラム、レントゲン写真、組織図、家系図、建築設計図などはすべて、シンボルや形という特殊な言語で私たちに語りかけ、その明確さに私は目を見張りました。とりわけ地図は幼い時から私の好奇心をそそってきました。それが自分の家のある一区画の地図でも、また新しい町や世界の地図でもよかったのです。地図は、独特な方法による情報の精製です。この私たちが住む空間の最も巧妙な表現に私は心を捕えられ、何度も何度も眺めました。なぜなら、私が魅せられたのは地図それ自身についてというより、情報を特殊な視覚的表現形式に変えていく過程だったからです。形を変えることの純粋な美しさと想像は、しばしば作品を創造します。これらの作品はそれ自身、単純さと優雅さの特殊

DIAGRAMS IN FOCUS.

In addition to my work as an illustrator and graphic designer is my work at UCLA where I teach communication design. My conversations with the students are often focussed on what I call the anatomy of graphic design: type, color, image, scale, form, texture, symbolism and, most importantly, imagination. The most consistent problem that I have found in the work of these young designers is the tendency, indeed the compulsion, to include too much information in a design solution, as if their confidence in communication was still too fragile to edit, distill, and crystallize the visual information. The task of encouraging students to think in graphic terms, to focus on the essence of the information, to organize and emphasize and not to just beautify seems to me to be precisely what the designers of diagrams are consistently challenged to do. In his introduction to Graphics Diagrams, Leslie Segal says "Charts and diagrams represent a synthesis of art and science". In some way, the process of synthesis is at the core of much creative work. The degree to which that synthesis is imbued with intelligence, taste and imagination, identifies the extent to which the diagram is successful and sometimes even memorable. The same can be said of computer graphics, a new tool for the graphic designer that is just beginning to make an impact on the way we create solutions to visual problems.

The work in this volume represents the best efforts of a kind of designer that I have always admired. The richness and variety of approaches to the process of synthesis as it relates to visual information reminds us that a truly creative force is at work here. It is easy to organize and classify information; it is not easy to transform that effort into a work of beauty, taste and memorability.

な美質を備えた芸術品なのです。

イラストレーター、グラフィック・デザイナーとしての仕事の外に、私にはカリフォルニア大学ロスアンゼルス校での仕事があります。そこで、私はコミュニケーション・デザインを教えているのですが、学生と話していてしばしば、私がグラフィック・デザインの解剖と呼んでいるものに話題が集中します。それは型、色、イメージ、大きさ、形、質感、シンボリズム、そして最も重要なのが想像力です。これらの若いデザイナーの作品に最も共通する問題は、ひとつのデザイン解答の中に余りにも多くの情報を入れ過ぎる傾向があるということです。それはもう傾向と言うより、強迫衝動といえるほどです。まるで、彼らのコミュニケーションについての確信が揺らいでいるため、視覚的情報を編集し、精製し、結晶させることができないかのようです。グラフィックの言葉で考え、情報の本質に焦点をしぼり、ただ美化するのではなく、組織し、強調するように学生に求めることは取りも直さず、ダイアグラム・デザイナーが常に要求されていることでもあるように思います。

レスリー・シーガルは「グラフィックス・ダイアグラムズ」の序文の中でこう述べています。「図表とダイアグラムは、美術と科学の統合である」。統合の過程はある意味で創作的仕事の核心をなすものです。その統合に知性、好み、想像力がどこまで加わるかによって、その図形の成功度と、時には印象度が決まるのです。同じことはコンピューター・グラフィックスについても言えます。それはグラフィック・デザイナーにとっての新しい道具で、私たちが視覚的問題に対する解答を模索する過程に対する影響を与え始めたところです。

この本の中の作品は、私が常に賞賛してきたデザイナー達のベストを尽くした力作です。視覚的情報を統合する過程への豊かで多様なアプローチは、作品の中に真に創造的な力が働いていることを想起させてくれます。情報を組織し分類することは簡単です。しかし、その努力を美しく、センスのよい、印象的な作品に変えていくことは容易ではありません。

（ビル・ブラウン
カリフォルニア大学・教授
ICOアメリカ／アートコンサルタント）

DIAGRAMS IN FOCUS.

Hideya Kawakita
President
Bélier
Japan

Many magazine editors have asked me the same question, "Do you know of any designers who can make good charts and diagrams?"

Diagrams occupy the main position in the field of graphic design, however, surprisingly few people specialize in them. Most of the charts and diagrams in magazines cannot be considered as having been designed seriously.

In the case of magazines, the amount of time available for design production is very short. Once the data has been provided, the designers will be told, for example, "Have it done by tomorrow evening." In addition, budgets are small.

Under such conditions, it is not surprising that good diagram designers do not generate. Diagram design is a monotonous job. Probably the most glamorous job for graphic designers is the creation of posters. A designer may put into a poster as much sensitivity and as many opinions as he wishes, and while creating it he lives in a colorful and exciting atmosphere.

For promotional posters, there are often opportunities to go abroad for a filming trip, and working with models, actors, photographers, copy-writers, and stylists is glamorous. The budget is always large and the pay is high.

But what about diagrams? Well, when designing a flow chart or statistics report, the client or editor presents you with complex tables and difficult charts and says, "Design these in a form that readers and consumers will easily comprehend."

First, the designer must completely understand the figures, and then he must carefully transform the data into a design. This is very tedious work, and the designer must be patient. Compared to the excitement of promotional design, diagrams appear to be in the opposite direction, in spite of the fact that both are forms of graphic design.

Japan is now considered an economic power, but the Western culture it absorbed after World War II is still superficial. Japan only took a small portion of Western culture and discarded the rest. Japan is definitely an advanced nation, but it is narrow, like Tokyo Tower, and does not have broad views.

Economic efficiency has been given the highest priority. Telephone poles have been planted incessantly along all roads, cars come and go through narrow streets, housing conditions in this huge city (Tokyo) are becoming extremely bad . . . I don't want to hear about GNP and so forth.

雑誌の編集者の何人もから聞かれた。「図表や説明図をうまくデザインできるデザイナーはいませんか」と。グラフィック・デザインの分野では、ダイヤグラムは重要なポジションであるにもかかわらず専門にやっている人は意外に少ない。特に一般の週刊誌ともなると、図表や説明図はとても真剣にデザインされたとは思いがたいものが多い。週刊誌の場合、データが渡されて、「明日の夕方まで」というふうに作業時間が短く、ギャラも安い。これでは優秀なダイヤグラムのデザイナーが育たないのは当然である。その上この仕事は地味である。グラフィック・デザインで一番派手なものといえばポスターなどであろうか。ポスターには、自分自身の感性や主張も存分に織りこめるし、現場の状況もいきいきとしている。広告ポスターの場合、海外にロケへ行くチャンスもあるし、モデル、タレント、カメラマン、コピーライター、スタイリスト等との共同作業も華やかである。予算も豊富だし、ギャラも高い。

一方、ダイヤグラムの方はどうか。たとえば、フローチャートや統計図表をデザインする場合。クライアントや編集者に難しい数表や、分かりにくいグラフを渡されて「これを、読者や消費者にわかりやすくデザインして欲しい」と頼まれる。デザイナーはまず、その数字を完璧に理解しなければならない。次にそれを冷静に判断してデザイン化していくわけだ。職人の根気がいる地味な作業である。広告デザインの派手さと比べれば、同じグラフィック・デザインでも180度方向が異なるように思う。

日本が経済大国になったとはいえ、第二次世界大戦後、急速に消化していった欧米型文化の深度は浅い。欧米の効率のよい部分ばかりを取り入れて、各文化分野のディテールを軽んじてきた。確かに日本は先進国ではあるが、その型は東京タワー的なやせ細った型であり、雄大な視野を持つ台形ではない。経済効率最優先で電柱を道路に立て続け、狭い道路には車が行き交う。都市の住宅事情は最悪である。GNPうんぬんなんて聞きたくもない。

しかし、電子技術は発達し、オーディオ、ビデオは世界一とか、車もカメラも……。それだけではない。なんと我が国のグラフィック・デザインもついに世界一になったという人さえいる。たしかに、日本の印刷技術が世界のトップクラス、華麗なポスターがデザインされていることは確かだ。が、そのことと日本のグラフィック・デザインが世界のナンバーワンであると

DIAGRAMS IN FOCUS.

On the other hand, Japan's electronic technology has developed to a point where its audio and video devices rank first in the world, along with its cars and cameras. Furthermore, there are many people who consider Japanese graphic design to be the best in the world. It is true that Japanese printing technology is top-class and that many splendid posters are designed in Japan, but I don't think this means that our graphic design is number one in the world. Just because we have a few designers who are capable of creating outstanding works, doesn't mean we're the best. Perhaps it is more important to consider their careers as graphic designers.

Another point to consider is the aesthetic quality of graphic design. Posters, for example, have characteristics which make them very similar to paintings. It is inevitable that even the most original designer will choose to work in this direction.

What about designing diagrams? This job is quite similar to that of the artist. In general, many of the tasks of a graphic designer are the same as those of an artist. Graphic design's development as an art form coincides with its rapid growth in use, which is caused in part by the economic development of Japan.

There has been little opportunity for education in the field of visual communication design in Japan. The social, political, and economic power of design has not been appreciated, and at this time graphic design is employed for more personal uses. Until now this may have been the most accepted and effective method for the Japanese design business. But, from now on, we must make an effort to give attention and constructive criticism to graphic designers working in the field of design communication, or Japan's design industry will not develop to meet world standards.

At present, 20,000 graphic designers graduate from universities in Japan each year. However, it is difficult to believe that these students have studied sufficient materials or have received adequate training in diagraphic communication.

Under these conditions, JCA Diagraphics will make a fundamental contribution towards the development of the graphic design business.

（河北秀也
ベリエール
代表取締役社長）

いうこととは話がいささか違うのではないだろうか。傑出したポスターを作る数人のデザイナーが日本にいるというだけでは決してそうはならない。問題はグラフィック・デザイナーの層の厚さではないだろうか。

もう一つの問題は、グラフィック・デザインの芸術性についてである。ポスターなどは限りなく絵画に近い要素を持っているので、個性豊かなデザイナーはどうしてもそちらの方向に行きたがるのはやむをえないだろう。

ダイヤグラムについてはどうか。これは限りなく職人に近い仕事である。この職人に近い部分の仕事がグラフィック・デザイン全般には多い。グラフィック・デザインの絵画性への傾斜はそのままグラフィック・デザインが日本で急成長した過程、つまり日本が経済的に急発展した状況と符合する。ビジュアル・コミュニケーション・デザインとして体系的教育がほどこされず、デザインが本来持っている社会的、政治的、経済的パワーを高めることもなく、パーソナルな世界に帰趨してしまった。今まではそれで日本のデザイン界で通用し、有効だったかもしれない。しかし、これからはもっとコミュニケーションとしてのデザイン分野で地道に（と今までは思われていたが）仕事をしているグラフィック・デザイナーにスポットを当てて、その評価を高めていく体制を取らなければ日本のグラフィック・デザインが世界レベルに達することなどないだろう。現在、大学や専門学校を卒業するグラフィック・デザイナーは年間2万人だそうである。彼らが充分な資料で研究し適切な教育を受けているとはとても思いがたい。こうした時期に日本クリエイターズ協会からJCA DIAGRAPHICSが発刊されることは、今後グラフィック・デザイン界発展のために大きく寄与するだろう。

DIAGRAMS IN FOCUS.

Gordon Tani
Creative Director
Ellis/Ross/Tani
Los Angeles, California
USA

VISUAL ORGANIZERS ELEVATED TO AN ARTFORM

I have always been fascinated by diagrams, graphs and maps. They seem to be "visual organizers" of assorted facts, figures and schedules. Sometimes related. Other times not. But they help us quickly absorb a wealth of information and comparisons in a comfortable edited fashion.

One high school math teacher of mine was instrumental in my early interest in this area. He taught me a valuable "reality" lesson: Graphs and diagrams can visually distort one's perception of the facts and figures. For example, he pointed out that by changing the units of measurement on a simple graph from increments of 10 to 2, the percentage of growth or decline would thus be exaggerated. This is an obvious truism the viewer has to keep in mind when looking at comparative statistics in chart form.

Access to "visual organizers" took a giant leap in the 1980's, with the advent of the personal computer and graphics software. Pie charts, bar graphs, line charts and comparative statistics are now available at the push of a button. Massive amounts of computer data can be charted in seconds compared to the past task of hand drawings. In business meetings, computer-generated charts and graphs are now commonplace. The visual distortion my teacher described has become a popular method for giving management a rosy picture of sales figures, sales growth and profits as well as to downplay losses to the stockholders.

But "visual organizers" were not elevated to their present day "artform" status until the publisher and editorial staffs began to push for more color and visual communication on their pages. Their push probably began more out of a need to increase readership but resulted in an effective and colorful visual medium to communicate sometimes complicated data.

On a daily basis, USA Today publishes a newspaper full of charts, diagrams and maps from sophisticated political analysis to trivia facts and figures on daily living. USA Today is the forerunner in this area and has been influential in other newspapers' presentation and use of "visual organizers".

The top star of "visual organizers", in my opinion is Nigel Holmes of Time Magazine. Every week, I look forward to his visual interpretations of the Chinese economic reforms, the USSR-USA arms race, changes in population, tax reform or living costs. For those of us who have been weaned on television and lack time enough to read a

アートフォームにまで高められた
ビジュアル・オーガナイザー

　私はいつも図表やグラフや地図に魅惑されて
きました。これらは事実の集合であり、数字、
予定表の"ビジュアル・オーガナイザー"（視覚
形成体）のようにみえます。情報との間に関連
がある場合もそうでない場合もありますが、こ
れらは多くの情報の理解や、適切に編集された
形での比較の手助けとなるのです。

　この分野への私の関心を目覚めさせてくれた
のは、私の高校の数学教師でした。彼は私に貴
重な"現実"の教訓を教えてくれました。それ
は、グラフや図表が事実や数字に対する人々の
知覚を視覚的に歪めることができるということ
です。例えばこの先生は、単純なグラフの測定
単位を10から2へ変えることによって、増加ま
たは減少の割合がそれぞれ強調されることを指
摘しました。これは、図表による比較統計を見
る際に注意しなければならない明白な事実です。

　パーソナル・コンピューターとグラフィック
ス・ソフトウェアの出現によって、1980年代に
"視覚形成体"は長足の前進をとげました。今
は、円形グラフ、棒グラフ、線グラフ、比較統
計はボタンを押せば作れるのです。かつての手
描きの仕事と異なり、ぼう大な量のコンピュー
ター・データを数秒間で図表にすることができ
ます。会社の会議でコンピューターが作成した
図表やグラフが、いまでは当たり前に使われて
います。先生が説明してくれた視覚的歪みは、
経営陣に売り上げの数字、売り上げの成長や利
益についてバラ色の楽観的予想図を提示し、同
様に株主には損失を軽視させるための人気のあ
る方法になっています。

　しかし、"ビジュアル・オーガナイザー"は、
出版者や編集担当者が出版物のページにより多
くの色と視覚的コミュニケーションをのせる努
力を始めたことによって、今日の"アートフォ
ーム"（芸術の表現媒体としてのフォルム）にま
で高められたのです。どちらかといえば読者を
増やす必要性からスタートした彼らの努力は、
一方で複雑なデータを伝える効果的で色彩豊か
な視覚媒体を生みだしました。

　日刊新聞 USA Today には、高度な政治的分
析から日常生活のささいな事実、数字に至るま
て、たくさんの図表、図形、地図がのっていま
す。USA Today はこの分野の先駆者であり、
他の新聞の"ビジュアル・オーガナイザー"に
影響を与えています。

　私の意見では"ビジュアル・オーガナイザ

DIAGRAMS IN FOCUS.

magazine cover-to-cover, Holmes has, in a single visual metaphor, captured the essence of a topic.

The high visibility of Time and USA Today in America has had a profound influence on graphic designers in this country. Designers of annual reports, brochures and catalogues are more aware and have more options in treating facts and figures beyond just listing them.

It seems timely that JCA publishes this new type of annual. "Visual organizers" should be recognized for their unique role in visual communications and as a bridge to better understanding of our increasingly complex and sophisticated world. To me, they blend the best of form and function and beauty. And besides, they're fun to look at.

ー"のトップスターは雑誌タイムのナイジェル・ホームズです。毎週私は中国の経済改革、米ソの軍備競争、人口の変化、税制改革、または生活費などについての彼の視覚的解釈を楽しみにしています。幼時からテレビを見て育ち、雑誌を隅から隅まで読むための十分な時間のない私たちのために彼はひとつの視覚的暗喩で話題の本質を捉えてくれます。

アメリカのタイム誌とUSA Todayの高度な視見性は、この国のパブリック・デザイナーたちに底知れない影響を与えています。年次報告、パンフレット、カタログのデザイナーたちは、事実や数字を単に列記するだけでなく、それらの扱い方も熟知しており、自由選択の余地もたくさん与えられています。

JCAがこのたび、新しい型の年鑑を発行することは時機を得たものと思われます。"視覚形成体"は、視覚コミニケーションにおけるその独特な役割によって、ますます複雑、高度化するこの世界の相互理解のかけ橋として認められるべきです。私にとってのビジュアル・オーガナイザーは、フォルム 機能 美のブレンドそのものですからなにしろ、それは見るだけでも楽しいのです。

（ゴードン・タニ
クリエイティブ・ディレクター
エリス／ロス／タニ）

DIAGRAMS IN FOCUS.

Koichiro Inagaki
President
Inagaki & Associates
Japan

INFORMATION-ORIENTED SOCIETY AND GRAPHIC COMMUNICATION

I usually work closely with statisticians because of my weakness with numbers.

Usually designers do not like working with numbers, although some of them can easily solve even the most difficult of university-level mathematics problems when they are over 40 years old. Generally, people engaged in work centered on visual and emotional communication are not good with figures, needless to say mathematics. I am one of these. I get headaches just looking at numbers. Anyways, I try to avoid statistical tables and groups of figures as much as possible.

While still a student, I was advised to refer to graphs in "Fortune Magazine." However, I didn't pay much attention to the problems of handling statistics and understanding both the questions and answers behind diagrams. Unintentionally, my interests were always directed towards the aesthetic aspects of graphs.

Things are different now. I have done some statistical designs since that time. Occasionally, enduring a headache, I've had to express the meaning of statistical data through diagrams. Talking with the statistician until late at night, I am able to evaluate the best way to express his intensions in graph form.

At first, I was surprised at the thought of a person becoming a statistician and dealing solely with figures. I think a lot of designers share my apprehension, but this attitude is counter-productive. Statistics are vital for comprehension of today's world.

The yen's increasing value is a popular topic of conversation, and hundreds of words would be necessary to explain its transitions. However, when expressed in graph form, the present position of the yen in relation to its past performance can be easily understood. Furthermore, its future trends may be roughly estimated.

A graph is the expression of uninteresting numbers in an exciting format. It can make people instantly recognize and understand a problem which would require hundreds of words if explained in an article. Recently, when Prime Minister Nakasone made a televised speech to gain the understanding and cooperation of the people on the issue of Japanese/American trade relations, he used several types of graphs which clarified his speech. Those graphs were created by designers, but the technical instructions were supplied by professional statisticians.

In the past, designers tried to avoid meeting people like statisticians, and when making a graph they would go about it in a very dogmatic

情報化社会とグラフ

私は統計専門家との接触を心がけている。数字に弱いからである。

デザイナーは一般に数字がきらいだ。なかには、40歳過ぎても大学入試の数学問題をすらすら解いてしまう人もいるが、そういうのは例外で、一般に美とか情緒を中心とする仕事に携わる人は数学どころか数字が苦手である。私もその一人で、数字を見るだけで頭痛のするほうだった。もっとも、収支をベースに見積りを出したりする時は結構冴えたりするのだが……。とにかく、数字がずらりと並ぶ統計表などにはできれば近づきたくない。学生の頃「フォーチュン」のグラフを参考にするように勧められたが、数字の料理の仕方や問答理解のほうはおざなりで、ついついその美的側面にのみ関心が向くようだった。

しかし、今は違う。その後多少の勉強はしたからだ。時には頭痛に堪えながらも統計数値の意味を図形に表現したり、統計専門家の意図を汲んで図形に反映する方法を深夜まで話し合ったりもしている。

最初は相手が統計学者と聞いただけでゲンナリした。何しろ数字を羅列する専門家だからだ。デザイナーには私と同じ人が少なくないだろう。しかし、それでは時流から取り残される。統計はある事象の実体を捉えるうえで不可欠である。円高、円高と騒がれても、それがどういう推移を辿っているかを説明するには数百語を必要とする。しかし、グラフで示せば、ごく簡単に全体の流れの中における現位置が分かり、さらには今後の動向までもおよその見当がつけられる。

グラフは無味乾燥な数値をドラマ化して一枚の劇画に仕立てるようなものだ。文章にすれば数百語を必要とする内容を一瞬にして認識・理解させることができる。先般、中曽根総理が日米貿易摩擦をめぐって、国民の理解協力を求めるべくTV放送を行ったが、数種類のグラフの利用が話を大変分かりやすいものにした。グラフはもとよりデザイナーの手になったものだが、背後に統計専門家の指導があったことは言うまでもない。

これまで、われわれは統計学者といった人たちを敬遠して、たぶんに独断で数字をグラフ化したものである。その大部分は幸いにも素人なりに的を射ていたが、しかし、そうでないものも少なくなかった。部分のみにとらわれて全母集団に対する関係が分からなかったりというのは序の口で、なかには本分と矛盾するものさえ

DIAGRAMS IN FOCUS.

manner. Luckily, many of these graphs were accurately expressed, but there were also many which failed to convey correct information.

Some of these designers were only concerned with the graph itself and not with its relationship to the field of research. Graphs often contradicted the accompanying written information. A single graph is equivalent to an article composed of hundreds of words. Misunderstandings can cause disastrous results. Amateur precision cannot be tolerated

Entering the computer age, statistical processing will expand to many fields, and its analytical methods will be diversified. Regarding these methods, there are many which require several months' study for basic

見られた。一枚のグラフは数百語の情報に匹敵する。誤解は恐るべき結果を生じかねない。素人の独善は許されない。

コンピューター時代を迎え、統計処理とその分析方法は多様になった。分析方法に関しては、一応の理解をするだけで数カ月、数値群に適用する能力を収得するには数年以上を要するものが少なくない。また、作図には専門家のアドバイスが不可欠である。もはや統計専門家に依頼して済まされる時代ではない。われわれは時折彼らと接触し、その知見を吸収し、親交を深めるようにしなければならない。

ここ2～3年目立ってきたことは、これまで

DIAGRAMS IN FOCUS.

Koichiro Inagaki
President
Inagaki & Associates
Japan

comprehension and several years to develop the ability to understand specific numerical values. The advice of professionals is vital when creating these graphs. This is not an age when designers will be able to work without the help of statistics experts. We must confer with them occasionally, absorb their knowledge, and promote cooperative relationships.

In the last few years, various forms of graphs have been introduced into account reports which until then displayed only numerical data. These are more readily understood by amateurs and are one of the many changes accompanying the internationalization of business. It is often said that music has no limits. This is also true of art and, moreover, of graphic communication. I am sure that with the internationalization of business, many graphs will appear more frequently in diverse fields.

Computers are the basis of our information-oriented society which focuses on international trends in politics, economy, and culture. It is a new age. In this era of continuous change, diverse methods of communication will inevitably appear. We cannot be ignorant of the existance of diagraphic communication.

When making graphs and working with statistic experts, the designer may not always agree with the material. He is an amateur when it comes to figures. In many cases a graph that is considered by experts to be very interesting is unclear to the amateur. Considering this factor, designers, as representatives of the general public, must express these opinions. Some study is necessary before creating a diagram. For this reason, you should listen to experts' explanations with an open mind, making sure you sufficiently understand the context, and then discuss what method of expression will best convey the information. For such devices as printed materials, billboards, and neon signs, each medium's characteristics and relation to the message to be communicated must be carefully considered. Depending on the data, each graph's composition will be different and unique. This is where a designer's ability becomes obvious. At present, most designers are too concerned with "appearance." I was the same when I first discovered "Fortune" magazine. As we repeat a habit, it often becomes second nature. But we must keep in mind that substance and content are more important than appearance. Content is the base of the entire design. Color and style are significant, but it is more important to convey the content accurately so that it can be easily understood.

Recently, I haven't had my usual headaches when I am presented with numerical data. This is because I started studying mathematics five years ago. In Japan, we consider the sixtieth birthday a new beginning of education, but fortunately, I have many years before I reach that age.

数値ばかり並んでいた決算報告書などにもさまざまな形でグラフが導入されるようになったことである。これは素人に分かりやすい故でもあり、また事業の国際化の表れでもあろう。音楽に国境はない、とよく言われるが、これは勿論絵画にも通用し、他ならぬグラフにも当てはまることである。さまざまな面でのグラフの多様な出現は事業その他が国際化するにつれて盛んになる。

　情報化社会のベースをなすコンピュータ、情報化を推し進める政治・経済・社会の国際動向など、新しい時代を迎えている。とうとうたる時代の流れは、その一面にグラフの多様な出現を必然たらしめる。われわれはグラフ音痴では生きていけない。

　しかし、グラフ作成に際して統計専門家と接する時、デザイナーはただ指示に従えばよいというのではない。われわれの強みは数字に対して素人だという点にある。つまり、一応の常識を備えた素人に理解できないグラフは、それが専門家にどれほど興味深くても半ば意味がないということである。対象が一般大衆の場合はこう言って差支えない。自分の主張を持てということである。

　それにはある程度の勉強が必要である。その上で、専門家の説明に虚心に耳を傾けその内容を十分理解し、テーマを生かした表現法を検討し合うのである。印刷物、オーバーヘッド・プロジェクター、ブラウン管スクリーン、それぞれの特性と伝えるべき内容の関係を十分考えなければいけない。テーマをどのように伝えるかによって、グラフの連続や複合の仕方が異なってくる。今後、われわれの能力差はこの辺に表れてくるだろう。

　従来、デザイナーは「見せかけ」にこだわりすぎていた。私自身『フォーチュン』に接した時の姿勢がそうであったように。これを繰返すうちに習い性となり、生活が、さらには性格が見せかけになる危険がある。見せかけより実質である。グラフではそれがはっきりする。色彩効果なども大切だが、それより内容を適切にストレートに理解できるように伝えることが重要である。

　最近、数字を見てもさほど頭痛がしなくなった。5年前から数学を（60にはまだ間があるが）手習い始めたからである。

（稲垣アソシエイツ
代表取締役社長
稲垣行一郎）

DIAGRAMS IN FOCUS.

Fátima Gil
Copywrighter
Portugal

BEFORE STARTING TO WORK FOR JCA, MY MAIN CONCERNS REGARDED MUSIC AND THE SOUND UNIVERSE, RATHER THAN THE VISUAL WORLD. I WAS, HOWEVER, QUITE FOND OF FINE-ARTS, ATTENDING EXHIBITIONS WHENEVER POSSIBLE AND BEING IN CONSTANT TOUCH WITH NOWADAYS ART PROBLEMS, FOR MY HUSBAND IS A PAINTER AND WE UPHOLD A PERMANENT DIALOGUE ON HIS WORK, THE ACHIEVEMENT OF DIAGRAPHICS BROUGHT A NEW POINT INTO MY CONSIDERATION: THE IMPORTANCE OF DIAGRAMS INSIDE THE WORLD OF DESIGN, AND WHILE WORKING FOR THIS PUBLICATION, I PROGRESSIVELY STARTED TO REMEMBER OLD IMPRESSIONS OF THEM. THE FOLLOWING TEXT IS A PRODUCT OF THESE CONSIDERATIONS AND OF THE GOOD CHALLENGE THAT WORKING FOR JCA REPRESENTS, MAKING ME AWARE OF A GREAT DEAL OF MATTERS WITHIN THE DESIGN WORLD:

When did I get acquainted with diagrams for the first time?Long

JCA に勤務する以前の私の主要関心事は、視覚的なものよりもむしろ音楽と音の世界にありました。もっとも私は、ファインアーツがとても好きで、できる限り展覧会にも出かけアーツにおける今日の問題点にも常に接してきました。というのも私の夫は画家なので、その創作活動については恒久的に対話が持たれるという状況にいるのですから、ダイアグラフィックスの完成に触発されて私は次のような新しいポイントを考えるようになりました。それはデザイン界におけるダイアグラムの重要性ということです。当 JCA 出版社に勤務しながら、私は積極的にダイアグラムに関する過去の印象などを思い起こし始めたのです。 JCA に勤務することがすなわち、デザイン界における諸問題について実に多くのことを気付かせてくれる素晴らしい機会になっているかについて述べてみたいと思います。

DIAGRAMS IN FOCUS.

Fátima Gil
Copywrighter
Portugal

ago, through very old graphics used by the European Alchemists, maps, genealogical trees, ancient Chinese representations of the body functions and energy channels, or even schemes of philosophical considerations on life, man's origin, etc., used since (or even before) middle ages by many hermetic thinkers, producers of mysterious explanations on the common mysteries of life.

These images used to fascinate me through the abstract or realistic surrealism they contained within their shapes, movements, color or its absence, strange symbols, hidden concepts or very practical, precise information (to the point of being unbelievable — I am referring, for instance, to the Chinese illustrations of body functions from I Tsung Pitu, compiled about 1575 A.D., or the ones from Ling Shu Su Wên Chieh Yao, both displayed in the "Yellow Emperor's Classic of Internal Medicine" translated by Ilza Veith).
Impressive also are the very simple diagrams (Pa Kua)
which invention is attributed to Fu-hsi (2800 B.C.) and that consist of broken and unbroken lines illustrating the Chinese Universalistic Philosophy.

Not all these charts have much to do with accuracy of information, or quick transmission of a message, but they are beautiful synthesis of thought and formed my way of being attracted by diagrams. This means that today's diagrams with all their clear way of transmitting information, if not accompanied by an equal quality of aesthetic achievement, aren't sufficient in their manner of catching the reader's eye.

How much did we evolve since these old diagrams full of creativity were made? Technically speaking, a lot, so much that it is even hard to establish a comparison, but the great part of today's diagrams, good witnesses of the scientific thought's evolution, are poor and boring schemes, vehicles of insipid knowledge.

There are some artistical manifestations which contain the essence of diagrams, being, however, unrelated to them. They are for instance the Japanese "Haiku", short, synthetic, poetical sentences bringing a multitude of sensations within the brief way of communicating them. Here also, we face a certain hermetism or ambiguity of sense which cannot coexist with the accuracy diagrams are asked, yet, they can be for the designer a good source, showing where synthetic expression and its poetical counterpart meet.

Musical scores are another example, even if they cannot be completely considered as real diagrams. They possess several qualities to

初めて私がダイアグラムと知り合いになったのは、いつのことだったでしょう。もう随分前、ヨーロッパの練金術師の使っていたとても古いグラフィックを通して、地図を通して、家系図を通して、また体の機能やエネルギーの経路に関する古代中国人による描写を通して、さらには生命、人類の起源に関する哲学的スキームなどを通してです。そして、ダイアグラムは、中世以前から多くの練金術師である思想家や力人共通の生命の神秘について不可思議な説明を行う創作家たちによって用いられてきたものなのです。

これらのイメージは、それらの形、動き、色もしくは色の欠如、奇妙な記号、隠された概念、あるいは信じられないほど実用的かつ詳細な情報—例えば私は、1575年頃に編さんされた「アイ・トゥング・ピトュ」に見られる身体の機能についての中国のイラストや「リング・シュースー・ウェン・チー・ヤオ」に見られるもののことを言っているのですが（二つ共出典はイルザ・ベイス訳による「黄帝の内臓医学古典」）—その中に含まれる抽象的、あるいは現実的シュールレアリズムを通して私を魅了したものでした。

フシー（起源前2800年）が発明し、中国における普遍的哲学を描写している実線や途中の欠けた線で構成される非常にシンプルなダイアグラム（八卦、パクァ）もまた、見る者の心を動かします。

こうしたチャートのすべてが必ずしも情報を正確に伝え、またメッセージを迅速に伝えるわけではありませんが、思想が美しく統合されたものであり、それがとりもなおさず私をダイアグラムの虜にしてしまったのです。つまり、今日の情報伝達法においては、どんなに明晰なダイアグラムも同時に美学的見地から見て優れたクオリティーを兼ね備えていなければ読者の目をひくに至らないということです。

創造性に富んだ古代のダイアグラムから私たちは一体どれだけ進歩したといえるでしょうか。技術面では多大の進歩—あまりに大きすぎて比較もできないほどの進歩—を遂げました。しかし、科学的思考の進化の良き証人ともいうべき今日のダイアグラムの大部分は、貧弱で退屈なスキームや、つまらない情報の媒体でしかないのです。

ダイアグラムと直接関係はありませんが、ダイアグラムの本質を内包する芸術作品もなかにはあります。例えば、日本の俳句がそれで、簡

DIAGRAMS IN FOCUS.

be pondered: accuracy and universality of message, practical and very direct although not synthetic information and sober but beautiful plastic expression, reminding me of the Japanese calligraphy, each time that I am confronted with an original by an author who gave his most "gestural" interpretation to the conventioned graphisms.

All these examples mean to open a world at first sight of little interest and show how much the designer can find pleasure by doing what he could otherwise feel like a condemnation, how much he can transform it in a good defiance to his imagination.
The artists we are displaying in this present edition accepted the challenge a long time ago, and I suppose they spent good moments with it. Their works are not only useful when looked in search for information, but also a source of delight for the eyes.

Designers are these people able to bring a magic touch of dream (the one we were about to lose with the establishment of a new technological era) into the most disagreeable, technocratic business. We invite you, therefore, to get acquainted with these artists and allow them to bring beauty into your business, magazine, research book, etc., as a condiment to full success.

潔でありながら見事に合成されており、詩的な響きを持った文章が短い感情伝達法の中でははるかに多くの感情を生み出しているのです。ここでもまた、ダイアグラムに求められる正確性とは共存し得ない一種の密封性、言い換えれば感覚のあいまいさ、というものに私たちは当面するのですが、俳句の例はデザイナーにとって統合された表現がその詩的表現とどのように結合しているかを示す格好の材料となりうるでしょう。

真のダイアグラムとは100パーセント見なせないとしても、楽譜もまた別の例として挙げることができます。楽譜は次のような特長を備えています。メッセージの正確性および普遍性、実用的で非常に直接的、かつ情報は統合されておらず色彩的には単調だけれども美しい造形的形態をしています。楽譜を従来のように描かずにボデーペインティングのような独自の「ジェスチュラル」的、つまり姿態的解釈をつけ加えて楽譜を描くアーチストのオリジナルに向かいあう時、私はいつも日本の書道を思い起こすのです。

これらの例のすべてが、一見しただけではあまり興味をそそりそうにない世界の扉を開く鍵となり、見ようによってはタブーへの挑戦ととられかねないことを敢えて試みることによって、デザイナーがどれほどたくさんの喜びを見い出すことができ、またどれだけたくさんのデザイナーがそれを自己の想像力へのチャレンジに変えているかを示してもいるのです。

この版に掲載されたアーチストたちは、ずっと以前からタブーに挑戦し、果敢にそれと戦ってきた皆さんです。彼らの作品は情報源として有益なだけではなく、私たちの目にも喜びを与えてくれます。

デザイナーとは、魔法のような感触の夢（新しい技術の時代の定着と共に私たちが失いかけている夢）を、この不快なテクノクラート万能の実世界に持ち込むことのできる人々なのです。ですから、みなさまがたもこれらのアーチストをお知りになり、みなさまがたのビジネス、雑誌、研究書などの大いなる成功への調味料として、また、美の使者として活用なさってみてはいかがでしょうか。

（コピーライター　ファティマ・ジル）

WHAT IS JCA ?

JCA HEADQUARTERS

This is the brain and heart of Japan Creators' Association (JCA), the international art agency which plays the role of negotiator between clients and creators scattered all over the world.
● Promotes Japanese creators in foreign countries and foreign creators in Japan. ● Formulates JCA's policies and objectives. ● Exchanges information with art-related groups in Japan and abroad. ● Plans cooperative activity, events, exhibitions, etc. ● Experiments with new techniques to better diffuse creative work.

JCA (Japan Creators' Association)

This association of highly qualified creators from Japan and overseas presently has approximately 4,000 members.
● Seeks to match supply to demand by expanding markets and increasing business exchanges.

JCA ART AGENCY

This division mediates between creators and clients to facilitate business connections. Presently over 60,000 artworks are registered and over 4,000 clients are using them.
● Introduces creators and their styles to clients worldwide. ● Serves clients by selecting appropriate artists, negotiating prices and terms, aiding in communication, arranging for delivery of finished artwork, etc. ● Areas dealt with are illustration, photography, graphic/package/product design, corporate identity, copywriting, etc. ● Establishes project teams of illustrators, graphic designers, and copywriters, as necessary, to meet client needs.

JCA PRESS, INC.

This department plans and publishes JCA's annuals.
● Presently publishes four annuals: JCA ANNUAL (illustration), International Photography Exposed, IPE (commercial photography), noAH (package and corporate identity design), and Diagraphics (diagrams). THE ILLUSTRATION BANK, which compiles images from the Illustration/Photo Bank is planned for the near future. ● Publishes JCA's newsletter, "Creators."
● Plans JCA Annual competitions.

JCA本部（ICO JAPAN）

日本クリエイターズ協会（JCA）の頭脳・心臓部。世界各地に点在するクリエイターとクライアンツとの橋渡し的役割を果たす国際的なアート・エージェンシーです。
●国内クリエイターを海外へ、海外クリエイターを日本へ紹介。
●JCA主要部門の施策、方針、決定。
●内外の関連各団体との交流。
●クリエイターのための共済活動、イベント企画、展示会などを開催。
●世界中のクリエイティブ・ワーク発展のための研究、開発、改善などを遂行。

JCA／日本クリエイターズ協会

日本、海外の優秀なクリエイターによって結成された組織団体。現在の会員数は内外合わせて4,000余名。
●クリエイターとクライアンツの需給促進及びマーケット拡大、ビジネス交流などを主な行務とする。

JCAアートエージェンシー事業部

クリエイターとクライアンツの間にあって、需給、ビジネスを円滑に進める部門。現在、登録作品数は60,000点以上。利活用するクライアンツは4,000社以上。
●世界中のあらゆる業種のクライアンツに対して、クリエイター及び作風の紹介。
●クライアンツの要望に添ったクリエイターの選定、制作進行、管理、予算調整、納品、から輸送に至るまですべてのマネージメントを遂行。
●全会員の中から、それぞれのスペシャリティを選び、1つのプロジェクトチームを結成。
●扱い種目は、イラストレーション、フォトグラフィ、グラフィック・パッケージ・プロダクツの各デザイン、コピーライティング、コーポレーション・アイデンティティなど。

JCA出版

アートビジネスに関する出版物の企画。制作部門。
●現在、イラスト中心の「JCA ANNUAL」、コマーシャルフォトグラフィーを中心とした「IPE」、パッケージ及びCIの「noAH」、統計図表の「ダイヤグラフィクス」の4年鑑を定期的に刊行、近く、イラスト／フォト／キャラクターの全作品を収録した「THE ILLUSTLATION BANK」を新しく刊行の予定。

WHAT IS JCA ?

JCA INTERNATIONAL DIVISION

This office screens incoming foreign communication and directs it to the appropriate JCA division.
For any inquiries please do not hesitate to contact:
International Division, 5-12-3 Higashikaigan Kita, Chigasaki, Kanagawa, JAPAN. Tel: 0467 (85) 2725. Fax: 0467 (86) 1501.

JCA of AMERICA Inc.

JCA's America branch, located in Los Angeles, aims to promote business exchanges between Japan and the U.S.A.
● Promotes clients and creators of both Japan and the U.S.A. ● Finds new and highly qualified creators within the U.S.A. ● Every day contacts JCA headquarters by facsimile machine and is prepared to receive information, inquiries, and mid-rough sketches.

WHAT IS ICO?

JCA and its network of 49 overseas bureaus has long recognized the need for a formal organization to facilitate communication between artists, artists' representatives, and their clients world-wide. In the spring of 1985, the JCA network met that need by organizing itself into the International Creators' Organization (ICO). Though still in its planning phase, this new network is clearly just what was needed to break the barriers of time, distance, and language which for so long have kept most artists out of the international market. Through ICO a client can easily commission foreign talent, and creators everywhere now have ICO as a representative to sell their skills internationally.

Later this year or early in 1987, when JCA and ICO complete their planned computer linkup and laserdisc image-storage and transfer system, international jobs will become nearly as quick and easy as local ones. Finally the dream is reality: an art director can hire the artist he wants, anywhere in the world, without worrying about missing deadlines or wasting time and money due to misunderstandings. With ICO, the right artist for the job is always available.

●クリエイターに情報を提供するJCAニュース「クリエイターズ」を発行。
●各年鑑のためのコンペ開催計画の立案など。

JCA国際部

JCAの諸外国向けの連絡窓口。
●各種情報や問い合わせなどの翻訳作業。
●海外からの来客に対する通訳。
●JCAの出版物の編集・翻訳作業。

JCAof America Inc.（ICOアメリカ）

ロスアンジェルスに置かれたJCAのアメリカ支社、日米間のビジネス交流。促進が目的。
●日米双方のクリエイターやクライアンツをお互いに紹介
●米国内の優秀なクリエイターや新人の発掘
●毎日、JCA本部とファクシミリで連絡をとり、情報交換、問い合わせ、中間ラフスケッチなどができる態勢を整えています。

ICOビューローとは

JCAと世界49地点にも及ぶ海外ビューローは、作家やその代理人、クライアンツとコミュニケートする公的な機関の必要性をかねてより感じていました。そして、1985年春、その第一段階としてインターナショナル・クリエイターズ・オーガニゼーション（ICO）を発足させたのです。まだ、いろいろ計画中ですが、この新しいネットワークが完成した暁には、長い間アーティストと国際マーケットの間に立ちはだかっていた時間、距離、言葉の障害を取り除くことができるに違いありません。例えば、クライアンツは海外の作家を自在に起用することができ、一方、作家側はICOを代理人に、自己の才能を国際的にアピールしやすくなるというわけです。本年末か来春早々に、JCAとICOが予定しているレーザーディスクによる作品の保存と転送、コンピューターのオンラインシステムが完成したとき、国際的な仕事は国内のそれとほぼ同じくらい速く、簡単になるでしょう。アートディレクターは連絡不十分なための時間や経費のロスに頭を悩ませることなく、仕事に最も適したアーティストを、いつまでも、世界のどこからでも自由に選び、使うことができます。

ICO BUREAUS

The International Creators' Organization is a unique bridge connecting Artists, Art Directors, Agents and Companies world-wide. Through this organization the world becomes an international network where full communication is easy and possible.

ICO Headquarters
c/o JCA/ Japan Creators' Association
ICO Organizing Committee
JCA Art Agency & Illus. Bank
Umehara Bldg. 3 & 4 Floor
3-1-29 Roppongi, Minato-ku, Tokyo 106
Tel: 03 (582) 4201/Fax: 03 (586) 4018

ICO JAPAN
c/o JCA Press Inc.
International Division
5-12-3 Higashikaigan Kita
Chigasaki, Kanagawa 253
Tel: 0467 (85) 2725/
Fax: 0467 (86) 1501

JCA OF AMERICA INC.
Mr. Koichi M. Yanagisawa
Iwasaki-Thomas Bldg. 4F
420 Boyd St.,
Los Angeles CA 90013
Tel: (213) 626-6462/
Fax: (213) 626-8203

ICO AMERICA
(Art Consultant)
Mr. William Brown
Bill Brown & Associates
4121 Wilshire Blvd., Suite 315
Los Angeles, CA 90010
Tel: (213) 386-2455

ICO AMERICA
LAX Branch
Mr. Howard Goldstein/Illustrators' Rep.
Howard Goldstein Design, Inc.
7031 Aldea Ave.,
Van Nuys, CA 91406
Tel: (818) 987-2837

ICO AMERICA
NY Branch
Mr. Gerard Caron
c/o Carré Noir Inc.
780 Third Avenue, Suite 2803
New York NY 10017
Tel: (212) 593-0355/Fax: (212) 593-0381

ICO AMERICA
SF Branch
Mr. Yasushi Okita
Yasushi Okita Design
87 Stillman
San Francisco, CA 94107
Tel: (415) 974-6070

ICO AMERICA
HAWAII Branch
Mr. Ric Noyle/Visual Impact
733 Auahi St.,
Honolulu HI 96813
Tel: (808) 524-8269
Fax: (808) 533-2088

ICO AUSTRALIA
Mr. Malcolm Holmes/
Asia Pacific Photo Service
GPO Box 5157, Sydney
NSW 2001
Tel: 929-3133

ICO CANADA
Ms. Nura Aidin Silver/
Silverfilm Inc.
863 King St. West
Toronto, Ontario M5V IP2
Tel: (416) 367-5063

ICO CANADA
Mr. Katsuyoshi Yamamoto
20 Monarch Park Ave.
Toronto, Ontario M4J 4P9

ICO CHINA (PRC)
Black Horse
49 Da Nan Rd.
Guangzhou
Tel: 31298/34188

ICO CZECHOSLOVAKIA
(Cultural Connection)
Mr. Jan Rajlich
Jiraskova 4-602 00 Brno
Tel: 5-752807

ICO FINLAND
Mr. Jukka Veistola
Tehtaankatu 34 E
00150 Helsinki 15
Tel: 9 (0) 608902

ICO FRANCE
Mr. Gerard Caron/Carre Noir
Square Monceau
82, Blvd. des Batignolles
75017 Paris
Tel: 42.94.02.27/
Fax: 42.94.06.78

ICO FRANCE
Ms. Claire Prebois/Agent
d'illustrateurs
90 Ave. Ch De Gaulle
92200 Neuily
Tel: (1) 4-624-1222

ICO FRANCE
Ms. Francoise Chassaing
3, quai Stalingrad 92100
Boulogne France
Tel: (1) 4 776-4121

JCA FRANCE BUREAU
Ms. Eiko Sekine
6 av. de la Republique
94110 Arcueil
Tel: 4-664-5200

ICO GREECE
Mr. Eugen Papapanagopoulos
Studio Pap 62 Omirou St.
Athens 135
Tel: 36 23 690

ICO HONG KONG
(HCA/Hong Kong Creators' Association)
Mr. Lui Lup Fun/Design First
3 & 4 Floor
195-197 Johnston Rd.
Tel: H8910868

ICO INDIA
Mr. Pradip Gupta
71, Birya House 1st Fl.
265 Bazargate St.
Fort Bombay 400 001
Tel: 263633

ICO INDONESIA
Mr. Gauri Nasution/GUA
JL Salemba 1
No. 20 Jakarta 10320
Tel: 021-331160

ICO INDONESIA
Mr. Paul Zacharia
JL K.H.S. Dakhlan 33
Malang 65118
PO Box 79
Tel: 23216

ICO IRAN
Mr. Dariosh Mokhtari
Dr. Shariati Ave.
No. 32 Meysag 6 St.
Tehran 15649

ICO ISRAEL
Mr. Raffi Rondel/Raffi Rondel
Photography
8A Hazanchanim St.,
Magdiel
Tel: 052-443159

ICO ITALY
Ms. Hilary Bradford
Via Bianca di Savoia 17
20122 Milano
Tel: 02-546-9141

ICO ITALY
Ms. Elisabetta Levorato
Idee Nuove sas
Via Cesare da Sesto, 24
Milano
Tel: 83.23.507/83.61.381

ICO KOREA
Mr. Ho Rim Han
26-205 Woo Sung Apt.
Jam Sil 1 Dong
Gang Dong Gu, Seoul
Tel: 422-9585

JCA OF AMERICA INC. IN HAWAII

ICO DENVER
JCA OF AMERICA INC.
(ICO AMERICA)

JCA OF AMERICA INC.
(ICO AMERICA)

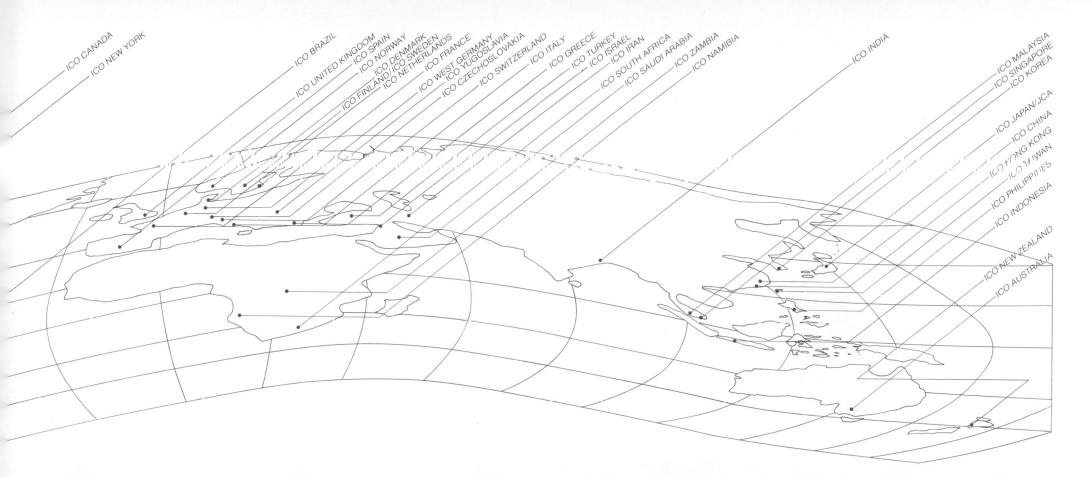

ICO CANADA
ICO NEW YORK
ICO BRAZIL
ICO UNITED KINGDOM
ICO SPAIN
ICO NORWAY
ICO DENMARK
ICO FINLAND/ICO SWEDEN
ICO NETHERLANDS
ICO FRANCE
ICO WEST GERMANY
ICO YUGOSLAVIA
ICO CZECHOSLOVAKIA
ICO SWITZERLAND
ICO ITALY
ICO GREECE
ICO TURKEY
ICO ISRAEL
ICO IRAN
ICO SOUTH AFRICA
ICO SAUDI ARABIA
ICO ZAMBIA
ICO NAMIBIA
ICO INDIA
ICO MALAYSIA
ICO SINGAPORE
ICO KOREA
ICO JAPAN/JCA
ICO CHINA
ICO HONG KONG
ICO TAIWAN
ICO PHILIPPINES
ICO INDONESIA
ICO NEW ZEALAND
ICO AUSTRALIA

ICO MALAYSIA
Mr. Stan Lee
199 Persiaran Zaaba
Taman Tun Dr.
Ismail, Kuala Lumpur
Tel: 782227

ICO MEXICO
Mr. Felix Beltran
Apartado de Correos M10733
Mexico 06000 D.F.

ICO NETHERLANDS
Mr. Edward Archer/Archer Art
Hoowfeg 50, 1058 BD
Amsterdam
Tel: 830-535/124-136/
Fax: 837-295

ICO NORWAY
Mr. Karl Orud/KO Studio
Teglverksgt 2C
0553 Oslo 5
Tel: 35 23 65/
Fax: 41 99 93

ICO PHILIPPINES
Mrs. Desiree Wright
88-C, Bahay Toro
Project 8, Quezon City

ICO SAUDIARABIA
Mr. Marjo Wright/United
Outdoors Ad Co.
PO Box 11919 Jeddah 21463
Tel: 6676157/
Fax: 401453

ICO SINGAPORE
Mr. Jimmy Kang Meng Hiang
BLK 511 #10-72
Jurong W. St. 52
Tel: 2264

ICO SOUTH AFRICA
Mr. Hilton Dawson/Design
International
1st Fl. Killarney Mall, Box 87629
Houghton 2041 Johannesburg
Tel: 646 1662/646 4769/646 5723
Fax: 726 1819

ICO SPAIN
Mr. Ramon Gonzalez Teja
Cartagena 16 5th C 28028
Madrid, Spain
Tel: 245-1443

ICO SWEDEN
Mr. Ove Granstrand
Bigatan 3, S-43139
Molndal
Tel: 031 (43) 4177

ICO SWITZERLAND
Mr. Vladislav Stransky
Birchienst 79
8600 Dubendorf
Tel: 01-820-2618

ICO TAIWAN (ROC)
Mr. Jeffery Su/Focus & Lemon Yellow
Associates
9th Floor #512
Chung-Hsiao E. Rd. Sec. 4
Taipei
Tel: 7002240-1/7001538-9/
Fax: 7412251

ICO TURKEY
Mr. Muhittin Uzal/Reba Reklam & Basin
Ticaret Ltd. Stl.
Nuruosmaniye CAD 40/2 Cagaloglu,
Istanbul
Tel: 520 74 69

ICO UNITED KINGDOM
Mr. George Underwood
21A Well Walk
London NW3
Tel: 01 (794) 0911

ICO WEST GERMANY
Ms. Margarethe Hubauer/Illustrators' Rep.
Isestrasse 96, D-2000
Hamburg 13
Tel: 040 (48) 6003
Fax: 47-77-84

ICO WEST GERMANY
Mr. Jeffrey Su/Photographers' Rep.
Mayer Norten Group
D-8000 Munchen 80
Kufsteiner Platz 5
Tel: 089-986230

ICO BRAZIL
Ms. Alicia Monica Guzovsky
Rua Jose Maria Lisboa 445
CEP 01423 Sao Paulo
Tel: (011) 288-9073

ICO UNITED KINGDOM
Mr. Andrew Archer
Archer Art
5 Park Road London NW 1
Tel: 01 (262) 5893/Fax: 01 (262) 9871

ICO DENMARK
Mr. Barry Pringle
Teglgardsstraede 12A
Mellembuset 1 sal
1452 Copenhagen K
Tel: 01 15 2824

ICO NAMIBIA
Mr. Dudley Viall
Box 22626, Windhoek 9000

ICO ZAMBIA
Mr. M.R.K. Banda
Ministry of General Education
and Culture
PO Box 50093 Lusaka Tel: 21100

ICO YUGOSLAVIA
Sintum
11000 Beograd
Terazije 26/11
Tel: 011 (687) 291

ICO NEW ZEALAND
Russell & Mary Lodge
12 Springcombe Rd.
St. Heliers, Auckland 5
Tel: 09-557-199

JCA AMONG THE ISLANDS

Our domestic network links the most distant parts of Japan in order to supply the best services to our designers and to their clients.

JCA/HEADQUARTERS

Japan Creators' Association
Art Agency & Illus. Bank
Tel: 03 (582) 4201,
Fax: 03 (586) 4018
3-4F Umehara Bldg. 3-1-29
Roppongi, Minato-ku, Tokyo
〒106

JCA PRESS INC./ International Div.

Tel: 0467 (85) 2725,
Fax: 0467 (86) 1501
5-12-3 Higashikaigan Kita,
Chigasaki, Kanagawa 〒253

SENDAI JCA

Tel: 0222 (27) 7667
Mr. Hiroo Hanzawa
Sendai-chuo Mansion 405
4-9-15 Chuo, Sendai 〒980

NAGANO JCA

Tel: 0262 (21) 8101
Mr. Toshiaki Kiguchi
920-1 Nakakawahara Inaba,
Nagano

TOYOHASHI JCA

Tel & Fax: 0532 (48) 2764
Mr. Kimihiko Narita
Naaru Design Room
17-11-5 Ohike-cho
Mukouyama, Toyohashi 〒440

KYOTO JCA

Tel: 075 (591) 1421
Mr. Kozo Ishikura
27-16 Sakawaki-cho Hinooka,
Yamashina-ku Kyoto 〒607

HIROSHIMA JCA

Tel: 0822 (48) 1688,
Fax: 0822 (47) 3779
Mr. Minoru Makino
Maki Design
5-5 Fukuromachi, Naka-ku
Hiroshima 〒730

JCA NAGOYA INC.

Tel: 052 (261) 2288,
Fax: 052 (261) 0173
Mr. Masahiko Kawai
Asukai Bldg. 3-9-10 Sakae
Naka-ku Nagoya 〒460

JCA Distribution Div.

c/o JCA Press Inc.
Mr. Takmich Homma
Tel: 0467 (82) 9271
Fax: 0467 (86) 1501

NIIGATA JCA

Tel: 0252 (41) 8861
Mr. Mitsuo Matsuoka
AD BRAIN
Hokuetsu Daiichi Bldg. 4F 1-2-25, Higashi Odori Niigata
〒950

HAMAMATSU JCA

Tel: 0534 (64) 2252
Mr. Yoshiyuki Takabayashi
Toyo Shuppan Service
643 Nakajima-cho,
Hamamatsu 〒430

GIFU JCA

Tel: 0582 (63) 2558,
Fax: 0582 (66) 9707
Mr. Yoshiro Amano
Amano Design Office
Nomura Bldg. 2F 2-10
Umegae-cho, Gifu 〒500

HIMEJI JCA

Tel: 0792 (89) 0160,
Fax: 0792 (88) 8063
Mr. Hisashi Ishii
Ishii Design
91-10 Aza Kawada, Nozato
Himeji 〒670

OSAKA JCA

Tel & Fax: 06 (358) 3920
Mr. Matsutaro Yoshida
3F Dodo Bldg. 2-1-31 Tenma,
Kita-ku Osaka 〒530

JCA HIROSHIMA INC.

Tel: 082 (291) 6118,
Fax: 082 (291) 9380
Mr. Takashi Morimoto
#201 Neolife Funairi 13-13
Kawahara-machi, Naka-ku
Hiroshima 〒733

JCA Distribution Div.

Tel: 06 (453) 5780
Mr. Yoshiaki Tsujinami
3F Hasegawa Bldg. 1-4-20
Oyodominami, Oyodo-ku
Osaka 〒531

SAPPORO JCA

Tel & Fax: 011 (831) 9919
Mr. Yusuke Toda
#808 33rd Fujii Bldg 3jyo
7 chome, Hiragishi Toyohira-ku, Sapporo 〒062

SHIZUOKA JCA

Tel: 0542 (63) 6171
Mr. Akiyoshi Shigeta
Shigeta Display
272-8 Kawai, Shizuoka-shi
Shizuoka 〒420

NAGOYA JCA

Tel: 052 (912) 6633
Mr. Hiromichi Takagi
53-4 Kouun-cho Kita-ku.
Nagoya 〒462

KANAZAWA JCA

Tel: 0762 (23) 2026
Mr. Toshitaka Shibahata
Madison 26
8F Hokkoku Bldg. 2-2-15
Katamachi, Kanazawa 〒920

MATSUE JCA

Tel: 0852 (21) 7765,
Fax: 0852 (27) 6542
Mr. Setsuo Aoto
Seigadou
4-54 Chuodori,
Higashihonmachi Matsue
〒730

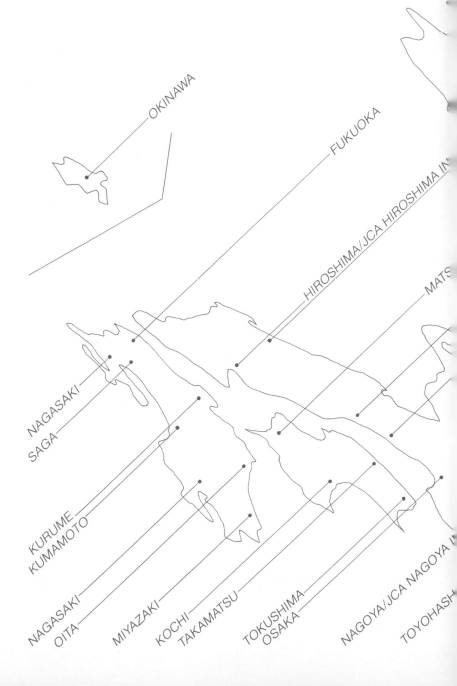

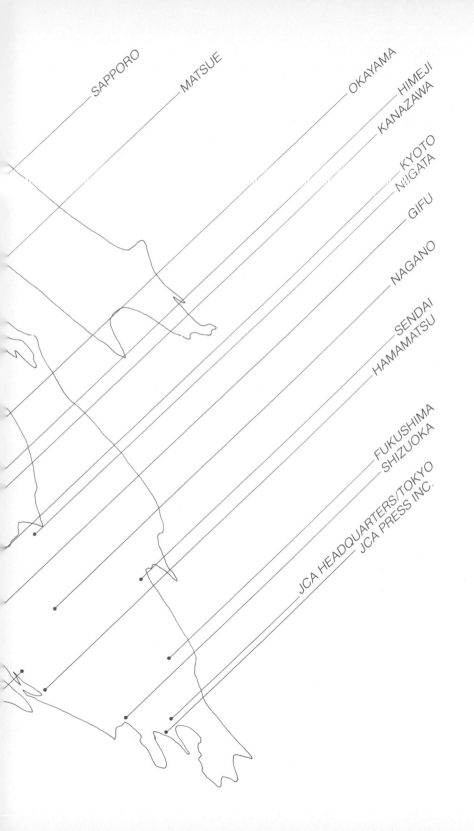

SAPPORO
MATSUE
OKAYAMA
HIMEJI
KANAZAWA
KYOTO
NIIGATA
GIFU
NAGANO
SENDAI
HAMAMATSU
FUKUSHIMA
SHIZUOKA
JCA HEADQUARTERS/TOKYO
JCA PRESS INC.

TOKUSHIMA JCA

Tel: 0886 (92) 2349,
Fax: 0878 (62) 3892
Mr. Michikazu Sakamoto
481-5 Nada, Aisumi-cho
Itanogun, Tokushima 〒771-12

TAKAMATSU JCA

Tel: 0878 (86) 6339
Mr. Tsuyoshi Miyake
Create House Makishimu
952-8 Nariai-cho Takamatsu
〒760

KOKURA JCA

Tel: 093 (921) 2131
Mr. Nobuyoshi Shigematsu
Total Design Senken
2-1-1 Saburomaru, Kita-ku
Kokura, Kitakyushu 〒802

OITA JCA

Tel: 0975 (45) 0959
Mr. Tetsuo Kojima
Urban Tamuro Room 403
9-80 Tamurocho, Oita 〒870

MIYAZAKI JCA

Tel: 0985 (24) 4407
Mr. Osamu Aoki
c/o Aoki Gazai
5-6-59 Nishi, Tachibanadori
Miyazaki 〒880

OKINAWA JCA

Tel: 0988 (62) 6269,
Fax: 0988 (66) 1957
Mr. Takezo Sakai
Brain Okinawa
4F Miebashi Bldg. 3-17-5
Kumoji Naha, Okinawa 〒900

MATSUYAMA JCA

Tel: 0899 (41) 9580,
Fax: 0899 (41) 9584
Mr. Tetsushi Yamaguchi
Creative House Tom Olly Bldg.
2F, 2-14-37 Misake
Matsuyama 〒790

FUKUOKA JCA

Tel: 092 (771) 9240
Mr. Keijiro Ozumi
3-3-4 Sasaoka, Chuo-ku
Fukuoka 〒814-01

NAGASAKI JCA

Tel: 0958 (62) 4452
Mr. Hidenobu Maeda
Nakamura Apt. 202
659 Yanagawa-machi
Nagasaki 〒852

OITA JCA

Tel: 0975 (51) 9701
Mr. Kunio Sato
18-11 Maki Kamimachi 〒870

KAGOSHIMA JCA

Tel: 0992 (24) 2735
Mr. Toshiaki Imamura
12-18 Shiroyama 1-chome
Kagoshima 〒892

OKAYAMA JCA

Tel: 0862 (31) 8790
Mr. Tadashi Nakamura
Total Design Center
15-23 Honmachi, Okuda
Okayama 〒700

KOCHI JCA

Tel: 0888 (22) 2111
Mr. Katsuhiro Sueoka
R.K.C. Productions
Kochi Hoso Kaikan 3-2-15
Honmachi, Kochi 〒780

KURUME JCA

Tel: 0942 (32) 6477
Mr. Tomohide Hieda
c/o Hieda Design
Kenkyushitsu
18-37 Hiyoshi-cho Kurume
〒830

NAGASAKI JCA

Tel: 0958 (24) 6989
Mr. Sumio Tani
Sun Design
3F Yamaguchi Bldg. 4-14
Sakaemachi, Nagasaki 〒850

SAGA JCA

Tel: 0952 (32) 0221
Mr. Katsutoshi Ikeda
Ikeda Katsutoshi Design Office
1-14-26 Hinode, Saga 〒840-01

KUMAMOTO JCA

Tel: 09632 (2) 6167
Mr. Yusaku Tomoeda
c/o T.I. Planning
Kamidori Central Heights 218
5-20 Kamidori-cho
Kumamoto 〒860

FUKUOKA JCA

Distributing Div.
Tel: 092 (751) 4342,
Fax: 092 (714) 0610
Mr. Takashi Oyama
Yamamoto Bunpodo
2-4-32 Daimiyo, Chuo-ku
Fukuoka 〒810

JCA ILLUS. BANK

ARE YOU AN ART BUYER?
JCA ILLUSTRATION BANK will meet all your needs with its rich stock of images from all parts of the world.

ARE YOU AN ILLUSTRATOR?
JCA ILLUSTRATION BANK will give your work world-wide exposure and turn your talents into profit in the second rights market.

Yes, you've probably heard of other image banks before, but you may not have tried them because you thought that within your original copyrighted area it wasn't worth the effort; you might as well do your own business. But what about the rest of the world? Who can show your work on five continents and deal with international clients for you, whatever the language may be?

We can!

In order to register your images (in an unlimited amount) you must submit them in transparency form, preferably 6 × 7 or larger. We will then classify the images by style and subject matter and file them together with our catalog of over 60,000 images. With the JCA Illustration Bank, we will always have just the image Art Directors are looking for, and this second rights system will fully satisfy their deadlines or budgets, because your images are readily available and cheaper than originals.

For further details, please contact
the ILLUSTRATION BANK DIVISION at:

Illustration Bank Division
c/o JCA
4F Umehara Bldg.
3-1-29 Roppongi, Minato-ku
Tokyo, Japan
Tel. (03) 582-4201
Fax. (03) 586-4018

あなたはアートバイヤーですか？
JCAイラストバンクは世界各地のアーチストから寄せられた豊富な在庫作品を通して皆様のあらゆるニーズにお応えします。

あなたはイラストレーターですか？
JCAイラストバンクは、あなたの作品を全世界に公開し、再利用のため販売いたします。

そうです。以前に他のイメージバンクなるものについてお聞きになったことがおありでしょう。でも、あなたが最初に著作権を得た地域内では、それらイメージバンクに登録するだけの価値はないと思われて一度もお試しになったことがないのではないでしょうか。でも、この広い地球上の別の地域ではどうでしょうか。まったく言葉の違う世界で、あなたに代わってあなたの作品を五大陸に発表し、クライアンツと交渉することのできるのは誰でしょうか。

私たちができます！

あなたのイメージを（何点でもご希望なだけ）登録なさる時は、それをポジフィルムにして提出してください。6×7のサイズ、もしくはそれ以上が望ましいのです。わたくしどもでは、これらの作品をカテゴリー別に分類し、既にわたくしどもが保有している6万点以上のイメージとともに保管いたします。これによってアートディレクターが探し求めるイメージを常時ストックできることになります。クライアンツの〆切や予算—それがどんなに差し迫った厳しいものであれ—それを再利用によって十分に満たすことができるのです。なぜなら、これらのイメージは即座に利用でき、オリジナルより安いからです。

なお、詳細につきましては下記のJCAイラストバンクまでお問い合わせ下さい。

イラストバンク事業部
東京都港区六本木3－1－29
梅原ビル4F
Tel（03）582－4201 Fax（03）586－4018

JCA CHARACTERS BANK

JCA is now beginning a new and completely revolutionary project: a Characters Bank!

We will gather images from all over the world and from all possible fields: logos, comics, advertisements, animated movies, etc. From this collection of characters we will compile a full-color annual publication and act as licensor for the concerned designers on a consignment basis, the copyright still belonging to the artist, but the exclusive market rights being handled by JCA.

For contributing designers this will mean world-wide exposure as never before possible and an effective method of international promotion through the services of our incredible ICO (International Creators' Organization) network spread over five continents.

Designers' images will be used for a wide variety of purposes: stationery, packaging, corporate identity, the food market, banks and other service businesses, clothing, advertising, TV, and much more. Artists will have access to international business opportunities without the trouble and cost of leaving home to search for commissions abroad.

The first deadline for application is the end of January 1987. However, applications will no longer be accepted when the annual's capacity is filled.

For further information, please feel free to contact us at the following address:

JCA Press Inc.
5-12-3 Higashikaigan Kita
Chigasaki, Kanagawa, Japan
Tel : (0467) 85-2725
Fax : (0467) 86-1501

JCAは今、まったく新しい革命的とも呼ぶべきプランを実行しようとしています。
キヤラクターバンク！

コミックス、ロゴマーク、広告、アニメーション映画など、あらゆる分野におけるキャラクターを世界各地から募集いたします。このようにして造られたキャラクターを集大成して総ページカラーのキャラクター年鑑を発刊し、委託ベースにし、掲載作家のサブモニリーとして皆様に奉仕いたします。著作権はあくまで作家に属しますが、両当事者の取り決めによる独占販売権はJCAが保有します。

これにより、キャラクター作家はこれまで考えられなかったような世界的規模で作品を公表することができ、37ヶ所にも及ぶILO（国際クリエーターズ機構）のネットワークを利用して容易に、かつ効果的にビジネスを進め、利益を上げることができます。

皆様から寄せられたキャラクターは、文房具、パッケージ、コーポレートアイデンティティ、食品市場、銀行および多業種にわたる会社、服飾、広告、テレビコマーシャル、そのほか諸々の目的に使用されます。あなたは世界的に有名になり、とても効率のよいビジネスチャンスが与えられます。しかも、自国を出て、自分の足でビジネスの可能性を探る煩わしさもなく、よくあるように無駄な時間、予算を費やすこともなく、したがってそうした徒労によって気力を失ってしまうこともありません。

皆様の作品の応募〆切は1987年1月といたしますが、年鑑のキャパシティを満たした時点で締切らせていただきます。

なお、詳細につきましては、どうぞお気軽にご連絡ください。
お問い合わせ先　：　JCA出版
神奈川県東海岸北5-12-3
Tel 0467－85－2725　FAX 0467－86－1501

BUSINESSES WHICH SUPPORT JCA

Diagrams, which are a universal means of communication applicable to even the most diversified fields, were considered a worthy theme for the new JCA annuals. Their wide range of applications, combined with the talents of the artists who produce diagrams, fully justify this publication. The following companies share our enthusiasm and have been instrumental in the creation of useful diagrams by supporting our company with consistent business exchanges and utilization of our services.

FOOD INDUSTRY WORLD. 食品業界
AJINOMOTO CO., INC. 味の素
THE CALPIS FOOD INDUSTRIES CO., LTD. カルピス
COCA-COLA (JAPAN) CO., LTD. 日本コカコーラ
FUJIYA CONFECTIONERY CO., LTD. 不二家
KAGOME CO. カゴメ
KATAOKA & CO., LTD. 片岡物産
KIKKOMAN SHOYU CO., LTD. キッコーマン醤油
KIRIN BREWERY CO., LTD. キリンビール
KOKUBU & CO., LTD. 国分
MEIJI CONFECTIONERY CO., LTD. 明治製菓
MORINAGA CONFECTIONERY CO., LTD. 森永製菓
PRIMA MEAT PACKERS LTD. プリマハム
SANRAKU-OCEAN CO., LTD. 三楽オーシャン
SNOW BRAND MILK PRODUCTS CO. 雪印乳業
SUNTORY LTD. サントリー
YAKULT CO., LTD. ヤクルト

COSMETICS, DETERGENT, CLOTHING JEWELRY WORLD. 化粧・洗剤・衣料・装飾品業界
DESCENTE LTD. デサント
MAX FACTOR JAPAN BRANCH マックスファクター
K. HATTORI CO., LTD. 服部時計店
KANEBO COSMETICS INC. カネボウ化粧品
KAO CORPORATION 花王

LION CORP. ライオン
K. MIKIMOTO AND CO., LTD. 御木本パール
MIZUNO CO. 美津濃
RENOWN INC. レナウン
SHISEIDO CO., LTD. 資生堂
WACOAL CO. ワコール
WAKO. 和光

ELECTRIC INDUSTRY WORLD. 電気(機)業界
AIWA CO., LTD. アイワ
AKAI TRADING CO., LTD. 赤井商事
SONY INC. ソニー
FUJI ELECTRIC CO., LTD. 富士電機
FUJITSU LTD. 富士通
HITACHI LTD. 日立製作所
MATSUSHITA ELECTRIC INDUSTRIAL CO., LTD. 松下電気
MITSUBISHI ELECTRIC CORPORATION. 三菱電機
NEC CORPORATION 日本電気（NEC）
PIONEER ELECTRIC CO. パイオニア
SHARP CORPORATION. シャープ
TEAC CORPORATION. ティアック
TOKYO SHIBAURA ELECTRIC CO., LTD. 東京芝浦電気
TRIO-KENWOOD CORPORATION. トリオ
UTSUNOMIYA ELECTRIC MFG., CO., LTD. 宇都宮電機製作所
YASUKAWA ELECTRIC MFG., CO., LTD. 安川電機
OLIVETTI CO., JAPAN 日本オリベッティ

COMPUTER WORLD. コンピューター業界
CASIO CORPORATION. カシオ
FUJITSU LTD. 富士通
IBM JAPAN LTD. 日本IBM
NIPPON ELECTRIC CO., LTD. NEC (NEC) 日本電気
SHARP CORPORATION. シャープ
SPN CO., LTD. エスピーエヌ
TOYO LINKS CO., LTD. トーヨー・フィルム・リンクス
NIPPON UNIVAC INFORMATION SYSTEMS 日本ユニバックインフォメーションシステム

RECORD WORLD. レコード業界
CBS SONY INC. CBSソニー
KING RECORD キングレコード
NIHON PHILIPS CORPORATION. 日本フィリップス
NIPPON COLUMBIA CO., LTD. 日本コロンビア
TOSHIBA EMI CO. 東芝EMI
VICTOR MUSICAL INDUSTRIES INC. ビクター音楽産業

WARNER PIONEER CO. ワーナーパイオニア

AUTOMOBILE INDUSTRY WORLD.
自動車業界
BRIDGESTONE TIRE CO., LTD.
ブリヂストンタイヤ
HONDA MOTOR CO., LTD. 本田技研工業
ISUZU MOTORS LTD. いすゞ自動車
MITSUBISHI MOTORS CO., LTD.
三菱自動車
NISSAN MOTOR CO., LTD. 日産自動車
TOYO INDUSTRY CO., LTD. 東洋工業
TOYOTA MOTOR SALES CO., LTD.
トヨタ自動車
YAMAHA CO., LTD. ヤマハ発動機

CONSTRUCTION WORLD. 建設業界
NOMURA DISPLAY CO., LTD. 及村工芸社
TAISEI CORPORATION. 大成建設
TAKENAKA KOUMUTEN CO., LTD.
竹中工務店
THE SHIMIZU CONSTRUCTION
CO., LTD. 清水建設

DEPARTMENT STORE WORLD.
百貨店業界
I WORLD CO., LTD. アイワールド
ISETAN CO., LTD. 伊勢丹
ITO-YOKADO CO., LTD. イトーヨーカ堂
PARCO CO., LTD. パルコ
MARUI CO., LTD. 丸井
MATSUYA CO., LTD. 松屋
MATSUZAKAYA CO., LTD. 松坂屋
MITSUKOSHI LTD. 三越
THE SEIBU DEPARTMENT STORES
LTD. 西武百貨店
TAKASHIMAYA CO., LTD. 高島屋
TOKYU DEPARTMENT STORE CO.,
LTD. 東急百貨店

MEDICINE WORLD. 薬品業界
DAI-ICHI SEIYAKU CO., LTD. 第一製薬
OOTSUKA PHARMACEUTICAL
CO., LTD. 大塚製薬
SANKYO CO., LTD. 三共
TAKEDA PHARMACEUTICAL CO.,
LTD. 武田薬品工業
YAMANOUCHI PHARMACEUTICAL
CO., LTD. 山之内製薬

OIL INDUSTRY, INSURANCE WORLD.
石油・保険業界
ESSO SEKIYU K.K. エッソ石油
IDEMITSU KOSAN CO., LTD. 出光興産
THE KYOEI LIFE INSURANCE CO.,
LTD. 協栄生命
KYODO SEKIYU CO., LTD. 共同石油
NIHON SEKIYU CO., LTD. 日本石油
SHELL SEKIYU K.K. シェル石油
THE YASUDA MUTUAL LIFE
INSURANCE CO. 安田生命保険

AVIATION WORLD. 航空業界
AIR FRANCE. エールフランス
ALL NIPPON AIRWAYS. 全日空
JAPAN AIR LINES CO., LTD. 日本航空
TOA DOMESTIC AIRLINES CO., LTD.
東亜国内航空

ARTIST SUPPLIES, BOOK STORE
WORLD. 画材・紙・書籍業界
ASAHIYA BOOK-STORE CO., LTD.
東京旭屋書店
ITO-YA LTD. 伊東屋
IZUMIYA CO., INC. いづみや
KINOKUNIYA BOOK-STORE CO.,LTD.
紀伊国屋書店
KOKUYO CO., LTD. コクヨ
MIDORI CO., LTD. ミドリ
MITSUBISHI PENCIL CO., LTD. 三菱えんぴつ
SANRIO CO., LTD. サンリオ
TAKEO CO., LTD. 竹尾
TOMBO PENCIL CO., LTD. とんぼえんぴつ
YURIN-DO CO., LTD. 有隣堂

PRINTING WORLD. 印刷業界
DAINIPPON INK CHEMICALS INC.
大日本インク化学工業
DAINIPPON PRINTING CO., LTD.
大日本印刷
KYODO PRINTING CO., LTD. 共同印刷
MITSUMURA PRINTING CO. 光村原色版印刷
SHA-KEN CO., LTD. 写研
TOPPAN PRINTING CO., LTD. 凸版印刷

NEWS PRESS, TV STATION WORLD.
新聞・放送・通信業界
ASAHI SHIMBUN. 朝日新聞社
KYODO TELEVISION. 共同テレビ
THE MAINICHI NEWSPAPER. 毎日新聞
NIHON KEIZAI SHIMBUN INC.
日本経済新聞
THE SANKEI SHIMBUN. サンケイ新聞社
NIPPON TELEVISION NETWORK
CORPORATION. 日本テレビ
TOKYO BROADCASTING SYSTEM
東京放送
TELEVISION KANAGAWA UHF
CHANNEL テレビ神奈川
TOKYO FM BROADCASTING CO.,
LTD. FM東京

ADVERTISING WORLD. 広告・宣伝業界
ASAHI KOKOKUSHA CO., LTD.
朝日広告社
ASAHI TSUSHINSHA ADVERTISING
AGENCY. 旭通信社
CHUO SENKO ADVERTISING CO.,
LTD. 中央宣興
DAI-ICHI ADVERTISING CO., LTD.
第一広告社
DAI-ICHI KIKAKU CO., LTD. 第一企画
DAIKO ADVERTISING INC. 大広東京本部
DENTSU INC. 電通
FRANKLIN MINT CO., LTD.
フランクリンミント
HAKUHODO INC. 博報堂
JAPAN MARKETING SERVICE.
ジャパン・マーケティング・サービス
KYODO ADVERTISING INC. 協同広告
KYODO SENDEN ADVERTISING
AGENCY INC. 協同宣伝
LIGHT PUBLICITY LTD. ライトパブリシティ
McCANN ERICKSON-HAKUHODO.
マッキャンエリクソン博報堂
NATIONAL ADVERTISING.
ナショナル宣伝研究所
THE NIPPON DESIGN CENTER INC.
日本デザインセンター
ORIKOMI ADVERTISING LTD. オリコミ
SHINWA INC. 真和
SOBI KIKAKU CORPORATION. 創美企画
SOUGEI CO., LTD. 創芸
J. WALTER THOMPSON CO., JAPAN.
J・ウォルター・トンプソン
TOKYU ADVERTISING. 東急エージェンシー
YOMIKO ADVERTISING. 読売広告社

PUBLISHING WORLD. 出版業界
AKITASHOTEN PUBLISHING CO.
秋田書店
KYOIKUSHA 教育社
FROEBEL-KAN CO., LTD. フレーベル館
GAKKEN CO., LTD. 学習研究社
HEIBON PUBLISHING COMPANY.
平凡出版
JIJIGAHO PUBLISHING CO., LTD.
時事画報社
KOKI PUBLISHING CO. コーキ出版
OBUNSHA PRESS. 旺文社
PRESIDENT INC. プレジデント社
SEIBUNDO SHINKOSHA CO., LTD.
誠文堂新光社
THE SENDENKAIGI INC. 宣伝会議
SHOBUNSHA PRINTING CO. 昭文社

SHOGAKUKAN PUBLISHING CO.,LTD.
小学館
TOKUMA SHOTEN PUBLISHING CO.
徳間書店
SHUEISHA PUBLISHING CO., LTD.
集英社
THE SHUFU TO SEIKATSU CO., LTD.
主婦と生活社

CAMERA (PHOTOGRAPHY)
INDUSTRY WORLD. カメラ（写真）業界
ASAHI PENTAX OPTICAL CO., LTD.
旭光学商事
BRONIKA CO., LTD. ブロニカ
CANON INC. キヤノン
CANON SALES CO. キヤノン販売
HASSELBLAD. ハッセルブラット
KONISHIROKU PHOTO INDUSTRY
CO., LTD. 小西六写真工業
MINOLTA CAMERA SALES CO., LTD.
ミノルタカメラ販売
NIPPON KOGAKU K.K. 日本光学
OLYMPUS OPTICAL CO., LTD.
オリンパス工業
ORIENTAL PHOTO SUPPLY CO.
オリエンタル写真商事
RICOH CO., LTD. リコー
YASHIKA CO., LTD. ヤシカ

PHOTOGRAPHIC PRODUCTS AND
LABORATORIES INDUSTRY.
写真周辺器材・関連業界
CHROMART LABORATORY INC.
クロマート
COMET CO., LTD. コメット
FUJI PHOTO FILM CO., LTD. 富士写真フィルム
FUJI XEROX CO., LTD. 富士ゼロックス
KODAK FILM CO., LTD. コダック
NIHON HASSHOKU CO., LTD. 日本発色
SIGMA CO., LTD. シグマ
SLIK TRIPOD CO., LTD. スリック
TOYO FAR EAST LABORATORIES
CO., LTD. 東洋現像所
YODOBASHI CAMERA CO., LTD.
ヨドバシカメラ

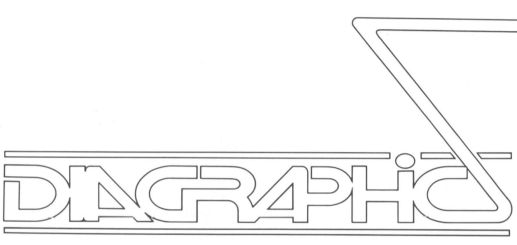

In the following pages you will be introduced to what was once considered impossible: precise and effective diagrams presented in an aesthetically pleasing and imaginative manner. This collection of diagrams owes its creation to the efforts of the JCA international network of ICO bureaus, and to the talents and cooperation of the artists who agreed to contribute their works to our publication. We hope that companies world-wide who are in need of such talent will refer to these artists' works through the services of our JCA Art Agency. We will be more than happy to supply clients with requested information or to initiate negotiations between clients and artists.

For further details, please contact the nearest ICO bureau (listed on pp.24,25), the JCA domestic bureaus, or our International Division located at 5-12-13 Higashikaigan Kita, Kanagawa, Japan. Tel. 0467-85-2726 Fax. 0467-86-1501

　ページをお開けください。あなたはそこに、これまで不可能と考えられていた新しいダイヤグラフィックスの姿を発見されることでしょう。正確で入念であっても死ぬほど退屈だった、あのダイアグラフィックスが正確、かつ細心、しかも楽しく、美しいダイアグラフィックスに　変身した姿を…。

　ダイアグラフィックスの　集大成とも呼ぶべきこの年鑑は JCA 国際ネットワークである ICO ビューローの努力の結晶であり、また作品を送ってくださったアーチストたちの想像力と善意の贈り物です。

　新生ダイアグラフィックスを探し求めている世界中の企業が、アートエージェンシーとしての JCA のサービスによって、このようなアーチストの作品を積極的に活用していただけるならば…。それが、わたくしどもの切なる願いです。わたくしどもは、みなさまからご要望があれば、いつでも喜んで情報を提供し、クライアンツとアーチストの間に立って必要な交渉のお手伝いをいたします。

In order to present each image in an organized and interesting manner, we have used the following data categories:

TITLE: Artist's name and image number
1. Artist's country
2. Artist's studio or design firm (if not independent)
3. Diagraphics image-category (i.e. Maps, Computer Graphics, etc.)
4. The medium or publication for which the image was created
5. Client
    A brief explanation of the image

Not every image is accompanies by all five data categories; sometimes because no information was provided by the artist and other times because we consider the images self-explanatory.

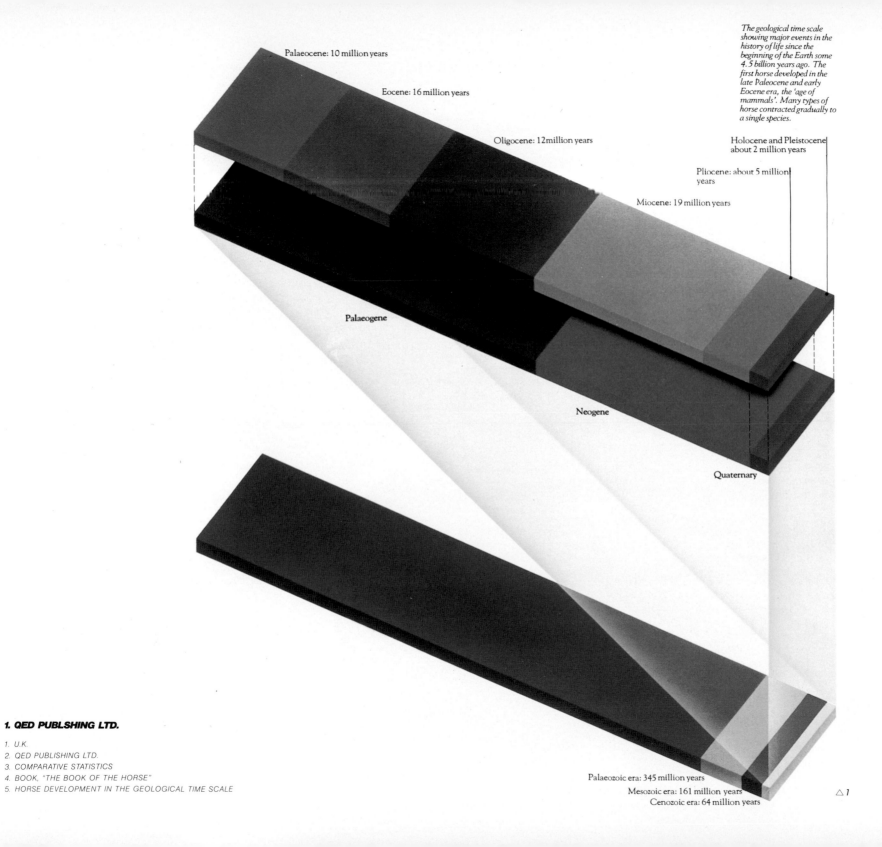

Palaeocene: 10 million years

Eocene: 16 million years

Oligocene: 12million years

The geological time scale showing major events in the history of life since the beginning of the Earth some 4.5 billion years ago. The first horse developed in the late Paleocene and early Eocene era, the 'age of mammals'. Many types of horse contracted gradually to a single species.

Holocene and Pleistocene about 2 million years

Pliocene: about 5 million years

Miocene: 19 million years

Palaeogene

Neogene

Quaternary

Palaeozoic era: 345 million years

Mesozoic era: 161 million years

Cenozoic era: 64 million years

△1

1. QED PUBLSHING LTD.

1. U.K.
2. QED PUBLISHING LTD.
3. COMPARATIVE STATISTICS
4. BOOK, "THE BOOK OF THE HORSE"
5. HORSE DEVELOPMENT IN THE GEOLOGICAL TIME SCALE

2. QED PUBLISHING LTD.

1. UK
2. QED PUBLISHING LTD.
3. COMPARATIVE STATISTICS
4. BOOK, "THE BOOK OF THE HORSE"
5. CARE SCHEDULE FOR PREGNANT MARES

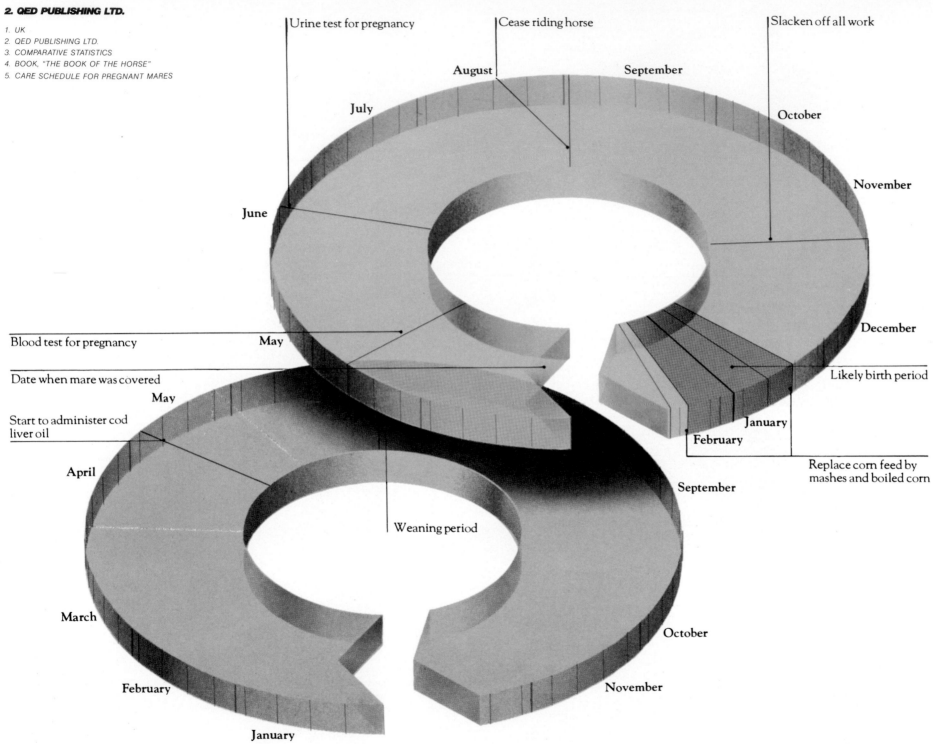

Urine test for pregnancy

Cease riding horse

Slacken off all work

August

September

July

October

June

November

Blood test for pregnancy

May

December

Date when mare was covered

May

Likely birth period

Start to administer cod liver oil

April

January

February

September

Replace corn feed by mashes and boiled corn

Weaning period

March

October

February

November

January

△2

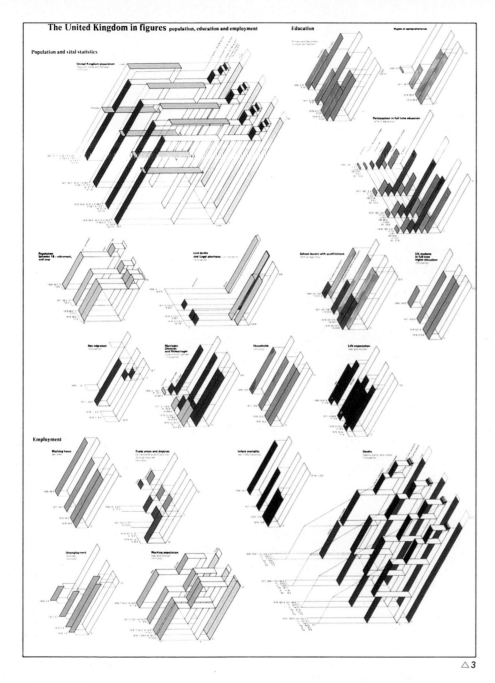

The United Kingdom in figures population, education and employment

Population and vital statistics

Education

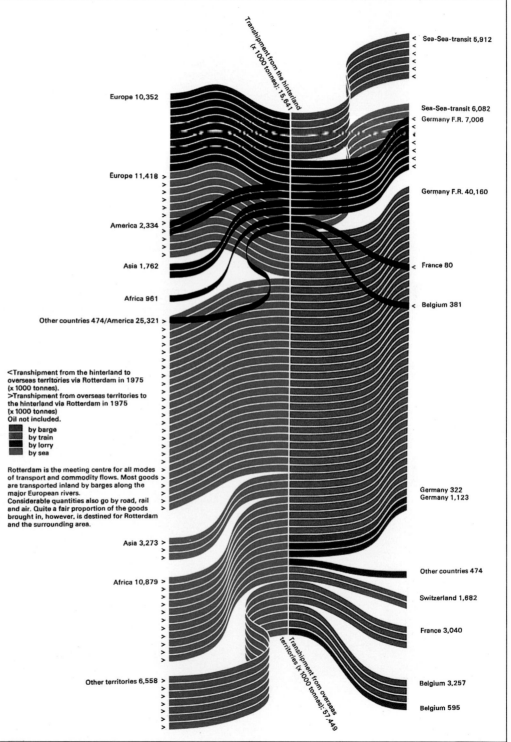

Europe 10,352

Transhipment from the hinterland (x 1000 tonnes): 15,641

< Sea-Sea-transit 5,912

< Sea-Sea-transit 6,082
< Germany F.R. 7,006

Europe 11,418 >

Germany F.R. 40,160

America 2,334 >

Asia 1,762

< France 80

Africa 961

< Belgium 381

Other countries 474/America 25,321 >

<Transhipment from the hinterland to
overseas territories via Rotterdam in 1975
(x 1000 tonnes).
>Transhipment from overseas territories to
the hinterland via Rotterdam in 1975
(x 1000 tonnes)
Oil not included.

by barge
by train
by lorry
by sea

Rotterdam is the meeting centre for all modes
of transport and commodity flows. Most goods
are transported inland by barges along the
major European rivers.
Considerable quantities also go by road, rail
and air. Quite a fair proportion of the goods
brought in, however, is destined for Rotterdam
and the surrounding area.

Germany 322
Germany 1,123

Asia 3,273 >

Africa 10,879 >

Other countries 474

Switzerland 1,682

France 3,040

Other territories 6,558 >

Belgium 3,257

Transhipment from overseas territories (x 1000 tonnes): 57,449

Belgium 595

△3

△4

3. EITETSU NOZAWA

1. UK
2. FREELANCE AT EDITORIAL DESIGN CONSULTANTS LTD.
3. COMPARATIVE STATISTICS
4. UNITED KINGDOM IN FIGURE
5. THE UNITED KINGDOM IN FIGURES-POPULATION,
   EDUCATION AND EMPLOYMENT

4. BENNO WISSING/JOHN STEGMEYER

1. U.S.A
2. THE WISSING GENGLER GROUP, INC.
3. COMPARATIVE STATISTICS
4. BOOK ON THE PORT OF ROTTERDAM DEVELOPMENT POTENTIAL
5. MEANS OF TRANSHIPMENT TO AND FROM OVERSEAS
   TERRITORIES VIA ROTTERDAM PORT IN 1975

5,6. BILL BROWN

1. U.S.A.
2. BILL BROWN & ASSOCIATES
ART DIRECTOR: BILL BROWN
DESIGNER: SHOJI TERAISHI
3. COMPARATIVE STATISTICS
4. CATALOGUE
5. DAMES & MOORE
DATA ON WASTE MANAGEMENT

Hazardous Waste Management Facility Closure — Dames & Moore

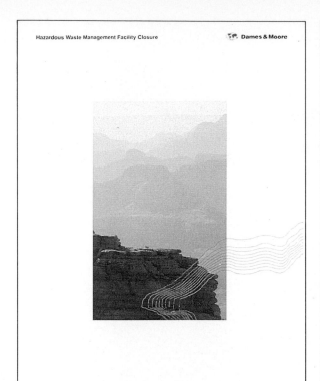

Facilitating the Closure Process

Developing a Certified Closure Plan

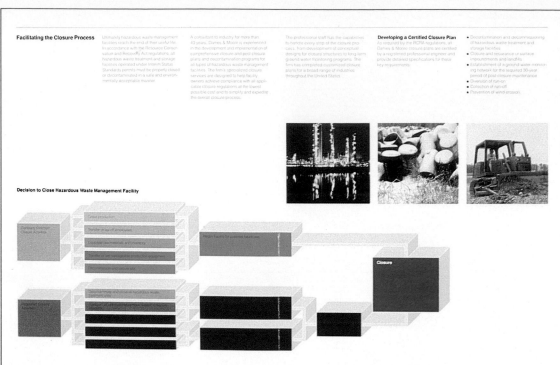

Decision to Close Hazardous Waste Management Facility

△5 ▽6

Siting and Permitting of Hazardous Waste Management Facilities — Dames & Moore

A Comprehensive Approach Designed to Facilitate Regulatory Compliance and Secure Public Acceptance

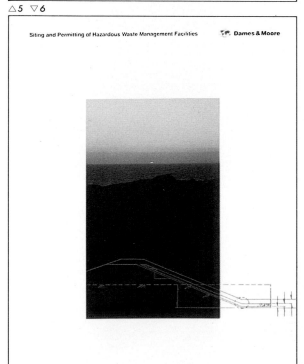

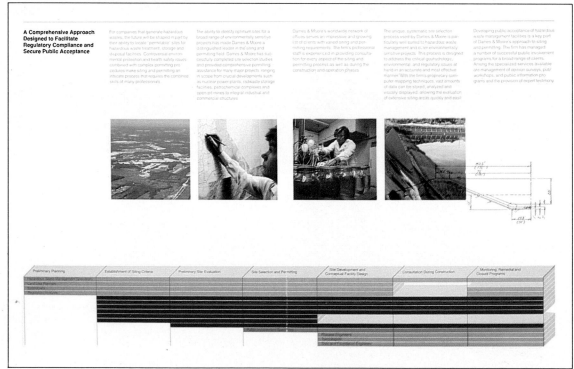

SUDARSHAN DHEER 7.

INDIA 1.
GRAPHIC COMMUNICATION CONCEPTS 2.
COMPARATIVE STATISTICS 3.
ANNUAL REPORT 4.
STATE BANK OF INDIA 5.

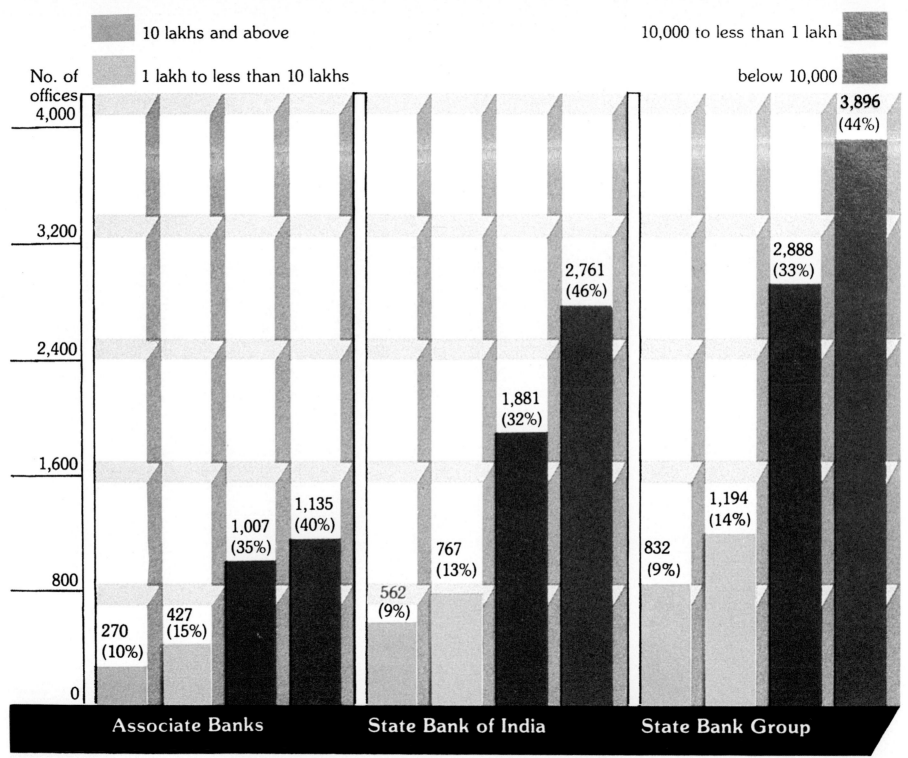

No. of offices

10 lakhs and above

1 lakh to less than 10 lakhs

10,000 to less than 1 lakh

below 10,000

Associate Banks

270 (10%)
427 (15%)
1,007 (35%)
1,135 (40%)

State Bank of India

562 (9%)
767 (13%)
1,881 (32%)
2,761 (46%)

State Bank Group

832 (9%)
1,194 (14%)
2,888 (33%)
3,896 (44%)

△7

5

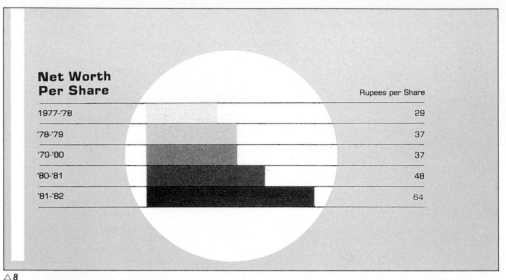

Net Worth Per Share

	Rupees per Share
1977-'78	29
'78-'79	37
'79-'80	37
'80-'81	48
'81-'82	64

△8

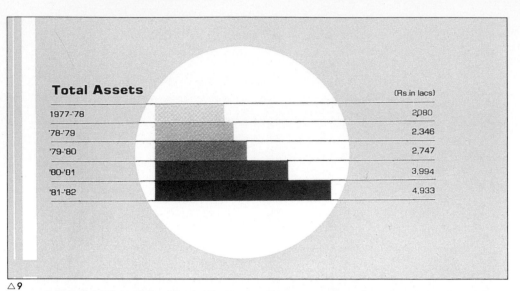

Total Assets

	(Rs. in lacs)
1977-'78	2,080
'78-'79	2,346
'79-'80	2,747
'80-'01	3,994
'81-'82	4,933

△9

Payment to Employees

	(Rs. in lacs)
1977-'78	506
'78-'79	626
'79-'80	743
'80-'81	742
'81-'82	1,080

△10

Shareholders' Funds

	(Rs. in lacs)
1977-'78	1,117
'78 70	1,400
'79-'80	1,724
'80-'81	2,207
'81-'82	3005

△11

8~11. SUDARSHAN DHEER

1. INDIA
2. GRAPHIC COMMUNICATION CONCEPTS
3. COMPARATIVE STATISTICS
4. ANNUAL REPORT
5. INDIAN RAYON CORPORATION LTD.

SUDARSHAN DHEER 12,13.

INDIA 1.
GRAPHIC COMMUNICATION CONCEPTS 2.
COMPARATIVE STATISTICS 3.
ANNUAL REPORT 4.
EXPORT IMPORT BANK OF INDIA 5.

Lending Programmes

Outstandings
(Rs. in million)

- Buyer's Credit
- Direct Financial Assistance
- Export Bills Rediscounting
- Export Credit Refinance
- Lines of Credit
- Overseas Investment Finance

96.34

269.31

814.05

1050.86

240.68

459.00

Lending Programmes

Sanctions
(Rs. in million)

- Buyer's Credit
- Direct Financial Assistance
- Export Bills Rediscounting
- Export Credit Refinance
- Lines of Credit
- Overseas Investment Finance
- Relending facility

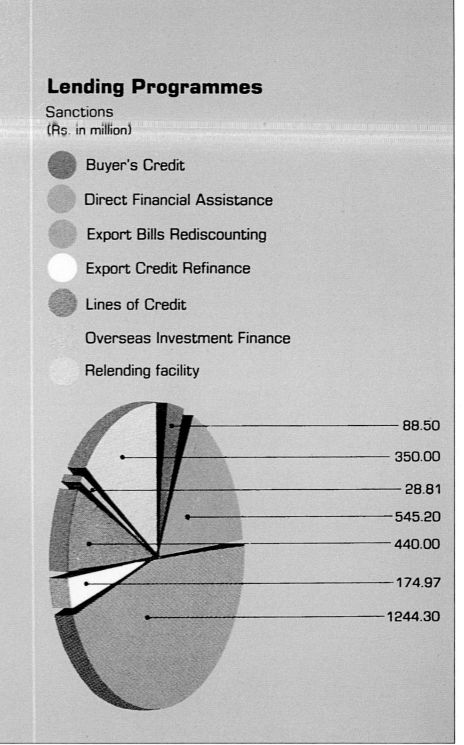

88.50

350.00

28.81

545.20

440.00

174.97

1244.30

△12   △13

7

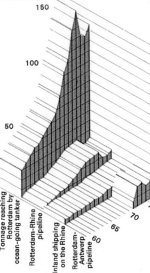

Mineral oils in super-tankers destined for Europe arrive continuously at the port of Rotterdam, the main distribution centre for energy (x mln. tonnes)

To manage means to be looking ahead and it was this insight that led to the decision to fit out the port to enable it to take more and larger ships. The infrastructure is provided by the city and made available to the industry. Some 3,800 ha, approximately 80% of the surface area of the port complex, is rented. New docks were built and provided with the right facilities to cope with the new types of ship. The mooring area for sea-going vessels has grown to the present 83 kilometres. In addition, there are 57 berths on buoys and dolphins.

The Botlek area is mainly for the transhipment and storage of oil, ores and dry bulk cargo such as grain, but there are also petro-chemical industries and some ship-building. Europoort, closer to the sea, was designed to enable supertankers to find a safe berth.

The Europoort docks to the east are intended for the new forms of transport such as containers, Ro-Ro, Seabea and Lash. Advanced techniques of transhipment ensure a fast turn-around time for the grain and ore tankers. The Maasvlakte, the last harbour expansion project which was completed in 1974, is almost entirely in the North Sea and its present function is to tranship and store fuels and ores but its ultimate function has yet

Nowadays the occupants of the harbour complex present a very diversified picture; about 1000 ha. of the harbour area still has to be allocated a purpose.

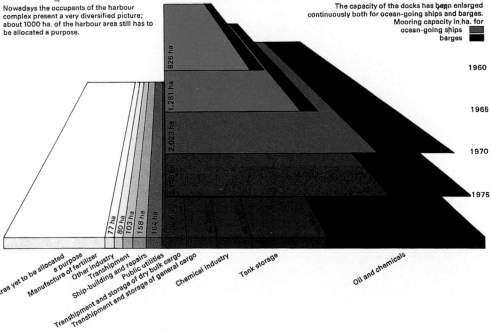

The capacity of the docks has been enlarged continuously both for ocean-going ships and barges.
Mooring capacity in ha. for
ocean-going ships
barges

drinking water, and civil engineering works such as the Maasvlakte and the dams and roads linking the islands of Zeeland, with its famous beaches and dunes.

It is not possible to sum up in a word what the port of Rotterdam actually does and what it signifies, still less what prospects are in store for the future. The city's unique geographical position combined with a waterway network extending deep into Europe and which is so important for the port because it can carry the most modern ships—these are the main foundations on which confidence in the port's future rest. Other favourable factors are: faith in the strength of purpose shown by the city council and trade and industry in anticipating and responding to new developments in trade, traffic and transport; the spirit of enterprise and will to succeed of the Rotterdam population.

The openess of the Dutch economy is well known. The significance of the foreign market for the various sectors is reflected in the percentage of foreign sales of gross production.
A yardstick for the broad and diversified economic structure is the number of man-years and the division of labour per branch.
man-years (x 1000)
foreign sales as % of gross production

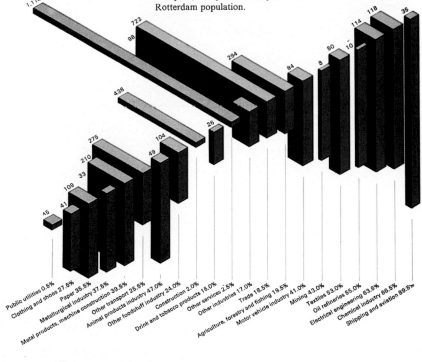

14,15. BENNO WISSING/JOHN STEGMEVER

1. U.S.A.
2. THE WISSING GENGLER GROUP, INC.
3. COMPARATIVE STATISTICS
4. BOOK ON THE PORT OF ROTTERDAM DEVELOPMENT POTENTIAL
5. MINERAL OIL TRANSPORT AND DOCK CAPACITY FOR ROTTERDAM PORT (14)
   FOREIGN SALES OF GROSS PRODUCTION (15)

△14

△15

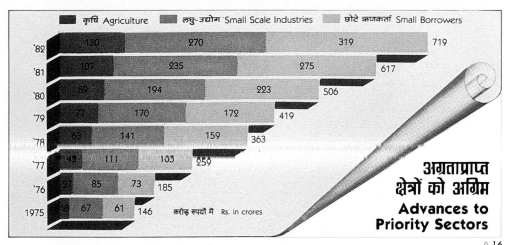

■ कृषि Agriculture ■ लघु-उद्योग Small Scale Industries ■ छोटे ऋणकर्ता Small Borrowers

'82	130	270	319	719
'81	107	235	275	617
'80	89	194	223	506
'79	77	170	172	419
'78	63	141	159	363
'77	49	111	103	259
'76	27	85	73	185
1975	18	67	61	146

करोड़ रुपयों में Rs. in crores

अग्रताप्राप्त
क्षेत्रों को अग्रिम
**Advances to
Priority Sectors**

△16

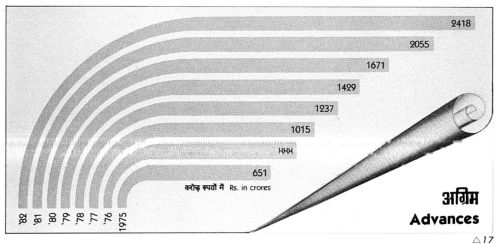

2418
2055
1671
1429
1237
1015
HHH
651

करोड़ रुपयों में Rs. in crores

'82 '81 '80 '79 '78 '77 '76 1975

अग्रिम
Advances

△17

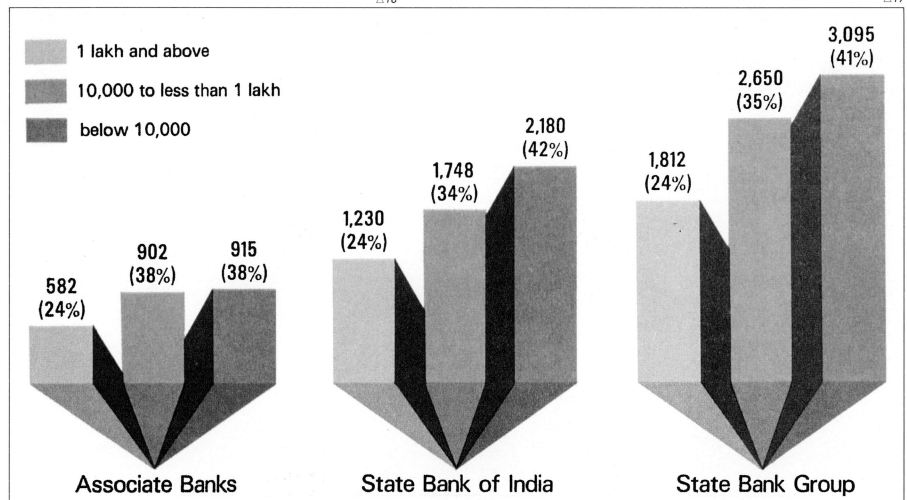

■ 1 lakh and above

■ 10,000 to less than 1 lakh

■ below 10,000

Associate Banks
582 (24%) 902 (38%) 915 (38%)

State Bank of India
1,230 (24%) 1,748 (34%) 2,180 (42%)

State Bank Group
1,812 (24%) 2,650 (35%) 3,095 (41%)

.SUDARSHAN DHEER

PHIC COMMUNICATION CONCEPTS
PARATIVE STATISTICS
UAL REPORT
E BANK OF INDIA
ADVANCES TO TYPES OF
NTS (16) AND BY YEARLY
ALS (17)

△18

Priority Sector Advances (December end)

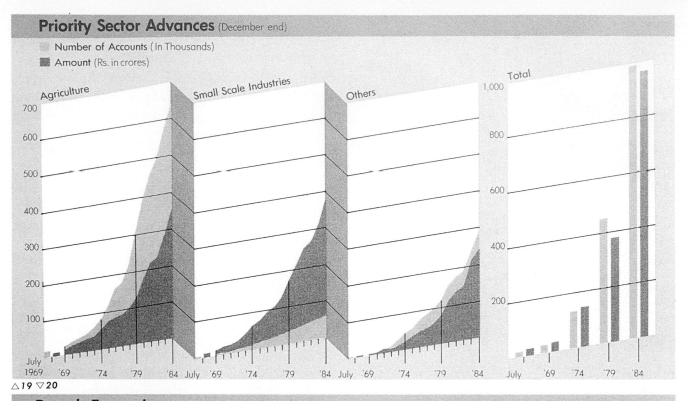

Number of Accounts (In Thousands)

Amount (Rs. in crores)

Agriculture   Small Scale Industries   Others   Total

△19 ▽20

Branch Expansion (December end-Numbers)

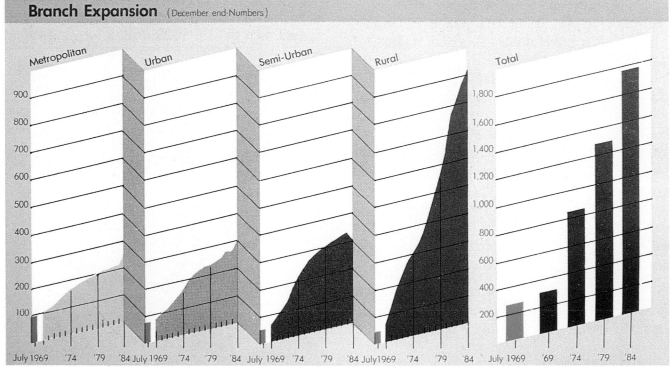

Metropolitan   Urban   Semi-Urban   Rural   Total

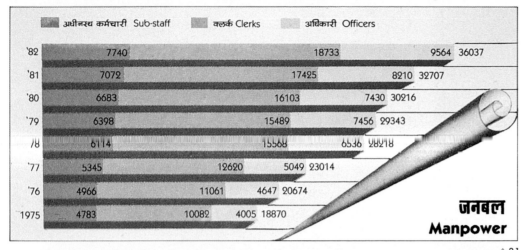

	अधीनस्थ कर्मचारी Sub-staff	वल्र्क Clerks	अधिकारी Officers	
'82	7740	18733	9564	36037
'81	7072	17425	8210	32707
'80	6683	16103	7430	30216
'79	6398	15489	7456	29343
'78	6114	15568	6536	28218
'77	5345	12620	5049	23014
'76	4966	11061	4647	20674
1975	4783	10082	4005	18870

जनबल
Manpower

△21

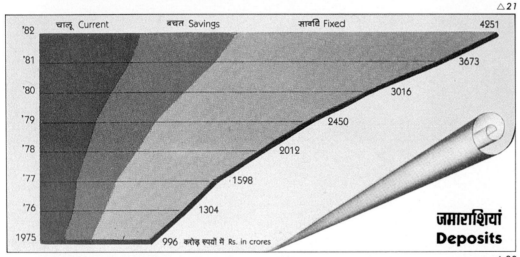

चालू Current   बचत Savings   सावधि Fixed

'82		4251
'81		3673
'80		3016
'79		2450
'78		2012
'77		1598
'76		1304
1975	996 करोड़ रुपयों में Rs. in crores	

जमाराशियां
Deposits

△22

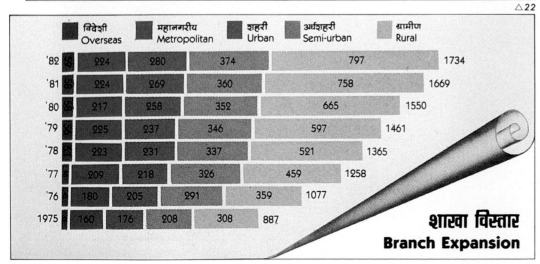

	विदेशी Overseas	महानगरीय Metropolitan	शहरी Urban	अर्धशहरी Semi-urban	ग्रामीण Rural	
'82		224	280	374	797	1734
'81		224	269	360	758	1669
'80		217	258	352	665	1550
'79		225	237	346	597	1461
'78		223	231	337	521	1365
'77		209	218	326	459	1258
'76		180	205	291	359	1077
1975	160	176	208	308	887	

शाखा विस्तार
Branch Expansion

△23

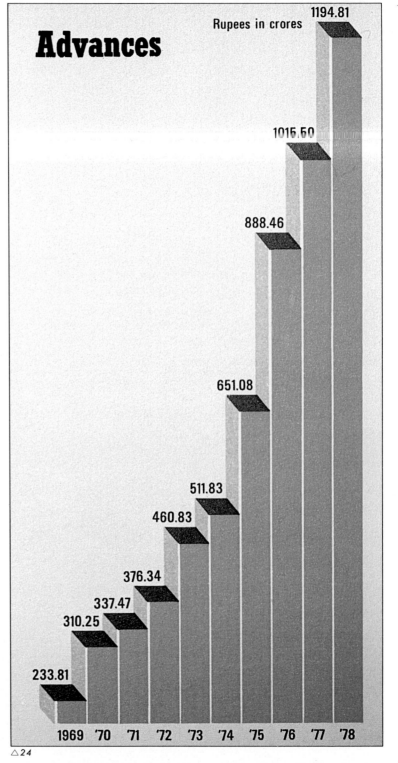

Advances

Rupees in crores

1969	233.81
'70	310.25
'71	337.47
'72	376.34
'73	460.83
'74	511.83
'75	651.08
'76	888.46
'77	1015.50
'78	1194.81

△24

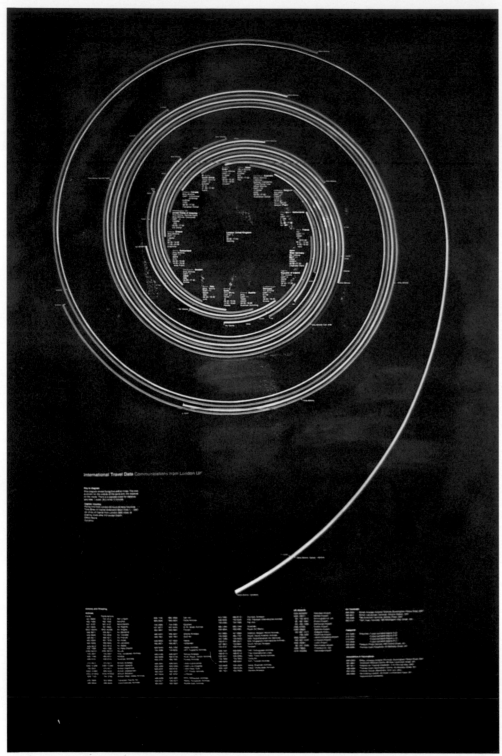

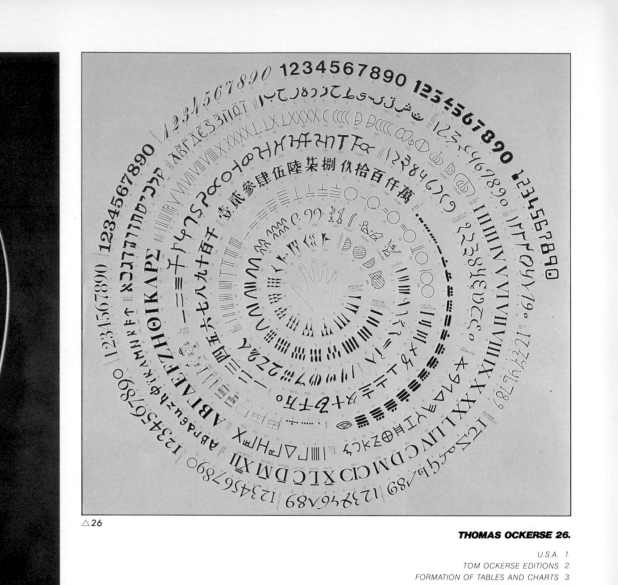

△26

THOMAS OCKERSE 26.

U.S.A. 1.
TOM OCKERSE EDITIONS 2.
FORMATION OF TABLES AND CHARTS 3.
WORLD MAGAZINE 4.
THE DEVELOPMENT AND HISTORY OF NUMBERS 5.

25. EITETSU NOZAWA

1. U.K.
2. FREELANCE AT EDITORIAL DESIGN CONSULTANTS LTD.
3. COMPARATIVE STATISTICS
4. INTERNATIONAL TRAVEL DATA
5. COMMUNICATIONS FROM LONDON, UK

EITETSU NOZAWA 27.

U.K. 1.
FREELANCE AT EDITORIAL DESIGN CONSULTANTS LTD. 2.
COMPARATIVE STATISTICS 3.
'PACKAGING REVIEW' 1983 IN UK 4.
READERSHIP ANALYSIS 5.

The following important findings have been extracted from the 1983 Packaging Review Readership Survey, based on 1533 returned questionnaires which were independently analysed and processed by Mass Observation (UK) Ltd.

1 Most regularly read packaging journal.

Packaging Review is read regularly by 95% of its readers – far more than any of its competitors.

1 Most regularly read packaging journal.

Packaging Review 98%

Packaging News 63%

Packaging Today 51%

Packaging 45%

No Preference/No Answer 6%

2 Readers preferred journal format.

Glossy Magazine 81%

Newspaper 8%

Glossy Newspaper 5%

2 Readers preferred journal format.

Glossy magazine format is preferred by 81% of readers.

3 Subjects of interest.

Packaging Review readers recorded high/fair interest ratings in the following subjects:-

Features on Packaging Industry Sectors 80%

Case Studies 73%

New Containers 72%

Legislation 74%

Packaging Equipment 81%

New Packaging Materials 94%

3 Subjects of interest.

The 1983 readership survey confirms that Packaging Review's requested circulation to readers in the UK packaging and packaging 'user' industries, is reaching not only those companies with a high manufacturing output, but also executives who have purchasing authority – the complete findings are available on request.

An analysis of enquiry cards from recent issues of Packaging Review showed the following reader response:

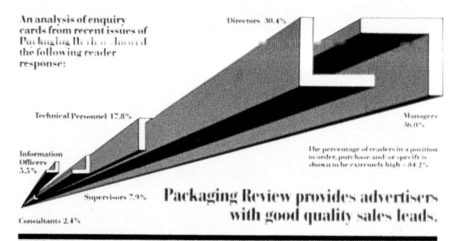

Directors 30.4%

Technical Personnel 17.8%

Information Officers 3.5%

Consultants 2.4%

Supervisors 7.9%

Managers 36.0%

The percentage of readers in a position to order, purchase and/or specify is shown to be extremely high – 84.3%

Packaging Review provides advertisers with good quality sales leads.

Packaging Review Product Information Cards

An additional marketing service giving advertisers direct contact with their potential customers at an extremely low cost. The cards are reply-paid postcards carrying an advertising message and are available as either a loose pack (despatched in a plastic wallet) or bound in the journal.

Loose Pack Publishing Frequency – Twice a year (March and October)

Circulation – All UK readers

Bound-in Cards Publishing Frequency – Monthly

Circulation – All copies of Packaging Review

Packaging Review Year Planner

The annual Packaging Review Year Planner is supplied free with the December issue and in addition a further 2500 copies are circulated to people on request. The Year Planner is an excellent and economical way of ensuring your company name and sales message is seen throughout the year by manufacturing industry.

Direct Mail

As a back-up to your advertising campaign Packaging Review can also offer you a direct mail facility. The entire controlled circulation computer database currently holds over 500,000 named individuals across industry, commerce and the professions. You can select these prospects by job title, industry, establishment size or by geographical area. Further details of this service are available on request.

Studio

Business Press International's studio can handle design and finished artwork for advertisers at a minimal cost.

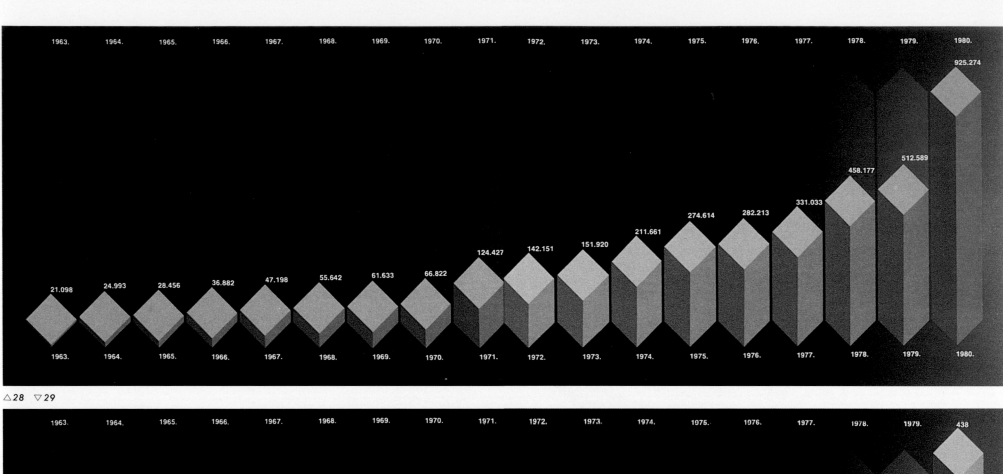

1963. 1964. 1965. 1966. 1967. 1968. 1969. 1970. 1971. 1972. 1973. 1974. 1975. 1976. 1977. 1978. 1979. 1980.

925.274

512.589

458.177

331.033

282.213

274.614

211.661

151.920

142.151

124.427

21.098 24.993 28.456 36.882 47.198 55.642 61.633 66.822

1963. 1964. 1965. 1966. 1967. 1968. 1969. 1970. 1971. 1972. 1973. 1974. 1975. 1976. 1977. 1978. 1979. 1980.

△28 ▽29

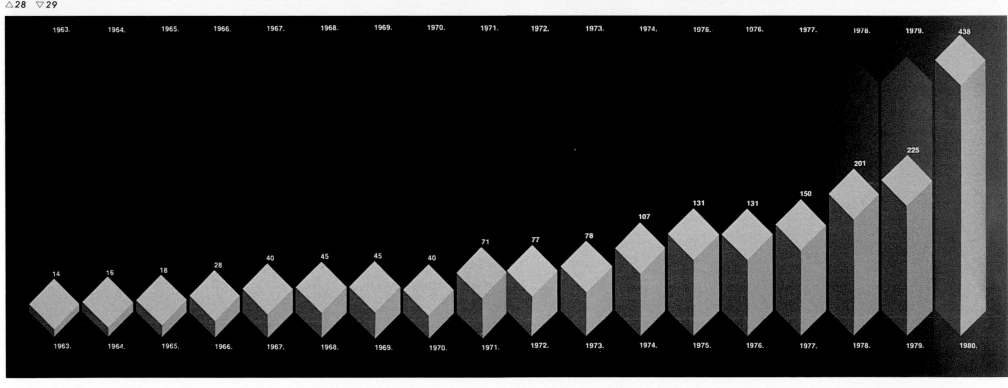

1963. 1964. 1965. 1966. 1967. 1968. 1969. 1970. 1971. 1972. 1973. 1974. 1975. 1976. 1977. 1978. 1979.

438

225

201

150

131 131

107

71 77 78

14 16 18 28 40 45 45 40

1963. 1964. 1965. 1966. 1967. 1968. 1969. 1970. 1971. 1972. 1973. 1974. 1975. 1976. 1977. 1978. 1979. 1980.

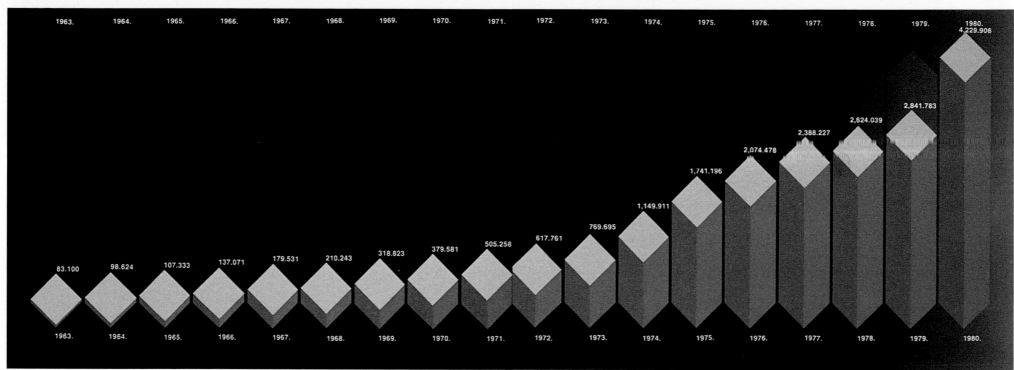

1963. 1964. 1965. 1966. 1967. 1968. 1969. 1970. 1971. 1972. 1973. 1974. 1975. 1976. 1977. 1978. 1979. 1980.
4,229.906

2,841.783

2,624.039

2,388.227

2,074.478

1,741.196

1,149.911

769.695

617.761

505.258

379.581

318.823

210.243

179.531

137.071

107.333

98.624

83.100

1963. 1964. 1965. 1966. 1967. 1968. 1969. 1970. 1971. 1972. 1973. 1974. 1975. 1976. 1977. 1978. 1979. 1980.

△30 ▽31

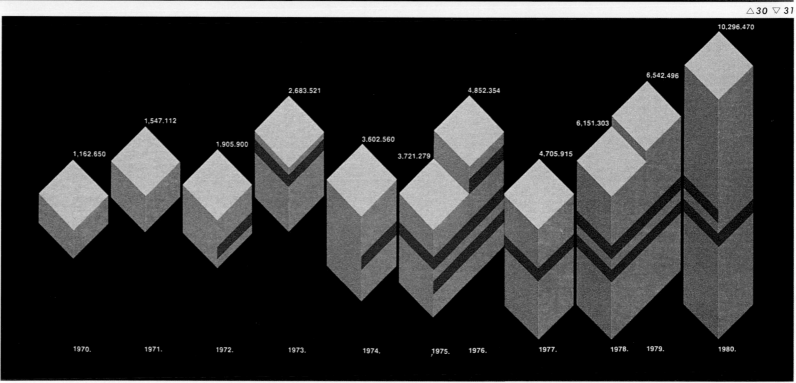

10,296.470

6,542.496

6,151.303

4,852.354

3,602.560

3,721.279

4,705.915

2,683.521

1,547.112

1,905.900

1,162.650

1970. 1971. 1972. 1973. 1974. 1975. 1976. 1977. 1978. 1979. 1980.

28~31. NINO KOVACEVIC

1. YUGOSLAVIA
3. COMPARATIVE STATISTICS
4. SAPONIA ANNUAL REPORTS
5. SAPONIA

15

Perkembangan Posisi Keuangan

1979-1983

Dalam Ribuan Rupiah

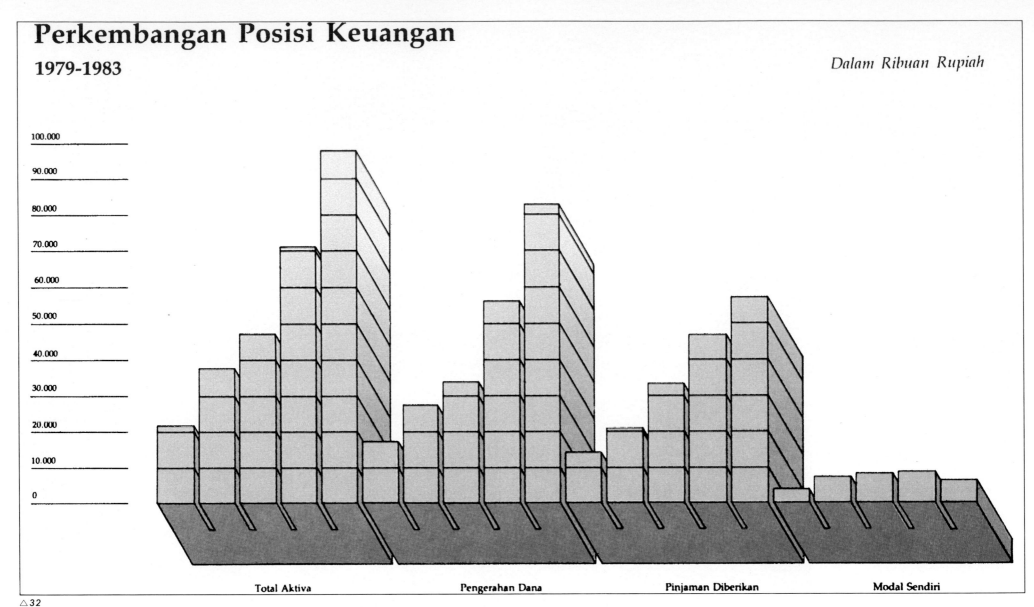

100.000
90.000
80.000
70.000
60.000
50.000
40.000
30.000
20.000
10.000
0

Total Aktiva   Pengerahan Dana   Pinjaman Diberikan   Modal Sendiri

△32

32. HAN KARDINATA

1. INDONESIA
2. PT CITRA INDONESIA
3. COMPARATIVE STATISTICS
4. GRAPHS FOR 1984 ANNUAL REPORT
5. OEB (OVERSEAS EXPRESS BANK)

33,34. HAN KARDINATA

1. INDONESIA
2. PT CITRA INDONESIA
3. COMPARATIVE STATISTICS
4. GRAPHS FOR 1984 ANNUAL REPORT
5. MERINCORP (MERCHANT INVESTMENT CORPORATION)

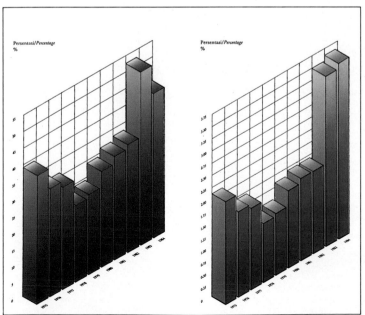

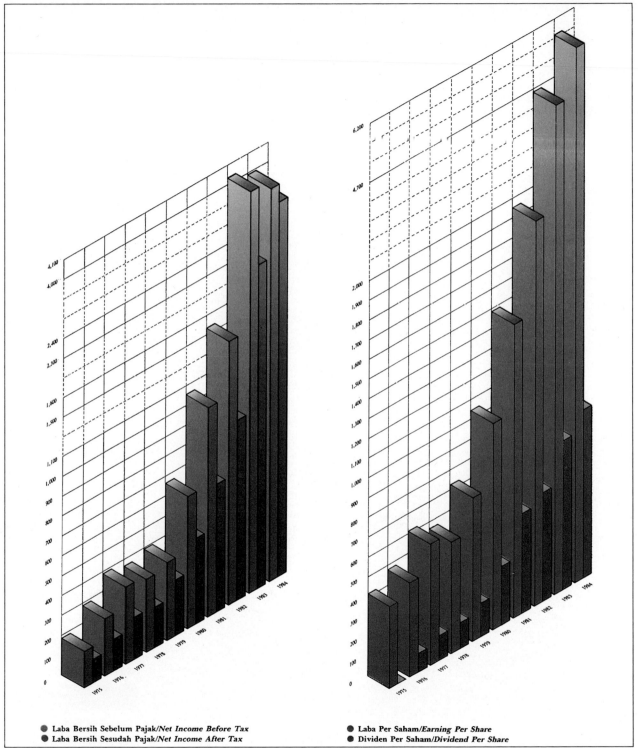

● Laba Bersih Sebelum Pajak/*Net Income Before Tax*
● Laba Bersih Sesudah Pajak/*Net Income After Tax*

● Laba Per Saham/*Earning Per Share*
● Dividen Per Saham/*Dividend Per Share*

△33   △34

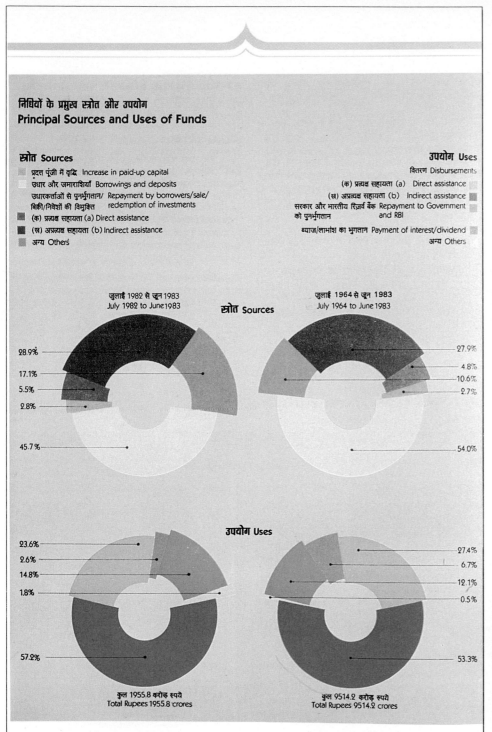

निधियों के प्रमुख स्रोत और उपयोग
Principal Sources and Uses of Funds

स्रोत **Sources**

- प्रदत्त पूंजी में वृद्धि Increase in paid-up capital
- उधार और जमाराशियाँ Borrowings and deposits
- उधारकर्ताओं से पुनर्भुगतान/ Repayment by borrowers/sale/
  बिक्री/निवेशों की विमुक्ति redemption of investments
- (क) प्रत्यक्ष सहायता (a) Direct assistance
- (ख) अप्रत्यक्ष सहायता (b) Indirect assistance
- अन्य Others

उपयोग **Uses**

वितरण Disbursements
(क) प्रत्यक्ष सहायता (a) Direct assistance
(ख) अप्रत्यक्ष सहायता (b) Indirect assistance
सरकार और भारतीय रिज़र्व बैंक Repayment to Government
को पुनर्भुगतान and RBI
ब्याज/लाभांश का भुगतान Payment of interest/dividend
अन्य Others

स्रोत Sources

जुलाई 1982 से जून 1983
July 1982 to June 1983

जुलाई 1964 से जून 1983
July 1964 to June 1983

28.9%
17.1%
5.5%
2.8%
45.7%

27.9%
4.8%
10.6%
2.7%
54.0%

उपयोग Uses

23.6%
2.6%
14.8%
1.8%
57.2%

27.4%
6.7%
12.1%
0.5%
53.3%

कुल 1955.8 करोड़ रुपये
Total Rupees 1955.8 crores

कुल 9514.2 करोड़ रुपये
Total Rupees 9514.2 crores

△35

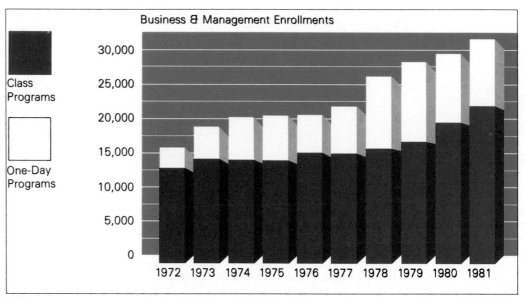

Business & Management Enrollments

Class Programs

One-Day Programs

30,000
25,000
20,000
15,000
10,000
5,000
0

1972 1973 1974 1975 1976 1977 1978 1979 1980 1981

△36

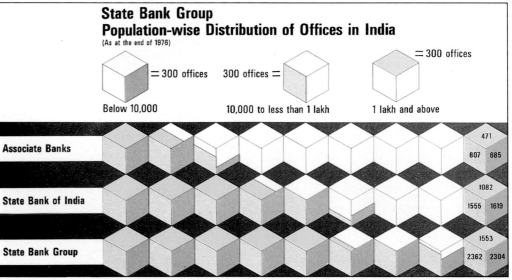

State Bank Group
Population-wise Distribution of Offices in India
(As at the end of 1976)

= 300 offices
300 offices =
= 300 offices

Below 10,000
10,000 to less than 1 lakh
1 lakh and above

Associate Banks

471
807 685

State Bank of India

1082
1555 1619

State Bank Group

1553
2362 2304

△37

38~40. ANDRZEJ J. OLEJNICZAK

1. U.S.A.
2. O & J DESIGN INC.
3. COMPARATIVE STATISTICS

5. CROSS & BROWN
   REAL ESTATE/AVAILABLE SPACE STATISTICS (38,39)
   CPI (CORPORATE PROPERTY INVESTORS)
   REAL ESTATE INVESTMENTS (40)

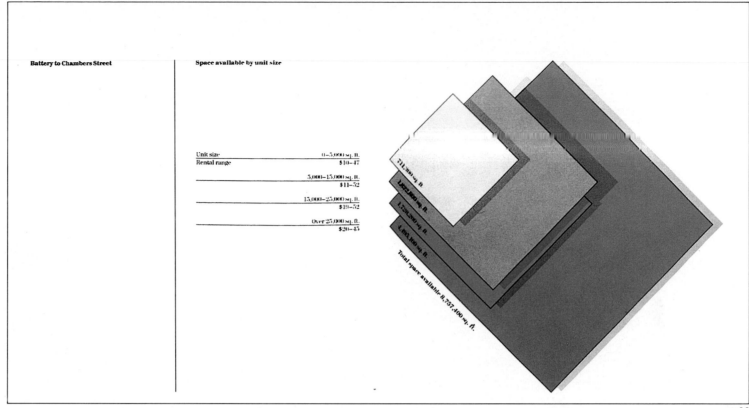

Battery to Chambers Street

Space available by unit size

Unit size	0–5,000 sq. ft.
Rental range	$10–47
	5,000–15,000 sq. ft.
	$11–52
	15,000–25,000 sq. ft.
	$19–52
	Over 25,000 sq. ft.
	$20–45

△38

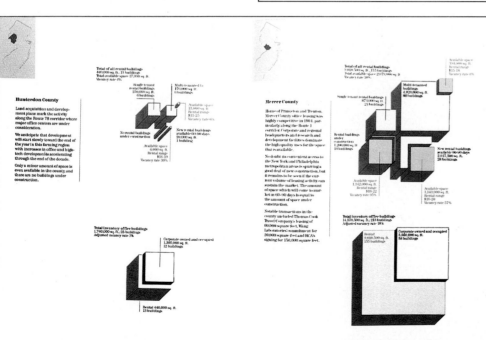

△39

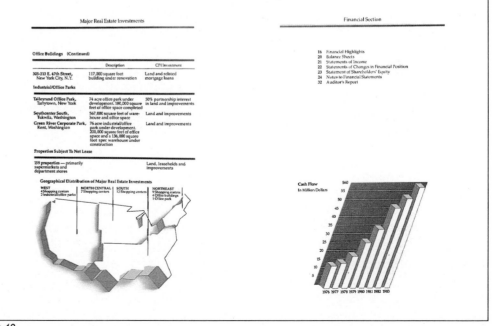

Major Real Estate Investments

Financial Section

△40

19

Appraised Net Asset Value and Contributed Capital

In million dollars

■ Appraised Net Asset Value
■ Contributed Capital

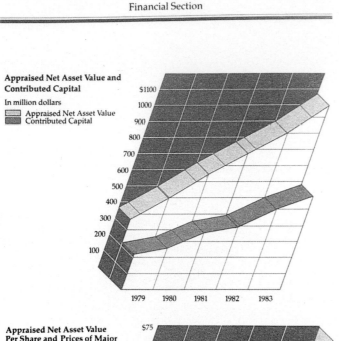

Appraised Net Asset Value Per Share and Prices of Major Sales of Common Shares

■ Appraised Net Asset Value
■ Price of Major Sales of Shares

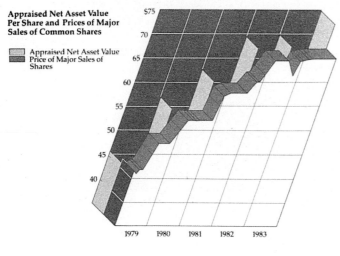

Comparative 10 Year Investment Performance Analysis

In million dollars

■ Common Shares: Corporate Property Investors
(Including reinvestment of dividends)
■ Common Stocks: S & P 500 Stock Index
(Including reinvestment of dividends)
□ Long Term Bonds: Salomon Brothers High Grade Corporate Bond Index
(Including reinvestment of interest)
■ Three Month U.S. Treasury Bills
(Including reinvestment of interest)
■ Consumer Price Index

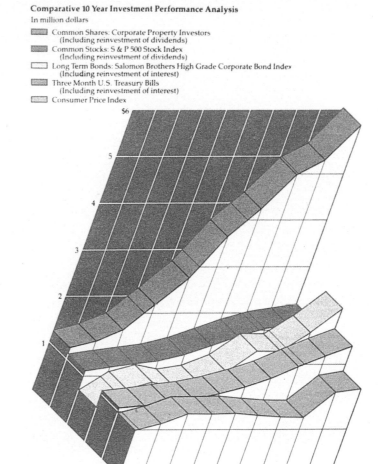

18

19

△ 41

41. ANDRZEJ J. OLEJNICZAK

1. U.S.A
2. O & J DESIGN INC.
3. COMPARATIVE STATISTICS
5. CPI (CORPORATE PROPERTY INVESTORS)/NET ASSET VALUES AND INVESTMENT PERFORMANCE ANALYSIS

MARJO R. WRIGHT 44.

PHILIPPINE 1.
UNITED OUTDOOR ADVERTISING CO. 2.
COMPARATIVE STATISTICS 3.
MAGAZINE COVER 4.
MANILA STOCK EXCHANGE 5.
CHART SHOWING GROWTH STOCKS OF THE YEAR 80

42,43. YASUSHI OKITA

1. U.S.A.
2. YASHI OKITA DESIGN
3. COMPARATIVE STATISTICS
4. SALES BROCHURE
5. EXAR INTEGRATED SYSTEMS, INC
   FAILURE RATE COMPARISON (42)
   REPAIR COSTS (43)

45. BENNO WISSING/JOHN STEGMEYER

1. U.S.A.
2. THE WISSING GENGLER GROUP, INC.
3. COMPARATIVE STATISTICS
4. BOOK ON THE PORT OF ROTTERDAM
   DEVELOPMENT POTENTIAL
5. INDUSTRIAL PRODUCTION INDEX AND DOMESTIC
   SALES/EXPORT OF GOODS AND SERVICES

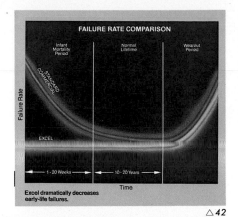

FAILURE RATE COMPARISON

Excel dramatically decreases early-life failures.

△42

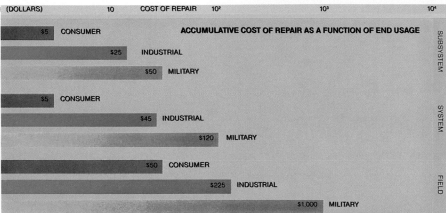

△43

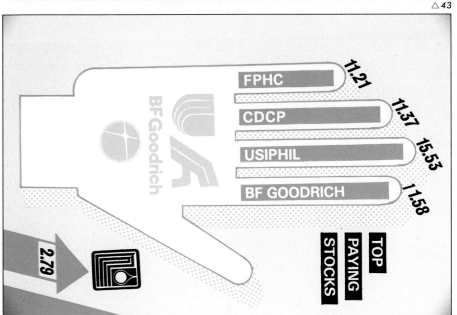

△44

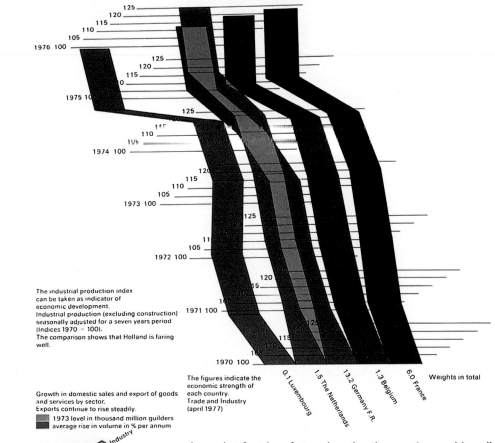

The industrial production index can be taken as indicator of economic development.
Industrial production (excluding construction) seasonally adjusted for a seven years period (Indices 1970 = 100).
The comparison shows that Holland is faring well.

The figures indicate the economic strength of each country.
Trade and Industry (april 1977)

Weights in total

0.1 Luxembourg
1.5 The Netherlands
13.2 Germany, F.R.
1.3 Belgium
6.0 France

Growth in domestic sales and export of goods and services by sector.
Exports continue to rise steadily.

1973 level in thousand million guilders
average rise in volume in % per annum

shown that for trips of around 400 km time can be saved by rail partly because of the fine and fast network of railways which has been standardised throughout Europe. You do not have to get to the airport and there are no formalities which means that time is saved. You travel comfortably and rapidly to the centres of other large towns from Rotterdam without changing trains or checking in and out.

A glance at the map quickly brings to light just how many towns and cities are within striking distance of 100 km of Rotterdam: Amsterdam, the capital; The Hague, the seat of government and diplomatic centre; Utrecht, the geographical centre; Roosendaal, Bergen op Zoom, Breda, Tilburg and Eindhoven (the Philips concern) in the province of Brabant; the Middelburg/Vlissingen area in Zeeland and the large Belgian cities of Brussels (capital, seat of government and EEC headquarters) and Antwerp (with its port and associated industries).

Living and working in Rotterdam not only gives you access to the numerous facilities and contacts that the city itself has to offer, you can also take advantage of the special attractions of all

△45

21

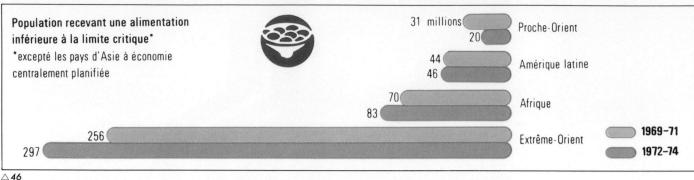

Population recevant une alimentation
inférieure à la limite critique*
*excepté les pays d'Asie à économie
centralement planifiée

31 millions — Proche-Orient
20

44 — Amérique latine
46

70 — Afrique
83

256 — Extrême-Orient
297

1969-71
1972-74

△ 46

THE DIAGRAM GROUP 46~48.

U.K. 1.
DIAGRAM VISUAL INFORMATION LTD. (D.V.I.) 2.
COMPARATIVE STATISTICS 3.
BOOK 4.
FAO IN AFRICA 5.
POPULATIONS RECEIVING A FOOD SUPPLY BELOW CRITICAL LIMITS (46)
WORLD FOREST RESOURCES (47)
WORLD RESOURCE LIMITATIONS (48)

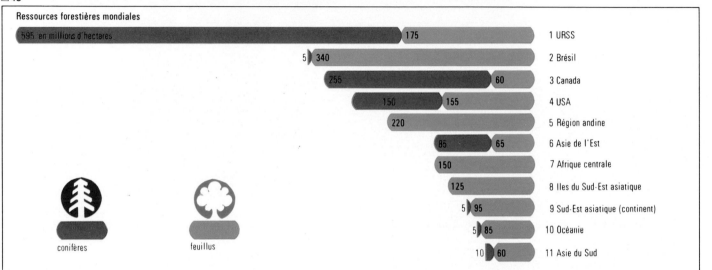

Ressources forestières mondiales

595 en millions d'hectares | 175 — 1 URSS
5 | 340 — 2 Brésil
255 | 60 — 3 Canada
150 | 155 — 4 USA
220 — 5 Région andine
85 | 65 — 6 Asie de l'Est
150 — 7 Afrique centrale
125 — 8 Iles du Sud-Est asiatique
5 | 95 — 9 Sud-Est asiatique (continent)
5 | 85 — 10 Océanie
10 | 60 — 11 Asie du Sud

conifères   feuillus

△ 47   ▽ 48

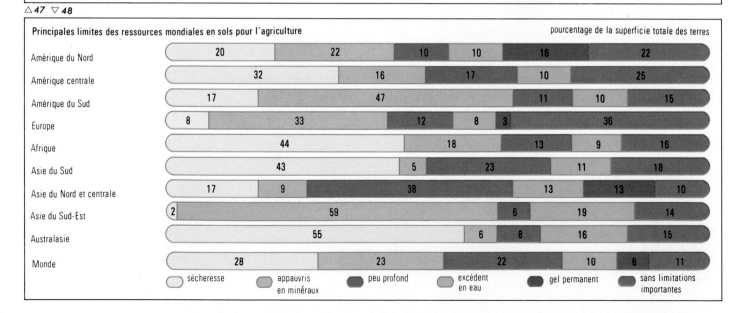

Principales limites des ressources mondiales en sols pour l'agriculture

pourcentage de la superficie totale des terres

	sécheresse	appauvris en minéraux	peu profond	excédent en eau	gel permanent	sans limitations importantes
Amérique du Nord	20	22	10	10	16	22
Amérique centrale	32	16	17	10		25
Amérique du Sud	17	47	11	10		15
Europe	8	33	12	8	3	36
Afrique	44	18	13	9		16
Asie du Sud	43	5	23	11		18
Asie du Nord et centrale	17	9	38	13	13	10
Asie du Sud-Est	2	59	6	19		14
Australasie	55		6	8	16	15
Monde	28	23	22	10	6	11

THE DIAGRAM GROUP 49~51.

U.K. 1.
DIAGRAM VISUAL INFORMATION LTD. (D.V.I.) 2.
COMPARATIVE STATISTICS 3.
BOOK 4.
FAO IN AFRICA 5.
AGRICULTURE EXPORT STATISTICS FOR DEVELOPED AND
DEVELOPING COUNTRIES (49)
AGRICULTURE EXPORT BY REGIONS (50)
WORLD FISH-CATCH STATISTICS (51)

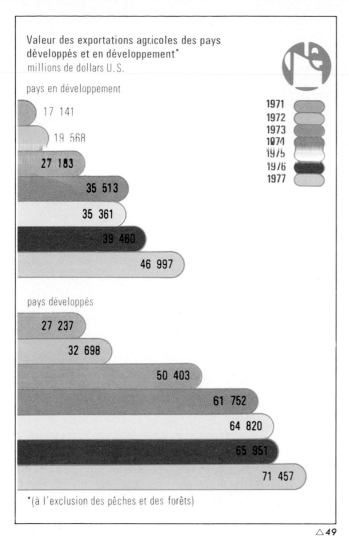

Valeur des exportations agricoles des pays développés et en développement*
millions de dollars U.S.

pays en développement

| 1971 |
| 1972 |
| 1973 |
| 1974 |
| 1975 |
| 1976 |
| 1977 |

17 141
19 568
27 183
35 513
35 361
39 460
46 997

pays développés

27 237
32 698
50 403
61 752
64 820
65 951
71 457

*(à l'exclusion des pêches et des forêts)

△49

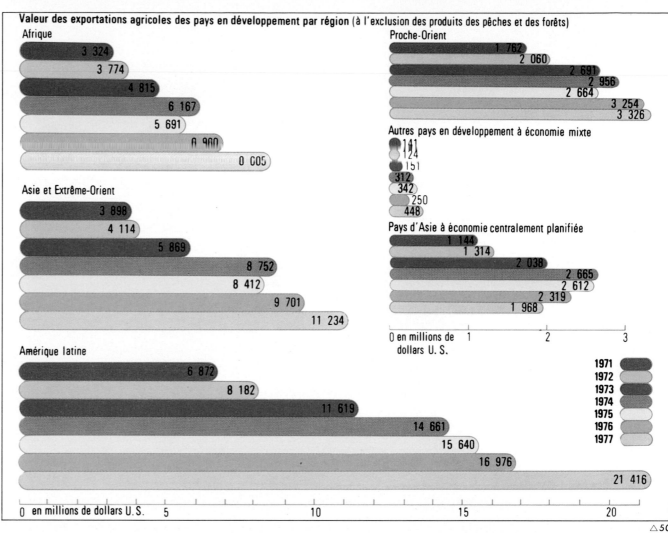

Valeur des exportations agricoles des pays en développement par région (à l'exclusion des produits des pêches et des forêts)

Afrique

3 324
3 774
4 815
6 167
5 691
6 900
8 005

Proche-Orient

1 762
2 060
2 691
2 956
2 664
3 254
3 326

Autres pays en développement à économie mixte

141
124
151
312
342
250
448

Asie et Extrême-Orient

3 898
4 114
5 869
8 752
8 412
9 701
11 234

Pays d'Asie à économie centralement planifiée

1 144
1 314
2 038
2 665
2 612
2 319
1 968

0 en millions de dollars U.S.   1   2   3

| 1971 |
| 1972 |
| 1973 |
| 1974 |
| 1975 |
| 1976 |
| 1977 |

Amérique latine

6 872
8 182
11 619
14 661
15 640
16 976
21 416

0 en millions de dollars U.S.   5   10   15   20

△50

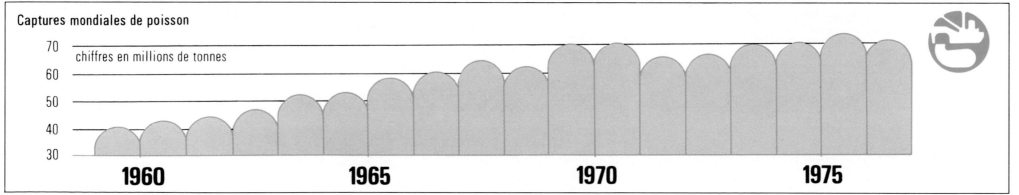

Captures mondiales de poisson

chiffres en millions de tonnes

70
60
50
40
30

1960   1965   1970   1975

△51

23

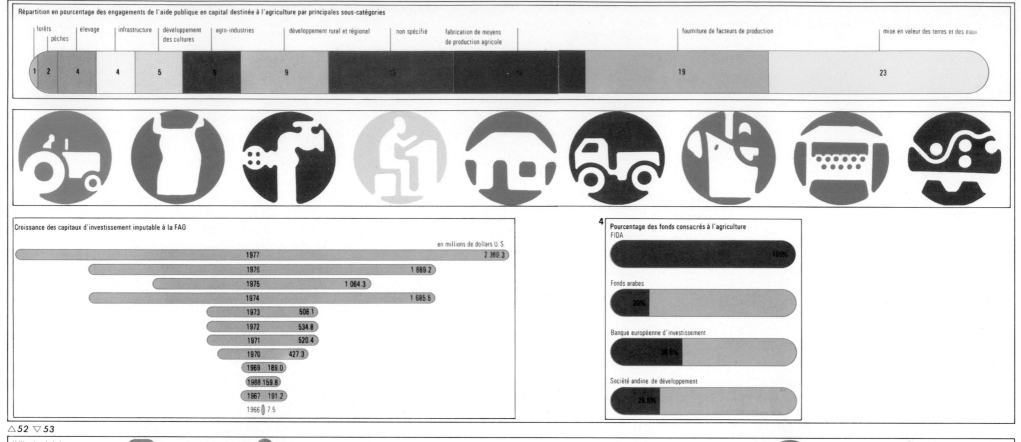

Répartition en pourcentage des engagements de l'aide publique en capital destinée à l'agriculture par principales sous-catégories

forêts	élevage	infrastructure	développement des cultures	agro-industries	développement rural et régional	non spécifié	fabrication de moyens de production agricole	fourniture de facteurs de production	mise en valeur des terres et des eaux

| 1 | 2 | 4 | 4 | 5 | 6 | 9 | 13 | 14 | 19 | 23 |

pêches

Croissance des capitaux d'investissement imputable à la FAO

en millions de dollars U.S.

1977	2 360.3
1976	1 689.2
1975	1 064.3
1974	1 685.5
1973	508.1
1972	534.8
1971	520.4
1970	427.3
1969	189.0
1968	159.8
1967	191.2
1966	7.5

4 Pourcentage des fonds consacrés à l'agriculture

FIDA — 100%

Fonds arabes — 20%

Banque européenne d'investissement — 38.8%

Société andine de développement — 26.5%

△ 52 ▽ 53

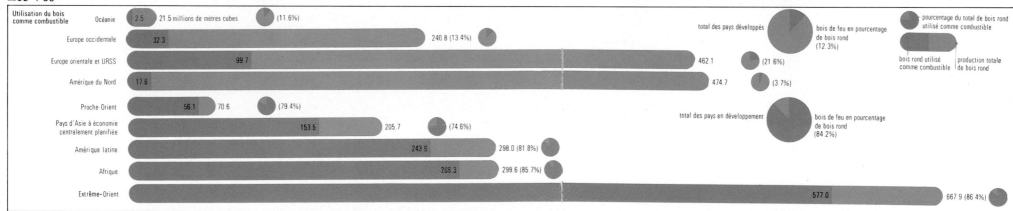

Utilisation du bois comme combustible

pourcentage du total de bois rond utilisé comme combustible

bois rond utilisé comme combustible │ production totale de bois rond

Océanie	2.5	21.5 millions de mètres cubes	(11.6%)
Europe occidentale	32.3	240.8 (13.4%)
Europe orientale et URSS	99.7	462.1
Amérique du Nord	17.6	474.7
Proche-Orient	56.1	70.6 (79.4%)
Pays d'Asie à économie centralement planifiée	153.5	205.7 (74.6%)
Amérique latine	243.9	298.0 (81.8%)
Afrique	288.3	299.6 (85.7%)
Extrême-Orient	577.0	667.9 (86.4%)

total des pays développés — bois de feu en pourcentage de bois rond (12.3%)

(21.6%)

(3.7%)

total des pays en développement — bois de feu en pourcentage de bois rond (84.2%)

52,53. THE DIAGRAM GROUP

1. U.K.
2. DIAGRAM VISUAL INFORMATION LTD. (D.V.I.)
3. COMPARATIVE STATISTICS
4. BOOK
5. FAO IN AFRICA

THE DIAGRAM GROUP 54~57.

U.K. 1.
DIAGRAM VISUAL INFORMATION LTD. (D.V.I) 2.
COMPARATIVE STATISTICS 3.
BOOK 4.
FAO IN AFRICA 5.

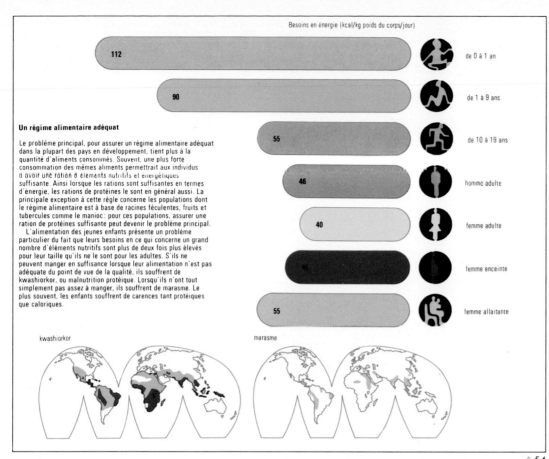

Besoins en énergie (kcal/kg poids du corps/jour)

112 — de 0 à 1 an
90 — de 1 à 9 ans
55 — de 10 à 19 ans
46 — homme adulte
40 — femme adulte
45 — femme enceinte
55 — femme allaitante

Un régime alimentaire adéquat

Le problème principal, pour assurer un régime alimentaire adéquat dans la plupart des pays en développement, tient plus à la quantité d'aliments consommés. Souvent, une plus forte consommation des mêmes aliments permettrait aux individus d'avoir une ration d'éléments nutritifs et énergétiques suffisante. Ainsi lorsque les rations sont suffisantes en termes d'énergie, les rations de protéines le sont en général aussi. La principale exception à cette règle concerne les populations dont le régime alimentaire est à base de racines féculentes, fruits et tubercules comme le manioc : pour ces populations, assurer une ration de protéines suffisante peut devenir le problème principal.

L'alimentation des jeunes enfants présente un problème particulier du fait que leurs besoins en ce qui concerne un grand nombre d'éléments nutritifs sont plus de deux fois plus élevés pour leur taille qu'ils ne le sont pour les adultes. S'ils ne peuvent manger en suffisance lorsque leur alimentation n'est pas adéquate du point de vue de la qualité, ils souffrent de kwashiorkor, ou malnutrition protéique. Lorsqu'ils n'ont tout simplement pas assez à manger, ils souffrent de marasme. Le plus souvent, les enfants souffrent de carences tant protéiques que caloriques.

kwashiorkor

marasme

△54

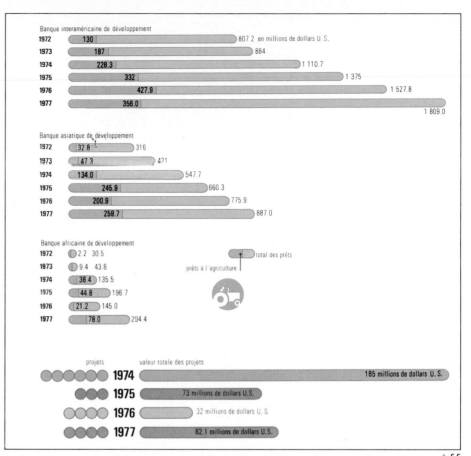

Banque interaméricaine de développement

1972	130	807.2 en millions de dollars U.S.
1973	187	884
1974	228.3	1 110.7
1975	332	1 375
1976	427.9	1 527.8
1977	356.0	1 809.0

Banque asiatique de développement

1972	32.8	316
1973	47.3	421
1974	134.0	547.7
1975	245.9	660.3
1976	200.9	775.9
1977	259.7	887.0

Banque africaine de développement

1972	2.2	30.5
1973	9.4	43.6
1974	38.4	135.5
1975	44.8	196.7
1976	21.2	145.0
1977	78.0	294.4

total des prêts

prêts à l'agriculture

projets — valeur totale des projets

1974 — 185 millions de dollars U.S.
1975 — 73 millions de dollars U.S.
1976 — 32 millions de dollars U.S.
1977 — 82.1 millions de dollars U.S.

△55

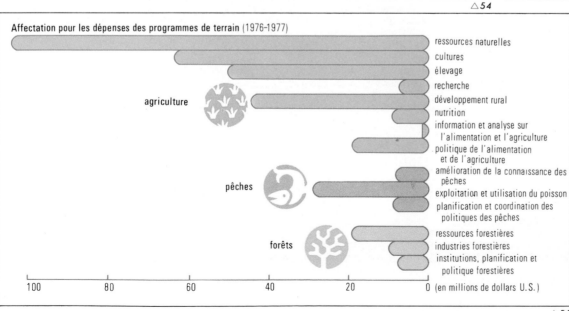

Affectation pour les dépenses des programmes de terrain (1976-1977)

agriculture
- ressources naturelles
- cultures
- élevage
- recherche
- développement rural
- nutrition
- information et analyse sur l'alimentation et l'agriculture
- politique de l'alimentation et de l'agriculture

pêches
- amélioration de la connaissance des pêches
- exploitation et utilisation du poisson
- planification et coordination des politiques des pêches

forêts
- ressources forestières
- industries forestières
- institutions, planification et politique forestières

100   80   60   40   20   0 (en millions de dollars U.S.)

△56

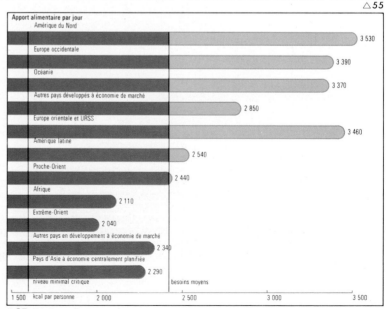

Apport alimentaire par jour

Amérique du Nord	3 530
Europe occidentale	3 390
Océanie	3 370
Autres pays développés à économie de marché	2 850
Europe orientale et URSS	3 460
Amérique latine	2 540
Proche-Orient	2 440
Afrique	2 110
Extrême-Orient	2 040
Autres pays en développement à économie de marché	2 340
Pays d'Asie à économie centralement planifiée	2 290

niveau minimal critique — besoins moyens

1 500   kcal par personne   2 000   2 500   3 000   3 500

△57

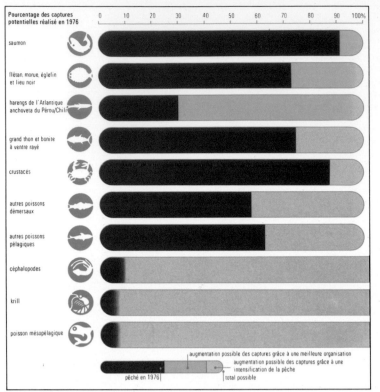

Pourcentage des captures potentielles réalisé en 1976

	0 10 20 30 40 50 60 70 80 90 100%
saumon	
flétan, morue, églefin et lieu noir	
harengs de l'Atlantique anchoveta du Pérou/Chili	
grand thon et bonite à ventre rayé	
crustacés	
autres poissons démersaux	
autres poissons pélagiques	
céphalopodes	
krill	
poisson mésopélagique	

augmentation possible des captures grâce à une meilleure organisation

augmentation possible des captures grâce à une intensification de la pêche

pêché en 1976 | total possible

△58 ▽60

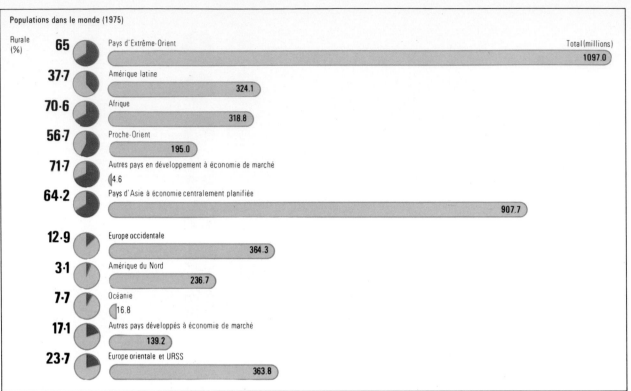

Populations dans le monde (1975)

Rurale (%) | | | Total (millions)

65	Pays d'Extrême-Orient	1097.0
37·7	Amérique latine	324.1
70·6	Afrique	318.8
56·7	Proche-Orient	195.0
71·7	Autres pays en développement à économie de marché	4.6
64·2	Pays d'Asie à économie centralement planifiée	907.7
12·9	Europe occidentale	364.3
3·1	Amérique du Nord	236.7
7·7	Océanie	16.8
17·1	Autres pays développés à économie de marché	139.2
23·7	Europe orientale et URSS	363.8

△59

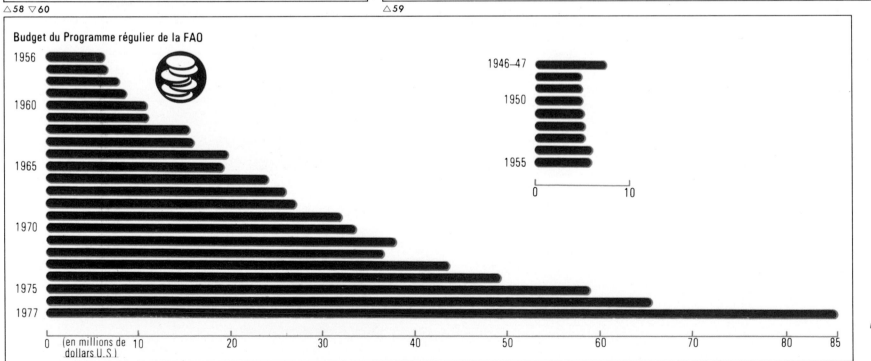

Budget du Programme régulier de la FAO

1956
1960
1965
1970
1975
1977

0 (en millions de dollars U.S.) 10 20 30 40 50 60 70 80 85

1946–47
1950
1955

0 10

THE DIAGRAM 58~60.
GROUP

U.K. 1.
DIAGRAM VISUAL INFORMATION 2.
LTD. (D.V.I.)
COMPARATIVE STATISTICS 3.
BOOK 4.
FAO IN AFRICA 5.
OCEAN FISHING STATISTICS (58)
WORLD POPULATION (59)
FAO BUDGET (60)

THE DIAGRAM GROUP 61~64.

U.K. 1.
DIAGRAM VISUAL INFORMATION LTD. (D.V.I.) 2.
COMPARATIVE STATISTICS 3.
BOOK 4.
FISHING WORLD HUNGER 5.

السمك كغذاء

التركيب الكيماوى لسمك
الكود بالنسبة المئوية

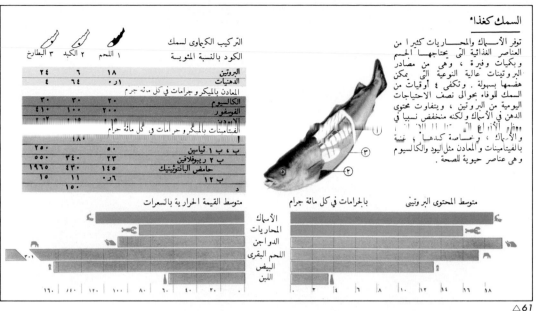

توفر الأسماك والمحاريات كثيرا من العناصر الغذائية التى يحتاجها الجسم وبكميات وفيرة ، وهى من مصادر البروتينات عالية النوعية التى يمكن هضمها بسهولة . وتكفى ٤ أوقيات من السمك للوفاء بحوالى نصف الاحتياجات اليومية من البروتين ، ويتفاوت محتوى الدهن فى الأسماك ولكنه منخفض نسبيا فى معظم الأنواع . . . . . والأسماك ، وخاصة كبدها ، غنية بالفيتامينات والمعادن مثل اليود والكالسيوم وهى عناصر حيوية للصحة .

	١ اللحم	٢ الكبد	٣ البطارخ
البروتين	١٨	٦	٢٤
الدهنيات	ر١	٦٤	٤

المعادن بالميكرو وجرامات فى كل مائة جرام

الكالسيوم	٢٠	٣٠	٣٠
الفوسفور	٢٠٠	١٠٠	٤١٠
	١٩ر١	١٩ر١	٤١٢

الفيتامينات بالميكرو وجرامات فى كل مائة جرام

	١٨٠		
ب ١ ثيامين	٥٠		٢٥٠
ب ٢ ريبوفلاوين	٢٣	٣٤٠	٥٥٠
حامض البانتوثينيك	١٤٥	٤٣٠	١٩٦٥
ب ١٢	٦ر١	١١	١٥
د	١٠٠		

متوسط القيمة الحرارية بالسعرات — بالجرامات فى كل مائة جرام — متوسط المحتوى البروتينى

	الأسماك
	المحاريات
	الدواجن
	اللحم البقرى
	البيض
	اللبن

محصول الأسماك العالمى — نسب توزيع المحصول فى ١٩٦٠ و ١٩٧٠

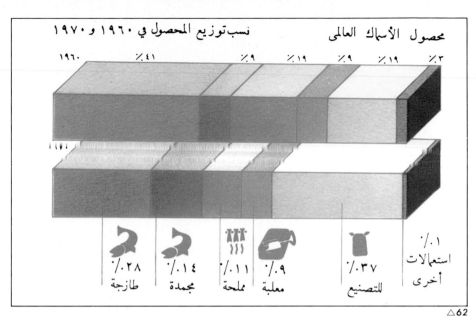

١٩٦٠   ٣٪   ١٩٪   ٩٪   ١٩٪   ٩٪   ٤١٪

طازجة ٢٨٪ — مجمدة ١٤٪ — مملحة ١١٪ — معلبة ٩٪ — للتصنيع ٣٧٪
استعمالات أخرى ١٪

الإنتاج السمكى فى الفيليبين منذ ١٩٦٢   بالاف الأطنان المترية (بالوزن الحى)

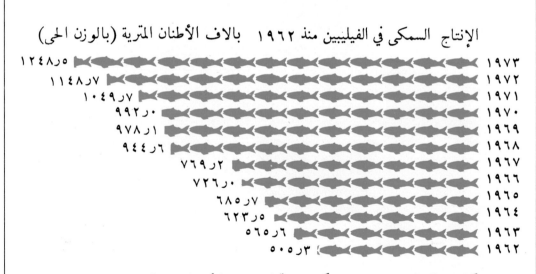

١٩٧٣	١٢٤٨ر٥
١٩٧٢	١١٤٨ر٧
١٩٧١	١٠٤٩ر٧
١٩٧٠	٩٩٢ر٠
١٩٦٩	٩٧٨ر١
١٩٦٨	٩٤٤ر٦
١٩٦٧	٧٦٩ر٢
١٩٦٦	٧٢٦ر٠
١٩٦٥	٦٨٥ر٧
١٩٦٤	٦٢٣ر٥
١٩٦٣	٥٦٥ر٦
١٩٦٢	٥٠٥ر٣

كانت الفيليبين تستورد كميات متزايدة من الأسماك خلال سنوات طويلة للوفاء بالطلب المحلى . ولم تعد هناك حاجة لهذه الواردات الباهظة ، إذ استطاعت الحكومة ، بمساعدة المنظمة ، استغلال الصيد العميق تجاريا ، كما أنها تعمل أيضا على تطوير الصيد الداخلى وتربية الأسماك . وكانت السفينة مايا مايا (الصورة اليسرى) أحد سفن التدريب على الصيد واستكشاف الأسماك . ويبين الرسم (أعلاه) تغير حالة المصايد فى هذا البلد . وقد بدأ تنفيذ أول مشروع لتنمية مصايد الأعماق فى مايو ١٩٦٥ .

محصول الأسماك العالمى (بملايين الاطنان المترية ، بالوزن الحى)

أهم عشر بلاد منتجة للأسماك
متوسط محصول الصيد فى ١٩٦٨/١٩٧٢ بالاف الأطنان المترية

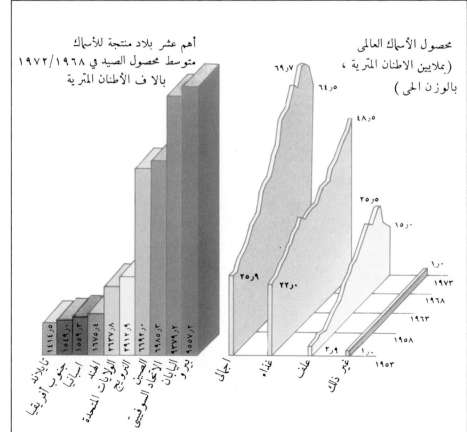

٦٩ر٧
٦٤ر٥
٤٨ر٥
٢٥ر٥
١٥ر٠

١٩٧٣
١٩٦٨
١٩٦٣
١٩٥٨
١٩٥٣

Ahlbergia ferra

Argynnis anadyomene

Thymelicus sylvaticus

Shirozua jonazi

Polytremis pellucida

Lethe diana

Parnassius stubbendorfi

April May June July August September October

Pieris rapae *crucivora*

Pieris *napi nesis*

April   May   June   July   August   September   October

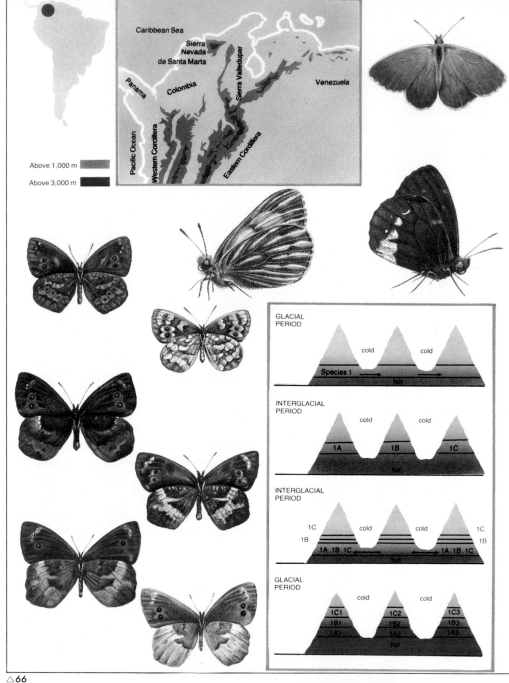

Caribbean Sea

Sierra Nevada de Santa Marta

Panama

Colombia

Sierra Valledupar

Venezuela

Pacific Ocean

Western Cordillera

Eastern Cordillera

Above 1,000 m

Above 3,000 m

GLACIAL PERIOD

cold   cold

Species 1

hot

INTERGLACIAL PERIOD

cold   cold

1A   1B   1C

hot

INTERGLACIAL PERIOD

1C   cold   cold   1C

1B   1B

1A 1B 1C   1A 1B 1C

hot

GLACIAL PERIOD

cold   cold

1C1   1C2   1C3

1B1   1B2   1B3

1A1   1A2   1A3

hot

65,66. ARNOLDO MONDADORI EDITORE, S.P.A.

1. ITALY
2. ARNOLDO MONDADORI EDITORE, S.P.A.
3. COMPARATIVE STATISTICS
4. BOOK, "THE WORLD OF BUTTERFLIES"
5. BUTTERFLY LIFE-SPAN AND POPULATION STATISTICS (65)
   LOCATION BY ALTITUDE AND HISTORICAL PERIODS (66)

△65   △66

67. ARNOLDO MONDADORI EDITORE, S.P.A.

1. ITALY
2. ARNOLDO MONDADORI EDITORE, S.P.A.
3. COMPARATIVE STATISTICS
4. BOOK, "THE WORLD OF BUTTERFLIES"
5. DEVELOPMENT OF BUTTERFLY SPECIES

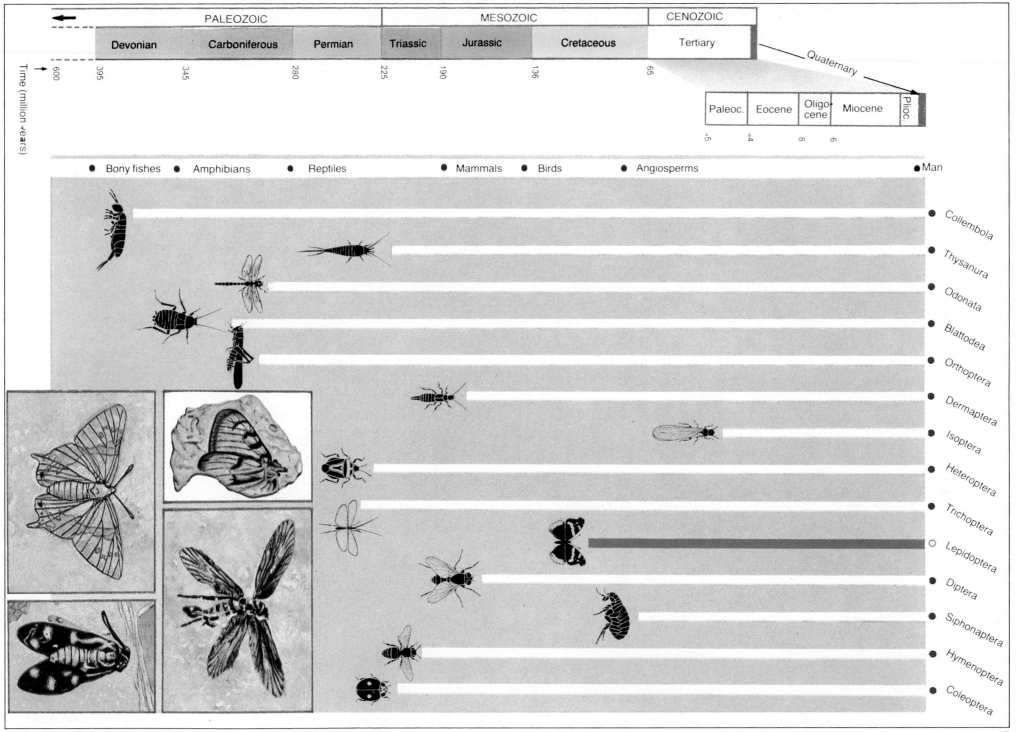

	PALEOZOIC			MESOZOIC			CENOZOIC	
	Devonian	Carboniferous	Permian	Triassic	Jurassic	Cretaceous	Tertiary	

Quaternary

Paleoc.	Eocene	Oligo-cene	Miocene	Plioc.

Time (million years)

600   395   345   280   225   190   136   65

• Bony fishes   • Amphibians   • Reptiles   • Mammals   • Birds   • Angiosperms   • Man

• Collembola
• Thysanura
• Odonata
• Blattodea
• Orthoptera
• Dermaptera
• Isoptera
• Heteroptera
• Trichoptera
○ Lepidoptera
• Diptera
• Siphonaptera
• Hymenoptera
• Coleoptera

△67

29

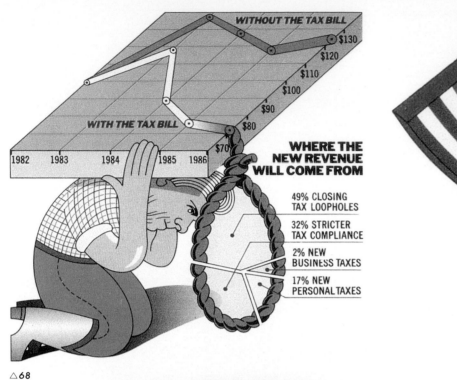

WITHOUT THE TAX BILL

$130
$120
$110
$100
$90
$80
$70

WITH THE TAX BILL

1982 1983 1984 1985 1986

WHERE THE NEW REVENUE WILL COME FROM

49% CLOSING TAX LOOPHOLES

32% STRICTER TAX COMPLIANCE

2% NEW BUSINESS TAXES

17% NEW PERSONAL TAXES

△68

+2
+1
0
-1

Quarters 1 2 3 4

RECESSION

FORECAST

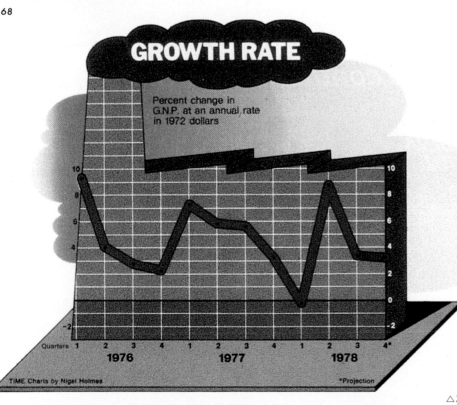

GROWTH RATE

Percent change in G.N.P. at an annual rate in 1972 dollars

10
8
6
4
2
0
-2

Quarters 1 2 3 4 1 2 3 4 1 2 3 4*

1976 **1977** **1978**

TIME Charts by Nigel Holmes

*Projection

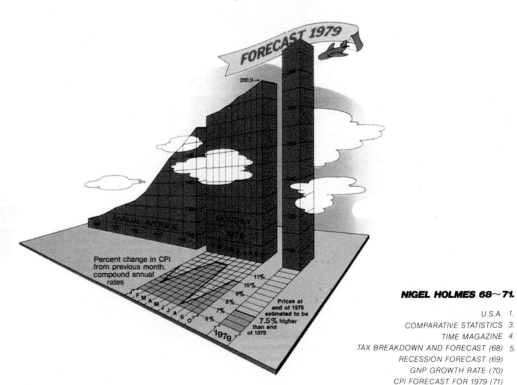

FORECAST 1979

200.9

ANNUAL AVERAGE

MONTHLY 1978

Percent change in CPI from previous month, compound annual rates

11%
10%
9%
8%
7%
6%

J F M A M J J A S O

Prices at end of 1979 estimated to be 7.5% higher than end of 1978

1979

△70   △71

Employment costs* for a steelworker per hour, average of first nine months 1982

U.S. $23.99
W. GERMANY $13.45
FRANCE $12.37
JAPAN $11.08
BRITAIN $9.32
S. KOREA $2.39

*includes benefits
Source: World Steel Dynamics
TIME Chart by Nigel Holmes

△72

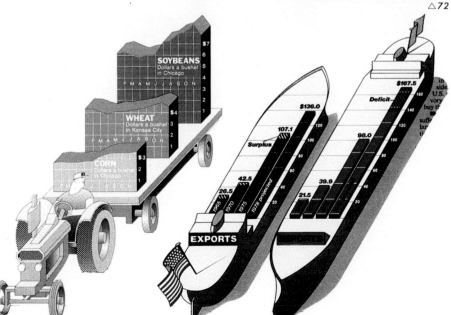

SOYBEANS
Dollars a bushel in Chicago

WHEAT
Dollars a bushel in Kansas City

CORN
Dollars a bushel in Chicago

EXPORTS

△73 △74

regulatory barriers that delay key energy projects. This week the Senate Finance Committee is expected to pass its version of the important windfall profits tax that will finance the new projects. The Senate is likely to approve a tax one-third smaller than the $104 billion House version; President Carter originally demanded a $142 billion tax.

The urgency for action on the energy program becomes clearer all the time. Brandishing the oil weapon in Belgrade, Saudi Arabia's Finance Minister Mohammed Ali Abdul Khail warned that continued depreciation of the dollars that the OPEC countries are paid for their oil might very well "evoke reactions." By that he presumably meant that the OPEC countries might force buyers to pay in a "basket" of many currencies rather than just in dollars; if this were to happen, demand for dollars would decline and they would slide further in value.

Though the greenback strengthened a bit late last week as the markets anticipated new dollar defense moves, worry remains deep about the future of the monetary system that helped create the world's postwar prosperity. The central problem is the roughly 1 trillion footloose dollars that slosh around banks and currency markets outside the U.S. For many years during the 1950s and 1960s, Europeans complained about a "dollar gap." Greenbacks were the only currency that was accepted everywhere, though there were not enough of them around to finance world trade and development. But the dollar gap has since become a dollar glut. Due to heavy foreign spending, first to pay for the Viet Nam War, more recently for oil imports, the U.S. has exported enough dollars in the past decade to boost the reserves held by foreign central banks from $24 billion to $300 billion. Private international banks hold another $600 billion in Eurodollars, which are dollars loaned abroad.

Central banks and private holders are reluctant to accept any more dollars, whose value declines almost daily. OPEC countries in particular are attempting to put new oil earnings into marks, yen or gold. Says Washington Economic Consultant Harald Malmgren: "The Arabs have learned that they pump oil out of the sand, hold the dollars, and the dollars turn back to sand." Nervous central bankers also fear that dollar holders will suddenly try to move large funds into another currency or into gold. Warns Karl Otto Pöhl, president-designate of the German Bundesbank: "If this mass of dollars ever begins to crumble, it could start an avalanche that would bury all other currencies."

The best-selling novel *The Crash of 79* described just such an avalanche. The result was a thumping destruction of all the foundations of industrial society as nations returned to barter economies. Financial experts tirelessly insist that in the nonfiction world such a collapse would be impossible. One reason is that well over half of foreign trade, including sales of oil, metals and grain, is billed in dollars. And despite attempts by central banks to diversify their currency holdings, 77% of all official reserves are still dollars; thus many governments have an interest in holding up the value of the dollar.

Ministers in Belgrade took a step to ensure that the crash of '79 remains fiction by reducing the hazardous excess of dollars. They agreed to press work on a plan to replace perhaps as much as $40 billion in dollars with bonds denominated in a basket of 16 currencies, including two from OPEC countries—Saudi Arabia and Iran. This could be approved at a meeting in April.

As the dollar is being eased out of the cornerstone position it has held since World War II, gold and some strong currencies are moving in. The American campaign to remove gold from the world money system has failed; as one example of bullion's continuing monetary role, the seven-month-old European Monetary System that links seven Common Market currencies has gold as a centerpiece. Fritz Leutwiler, the president of the Swiss National Bank, quotes from the *Book of Job:* "I have made gold my hope or have said to the fine gold, Thou art my confidence." Some leading Americans are even beginning to challenge Carter's policy of selling off the U.S. gold reserve. Former Federal Reserve Chairman William McChesney Martin says that if he were still in office, the U.S. would sell gold only "over my dead body."

The Bundesbank's Pöhl sees the world "moving inexorably toward a multicurrency arrangement." The European Monetary System is anchored on the German mark, while the Japanese yen is developing an important role in Asia as a trading currency. The oil-backed Saudi Arabian riyal could be a new powerhouse, but the Saudis have been reluctant to let it play a role in international loans.

While world moneymen continue slouching toward a new financial Bethlehem, it becomes clearer that the only real way to restore the dollar's health is to cut America's inflation. As long as prices continue climbing at a rate of 13% in the U.S., compared with 6% in West Germany, the dollar will sink and the mark will rise. In such circumstances the dollar is lost, and attempts to save it will only ruin the nation's industry by making such exports as computers, airplanes and chemicals vastly too expensive in Japan or Germany, and imports like autos far too cheap at home. Former Fed Chairman Arthur Burns told the Belgrade conference that the turmoil in world exchange markets would not end until "reasonably good control over inflationary forces has been achieved, especially in the U.S."

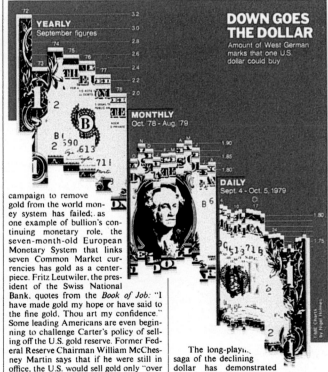

DOWN GOES THE DOLLAR
Amount of West German marks that one U.S. dollar could buy

YEARLY
September figures

MONTHLY
Oct. '78 - Aug. '79

DAILY
Sept. 4 - Oct. 5, 1979

The long-playing saga of the declining dollar has demonstrated that a weakening currency fosters a vicious circle. The dollar's decline not only causes more inflation in the U.S. but also gives OPEC an excuse to push petroleum costs still higher, because oil prices are set in dollars. As the latest run on the dollar continued to lose momentum, officials in Bonn and Washington recalled that in the battle of the buck the next round of speculation has always come more quickly and been more ferocious than the last. ■

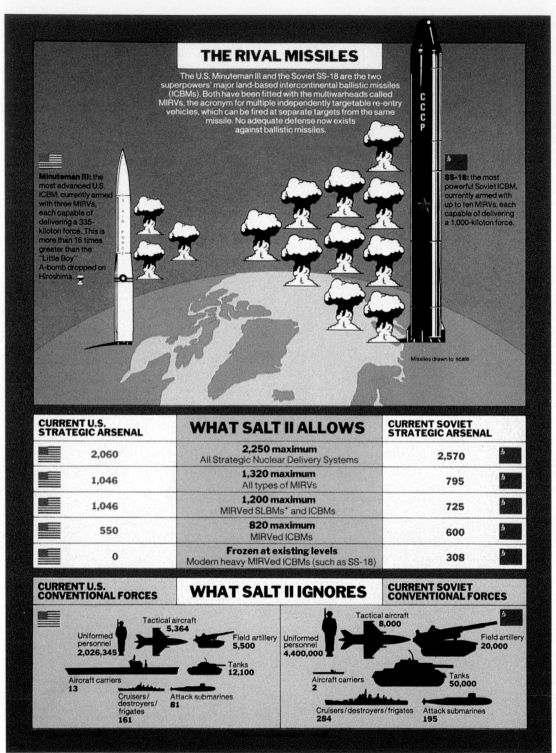

THE RIVAL MISSILES

The U.S. Minuteman III and the Soviet SS-18 are the two superpowers' major land-based intercontinental ballistic missiles (ICBMs). Both have been fitted with the multiwarheads called MIRVs, the acronym for multiple independently targetable re-entry vehicles, which can be fired at separate targets from the same missile. No adequate defense now exists against ballistic missiles.

Minuteman III: the most advanced U.S. ICBM, currently armed with three MIRVs, each capable of delivering a 335-kiloton force. This is more than 16 times greater than the "Little Boy" A-bomb dropped on Hiroshima.

SS-18: the most powerful Soviet ICBM, currently armed with up to ten MIRVs, each capable of delivering a 1,000-kiloton force.

Missiles drawn to scale

CURRENT U.S. STRATEGIC ARSENAL	WHAT SALT II ALLOWS	CURRENT SOVIET STRATEGIC ARSENAL
2,060	**2,250 maximum** All Strategic Nuclear Delivery Systems	2,570
1,046	**1,320 maximum** All types of MIRVs	795
1,046	**1,200 maximum** MIRVed SLBMs* and ICBMs	725
550	**820 maximum** MIRVed ICBMs	600
0	**Frozen at existing levels** Modern heavy MIRVed ICBMs (such as SS-18)	308

CURRENT U.S. CONVENTIONAL FORCES	WHAT SALT II IGNORES	CURRENT SOVIET CONVENTIONAL FORCES

CURRENT U.S. CONVENTIONAL FORCES
Uniformed personnel 2,026,345
Tactical aircraft 5,364
Field artillery 5,500
Tanks 12,100
Aircraft carriers 13
Cruisers/destroyers/frigates 161
Attack submarines 81

CURRENT SOVIET CONVENTIONAL FORCES
Uniformed personnel 4,400,000
Tactical aircraft 8,000
Field artillery 20,000
Tanks 50,000
Aircraft carriers 2
Cruisers/destroyers/frigates 284
Attack submarines 195

△75

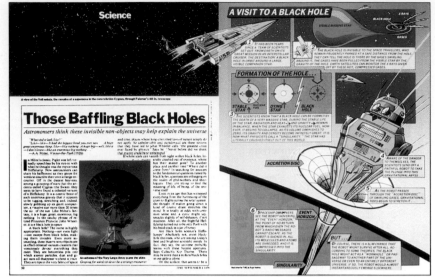

Those Baffling Black Holes

Astronomers think these invisible non-objects may help explain the universe

△76

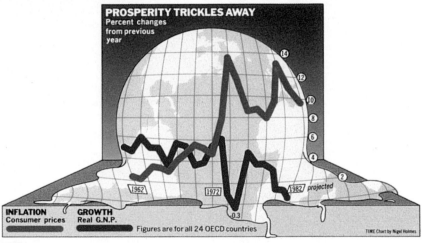

PROSPERITY TRICKLES AWAY
Percent changes from previous year

1962   1972   1982 projected

INFLATION Consumer prices
GROWTH Real G.N.P.
Figures are for all 24 OECD countries

TIME Chart by Nigel Holmes

△77

INFLATION
Percent change in C.P.I.
annualized

Sept. 12.7%*

18%
16%
14%
12%
10%
8%
6%
4%
2%

*Monthly increases at compound annual rate

PRIME RATE
Percent per year, effective date of rate change

20%
18%
16%
14%
12%
10%
8%
6%
4%

Oct. 17 14%

1980
1979
1978
1977

UNEMPLOYMENT
Percent of civilian labor force unemployed

Sept. 7.5%

7.5%
7%
6.5%
6%
5.5%

1977 1978 1979 1980

GROWTH
Percent change in real G.N.P. at annual rates

USA

8%
6%
4%
2%
0
-2.3%

3rd. qtr. +1%

1977 1978 1979 1980

TIME Charts by Nigel Holmes

△78

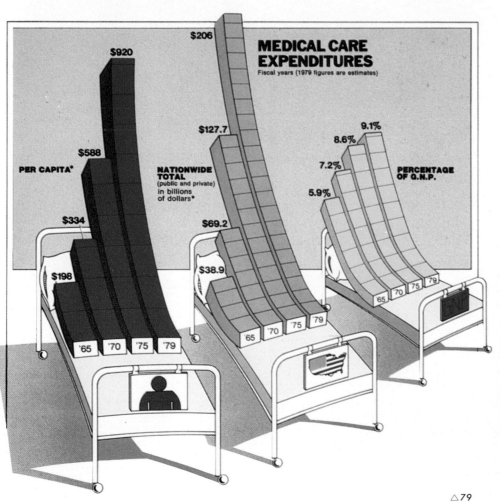

MEDICAL CARE EXPENDITURES
Fiscal years (1979 figures are estimates)

PER CAPITA*
$920
$588
$334
$198

NATIONWIDE TOTAL
(public and private) in billions of dollars*
$206
$127.7
$69.2
$38.9

PERCENTAGE OF G.N.P.
9.1%
8.6%
7.2%
5.9%

'65 '70 '75 '79

△79

78~80. NIGEL HOLMES

1. U.S.A.
3. COMPARATIVE STATISTICS
4. TIME MAGAZINE
5. AMERICAN ECONOMIC STATISTICS (78)
   MEDICAL CARE EXPENDITURES (79)
   REVENUES AND SALES OF MAJOR ELECTRONICS COMPANIES (80)

▽80

WHO'S WHO IN THE ELECTRONIC JUNGLE
Estimated 1981 revenues and sales in billions of dollars

AT&T $34†
IBM $29
ITT $17.7*
GTE $10.9*
RCA $8.1*
NIPPON ELECTRIC $5
MCI $0.5

†Does not include 22 companies soon to be divested *Estimated by Value Line

TIME Chart by Nigel Holmes

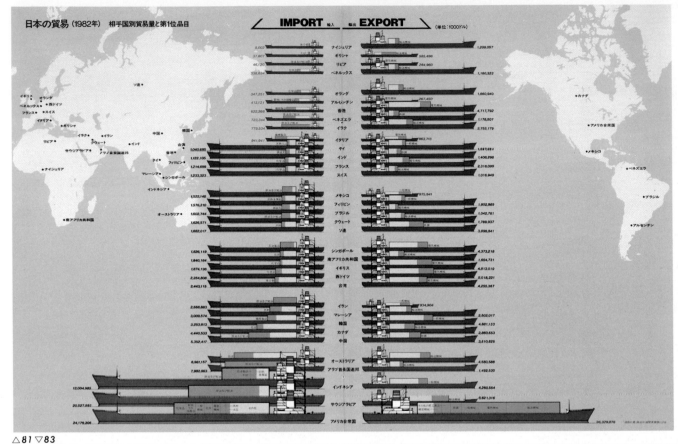

日本の貿易（1982年）　相手国別貿易量と第1位品目

IMPORT 輸入　輸出 EXPORT　（単位:1000ドル）

△81 ▽83

81～83. MORISHITA CO., LTD.

1. JAPAN
2. MORISHITA CO., LTD.
   NOBUO MORISHITA
   CAORI ISHIKAWA
   TAKAMOTO ISHII
   HIROSHI KIYONO
   HIROYUKI KIMURA/ART DIRECTION, DESIGN
   YUKO ISHIKAWA
3. COMPARATIVE STATISTICS
4. WEEKLY MAGAZINE "ASAHI HYAKKA-GEOGRAPHY IN THE WORLD"
5. ASAHI SHIMBUN SHA
   INTERNATIONAL COMMERCE IN JAPAN (1982)
   QUANTITY AND LEADING PRODUCTS SHOWN IN DIFFERENT COUNTRIES
   (UNIT: $1000)(81)
   INTERNATIONAL EXTENSION OF JAPANESE INDUSTRY (1982)(82)
   TYPICAL FOOD CONSUMED BY A NATION IN A DAY (83)

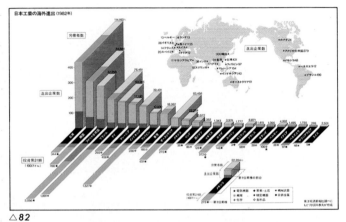

日本工業の海外進出（1982年）

△82

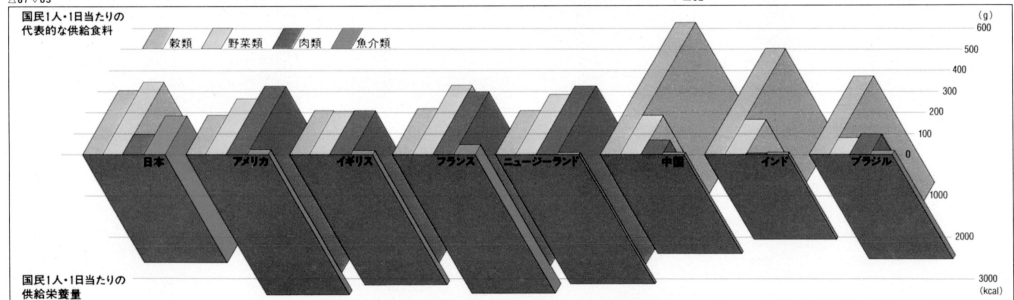

国民1人・1日当たりの代表的な供給食料

穀類　野菜類　肉類　魚介類

日本　アメリカ　イギリス　フランス　ニュージーランド　中国　インド　ブラジル

国民1人・1日当たりの供給栄養量

（g）600 500 400 300 200 100 0

1000 2000 3000（kcal）

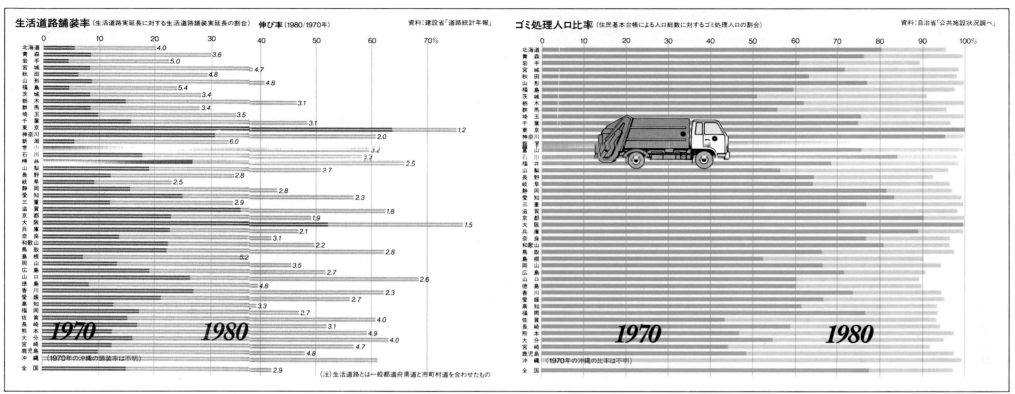

生活道路舗装率（生活道路実延長に対する生活道路舗装実延長の割合）　伸び率（1980/1970年）　資料：建設省「道路統計年報」

1970　1980

（1970年の沖縄の舗装率は不明）

（注）生活道路とは一般都道府県道と市町村道を合わせたもの

ゴミ処理人口比率（住民基本台帳による人口総数に対するゴミ処理人口の割合）　資料：自治省「公共施設状況調べ」

1970　1980

（1970年の沖縄の比率は不明）

▽85　△84

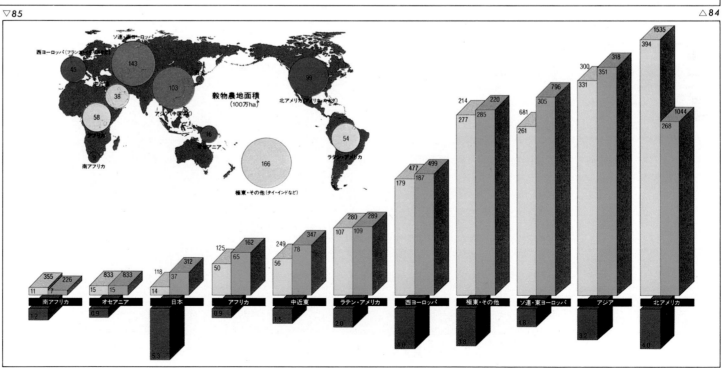

穀物農地面積（100万ha）

西ヨーロッパ（フランス・西ドイツなど）　45
ソ連・東ヨーロッパ　143
38
103
北アメリカ（アメリカ・カナダ）　99
58
アジア（中国など）　16
54
南アフリカ
オセアニア
166
ラテン・アメリカ
極東・その他（タイ・インドなど）

南アフリカ　355　226　1.2
オセアニア　833　833　0.9
日本　118　312　14　37　5.3
アフリカ　125　162　50　65　0.9
中近東　249　347　56　78　1.5
ラテン・アメリカ　280　289　107　109　2.0　4.0
西ヨーロッパ　477　499　179　187　3.8
極東・その他　214　220　277　285
ソ連・東ヨーロッパ　681　796　261　305　1.8
アジア　300　318　331　351　3.2
北アメリカ　1535　394　268　1044　4.0

84,85. MORISHITA CO., LTD.

1. JAPAN
2. MORISHITA CO., LTD.
   NOBUO MORISHITA
   CAORI ISHIKAWA
   TAKAMOTO ISHII
   HIROSHI KIYONO
   HIROYUKI KIMURA
   YUKO ISHIKAWA
3. COMPARATIVE STATISTICS
4. WEEKLY MAGAZINE "ASAHI HYAKKA-GEOGRAPHY IN THE WORLD"
5. ASAHI SHIMBUN SHA
   PERCENTAGES OF PAVED ROADS/PERCENTAGES OF THE NUMBER OF PEOPLE FOR GARBAGE DISPOSAL (84)
   PRODUCTION AND CONSUMPTION QUANTITIES OF GRAIN IN THE WORLD (85)

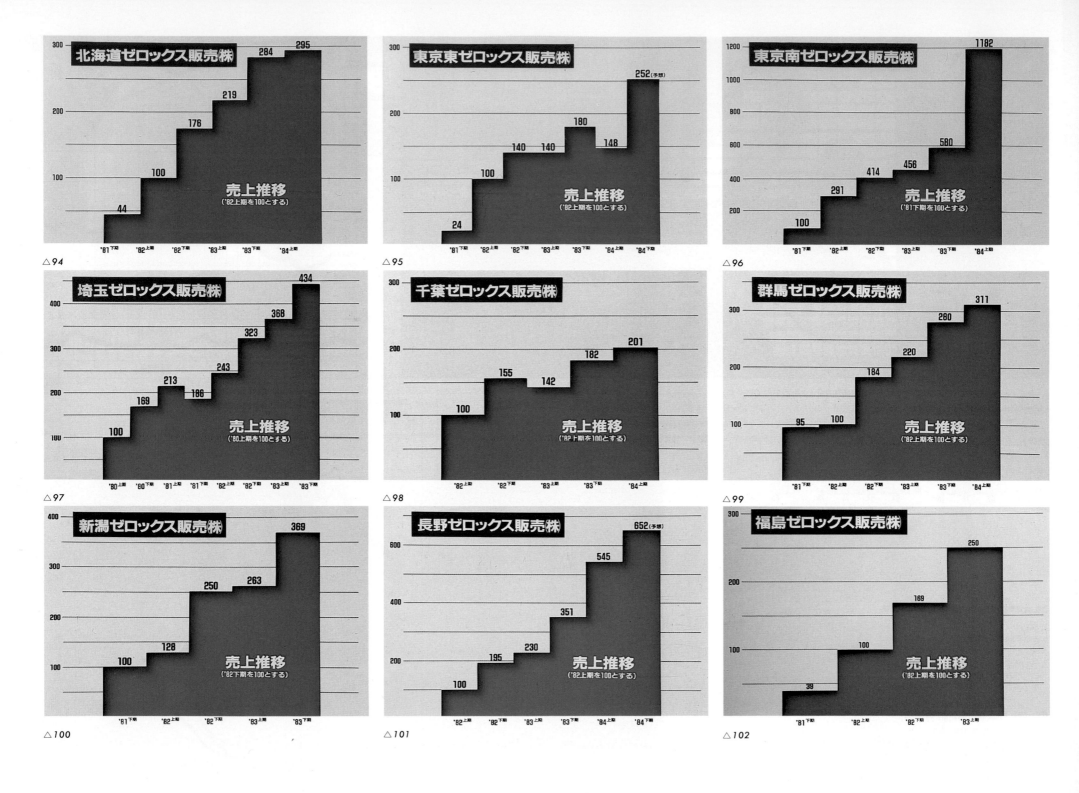

△94　△95　△96

△97　△98　△99

△100　△101　△102

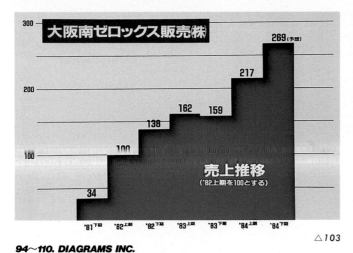

大阪南ゼロックス販売㈱

売上推移
('82上期を100とする)

300
269(予想)
217
200
162 159
138
100 100
34
'81下期 '82上期 '82下期 '83上期 '83下期 '84上期 '84下期

△103

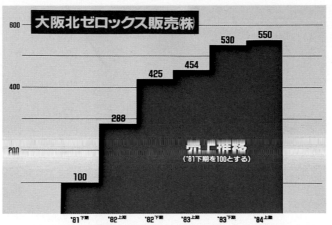

大阪北ゼロックス販売㈱

売上推移
('81下期を100とする)

600
550
530
454
425
400
288
200
100
'81下期 '82上期 '82下期 '83上期 '83下期 '84上期

△104

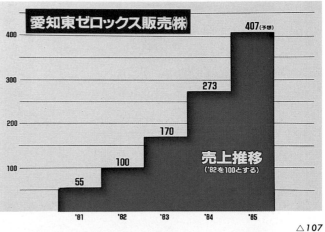

大阪中央ゼロックス販売㈱

売上推移
('82上期を100とする)

300
230
198
200
175
143
100 100
'82上期 '82下期 '83上期 '83下期 '84上期

△105

94～110. DIAGRAMS INC.

1. JAPAN
2. DIAGRAMS INC.
   ART DIRECTOR : TSUTOMU OKAMOTO
   DESIGNER : RYOCHI TAYA
            REIKO HAYASHI
            NORIKO YURI
   PHOTO : EISEI WAKATSUKI
3. COMPARATIVE STATISTICS
4. MARKETING REPORT FOR DEALERS
5. FUJI XEROX CO., LTD.
   SALES TRANSITIONS

京都ゼロックス販売㈱

売上推移
('80下期を100とする)

413 402
400
322
303
300
236
201
200
150
100 100
'80下期 '81上期 '81下期 '82上期 '82下期 '83上期 '83下期 '84上期

△106

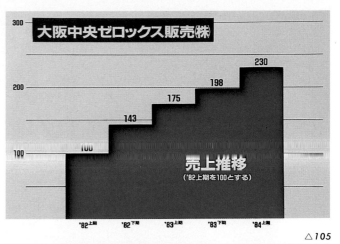

愛知東ゼロックス販売㈱

売上推移
('82を100とする)

407(予想)
400
300
273
200
170
100 100
55
'81 '82 '83 '84 '85

△107

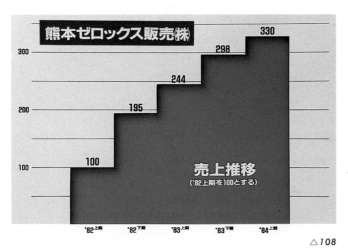

熊本ゼロックス販売㈱

売上推移
('82上期を100とする)

330
298
300
244
200 195
100 100
'82上期 '82下期 '83上期 '83下期 '84上期

△108

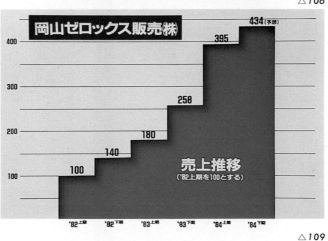

岡山ゼロックス販売㈱

売上推移
('82上期を100とする)

434(予想)
395
400
258
300
242
180
200
140
100 100
'82上期 '82下期 '83上期 '83下期 '84上期 '84下期

△109

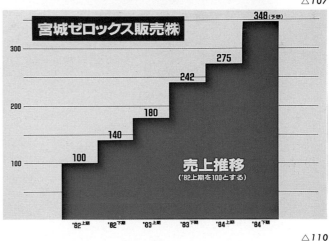

宮城ゼロックス販売㈱

売上推移
('82上期を100とする)

348(予想)
300 275
242
180
200
140
100 100
'82上期 '82下期 '83上期 '83下期 '84上期 '84下期

△110

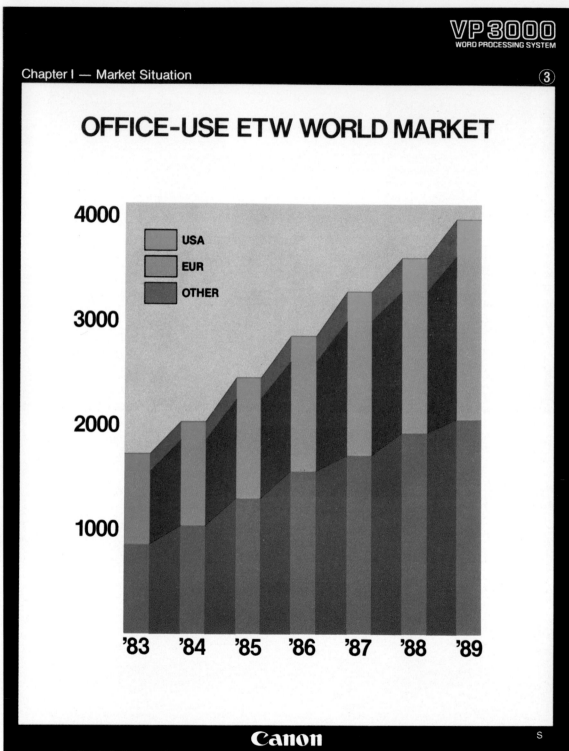

△111

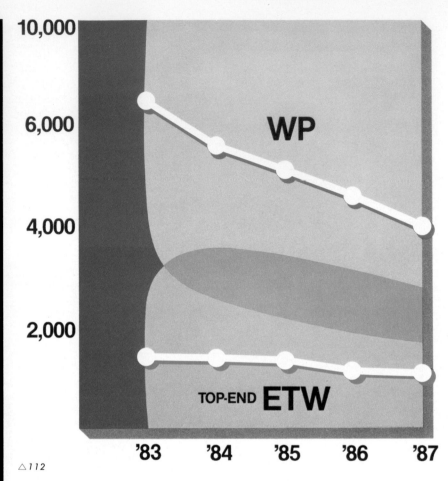

△112

111~118. HAKUHODO

1. JAPAN
2. HAKUHODO INC./DIAGRAMS INC.
   ART DIRECTOR: TAKASHI KITAMURA
              MASAYOSHI MORIOKA
   DESIGNER: TSUTOMU OKAMOTO
           REIKO HAYASHI
           RYÔCHI TAYA
3. FLOW CHARTS
4. PAMPHLET
5. CANON INC.

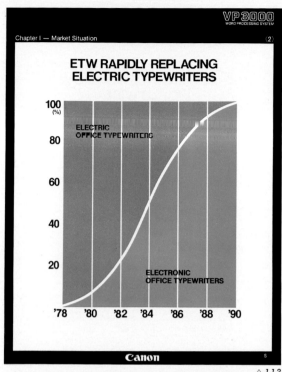

ETW RAPIDLY REPLACING ELECTRIC TYPEWRITERS

ELECTRIC OFFICE TYPEWRITERS

ELECTRONIC OFFICE TYPEWRITERS

'78 '80 '82 '84 '86 '88 '90

Canon

△113

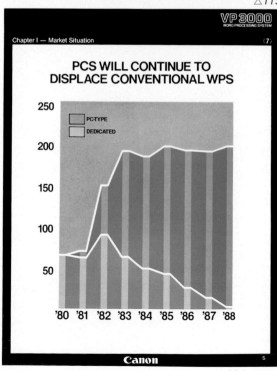

PCS WILL CONTINUE TO DISPLACE CONVENTIONAL WPS

PC-TYPE

DEDICATED

'80 '81 '82 '83 '84 '85 '86 '87 '88

Canon

△114 115▷

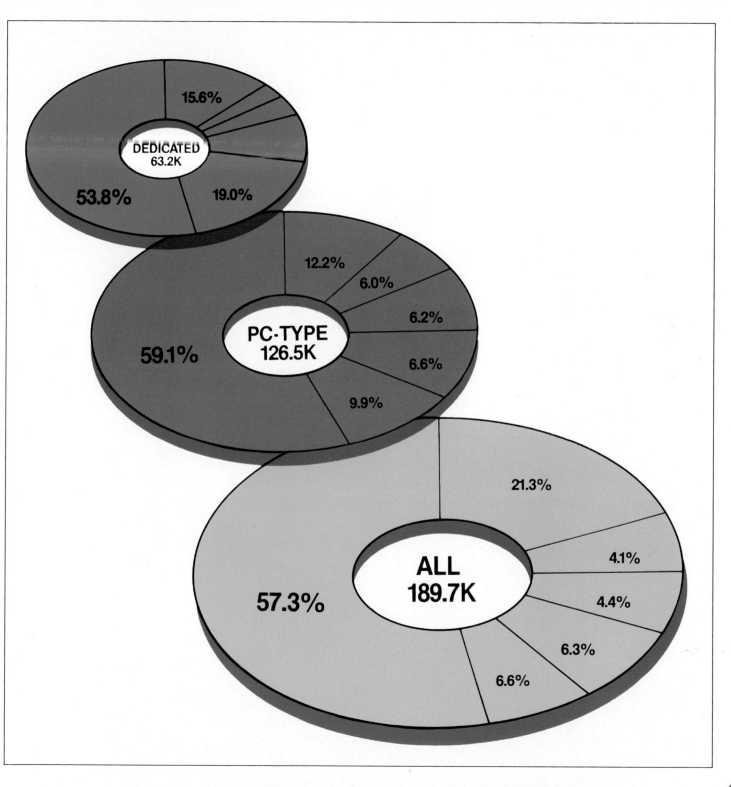

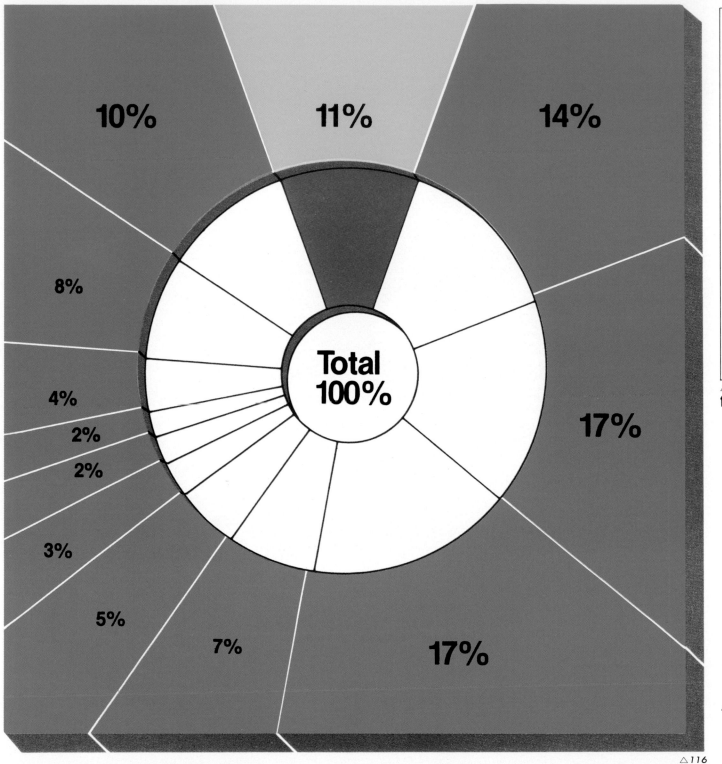

10%

11%

14%

8%

Total
100%

17%

4%

2%

2%

3%

17%

5%

7%

△116

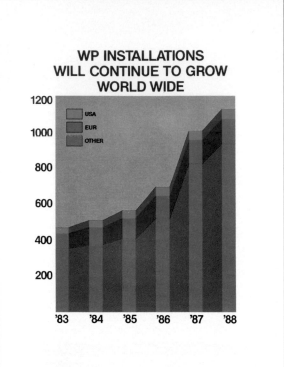

WP INSTALLATIONS WILL CONTINUE TO GROW WORLD WIDE

USA
EUR
OTHER

1200
1000
800
600
400
200

'83 '84 '85 '86 '87 '88

△117

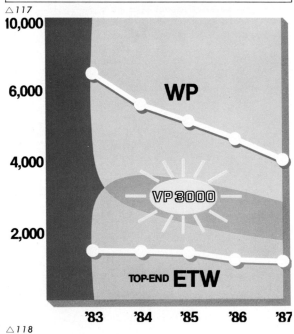

10,000

WP

6,000

VP 3000

4,000

2,000

TOP-END ETW

'83 '84 '85 '86 '87

△118

42

Imports

Exports

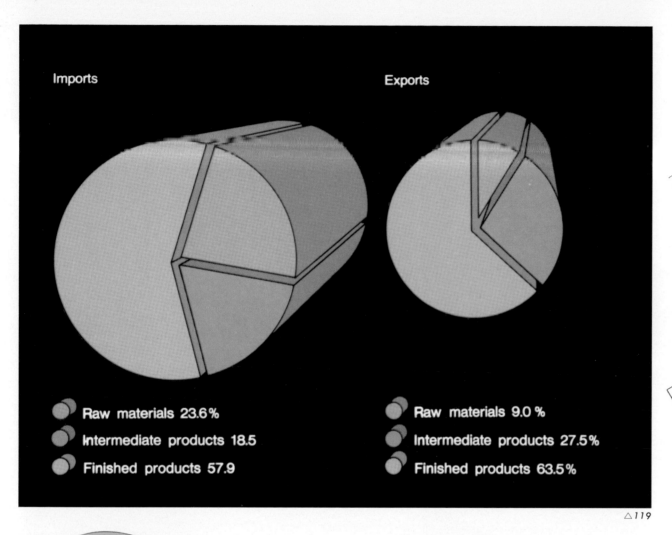

⬤ Raw materials 23.6%

⬤ Intermediate products 18.5

⬤ Finished products 57.9

⬤ Raw materials 9.0%

⬤ Intermediate products 27.5%

⬤ Finished products 63.5%

△119

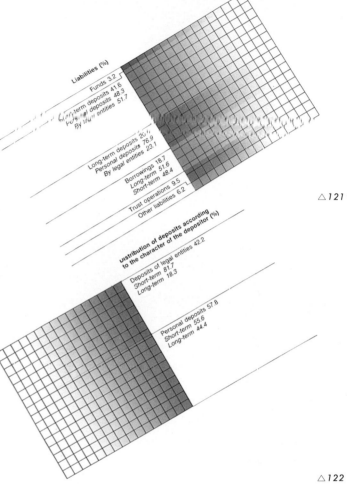

Liabilities (%)
Funds 3.2
Long-term deposits 41.6
By legal entities 48.3
By legal entities 51.7

Long-term deposits 20.7
Personal deposits 76.9
By legal entities 23.1

Borrowings 18.7
Long-term 51.6
Short-term 48.4

Trust operations 9.5
Other liabilities 6.2

△121

Distribution of deposits according to the character of the depositor (%)

Deposits of legal entities 42.2
Short-term 81.7
Long-term 18.3

Personal deposits 57.8
Short-term 55.6
Long-term 44.4

△122

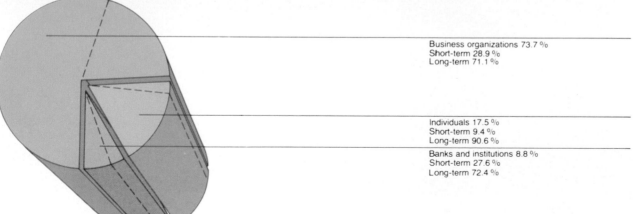

Business organizations 73.7 %
Short-term 28.9 %
Long-term 71.1 %

Individuals 17.5 %
Short-term 9.4 %
Long-term 90.6 %

Banks and institutions 8.8 %
Short-term 27.6 %
Long-term 72.4 %

△120

PETER SKALAR 120~122.

YUGOSLAVIA 1.
COMPARATIVE STATISTICS 3.
CATALOGUE 4.

Crude Oil Production
Thousands of barrels per day

TOMOKO HINO 123.

U.S.A. 1.
COMPARATIVE STATISTICS 3.
ANNUAL REPORT 4.
CRUDE OIL AND NATURAL GAS STATISTICS 5.

Sales of Natural Gas, North America
Millions of cubic feet per day

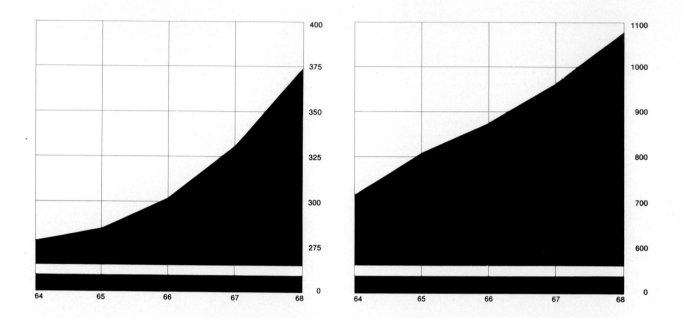

Crude Oil Refined
Thousands of barrels per day

Product Sales
Thousands of barrels per day

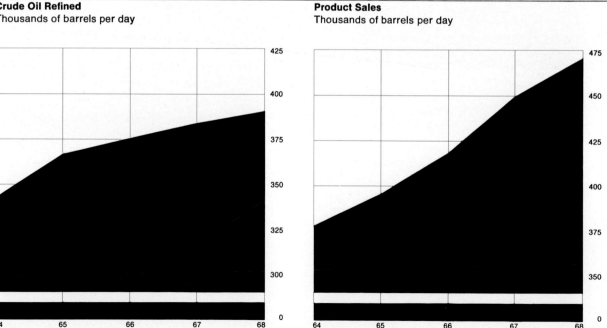

124. CHRISTOPH BLUMRICH

1. U.S.A.
2. NEWSWEEK
3. COMPARATIVE STATISTICS
4. NEWSWEEK MAGAZINE
5. ECONOMIC STATISTICS DURING "THE VOLCKER YEARS"

125. ROBERT M. RUNYAN

1. U.S.A.
2. ROBERT M. RUNYAN ASSOCIATES
3. COMPARATIVE STATISTICS
4. ANNUAL REPORT
5. HOME INSURANCE COMPANY

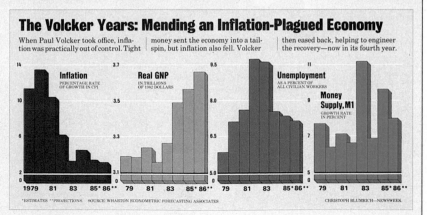

over which is the more effective way to conduct monetary policy—controlling the supply or the price. What's not debatable is that the supply of money circulating has much to do with the level of prices and economic growth. By the late 1970s, for example, the Fed had been rapidly pumping money into the system, mainly to accommodate dramatic oil-price hikes. Had it not done so there could have been an immediate, steep recession. People would have stopped buying other goods to pay for oil. But the Fed was merely delaying the inevitable. Too many dollars chasing too few goods generate price increases. By 1979 the Fed's effort to support the economy pushed inflation into double digits. With Volcker taking charge, the

Recession's impact: *Unemployment lines in Michigan, 1982*

ANDREW SACKS—BLACK STAR

Fed changed course: it tightened money, interest rates soared, and the inflation-fighting recession it had once hoped to forestall quickly followed.

Despite its pervasive impact, the Fed has a hard time fine-tuning the economy. A change in the money supply affects GNP and inflation only after erratic time lags. Over the last year, some economists have been warning that the rapid growth in cash and checking deposits—a measure of money known as M1—guaranteed a surge in inflation. But the recent advent of interest-bearing checking accounts has made people more willing to let money sit idly in their banks. The result has been weaker growth and less inflation than expected.

Now the pressure is on the Fed to ease even further. Some economists worry that Gramm-Rudman budget cutting threatens the current expansion. The Fed, they argue, should step in to keep the economy rolling. With oil prices plunging, this argument goes, it can do so without risking inflation. As usual, what the Fed will do is unclear. Only one thing is certain: its actions will affect everyone from Wall Street's happy stockbrokers to America's frightened farmers.

BILL POWELL in New York

The Volcker Years: Mending an Inflation-Plagued Economy

When Paul Volcker took office, inflation was practically out of control. Tight money sent the economy into a tailspin, but inflation also fell. Volcker then eased back, helping to engineer the recovery—now in its fourth year.

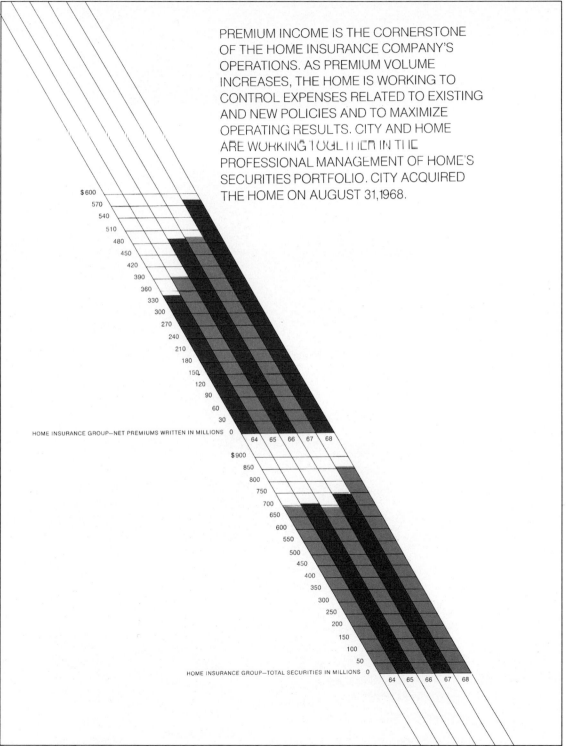

THE HANDGUN IN U.S. IS UNRIVALLED MURDER WEAPON

1980

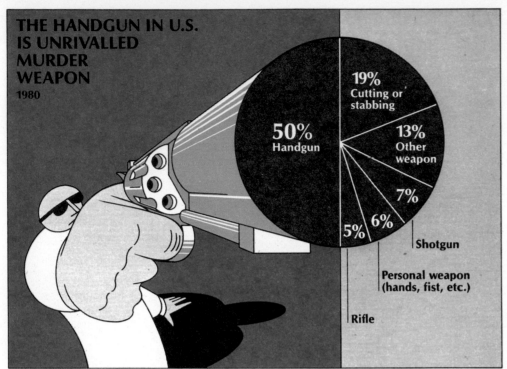

50% Handgun

19% Cutting or stabbing

13% Other weapon

7% Shotgun

6% Personal weapon (hands, fist, etc.)

5% Rifle

△126

HANDGUN BODY-COUNT HITS ALL-TIME HIGH

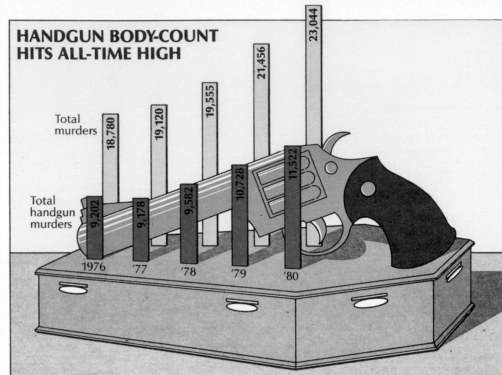

Total murders

Total handgun murders

	1976	'77	'78	'79	'80
Total murders	18,780	19,120	19,555	21,456	23,044
Total handgun murders	9,202	9,178	9,582	10,728	11,522

△127

SALES OF HANDGUNS KEEP SHOOTING UP

U.S. manufacturers, excluding purchases by military, in millions of dollars

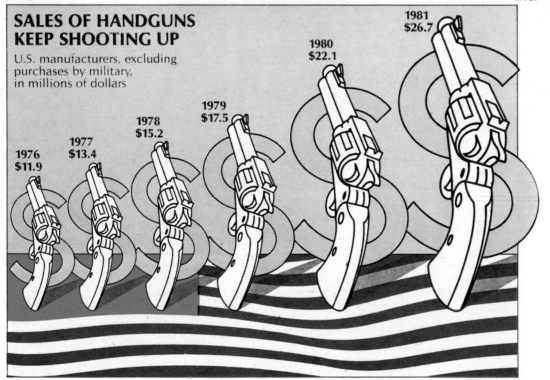

1976 $11.9

1977 $13.4

1978 $15.2

1979 $17.5

1980 $22.1

1981 $26.7

△128

Now a Middling-Size Downturn

It should bring relief from U.S. price rises, but not enough to cheer

Is it a bloom, an oddball mix of [...] and [...]? Is it an "expansionary recession," an expansionary recession? Is it merely a forward retreat? Whatever the U.S. economy is going through is as much a matter of semantics as statistics. But the confusing numbers will quickly clear up. Even if the economy is not now in a recession, the latest oil price rises by the OPEC cartel further ensure that a downturn will soon begin.

That is the view of almost all the experts, including the ten members of TIME's Board of Economists. Their unanimous opinion is that 1980 will be a year of middling-size recession. It will bring lower inflation, easier interest rates and higher unemployment, but not so much as to create either tremendous pain or fast, fast relief.

The current indicators are as perplexing and contradictory as a set of cooked books. Consider the liabilities: America's factories are producing less than they did last March; auto sales are moving like an [...] psalm car without antifreeze, and the [...] the traditional harbinger of economic swings, is down from a rate of 2.1 million a year ago to 1.5 million now. But count the assets: a record 97.6 million Americans are at work in civilian jobs, and their personal income and spending rose rather smartly last month, although many of the gains were the puffy results of inflation. People seem pessimistic about the economy, yet

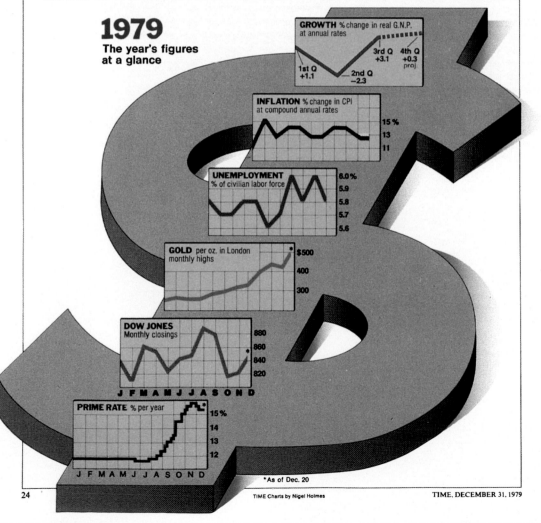

1979
The year's figures at a glance

GROWTH % change in real G.N.P. at annual rates
- 1st Q +1.1
- 2nd Q −2.3
- 3rd Q +3.1
- 4th Q +0.3 proj.

INFLATION % change in CPI at compound annual rates
- 15 %
- 13
- 11

UNEMPLOYMENT % of civilian labor force
- 6.0 %
- 5.9
- 5.8
- 5.7
- 5.6

GOLD per oz. in London monthly highs
- *$500
- 400
- 300

DOW JONES Monthly closings
- 880
- 860
- *840
- 820

J F M A M J J A S O N D

PRIME RATE % per year
- 15 %
- 14
- 13
- 12

J F M A M J J A S O N D

*As of Dec. 20

TIME Charts by Nigel Holmes

TIME, DECEMBER 31, 1979

24

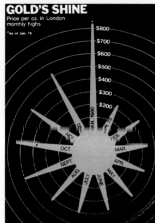

GOLD'S SHINE
Price per oz. in London monthly highs
*As of Jan. 18
- $800
- $700
- $600
- $500
- $400
- $300
- $200

△130

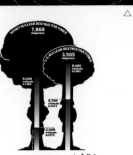

SOVIET NUCLEAR DESTRUCTIVE FORCE 7,868 megatons

U.S. NUCLEAR DESTRUCTIVE FORCE 3,505 megatons

△131

BACKBREAKING
Personal debt in billions of dollars at year's end

1981 PER CAPITA DEBT $6,737

1975 PER CAPITA DEBT $[...]

- $1,548.2
- $1,439.9
- $1,335.4
- $1,164.5
- $1,001.7
- TOTAL $862.3
- TOTAL $771.7

INSTALLMENT CREDIT and other borrowings

HOUSEHOLD MORTGAGES

- 1,400
- 1,300
- 1,200
- 1,100
- $1,000
- 900
- 800
- 700
- 600
- $500
- 400
- 300
- 200
- 100

'75 '76 '77 '78 '79 '80 '81

TIME Charts by Nigel Holmes

△132

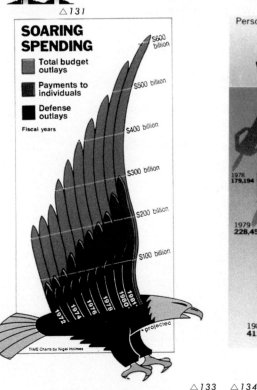

SOARING SPENDING
- Total budget outlays
- Payments to individuals
- Defense outlays

Fiscal years

- $600 billion
- $500 billion
- $400 billion
- $300 billion
- $200 billion
- $100 billion

1972 1974 1976 1978 1980 1981

*projected

TIME Charts by Nigel Holmes

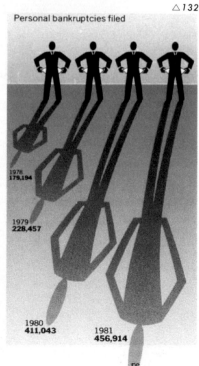

Personal bankruptcies filed

- 1978 179,194
- 1979 228,457
- 1980 411,043
- 1981 456,914

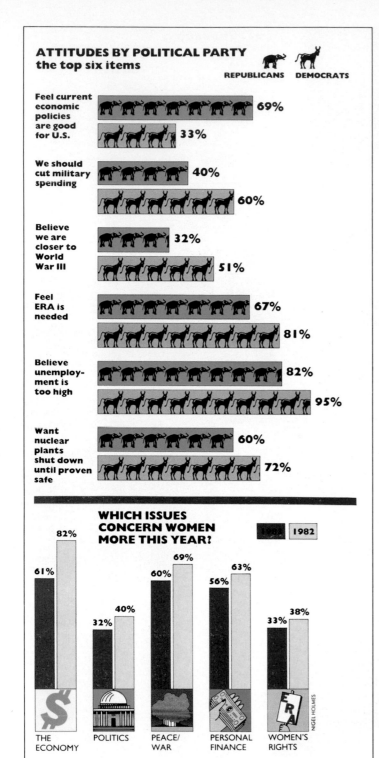

ATTITUDES BY POLITICAL PARTY
the top six items

REPUBLICANS   DEMOCRATS

Feel current economic policies are good for U.S.
69%
33%

We should cut military spending
40%
60%

Believe we are closer to World War III
32%
51%

Feel ERA is needed
67%
81%

Believe unemployment is too high
82%
95%

Want nuclear plants shut down until proven safe
60%
72%

WHICH ISSUES CONCERN WOMEN MORE THIS YEAR?

1981   1982

	THE ECONOMY	POLITICS	PEACE/WAR	PERSONAL FINANCE	WOMEN'S RIGHTS
1981	61%	32%	60%	56%	33%
1982	82%	40%	69%	63%	38%

NIGEL HOLMES

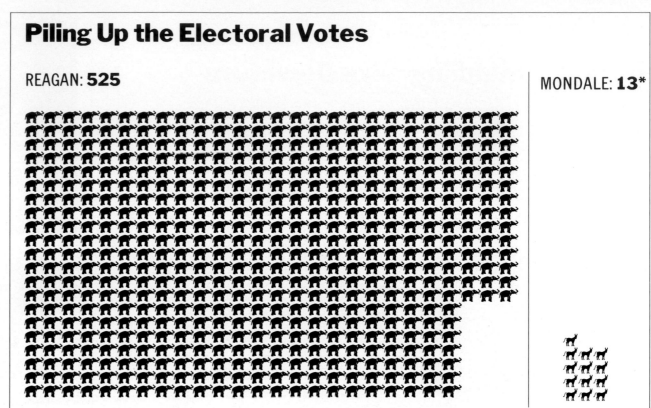

Piling Up the Electoral Votes

REAGAN: 525

MONDALE: 13*

Time Chart

*Washington, D.C. and Minnesota

△136

Ships of the Royal Navy

△137

NIGEL HOLMES 135~137.

U.S.A. 1.
COMPARATIVE STATISTICS 3.
GLAMOUR MAGAZINE (135) 4.
TIME MAGAZINE (136)
RADIO TIMES MAGAZINE (137)
POLITICAL PARTY PLATFORMS (135) 5.
ELECTORAL VOTES OF 1984 NATIONAL ELECTION (136)
SHIPS OF THE ROYAL NAVY (137)

△135

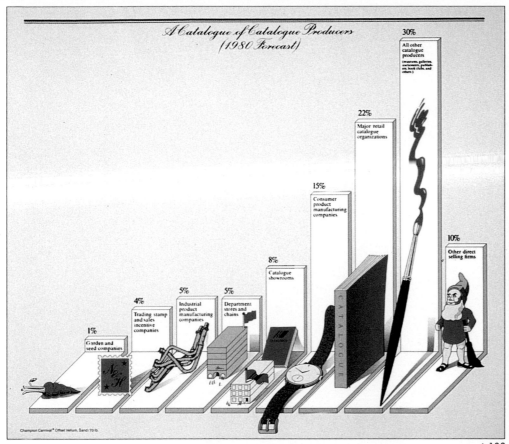

A Catalogue of Catalogue Producers
(1980 Forecast)

30%
All other catalogue producers
(museums, galleries, auctioneers, publishers, book clubs, and others)

22%
Major retail catalogue organizations

15%
Consumer product manufacturing companies

10%
Other direct selling firms

8%
Catalogue showrooms

5%
Department stores and chains

5%
Industrial product manufacturing companies

4%
Trading stamp and sales incentive companies

1%
Garden and seed companies

Champion Carnival® Offset Vellum, Sand/70 lb.

△138

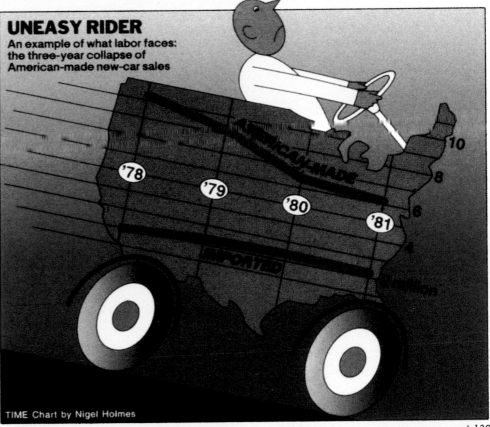

UNEASY RIDER
An example of what labor faces:
the three-year collapse of
American-made new-car sales

'78   '79   '80   '81

AMERICAN MADE

IMPORTED

10
8
6

TIME Chart by Nigel Holmes

△139

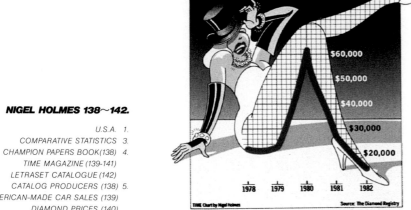

DIAMONDS *WERE* A GIRL'S BEST FRIEND
Average price of a one-carat D-flawless

$60,000
$50,000
$40,000
$30,000
$20,000

1978   1979   1980   1981   1982

TIME Chart by Nigel Holmes   Source: The Diamond Registry

△140

TEAMS' 1982 GROSS REVENUES
Estimated
Football* $600 m.
Baseball $400 m.
Basketball $120 m.

Football* $90,000   Baseball $240,000   Basketball $218,000

PLAYERS' 1982 AVERAGE SALARIES
*N.F.L. Players Association figures

TIME Chart by Nigel Holmes

△141

1981 19·2
1980 18·4
1979 17·8
1978 17·0
1977 16·2

SHARP PROFITS
Amount of electric shavers sold in the United States, in millions

△142

49

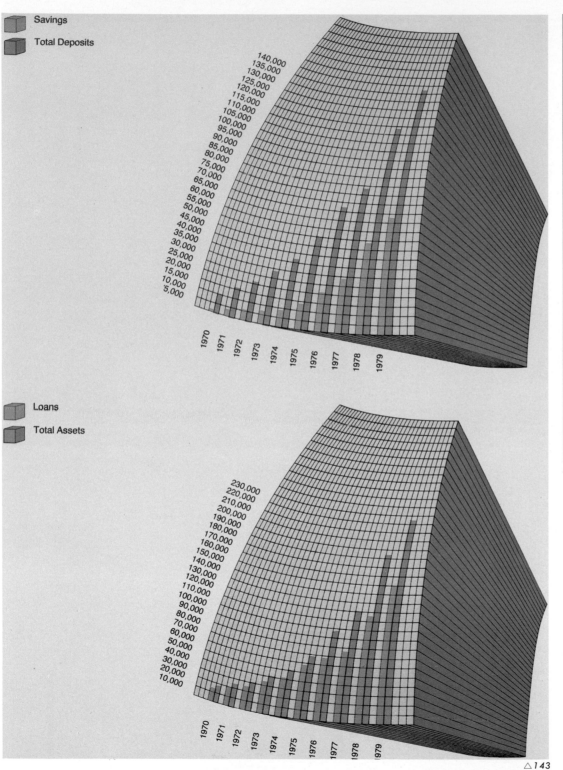

Savings

Total Deposits

140,000
135,000
130,000
125,000
120,000
115,000
110,000
105,000
100,000
95,000
90,000
85,000
80,000
75,000
70,000
65,000
60,000
55,000
50,000
45,000
40,000
35,000
30,000
25,000
20,000
15,000
10,000
5,000

1970 1971 1972 1973 1974 1975 1976 1977 1978 1979

Loans

Total Assets

230,000
220,000
210,000
200,000
190,000
180,000
170,000
160,000
150,000
140,000
130,000
120,000
110,000
100,000
90,000
80,000
70,000
60,000
50,000
40,000
30,000
20,000
10,000

1970 1971 1972 1973 1974 1975 1976 1977 1978 1979

△143

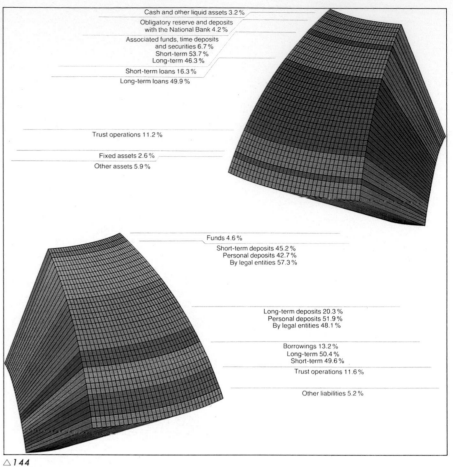

Cash and other liquid assets 3.2 %
Obligatory reserve and deposits with the National Bank 4.2 %
Associated funds, time deposits and securities 6.7 %
Short-term 53.7 %
Long-term 46.3 %
Short-term loans 16.3 %
Long-term loans 49.9 %

Trust operations 11.2 %

Fixed assets 2.6 %
Other assets 5.9 %

Funds 4.6 %
Short-term deposits 45.2 %
Personal deposits 42.7 %
By legal entities 57.3 %

Long-term deposits 20.3 %
Personal deposits 51.9 %
By legal entities 48.1 %

Borrowings 13.2 %
Long-term 50.4 %
Short-term 49.6 %
Trust operations 11.6 %

Other liabilities 5.2 %

△144

PETER SKALAR 143,144.

YUGOSLAVIA 1.
COMPARATIVE STATISTICS 3.

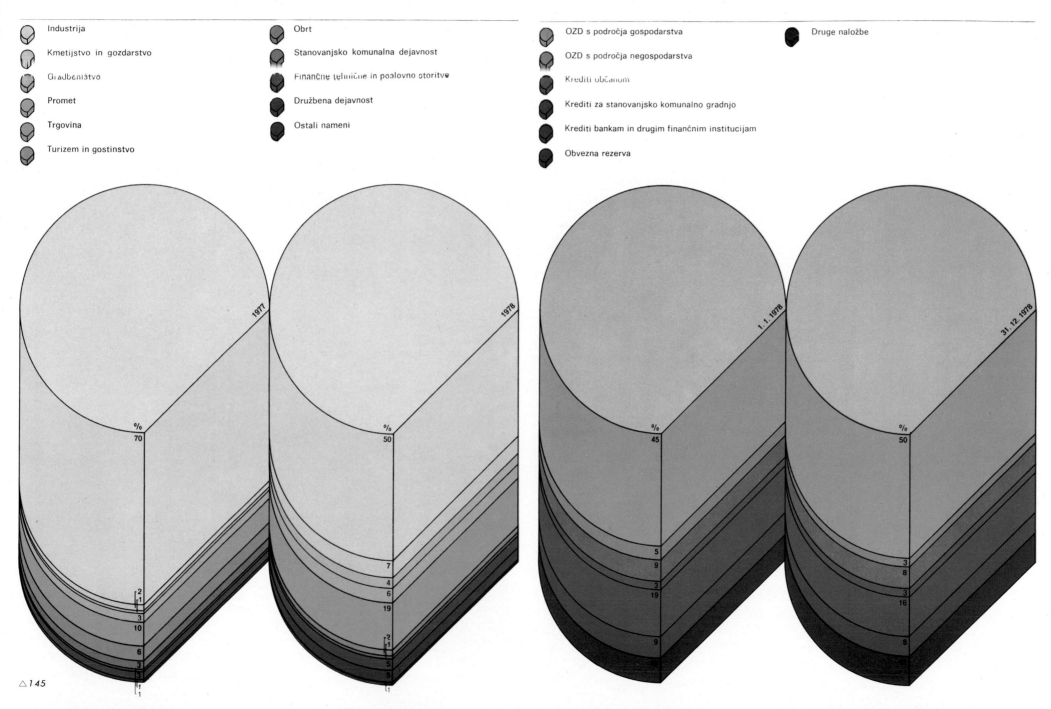

Industrija

Kmetijstvo in gozdarstvo

Gradbeništvo

Promet

Trgovina

Turizem in gostinstvo

Obrt

Stanovanjsko komunalna dejavnost

Finančne tehnične in poslovno storitve

Družbena dejavnost

Ostali nameni

OZD s področja gospodarstva

OZD s področja negospodarstva

Krediti občanom

Krediti za stanovanjsko komunalno gradnjo

Krediti bankam in drugim finančnim institucijam

Obvezna rezerva

Druge naložbe

△145

51

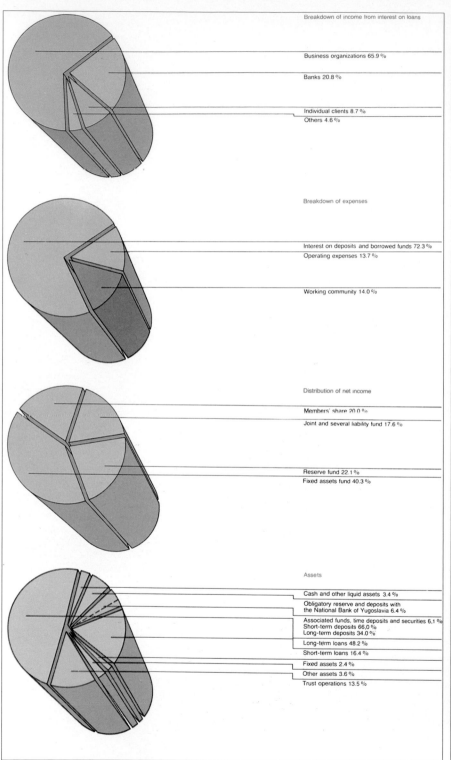

Breakdown of income from interest on loans

Business organizations 65.9 %

Banks 20.8 %

Individual clients 8.7 %
Others 4.6 %

Breakdown of expenses

Interest on deposits and borrowed funds 72.3 %
Operating expenses 13.7 %

Working community 14.0 %

Distribution of net income

Members' share 20.0 %
Joint and several liability fund 17.6 %

Reserve fund 22.1 %
Fixed assets fund 40.3 %

Assets

Cash and other liquid assets 3.4 %
Obligatory reserve and deposits with
the National Bank of Yugoslavia 6.4 %
Associated funds, time deposits and securities 6,1 %
Short-term deposits 66,0 %
Long-term deposits 34.0 %
Long-term loans 48.2 %
Short-term loans 16.4 %
Fixed assets 2.4 %
Other assets 3.6 %
Trust operations 13.5 %

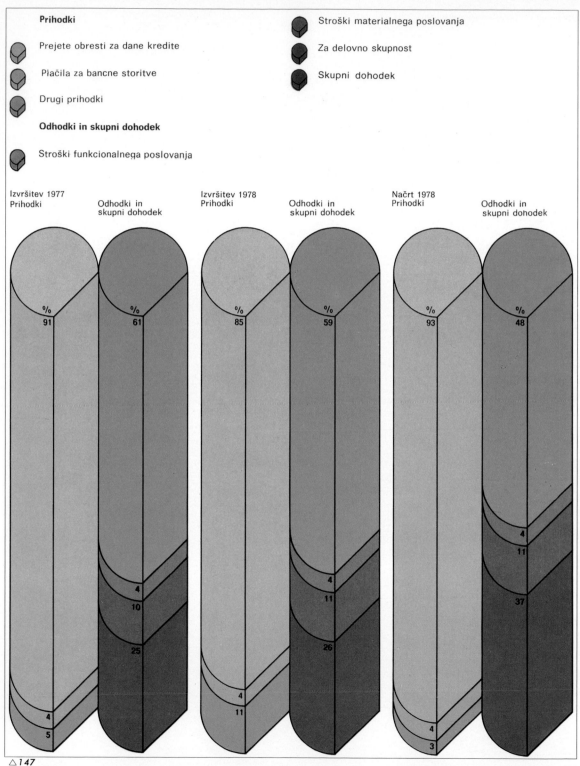

Prihodki

Prejete obresti za dane kredite

Plačila za bancne storitve

Drugi prihodki

Odhodki in skupni dohodek

Stroški funkcionalnega poslovanja

Stroški materialnega poslovanja

Za delovno skupnost

Skupni dohodek

Izvršitev 1977
Prihodki

Odhodki in
skupni dohodek

Izvršitev 1978
Prihodki

Odhodki in
skupni dohodek

Načrt 1978
Prihodki

Odhodki in
skupni dohodek

△146   △147

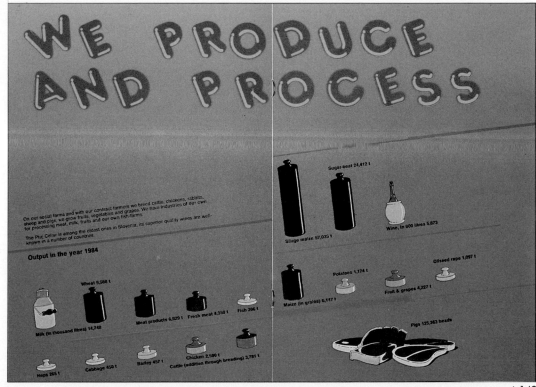

△149

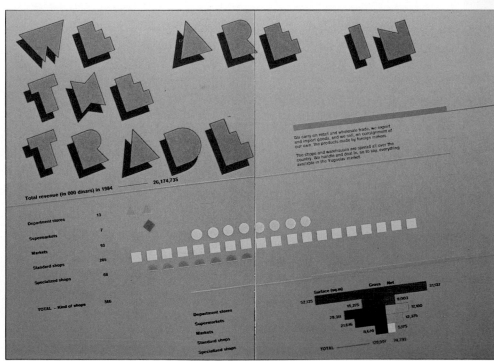

△148 △150

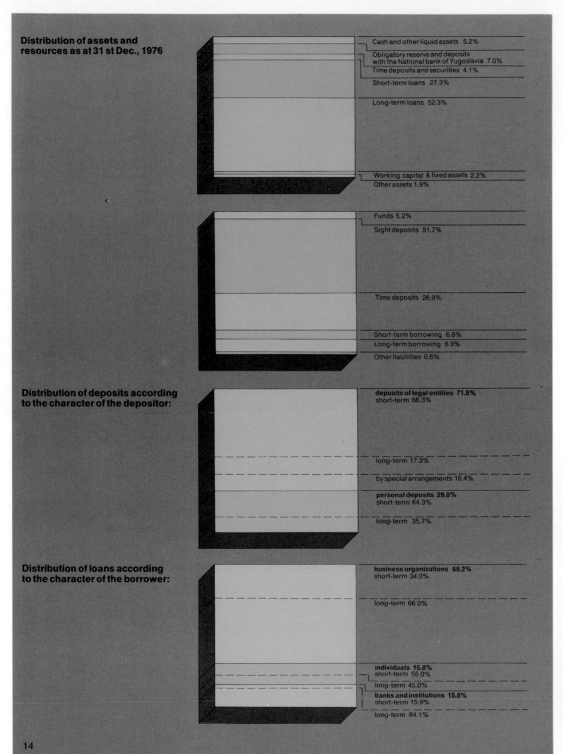

Distribution of assets and resources as at 31 st Dec., 1976

Cash and other liquid assets 5.2%

Obligatory reserve and deposits with the National bank of Yugoslavia 7.0%

Time deposits and securities 4.1%

Short-term loans 27.3%

Long-term loans 52.3%

Working capital & fixed assets 2.2%
Other assets 1.9%

Funds 5.2%
Sight deposits 51.7%

Time deposits 26.9%

Short-term borrowing 6.6%
Long-term borrowing 8.9%

Other liabilities 0.6%

Distribution of deposits according to the character of the depositor:

deposits of legal entities 71.0%
short-term 66.3%

long-term 17.3%

by special arrangements 16.4%

personal deposits 29.0%
short-term 64.3%

long-term 35.7%

Distribution of loans according to the character of the borrower:

business organizations 69.2%
short-term 34.0%

long-term 66.0%

individuals 15.0%
short-term 55.0%
long-term 45.0%

banks and institutions 15.8%
short-term 15.9%

long-term 84.1%

14

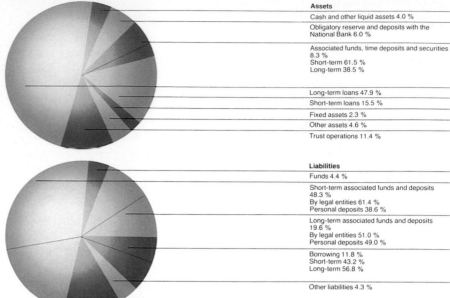

Assets

Cash and other liquid assets 4.0 %

Obligatory reserve and deposits with the National Bank 6.0 %

Associated funds, time deposits and securities 8.3 %
Short-term 61.5 %
Long-term 38.5 %

Long-term loans 47.9 %

Short-term loans 15.5 %

Fixed assets 2.3 %

Other assets 4.6 %

Trust operations 11.4 %

Liabilities

Funds 4.4 %

Short-term associated funds and deposits 48.3 %
By legal entities 61.4 %
Personal deposits 38.6 %

Long-term associated funds and deposits 19.6 %
By legal entities 51.0 %
Personal deposits 49.0 %

Borrowing 11.8 %
Short-term 43.2 %
Long-term 56.8 %

Other liabilities 4.3 %

Trust operations 11.6 %

151,152. PETER SKALAR

1. YUGOSLAVIA
3. COMPARATIVE STATISTICS

153. ABE GURVIN

1. U.S.A.
2. ABE GURVIN ILLUSTRATION & DESIGN
3. COMPARATIVE STATISTICS
4. MAGAZINE AD
5. PLESSEY SEMI CONDUCTORS

It's lonely at the top.

Mind you, we wouldn't have it any other way.
Because we deliberately set out to be the leader in integrated circuits for communications. And today, nobody else even comes close.
We developed the first and only 2 GHz counter. And a family of prescalers and controllers for your TV, radio and instrumentation frequency synthesizers.
We have a monolithic 1 GHz amplifier. And a complete array of complex integrated function blocks for radio communications and signal processing right down to DC.
We can supply an A-to-D converter with a propagation delay of just 2½ nanoseconds. And a range of MNOS logic that stores data for a year when you remove power, yet uses only a single supply and is fully TTL/CMOS-compatible.
Our processing was designed for quality, then applied to our

high volume lines. Process III has a projected MTBF of 400,000 hours, Process I is even better.
Most of our ICs are available screened to MIL-STD-883B, and our quality levels exceed the most stringent military, TV and automotive requirements.
Last year, millions of Plessey devices were built into TV sets and car radios; CATV, navigation and radar systems; frequency synthesizers and telecommunications systems.
This year, maybe you won't have to re-invent the wheel. Contact us for the complete information on Plessey high technology, high quality, high volume capabilities.
It could put you on top.
Plessey Semiconductors, Cheney Manor, Swindon, Wiltshire, SN2 2QW, U.K. Telephone 0793 36251.
1641 Kaiser Avenue, Santa Ana, CA 92714, U.S.A. Telephone (714) 540-9979.

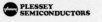
PLESSEY SEMICONDUCTORS

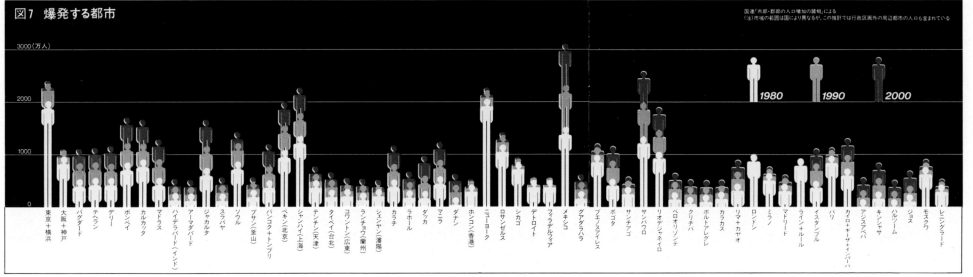

△154 ▽156 △155

図7 爆発する都市

国連「市部・郡部の人口増加の諸相」による
(注)市域の範囲は国により異なるが、この推計では行政区画外の周辺都市の人口も含まれている

3000(万人)

2000

1000

0

1980　**1990**　**2000**

東京＋横浜
大阪＋神戸
バグダード
テヘラン
デリー
ボンベイ
カルカッタ
マドラス
ハイデラバード（インド）
アーマダバード
ジャカルタ
スラバヤ
ソウル
プサン（釜山）
バンコク＋トンブリ
ペキン（北京）
シャンハイ（上海）
テンチン（天津）
タイペイ（台北）
コワントン（広東）
ランチョウ（瀋陽）
シェンヤン（瀋陽）
カラチ
ラホール
ダッカ
マニラ
ダナン
ホンコン（香港）
ニューヨーク
ロサンゼルス
シカゴ
デトロイト
フィラデルフィア
メキシコ
グアダラハラ
ブエノスアイレス
ボゴタ
サンチアゴ
サンパウロ
リオデジャネイロ
ベロオリゾンテ
クリチバ
ポルトアレグレ
カラカス
リマ＋カオ
ロンドン
ミラノ
マドリード
ラインルール
イスタンブール
パリ
カイロ＋ギザ＋インバーバ
アジスアベバ
キンシャサ
ハルツーム
ジョス
モスクワ
レニングラード

154,155. SOREN THAAE　　　　　　　　　　　　　　　　　　　　　　　　　　　　　　　　　　　**MORISHITA CO., LTD. 156.**

1. DENMARK　　　　　　3. COMPARATIVE STATISTICS　　　　　　ASAHI SHIMBUN SHA 5.　　　　　　COMPARATIVE STATISTICS 3.　　　　　　JAPAN 1.
2. 3-D ILLUSTRATIONS　　5. DANISH TELEVISION　　　INCREASE IN URBAN POPULATIONS　　WEEKLY MAGAZINE "ASAHI HYAKKA-GEOGRAPHY IN THE WORLD" 4.　　MORISHITA CO., LTD. 2.

157. ELLIS/ROSS/TANI

1. U.S.A.
2. ELLIS/ROSS/TANI
   CREATIVE DIRECTOR: JOHN ELLIS MARCIA ROSS
   DESIGNER: GORDON TANI
   PHOTOGRAPHER: JIM CORNFIELD
3. FLOW CHART
4. PAMPHLET
5. ARRAYS, INC

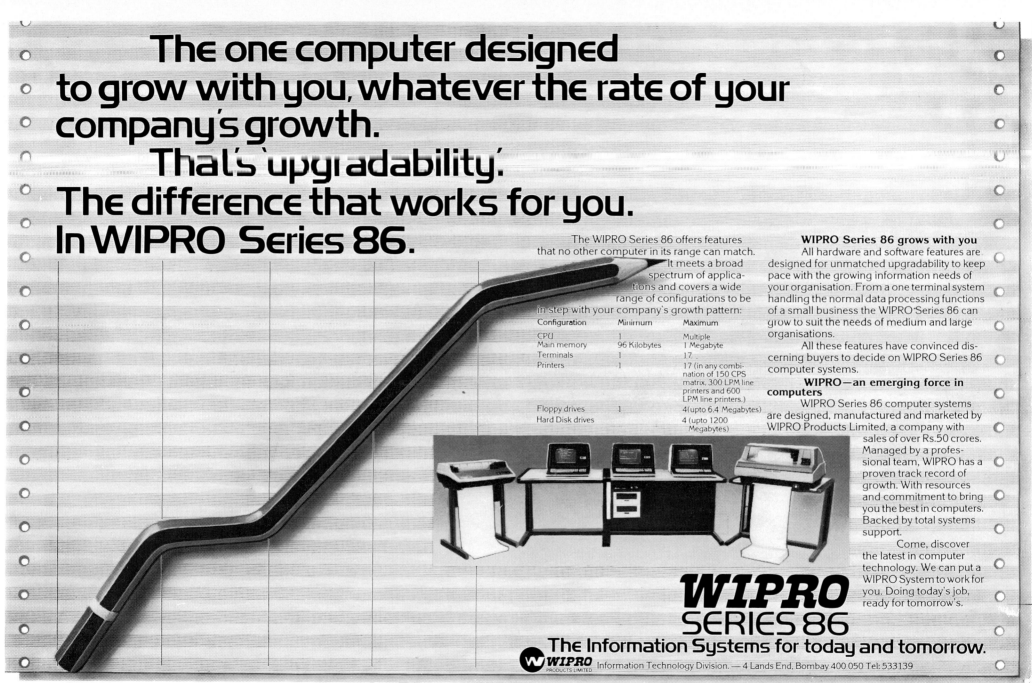

The one computer designed to grow with you, whatever the rate of your company's growth.
That's 'upgradability'.
The difference that works for you. In WIPRO Series 86.

The WIPRO Series 86 offers features that no other computer in its range can match. It meets a broad spectrum of applications and covers a wide range of configurations to be in step with your company's growth pattern:

Configuration	Minimum	Maximum
CPU	1	Multiple
Main memory	96 Kilobytes	1 Megabyte
Terminals	1	17
Printers	1	17 (in any combination of 150 CPS matrix, 300 LPM line printers and 600 LPM line printers.)
Floppy drives	1	4 (upto 6.4 Megabytes)
Hard Disk drives		4 (upto 1200 Megabytes)

WIPRO Series 86 grows with you

All hardware and software features are designed for unmatched upgradability to keep pace with the growing information needs of your organisation. From a one terminal system handling the normal data processing functions of a small business the WIPRO Series 86 can grow to suit the needs of medium and large organisations.

All these features have convinced discerning buyers to decide on WIPRO Series 86 computer systems.

WIPRO—an emerging force in computers

WIPRO Series 86 computer systems are designed, manufactured and marketed by WIPRO Products Limited, a company with sales of over Rs.50 crores. Managed by a professional team, WIPRO has a proven track record of growth. With resources and commitment to bring you the best in computers. Backed by total systems support.

Come, discover the latest in computer technology. We can put a WIPRO System to work for you. Doing today's job, ready for tomorrow's.

WIPRO SERIES 86
The Information Systems for today and tomorrow.

W WIPRO PRODUCTS LIMITED. Information Technology Division. — 4 Lands End, Bombay 400 050 Tel: 533139

△158

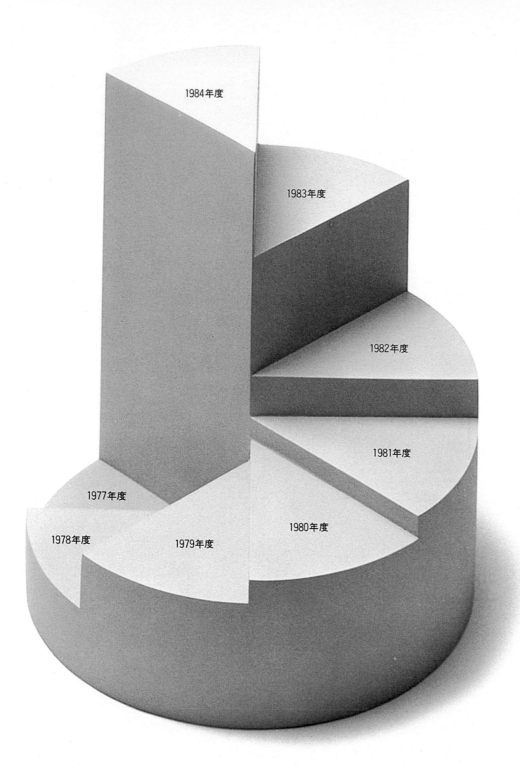

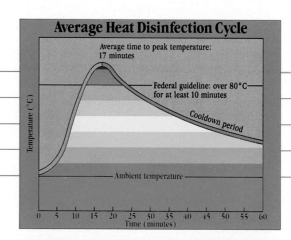

THE ALLERGAN HEAT DISINFECTION UNIT

PERFORMANCE RELIABILITY

BACKED BY EXTENSIVE TESTING

Average Heat Disinfection Cycle

Average time to peak temperature: 17 minutes

Federal guideline: over 80°C for at least 10 minutes

Cooldown period

Ambient temperature

Temperature (°C)

Time (minutes)

57,600 heat cycles tested with only one failure
160 units x 360 cycles/unit
57,600 heat cycles

Units were also tested at extremes of:
• voltage • ambient temperature • humidity • solution level • altitude
and successfully met all standards of performance.

You can recommend the new Allergan Heat Disinfection Unit with greater confidence to your soft lens patients.

161. ANTONIO DIAZ ASOCIADOS S.A.

1. SPAIN
2. ANTONIO DIAZ ASOCIADOS S.A.
3. COMPARATIVE STATISTICS
4. 1 FULL PAGE PRESS ADVERTISEMENT
   GRAPHIC OF AUDIENCES IN AM AND FM
5. CADENA SER (SER RADIO NETWORK), SPAIN'S FIRST PRIVATE RADIO NETWORK

162. VU S.R.L.

1. ITALY
2. VU S.R.L.
3. COMPARATIVE STATISTICS

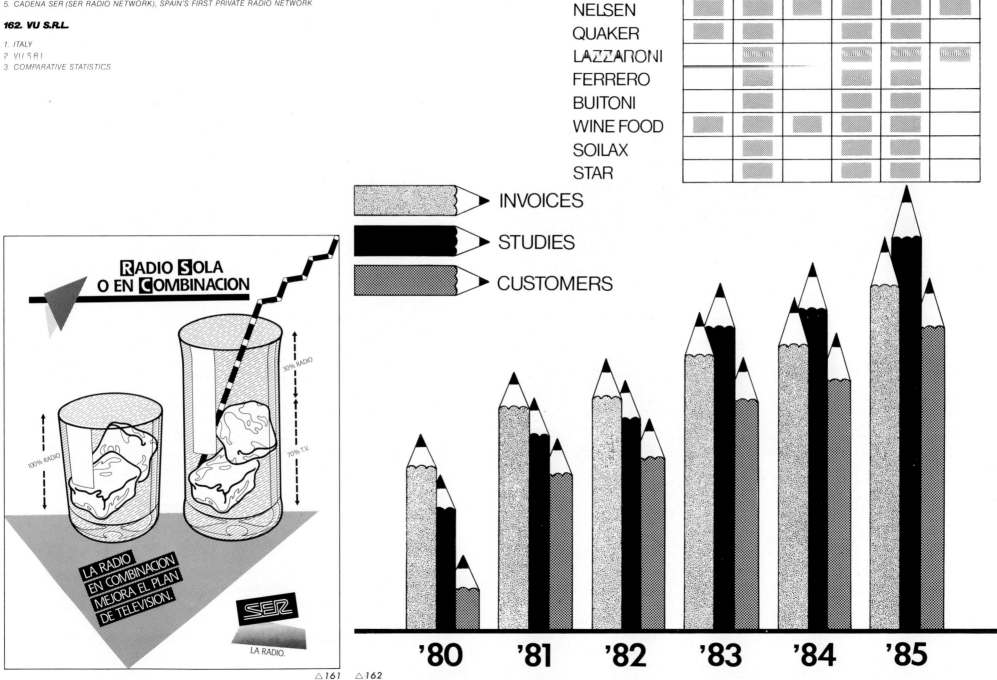

CUSTOMERS	FORM	PACKAGING	CORPORATE IMAGE	LOGOTYPE	EXTENTION OF PRODUCT LINE	SALES ORGANIZER
NELSEN	▨	▨	▨	▨	▨	▨
QUAKER	▨	▨			▨	
LAZZARONI		▨		▨	▨	▨
FERRERO		▨		▨	▨	
BUITONI		▨			▨	
WINE FOOD	▨	▨	▨		▨	
SOILAX		▨			▨	
STAR		▨		▨	▨	

INVOICES

STUDIES

CUSTOMERS

'80 '81 '82 '83 '84 '85

RADIO SOLA
O EN COMBINACION

30% RADIO

100% RADIO

70% T.V.

LA RADIO
EN COMBINACION
MEJORA EL PLAN
DE TELEVISION.

SER

LA RADIO.

△161   △162

59

In the selection of the ultimate solution, knowledge of regulatory and environmental issues is paramount. Dames & Moore's technical staff is familiar with waste and environmental regulations and can evaluate these factors early in the selection process to avoid delays in later phases of the project.

Critical to the analysis of various waste management alternatives is a consistent approach to cost/benefit analyses for both construction and operation. Cost information is obtained from readily available data used in combination with Dames & Moore's comprehensive in-house data base. More detailed analyses may require evaluation of current construction costs, surveys of recent bid information and cost quotations from equipment suppliers.

For each alternative, a realistic understanding of the performance and reliability of the system is essential. Though waste systems can be designed to provide a given factor of safety, many waste management alternatives operate optimally without being over designed. Dames & Moore's integrated approach to the broad range of technical issues related to waste management ensures that the alternative ultimately selected will be technically sound and reliable.

Computer mapping, aerial photo interpretation and seismic analysis are only a few techniques used to address the geohydrologic, environmental and regulatory issues of facility siting.

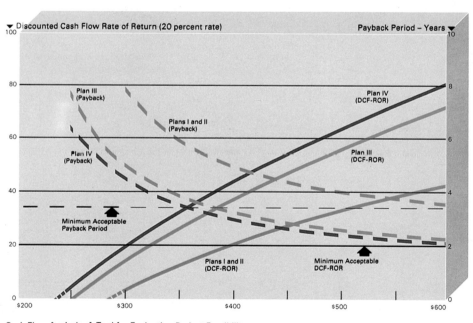

Cash Flow Analysis: A Tool for Evaluating Project Feasibility

△163

163,164. BILL BROWN

1. *U.S.A.*
2. *BILL BROWN & ASSOCIATES*
   ART DIRECTOR:BILL BROWN
   DESIGNER:SHOJI TERAISHI
3. *FLOW CHARTS*
4. *CATALOGUE*   5. *DAMES & MOORE ENVIRONMENTAL ISSUES AND PROJECTS*

Conceptualization: Assessing Alternative Waste Management Options

Upon identification of the waste-related problem, alternative solutions are assessed. These alternatives may include:

- Various strategies for cleanup and remedial actions
- Operation modifications
- Waste segregation and/or volume reduction
- Waste recycling and recovery of energy and/or materials
- Waste treatment or detoxification
- Waste disposal or isolation

Dames & Moore's range of technical expertise allows for a rapid and thorough consideration of feasible alternatives. The firm's extensive project experience with design alternatives, regulatory compliance and industry requirements facilitates the development of a broad range of creative options with an eye for practical, cost effective solutions.

Feasibility Study to Select and Implement Alternative Waste Management Options

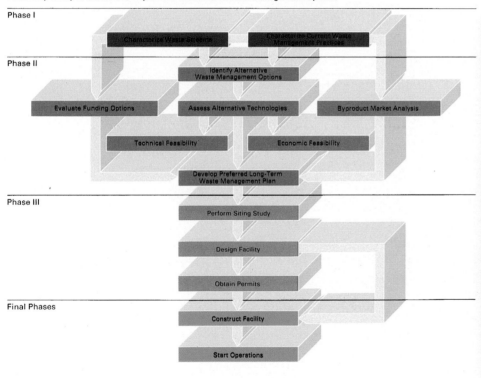

Phase I
- Characterize Waste Streams
- Characterize Current Waste Management Practices

Phase II
- Identify Alternative Waste Management Options
- Evaluate Funding Options
- Assess Alternative Technologies
- Byproduct Market Analysis
- Technical Feasibility
- Economic Feasibility
- Develop Preferred Long-Term Waste Management Plan

Phase III
- Perform Siting Study
- Design Facility
- Obtain Permits

Final Phases
- Construct Facility
- Start Operations

Should disposal options be considered, Dames & Moore provides extensive experience in selection of sites for hazardous and non-hazardous waste facilities.

△164

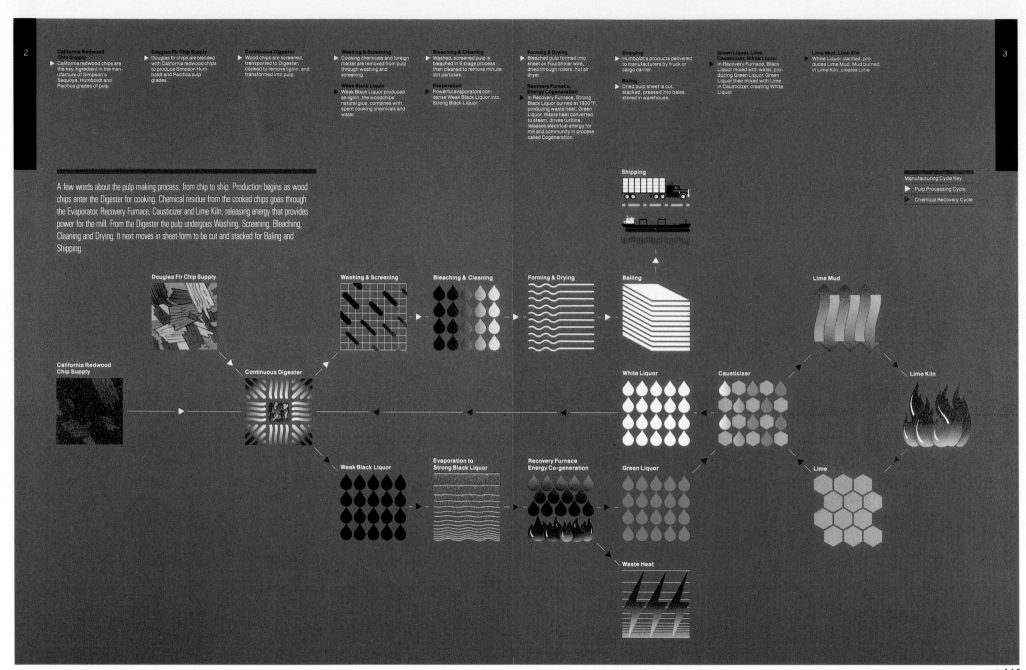

California Redwood Chip Supply
▶ California redwood chips are the key ingredient in the manufacture of Simpson's Sequoya, Humboldt and Pacifica grades of pulp.

Douglas Fir Chip Supply
▶ Douglas fir chips are blended with California redwood chips to produce Simpson Humboldt and Pacifica pulp grades.

Continuous Digester
▶ Wood chips are screened, transported to Digester, cooked to remove lignin, and transformed into pulp.

Washing & Screening
▶ Cooking chemicals and foreign matter are removed from pulp through washing and screening.

Weak Black Liquor
▶ Weak Black Liquor produced as lignin, the woodchips' natural glue, combines with spent cooking chemicals and water.

Bleaching & Cleaning
▶ Washed, screened pulp is bleached in 6 stage process then cleaned to remove minute dirt particles.

Evaporation
▶ Powerful evaporators condense Weak Black Liquor into Strong Black Liquor.

Forming & Drying
▶ Bleached pulp formed into sheet on Fourdrinier wire, dried through rollers, hot air dryer.

Recovery Furnace, Energy Cogeneration
▶ In Recovery Furnace, Strong Black Liquor burned at 1800°F, producing waste heat, Green Liquor. Waste heat converted to steam, drives turbine, releases electrical energy for mill and community in process called Cogeneration.

Shipping
▶ Humboldt's products delivered to manufacturers by truck or cargo carrier.

Baling
▶ Dried pulp sheet is cut, stacked, pressed into bales, stored in warehouse.

Green Liquor, Lime, Causticizer, White Liquor
▶ In Recovery Furnace, Black Liquor mixed with water, producing Green Liquor. Green Liquor then mixed with Lime in Causticizer, creating White Liquor.

Lime Mud, Lime Kiln
▶ White Liquor clarified, produces Lime Mud. Mud burned in Lime Kiln, creates Lime.

A few words about the pulp making process, from chip to ship. Production begins as wood chips enter the Digester for cooking. Chemical residue from the cooked chips goes through the Evaporator, Recovery Furnace, Causticizer and Lime Kiln, releasing energy that provides power for the mill. From the Digester the pulp undergoes Washing, Screening, Bleaching, Cleaning and Drying. It next moves in sheet-form to be cut and stacked for Baling and Shipping.

Manufacturing Cycle Key
▶ Pulp Processing Cycle
▶ Chemical Recovery Cycle

Shipping

Douglas Fir Chip Supply — Washing & Screening — Bleaching & Cleaning — Forming & Drying — Bailing — Lime Mud

California Redwood Chip Supply — Continuous Digester — White Liquor — Causticizer — Lime Kiln

Weak Black Liquor — Evaporation to Strong Black Liquor — Recovery Furnace Energy Co-generation — Green Liquor — Lime

Waste Heat

△165

DOUGLAS BOYD 165.

1. U.S.A.
2. DOUGLAS BOYD DESIGN AND MARKETING
3. FLOW CHARTS
4. BROCHURE
5. SIMPSON PAPER COMPANY
   PULP MAKING PROCESS

166,167. YASUSHI OKITA

1. U.S.A.
2. YASHI OKITA DESIGN
3. SYSTEMATICAL GRAPHS (166,167)
4. SALES BROCHURE
5. EXAR INTEGRATED SYSTEM, INC (166)
   INTEL CORPORATION (167)

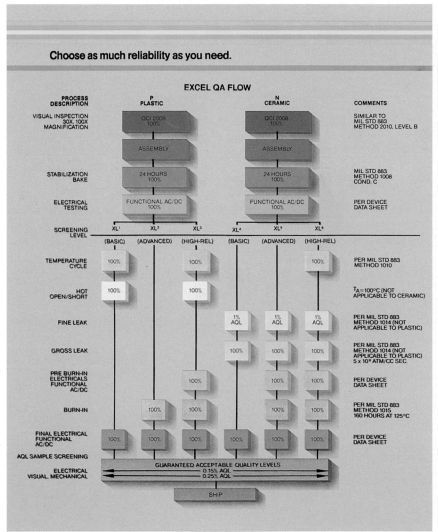

Choose as much reliability as you need.

EXCEL QA FLOW

PROCESS DESCRIPTION	P PLASTIC			N CERAMIC			COMMENTS
VISUAL INSPECTION 30X, 100X MAGNIFICATION	QCI 2008 100%			QCI 2008 100%			SIMILAR TO MIL STD 883 METHOD 2010, LEVEL B
	ASSEMBLY			ASSEMBLY			
STABILIZATION BAKE	24 HOURS 100%			24 HOURS 100%			MIL STD 883 METHOD 1008 COND. C
ELECTRICAL TESTING	FUNCTIONAL AC/DC 100%			FUNCTIONAL AC/DC 100%			PER DEVICE DATA SHEET
SCREENING LEVEL	XL¹ (BASIC)	XL² (ADVANCED)	XL³ (HIGH-REL)	XL⁴ (BASIC)	XL⁵ (ADVANCED)	XL⁶ (HIGH-REL)	
TEMPERATURE CYCLE	100%		100%			100%	PER MIL STD 883 METHOD 1010
HOT OPEN/SHORT	100%		100%				$T_A = 100°C$ (NOT APPLICABLE TO CERAMIC)
FINE LEAK				1% AQL	1% AQL	1% AQL	PER MIL STD 883 METHOD 1014 (NOT APPLICABLE TO PLASTIC)
GROSS LEAK				100%	100%	100%	PER MIL STD 883 METHOD 1014 (NOT APPLICABLE TO PLASTIC) 5 x 10⁸ ATM/CC SEC.
PRE BURN-IN ELECTRICALS FUNCTIONAL AC/DC			100%		100%	100%	PER DEVICE DATA SHEET
BURN-IN		100%	100%		100%	100%	PER MIL STD 883 METHOD 1015 160 HOURS AT 125°C
FINAL ELECTRICAL FUNCTIONAL AC/DC	100%	100%	100%	100%	100%	100%	PER DEVICE DATA SHEET
AQL SAMPLE SCREENING							
ELECTRICAL VISUAL MECHANICAL	GUARANTEED ACCEPTABLE QUALITY LEVELS 0.15% AQL 0.25% AQL						

SHIP

The distributed development approach—sharing a large data base among all users, with common interfaces, from editing to system integration.

Optimizing the development environment.

As microprocessor development projects increase in size and complexity, so too does the task of managing the development process effectively and efficiently.

Now there's a development system that helps *manage* microprocessor development projects as well as helping *develop* and *debug* the project itself—Intel's Network Development System II.

NDS-II has been optimized for large development projects. It integrates the entire process—from editing of source code to system integration—into a single environment. An environment that features consistent physical, logical and language interfaces throughout.

NDS-II provides both program development and project management capabilities that are achievable only through this "total system" approach. For example:

Multiple Users. NDS-II supports a large number of workstations and users, *all sharing the resources of the network.*

Large Storage Capacity. NDS-II supports hundreds of megabytes of on-line, shared disk storage capacity, which can be added in flexible increments as your project size increases.

Shared Data Base. NDS-II allows all users to share data base files from any workstation on the network, without being concerned about where the files are physically stored, and without having to sift through a single, massive directory.

An optimized development environment allows users to share resources, gain access to all necessary "tools" (debuggers, emulators, etc.) and to increase storage and users without affecting the network.

The user has interactive access to all the hardware and software engineering "tools" for product development.

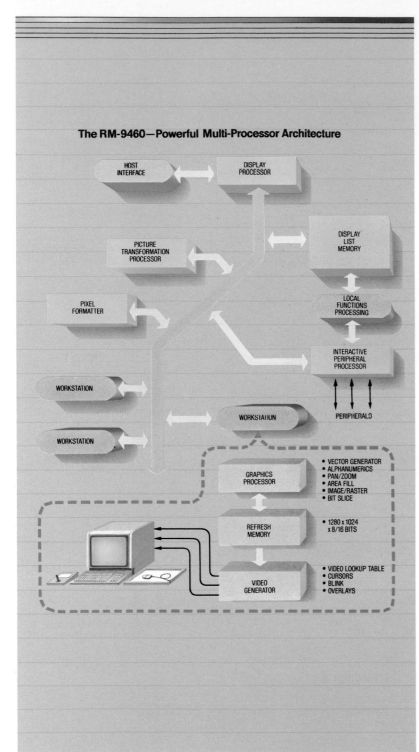

The RM-9460—Powerful Multi-Processor Architecture

HOST INTERFACE

DISPLAY PROCESSOR

PICTURE TRANSFORMATION PROCESSOR

DISPLAY LIST MEMORY

PIXEL FORMATTER

LOCAL FUNCTIONS PROCESSING

INTERACTIVE PERIPHERAL PROCESSOR

WORKSTATION

WORKSTATION

WORKSTATION

PERIPHERALS

GRAPHICS PROCESSOR
- VECTOR GENERATOR
- ALPHANUMERICS
- PAN/ZOOM
- AREA FILL
- IMAGE/RASTER
- BIT SLICE

REFRESH MEMORY
- 1280 x 1024 x 8/16 BITS

VIDEO GENERATOR
- VIDEO LOOKUP TABLE
- CURSORS
- BLINK
- OVERLAYS

△168

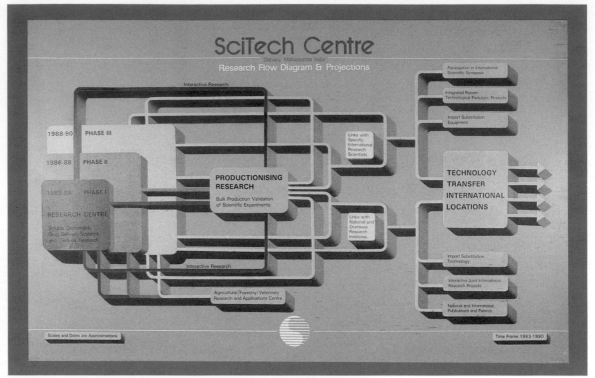

△169

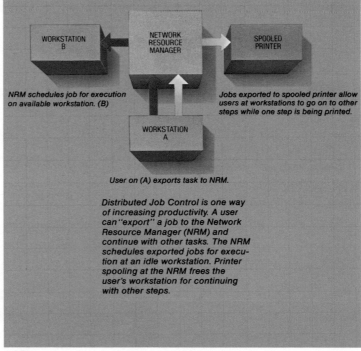

NRM schedules job for execution on available workstation. (B)

Jobs exported to spooled printer allow users at workstations to go on to other steps while one step is being printed.

User on (A) exports task to NRM.

Distributed Job Control is one way of increasing productivity. A user can "export" a job to the Network Resource Manager (NRM) and continue with other tasks. The NRM schedules exported jobs for execution at an idle workstation. Printer spooling at the NRM frees the user's workstation for continuing with other steps.

△170

The modular approach to development system investment ... now and in the future.

The NDS-II system is at once practical for customers with modest development system requirements, and for those already engaged in developing very large programs.

For example, you can start with a small local network—a single Network Resource Manager and two or three workstations, tied together with Intel's Network Architecture (iNA). Then as your needs expand, you can add workstations and additional NRMs, thereby continuously matching network resources with your requirements.

Looking into the future.

Even now, Intel is developing additional NDS-II-based products that will both expand your development capabilities and lower your cost per user—products that will become available over the course of the next two or three years. As these new products are added to the NDS-II network, your capabilities for handling large projects will continue to become both more efficient and more cost effective.

Future network options now on the drawing boards provide assurance that your investment in an NDS-II system today will continue to pay dividends tomorrow by expanding your development capabilities and reducing your cost per user.

Intel's development system products allow users to purchase systems suited to the level of product development complexity—from a standalone workstation (A), to a small network comprised of several workstations and a Network Resource Manager (B), to a large network supporting dozens of users and connecting several engineering labs (C). The network can be incrementally expanded to meet growth in customer development needs.

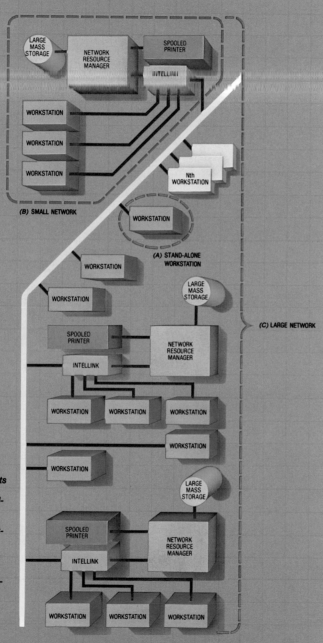

△171

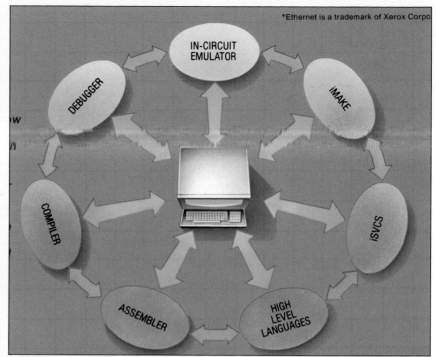

*Ethernet is a trademark of Xerox Corpo

△172

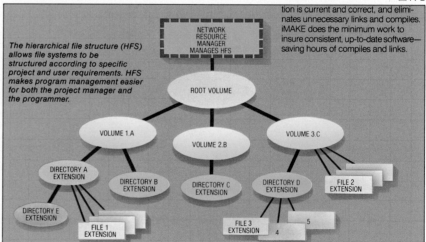

The hierarchical file structure (HFS) allows file systems to be structured according to specific project and user requirements. HFS makes program management easier for both the project manager and the programmer.

tion is current and correct, and eliminates unnecessary links and compiles. iMAKE does the minimum work to insure consistent, up-to-date software—saving hours of compiles and links.

△173

the cost of a standalone system. And installation is simple.

The result is a fully functional NDS-II workstation at every team member's desk—with full access to editors, compilers, Program Management Tools and Electronic Mail. No more waiting for workstations. No more inefficient communication. With all programmers "on-line", productivity is increased dramatically.

Peripheral options provide the flexibility to meet your growing data storage needs.

NDS-II allows you to add mass storage incrementally, as you need it. Start with the mass storage built into the Network Resource Manager, or use your existing mass storage devices. As your project data base grows, expand on-line storage to over 370 megabytes.

Communication options link your existing computers to the NDS-II network for the best of the micro and mainframe worlds.

If non-Intel computers are part of your current development environment, NDS-II will meet the communication challenge.

iRMX™ Link

iRMX-based microcomputer systems can be connected directly to NDS-II via Ethernet. iRMX system developers can use the program management, editing, compiling, and debugging tools of NDS-II to develop software. Using the iRMX link, developers can quickly download programs into their target iRMX host for execution. The iRMX link also provides a programmatic interface to NDS-II, which allows iRMX OEMs to develop customized networked environments.

As illustrated in the diagram and photo, ISIS cluster boards each contain their own CPU and memory. By installing these boards within a networked development system and connecting low cost terminals, you create fully functional workstations at a fraction of the usual cost.

Mainframe Link and Asynchronous Communication Link

The Mainframe Link offers the ability to integrate mainframe resources (IBM, for instance) with NDS-II resources. The Asynchronous Communication Link permits an NDS-II workstation to communicate with a Digital Equipment Corporation VAX* computer.

Engineers and engineering support groups can now take advantage of mainframe capabilities, and then download source code or documentation to the NDS-II for higher speed compilation plus execution, debug and system integration.

neering labs. NDS-II is designed to completely meet your changing needs.

HOST CRT

HOST PROCESSOR

ISIS CLUSTER PROCESSOR

ISIS CLUSTER PROCESSOR

ISIS CLUSTER PROCESSOR

ISIS CLUSTER PROCESSOR

ISIS CLUSTER PROCESSOR

ISIS CLUSTER PROCESSOR

ISIS CLUSTER TERMINALS

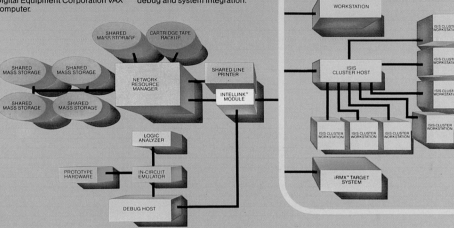

LARGE MAINFRAME

SHARED MASS STORAGE

CARTRIDGE TAPE BACKUP

SHARED MASS STORAGE

SHARED MASS STORAGE

SHARED MASS STORAGE

SHARED MASS STORAGE

NETWORK RESOURCE MANAGER

SHARED LINE PRINTER

INTELLINK™ MODULE

LOGIC ANALYZER

PROTOTYPE HARDWARE

IN-CIRCUIT EMULATOR

DEBUG HOST

WORKSTATION

ISIS CLUSTER WORKSTATION

ISIS CLUSTER HOST

ISIS CLUSTER WORKSTATION

ISIS CLUSTER WORKSTATION

ISIS CLUSTER WORKSTATION

ISIS CLUSTER WORKSTATION

ISIS CLUSTER WORKSTATION

iRMX™ TARGET SYSTEM

△174

NDS-II: The Intelligent Approach to System Development.

Network expansion is designed in.

NDS-II is ideal for customers with modest development requirements as well as those already engaged in very large scale system development. You can start with a small local network—a single Network Resource Manager and two or three workstations tied together with high speed Ethernet technology. Then, as needs expand, you can add workstations, mass storage and other network resources. In this manner, you can tailor the NDS-II configuration to a vast range of changing requirements.

NDS-II protects your development system investment.

As newer, more powerful products are developed, Intel is careful to protect the investment you have already made in Intel hardware and software. Every Intel development system introduced since 1975 can be incorporated into NDS-II with easy- to-install upgrade packages. And, your software investment is equally protected as all tools can be easily moved to the network for shared access on higher speed storage devices.

Intel provides a worldwide network of customer support.

Intel's comprehensive support for your development efforts goes far beyond providing superior products.

Intel is committed to offering future network-based products that will expand your development capabilities while lowering the cost per user. As new products are added to the network you will be able to successfully handle larger, more complex development projects involving the latest microprocessor architectures and languages.

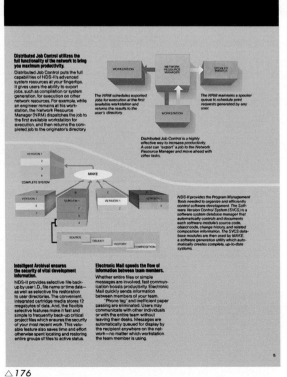

Distributed Job Control utilizes the full functionality of the network to bring you maximum productivity.

Distributed Job Control puts the full capabilities of NDS-II's advanced system resources at your fingertips. It gives users the ability to export jobs, such as compilation or system generation, for execution on other network resources. For example, while an engineer remains at his workstation, the Network Resource Manager (NRM) dispatches the job to the first available workstation for execution, and then returns the completed job to the originator's directory.

The NRM schedules exported jobs for execution at the first available workstation and returns the results to the user's directory.

The NRM maintains a spooler queue to schedule print requests generated by any user.

WORKSTATION

NETWORK RESOURCE MANAGER

SPOOLED PRINTER

WORKSTATION

Distributed Job Control is a highly effective way to increase productivity. A user can "export" a job to the Network Resource Manager and move ahead with other tasks.

VERSION 1

COMPLETE SYSTEM

MAKE

VERSION 1

VERSION 1

VERSION 1

SOURCE

OBJECT

HISTORY

COMPOSITION

NDS-II provides the Program Management Tools needed to organize and efficiently control software development. The Software Version Control System (SVCS) is a software system database manager that automatically controls and documents each software module's source code, object code, change history, and related composition information. The SVCS database modules are then used by MAKE, a software generation utility which automatically creates complete, up-to-date systems.

Intelligent Archival ensures the security of vital development information.

NDS-II provides selective file back-up by user I.D., file name or time data—as well as selective file restoration to user directories. The convenient, integrated cartridge media stores 12 megabytes of data. And, the flexible selective features make it fast and simple to frequently back-up critical project files which ensures the security of your most recent work. This valuable feature also saves time and effort otherwise spent locating and restoring entire groups of files to active status.

Electronic Mail speeds the flow of information between team members.

Whether entire files or simple messages are involved, fast communication boosts productivity. Electronic Mail quickly sends information between members of your team.

"Phone tag" and inefficient paper passing are eliminated. Users may communicate with other individuals or with the entire team without leaving their desks. Messages are automatically queued for display by the recipient anywhere on the network—no matter which workstation the team member is using.

△175   △176

YASUSHI OKITA 177,178.

U.S.A. 1.
YASHI OKITA DESIGN 2.
FLOW CHARTS 3.
SALES BROCHURE 4.
INTEL CORPORATION 5.

one system. With the I²ICE system you shorten debugging time and obtain easier to understand debug data—while reducing data and product development time.

The I²ICE system gives you full speed, real-time support for all Intel iAPX microprocessors. It also offers an arsenal of break and trace points so that your design team can set up complex, multi-nested test conditions.

The I²ICE system provides a single human interface across the spectrum of debugging and system integration tasks. This eliminates the slow-down problems inherent in multiple interfaces. And, there is never the need to leave the high-level language environment because the I²ICE system incorporates PSCOPE to ease the transition from software debug to hardware debug and hardware/software integration.

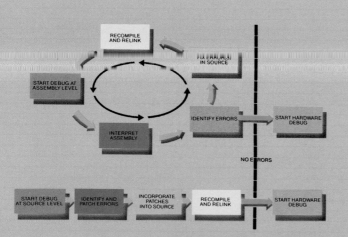

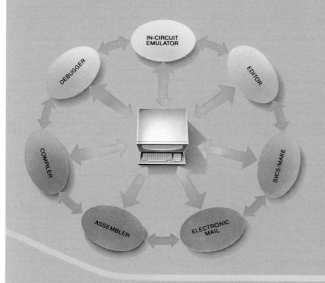

PSCOPE is an advanced, high-level language debugger that cuts many time consuming steps out of the software debugging process. PSCOPE enables users to correct software errors with "patches," eliminating many unnecessary edits, compiles and links. Using PSCOPE, software engineers produce the highest quality software in the shortest possible time.

Tools that share information can significantly improve engineering productivity. Intel's integrated tool set allows information gathered at one step in the development process to be used throughout the process. For example, symbol information

from a compiler is routinely passed to our advanced debugging tools, PSCOPE and I²ICE. Moreover, many Intel tools have similar human interfaces, minimizing tool learning time and user errors.

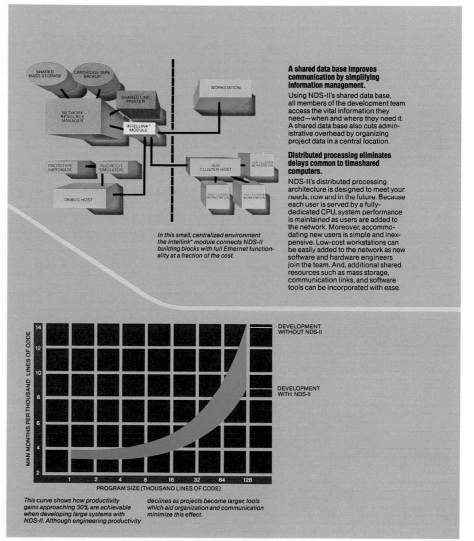

In this small, centralized environment the Intellink™ module connects NDS-II building blocks with full Ethernet functionality at a fraction of the cost.

A shared data base improves communication by simplifying information management.

Using NDS-II's shared data base, all members of the development team access the vital information they need—when and where they need it. A shared data base also cuts administrative overhead by organizing project data in a central location.

Distributed processing eliminates delays common to timeshared computers.

NDS-II's distributed processing architecture is designed to meet your needs, now and in the future. Because each user is served by a fully-dedicated CPU, system performance is maintained as users are added to the network. Moreover, accommodating new users is simple and inexpensive. Low-cost workstations can be easily added to the network as new software and hardware engineers join the team. And, additional shared resources such as mass storage, communication links, and software tools can be incorporated with ease.

This curve shows how productivity gains approaching 30% are achievable when developing large systems with NDS-II. Although engineering productivity declines as projects become larger, tools which aid organization and communication minimize this effect.

△177

△178

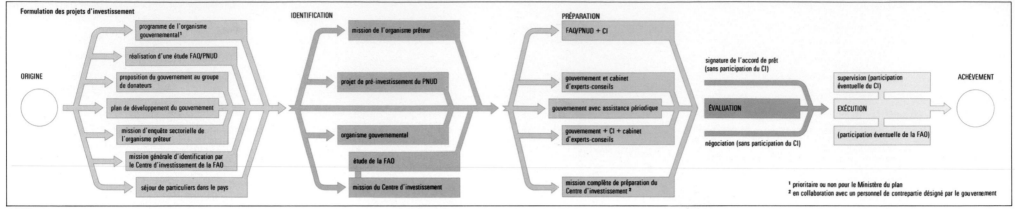

Formulation des projets d'investissement

IDENTIFICATION

PRÉPARATION

ORIGINE

- programme de l'organisme gouvernemental[1]
- réalisation d'une étude FAO/PNUD
- proposition du gouvernement au groupe de donateurs
- plan de développement du gouvernement
- mission d'enquête sectorielle de l'organisme prêteur
- mission générale d'identification par le Centre d'investissement de la FAO
- séjour de particuliers dans le pays

- mission de l'organisme prêteur
- projet de pré-investissement du PNUD
- organisme gouvernemental
- étude de la FAO
- mission du Centre d'investissement

- FAO/PNUD + CI
- gouvernement et cabinet d'experts-conseils
- gouvernement avec assistance périodique
- gouvernement + CI + cabinet d'experts-conseils
- mission complète de préparation du Centre d'investissement [2]

signature de l'accord de prêt (sans participation du CI)

ÉVALUATION

négociation (sans participation du CI)

supervision (participation éventuelle du CI)

EXÉCUTION

(participation éventuelle de la FAO)

ACHÈVEMENT

[1] prioritaire ou non pour le Ministère du plan
[2] en collaboration avec un personnel de contrepartie désigné par le gouvernement

△179

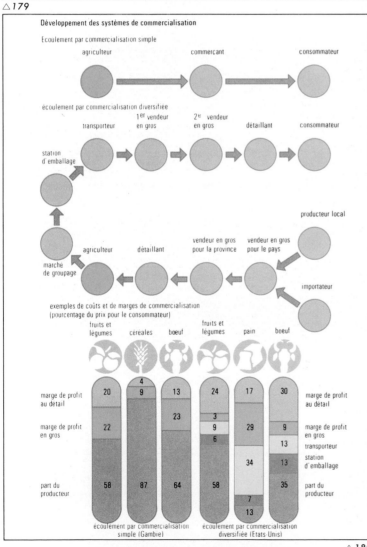

Développement des systèmes de commercialisation

Écoulement par commercialisation simple

agriculteur → commerçant → consommateur

écoulement par commercialisation diversifiée

transporteur / 1er vendeur en gros / 2e vendeur en gros / détaillant → consommateur

station d'emballage

producteur local

agriculteur / détaillant / vendeur en gros pour la province / vendeur en gros pour le pays

marché de groupage

importateur

exemples de coûts et de marges de commercialisation (pourcentage du prix pour le consommateur)

	fruits et légumes	céréales	bœuf	fruits et légumes	pain	bœuf
marge de profit au détail	20	4 / 9	13	24	17	30
marge de profit en gros	22	23	23	3 / 9 / 6	29	9
transporteur						13
station d'emballage					34	13
part du producteur	58	87	64	58	7 / 13	35

écoulement par commercialisation simple (Gambie)

écoulement par commercialisation diversifiée (États-Unis)

△180

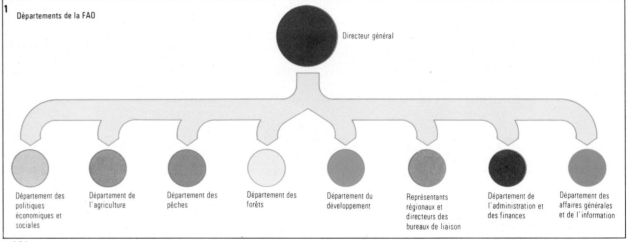

1 Départements de la FAO

Directeur général

- Département des politiques économiques et sociales
- Département de l'agriculture
- Département des pêches
- Département des forêts
- Département du développement
- Représentants régionaux et directeurs des bureaux de liaison
- Département de l'administration et des finances
- Département des affaires générales et de l'information

△181

THE DIAGRAM GROUP 179~181.

U.K. 1.
DIAGRAM VISUAL INFORMATION LTD. (D.V.I.) 2.
FLOW CHARTS 3.
BOOK 4.
FAO IN AFRICA 5.
FORMULATION OF INVESTMENT PROJECTS (179)
COMMERCIALIZATION SYSTEMS (180)
DEPARTMENTS OF FAO (181)

TIM ALT/KENNETH R. WEISS 182,183.

U.S.A. 1.
DIGITAL ART 2.
FLOW CHARTS 3.
PAMPHLET 4.
AEROJET ELECTRO SYSTEMS COMPANY 5.
GENCORP DIVISIONS (182)

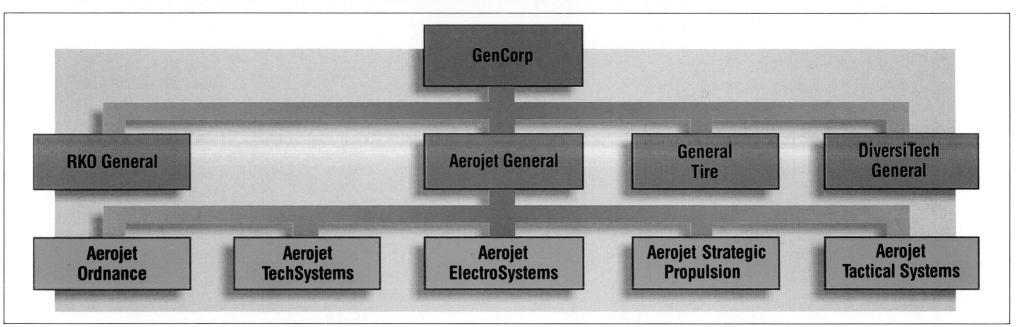

△182 ▽183

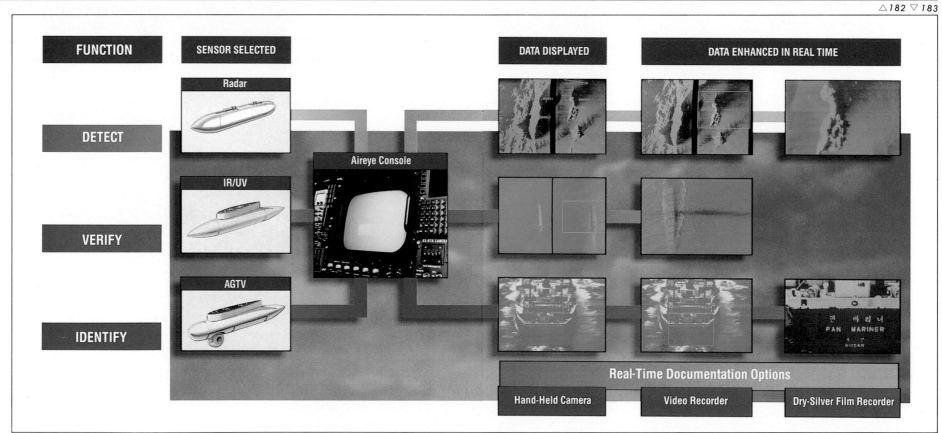

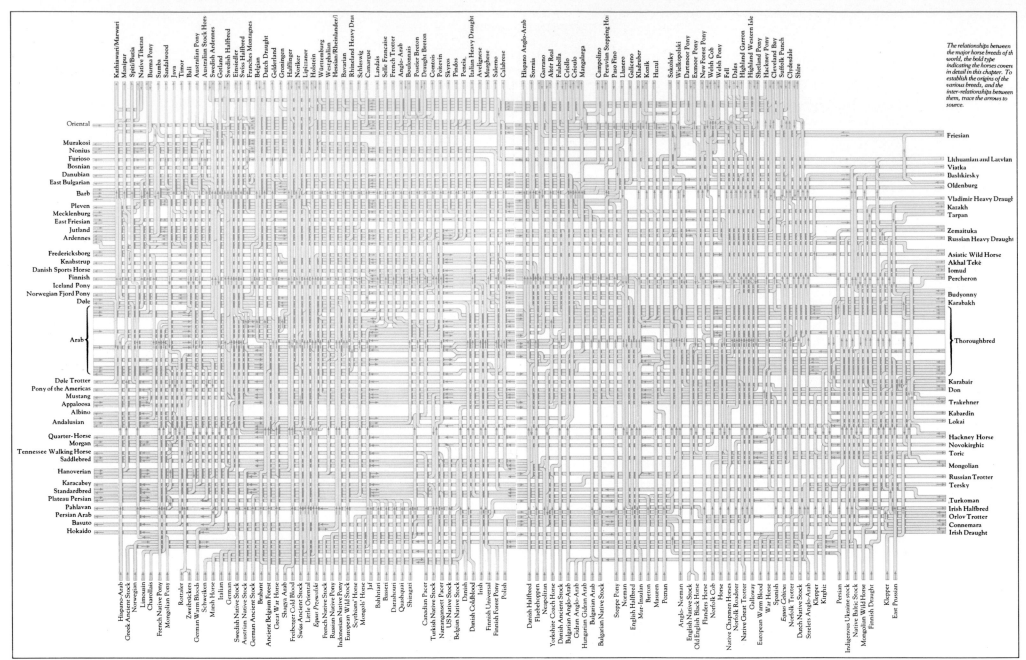

184. QED PUBLISHING LTD.

1. U.K.

2. QED PUBLISHING LTD.

3. FLOW CHARTS

4. BOOK, "THE BOOK OF HORSE"

5. RELATIONSHIPS BETWEEN THE MAJOR HORSE BREEDS OF THE WORLD

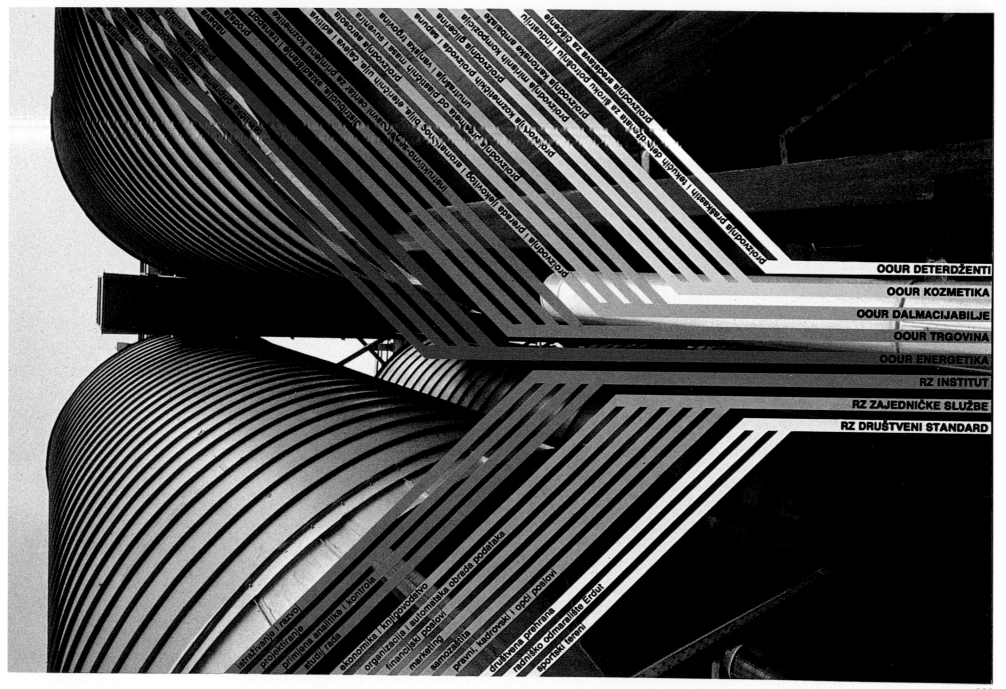

proizvodnja praškastih i tekućih detergenata i sredstava za čišćenje | industriju

proizvodnja mlinskih komponzicija i kanonske ambalaže

proizvodnja glicerina

proizvodnja plastičnih masa | vanjska trgovina

proizvodnja ulja, žejeva i aktiva

unutrašnja

proizvodnja sredstava za bilja, aerosola | sredstva

distribucija, prerada jakovica | atomatično-aserativni centar za primjenu kompanije

instruktivno-aserativni bilja, eterečnih ulja, čajeva i aktiva

pro-No/ja la kozmetičkih

pohraniranje za proizvodnju

radnice za obradevine

proizvodnja robinu

nabava tipita

zadrge

proizvodnja zglobova

OOUR DETERDŽENTI

OOUR KOZMETIKA

OOUR DALMACIJABILJE

OOUR TRGOVINA

OOUR ENERGETIKA

RZ INSTITUT

RZ ZAJEDNIČKE SLUŽBE

RZ DRUŠTVENI STANDARD

istraživanje i razvoj

projektiranje

primjena analitike i kontrole

studij rada

ekonomika i knjigovodstvo

organizacija i automatska obrada podataka

financijski poslovi

marketing

samozaštita

pravni, kadrovski i opći poslovi

društvena prehrana

radničko odmaralište Erdut

sportski tereni

△185

NINO KOVACEVIC 185.

YUGOSLAVIA 1.
FLOW CHARTS 3.
SAPONIA YEARS REPORT 4.

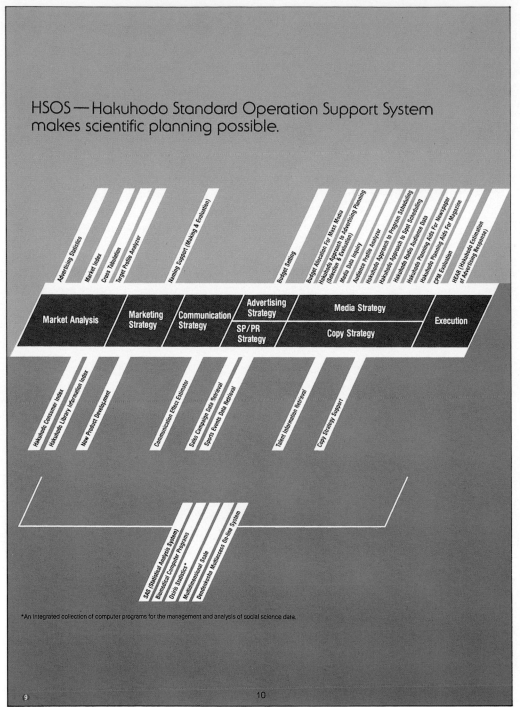

HSOS — Hakuhodo Standard Operation Support System makes scientific planning possible.

*An integrated collection of computer programs for the management and analysis of social science data.

9   10

△186

186. HAKUHODO INC./DIAGRAMS INC.

1. JAPAN
2. HAKUHODO INC./DIAGRAMS INC.
   ART DIRECTOR: TAKASHI KITAMURA
   DESIGNER: TSUTOMU OKAMOTO
              NORIKO YURI
3. FORMATION TABLES AND CHARTS
4. PAMPHLET FOR OVERSEAS
5. HAKUHODO INC
   COMPUTER RESOURCES

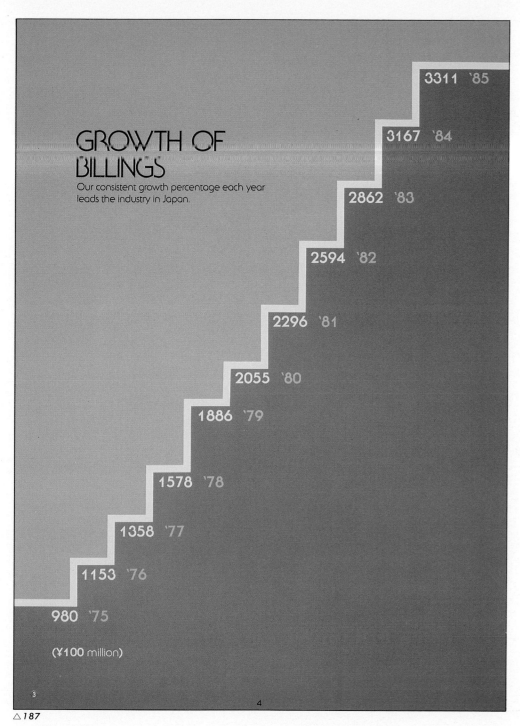

GROWTH OF BILLINGS
Our consistent growth percentage each year leads the industry in Japan.

3311 '85
3167 '84
2862 '83
2594 '82
2296 '81
2055 '80
1886 '79
1578 '78
1358 '77
1153 '76
980 '75

(¥100 million)

3
4

△187

187. HAKUHODO INC./DIAGRAMS INC.

1. JAPAN
2. HAKUHODO INC./DIAGRAMS INC.
   ART DIRECTOR: TAKASHI KITAMURA
   DESIGNER: TSUTOMU OKAMOTO
              NORIKO YURI
3. FORMATION TABLES AND CHARTS
4. PAMPHLET FOR OVERSEAS
5. HAKUHODO INC.

The scientific and production technologies required to bring lymphokines to the world as therapeutics already exist. Immunex is the first to bring it all together—central research facilities and a team of scientists from a variety of disciplines.

Immunex has moved quickly to adapt several recently developed biological technologies for use in research and in development of lymphokine products.

The central element for this research is a large collection of human and animal cells which multiply continuously in culture—cell lines. These cells produce particular lymphokines in quantities sufficient for laboratory work, including biochemical characterization—the process of defining the chemical structure of lymphokine molecules and their behavior.

Immunex scientists have developed assay techniques which allow them to identify which cells produce a particular lymphokine. They also have developed procedures to optimize lymphokine production from those cells.

Commercial quantities may be produced by using recombinant DNA technology to engineer micro-organisms that rapidly produce large quantities of lymphokines, or by synthesizing biologically active lymphokines chemically.

Another aspect of Immunex research involves the development of monoclonal antibodies through cell fusion technology. In this work, short-lived, antibody producing B-cells are fused with cells from a malignant B-cell line.

The cell fusion process results in a new cell type called a hybridoma which inherits some of the traits of each parental cell type. In this case, the hybridoma produces monoclonal antibodies (a trait inherited from the short-lived B-cell parent) but also is capable of continuous growth (a trait inherited from the malignant B-cell line).

Monoclonal antibodies are useful in detecting the presence of lymphokines—and therefore valuable in diagnostic kits that test for the presence of lymphokines in patient fluids. In addition, monoclonal antibodies may prove valuable in purifying lymphokines for large scale production.

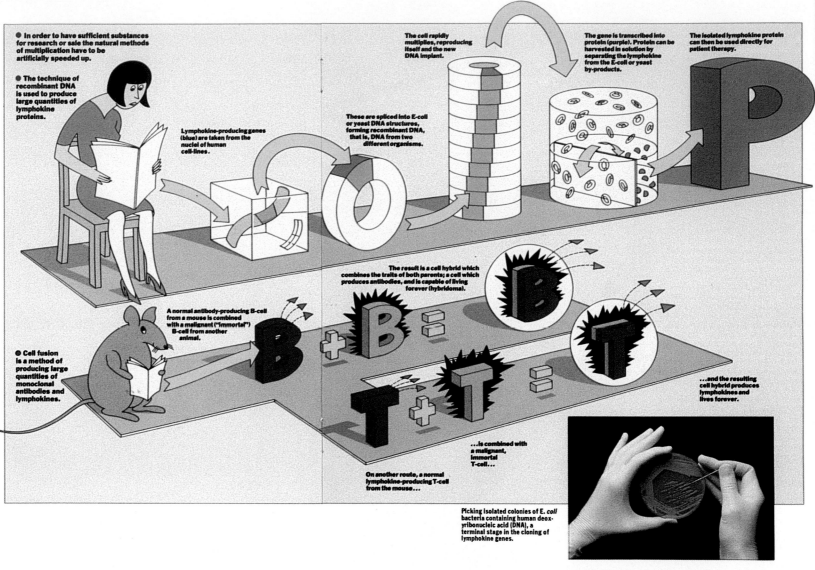

● In order to have sufficient substances for research or sale the natural methods of multiplication have to be artificially speeded up.

● The technique of recombinant DNA is used to produce large quantities of lymphokine proteins.

Lymphokine-producing genes (blue) are taken from the nuclei of human cell-lines.

These are spliced into E-coli or yeast DNA structures, forming recombinant DNA, that is, DNA from two different organisms.

The cell rapidly multiplies, reproducing itself and the new DNA implant.

The gene is transcribed into protein (purple). Protein can be harvested in solution by separating the lymphokine from the E-coli or yeast by-products.

The isolated lymphokine protein can then be used directly for patient therapy.

● Cell fusion is a method of producing large quantities of monoclonal antibodies and lymphokines.

A normal antibody-producing B-cell from a mouse is combined with a malignant ("immortal") B-cell from another animal.

The result is a cell hybrid which combines the traits of both parents; a cell which produces antibodies, and is capable of living forever (hybridoma).

...and the resulting cell hybrid produces lymphokines and lives forever.

On another route, a normal lymphokine-producing T-cell from the mouse...

...is combined with a malignant, immortal T-cell...

Picking isolated colonies of E. coli bacteria containing human deoxyribonucleic acid (DNA), a terminal stage in the cloning of lymphokine genes.

△188

188. NIGEL HOLMES

1. U.S.A.
3. SYSTEMATICAL GRAPHS
4. ANNUAL REPORT

5. IMMUNEX CORP.
   IMMUNEX REACTION PROCESS

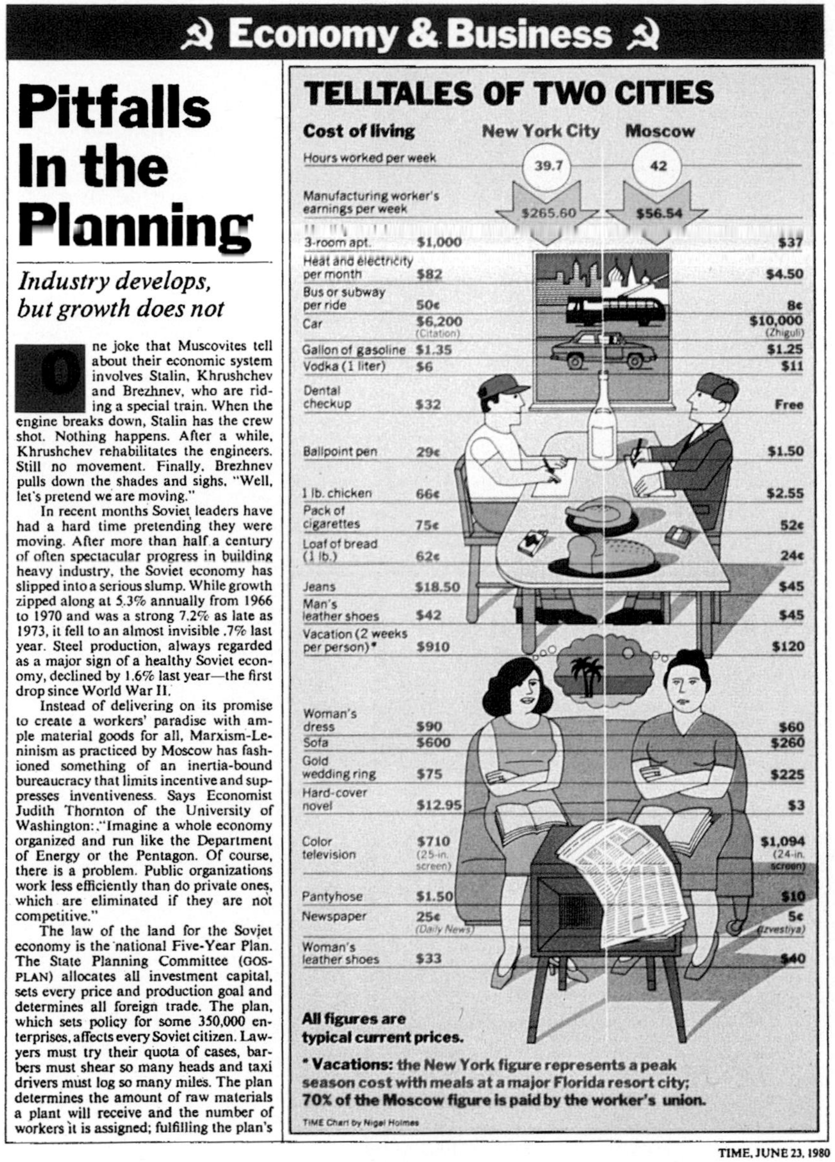

Economy & Business

Pitfalls In the Planning

Industry develops, but growth does not

One joke that Muscovites tell about their economic system involves Stalin, Khrushchev and Brezhnev, who are riding a special train. When the engine breaks down, Stalin has the crew shot. Nothing happens. After a while, Khrushchev rehabilitates the engineers. Still no movement. Finally, Brezhnev pulls down the shades and sighs, "Well, let's pretend we are moving."

In recent months Soviet leaders have had a hard time pretending they were moving. After more than half a century of often spectacular progress in building heavy industry, the Soviet economy has slipped into a serious slump. While growth zipped along at 5.3% annually from 1966 to 1970 and was a strong 7.2% as late as 1973, it fell to an almost invisible .7% last year. Steel production, always regarded as a major sign of a healthy Soviet economy, declined by 1.6% last year—the first drop since World War II.

Instead of delivering on its promise to create a workers' paradise with ample material goods for all, Marxism-Leninism as practiced by Moscow has fashioned something of an inertia-bound bureaucracy that limits incentive and suppresses inventiveness. Says Economist Judith Thornton of the University of Washington: "Imagine a whole economy organized and run like the Department of Energy or the Pentagon. Of course, there is a problem. Public organizations work less efficiently than do private ones, which are eliminated if they are not competitive."

The law of the land for the Soviet economy is the national Five-Year Plan. The State Planning Committee (GOSPLAN) allocates all investment capital, sets every price and production goal and determines all foreign trade. The plan, which sets policy for some 350,000 enterprises, affects every Soviet citizen. Lawyers must try their quota of cases, barbers must shear so many heads and taxi drivers must log so many miles. The plan determines the amount of raw materials a plant will receive and the number of workers it is assigned; fulfilling the plan's

TELLTALES OF TWO CITIES

Cost of living	New York City	Moscow
Hours worked per week	39.7	42
Manufacturing worker's earnings per week	$265.60	$56.54
3-room apt.	$1,000	$37
Heat and electricity per month	$82	$4.50
Bus or subway per ride	50¢	8¢
Car	$6,200 (Citation)	$10,000 (Zhiguli)
Gallon of gasoline	$1.35	$1.25
Vodka (1 liter)	$6	$11
Dental checkup	$32	Free
Ballpoint pen	29¢	$1.50
1 lb. chicken	66¢	$2.55
Pack of cigarettes	75¢	52¢
Loaf of bread (1 lb.)	62¢	24¢
Jeans	$18.50	$45
Man's leather shoes	$42	$45
Vacation (2 weeks per person)*	$910	$120
Woman's dress	$90	$60
Sofa	$600	$260
Gold wedding ring	$75	$225
Hard-cover novel	$12.95	$3
Color television	$710 (25-in. screen)	$1,094 (24-in. screen)
Pantyhose	$1.50	$10
Newspaper	25¢ (Daily News)	5¢ (Izvestiya)
Woman's leather shoes	$33	$40

All figures are typical current prices.

*** Vacations: the New York figure represents a peak season cost with meals at a major Florida resort city; 70% of the Moscow figure is paid by the worker's union.**

TIME Chart by Nigel Holmes

TIME, JUNE 23, 1980

△189

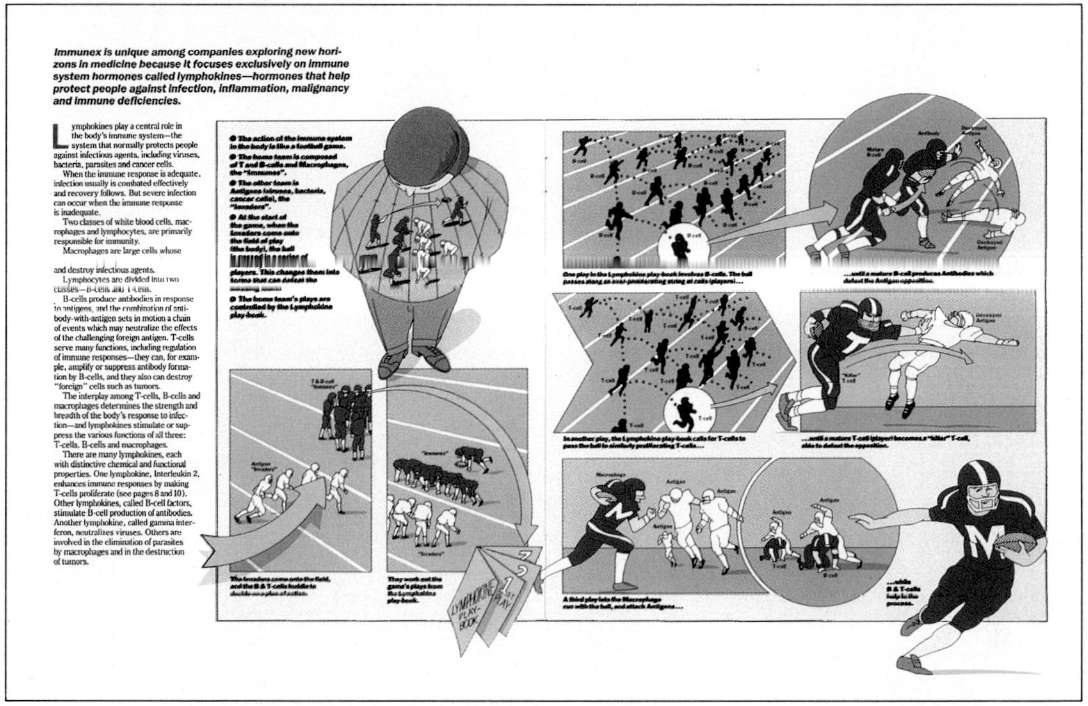

Immunex is unique among companies exploring new horizons in medicine because it focuses exclusively on immune system hormones called lymphokines—hormones that help protect people against infection, inflammation, malignancy and immune deficiencies.

Lymphokines play a central role in the body's immune system—the system that normally protects people against infectious agents, including viruses, bacteria, parasites and cancer cells.

When the immune response is adequate, infection usually is combated effectively and recovery follows. But severe infection can occur when the immune response is inadequate.

Two classes of white blood cells, macrophages and lymphocytes, are primarily responsible for immunity.

Macrophages are large cells whose

and destroy infectious agents.

Lymphocytes are divided into two classes—B-cells and T-cells.

B-cells produce antibodies in response to antigens, and the combination of antibody-with-antigen sets in motion a chain of events which may neutralize the effects of the challenging foreign antigen. T-cells serve many functions, including regulation of immune responses—they can, for example, amplify or suppress antibody formation by B-cells, and they also can destroy "foreign" cells such as tumors.

The interplay among T-cells, B-cells and macrophages determines the strength and breadth of the body's response to infection—and lymphokines stimulate or suppress the various functions of all three: T-cells, B-cells and macrophages.

There are many lymphokines, each with distinctive chemical and functional properties. One lymphokine, Interleukin 2, enhances immune responses by making T-cells proliferate (see pages 8 and 10). Other lymphokines, called B-cell factors, stimulate B-cell production of antibodies. Another lymphokine, called gamma interferon, neutralizes viruses. Others are involved in the elimination of parasites by macrophages and in the destruction of tumors.

△190

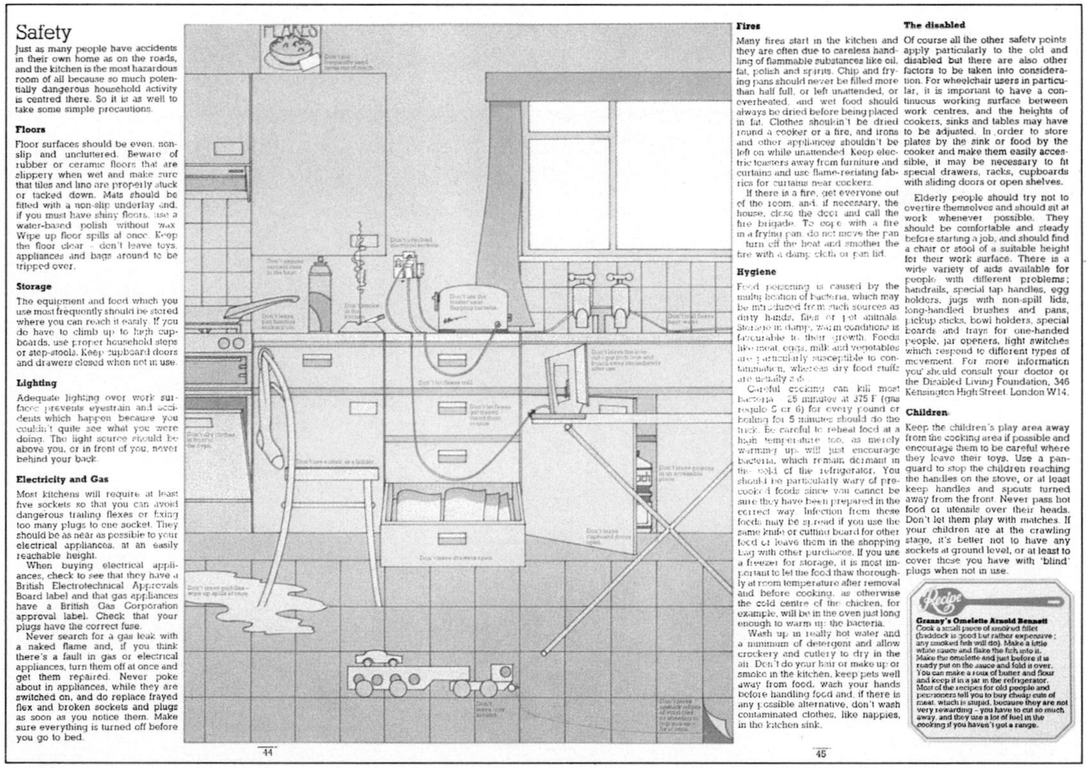

Safety

Just as many people have accidents in their own home as on the roads, and the kitchen is the most hazardous room of all because so much potentially dangerous household activity is centred there. So it is as well to take some simple precautions.

Floors

Floor surfaces should be even, non-slip and uncluttered. Beware of rubber or ceramic floors that are slippery when wet and make sure that tiles and lino are properly stuck or tacked down. Mats should be fitted with a non-slip underlay and, if you must have shiny floors, use a water-based polish without wax. Wipe up floor spills at once. Keep the floor clear – don't leave toys, appliances and bags around to be tripped over.

Storage

The equipment and food which you use most frequently should be stored where you can reach it easily. If you do have to climb up to high cupboards, use proper household steps or step-stools. Keep cupboard doors and drawers closed when not in use.

Lighting

Adequate lighting over work surfaces prevents eyestrain and accidents which happen because you couldn't quite see what you were doing. The light source should be above you, or in front of you, never behind your back.

Electricity and Gas

Most kitchens will require at least five sockets so that you can avoid dangerous trailing flexes or fixing too many plugs to one socket. They should be as near as possible to your electrical appliances, at an easily reachable height.

When buying electrical appliances, check to see that they have a British Electrotechnical Approvals Board label and that gas appliances have a British Gas Corporation approval label. Check that your plugs have the correct fuse.

Never search for a gas leak with a naked flame and, if you think there's a fault in gas or electrical appliances, turn them off at once and get them repaired. Never poke about in appliances, while they are switched on, and do replace frayed flex and broken sockets and plugs as soon as you notice them. Make sure everything is turned off before you go to bed.

Fires

Many fires start in the kitchen and they are often due to careless handling of flammable substances like oil, fat, polish and spirits. Chip and frying pans should never be filled more than half full, or left unattended, or overheated, and wet food should always be dried before being placed in fat. Clothes shouldn't be dried round a cooker or a fire, and irons and other appliances shouldn't be left on while unattended. Keep electric toasters away from furniture and curtains and use flame-resisting fabrics for curtains near cookers.

If there is a fire, get everyone out of the room, and, if necessary, the house, close the door and call the fire brigade. To cope with a fire in a frying pan, do not move the pan turn off the heat and smother the fire with a damp cloth or pan lid.

Hygiene

Food poisoning is caused by the multiplication of bacteria, which may be introduced from such sources as dirty hands, flies or pet animals. Storage in damp, warm conditions is favourable to their growth. Foods like meat, eggs, milk and vegetables are particularly susceptible to contamination, whereas dry food stuffs are usually safe.

Careful cooking can kill most bacteria – 25 minutes at 375 F (gas regulo 5 or 6) for every pound or boiling for 5 minutes should do the trick. Be careful to reheat food at a high temperature too, as merely warming up will just encourage bacteria, which remain dormant in the cold of the refrigerator. You should be particularly wary of precooked foods since you cannot be sure they have been prepared in the correct way. Infection from these foods may be spread if you use the same knife or cutting board for other food or leave them in the shopping bag with other purchases. If you use a freezer for storage, it is most important to let the food thaw thoroughly at room temperature after removal and before cooking, as otherwise the cold centre of the chicken, for example, will be in the oven just long enough to warm up the bacteria.

Wash up in really hot water and a minimum of detergent and allow crockery and cutlery to dry in the air. Don't do your hair or make up or smoke in the kitchen, keep pets well away from food, wash your hands before handling food and, if there is any possible alternative, don't wash contaminated clothes, like nappies, in the kitchen sink.

The disabled

Of course all the other safety points apply particularly to the old and disabled but there are also other factors to be taken into consideration. For wheelchair users in particular, it is important to have a continuous working surface between work centres, and the heights of cookers, sinks and tables may have to be adjusted. In order to store plates by the sink or food by the cooker and make them easily accessible, it may be necessary to fit special drawers, racks, cupboards with sliding doors or open shelves.

Elderly people should try not to overtire themselves and should sit at work whenever possible. They should be comfortable and steady before starting a job, and should find a chair or stool of a suitable height for their work surface. There is a wide variety of aids available for people with different problems; handrails, special tap handles, egg holders, jugs with non-spill lids, long-handled brushes and pans, pickup sticks, bowl holders, special boards and trays for one-handed people, jar openers, light switches which respond to different types of movement. For more information you should consult your doctor or the Disabled Living Foundation, 346 Kensington High Street, London W14.

Children

Keep the children's play area away from the cooking area if possible and encourage them to be careful where they leave their toys. Use a pan-guard to stop the children reaching the handles on the stove, or at least keep handles and spouts turned away from the front. Never pass hot food or utensils over their heads. Don't let them play with matches. If your children are at the crawling stage, it's better not to have any sockets at ground level, or at least to cover those you have with 'blind' plugs when not in use.

Recipe

Granny's Omelette Arnold Bennett

Cook a small piece of smoked fillet (haddock is good but rather expensive; any smoked fish will do). Make a little white sauce and flake the fish into it. Make the omelette and just before it is ready put on the sauce and fold it over. You can make a roux of butter and flour and keep it in a jar in the refrigerator. Most of the recipes for old people and pensioners tell you to buy cheap cuts of meat, which is stupid, because they are not very rewarding – you have to cut so much away, and they use a lot of fuel in the cooking if you haven't got a range.

44 45

△191

189~191. NIGEL HOLMES

1. U.S.A.
3. SYSTEMATICAL GRAPHS
4. TIME MAGAZINE (189)
   ANNUAL REPORT (190)
   HABITAT BOOK (U.K.)(191)
5. IMMUNEX CORP (190)
   INDUSTRIAL DEVELOPMENT (189)
   IMMUNEX HORMONAL PROTECTION (190)
   SAFETY HAZARDS (191)

JAPAN 1.
ILLUSTRATOR: ETSUKO TAKAHASHI 2.
ICHIMATSU MEGURO
SYSTEMATICAL GRAPHS 3.
NEWTON MAGAZINE 4.
©KYOIKUSHA NEWTON 5.
HUMAN IMMUNITY SYSTEM (192)
IRON MANUFACTURE AND
CASTING METHODS (193)

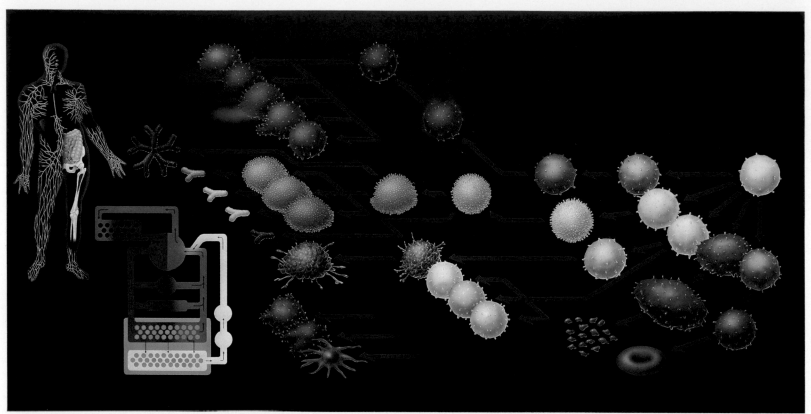

△192 ▽193

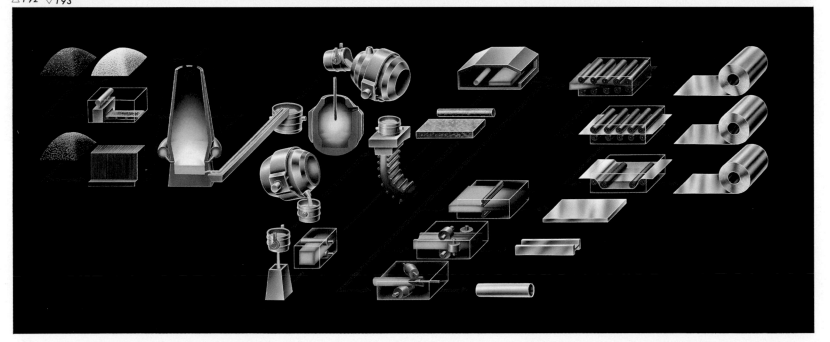

1. JAPAN
2. ILLUSTRATOR: KAZUHO ITOH
3. SYSTEMATICAL GRAPHS
4. NEWTON MAGAZINE
5. ©KYOIKUSHA NEWTON
   BLOOD MAINTAINING LIFE BY CONVEYING
   VARIOUS SUBSTANCES

△194

△195

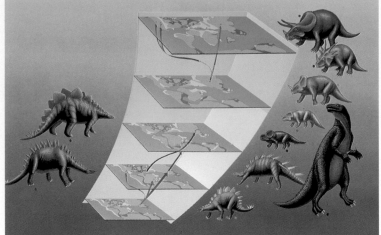

△196

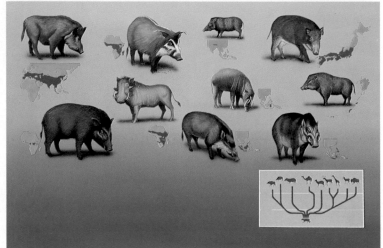

△197

NEWTON 195～197.

JAPAN 1.
ILLUSTRATOR: TAKUMI YAMAMOTO(195) 2.
HITOSHI ASANO(196)
YUYA KANAI(197)
SYSTEMATICAL GRAPHS 3.
NEWTON MAGAZINE 4.
©KYOIKUSHA NEWTON 5.
ELEPHANT EVOLUTION (195)
DINOSAUR EVOLUTION (196)
WILD BOAR DISTRIBUTION (197)

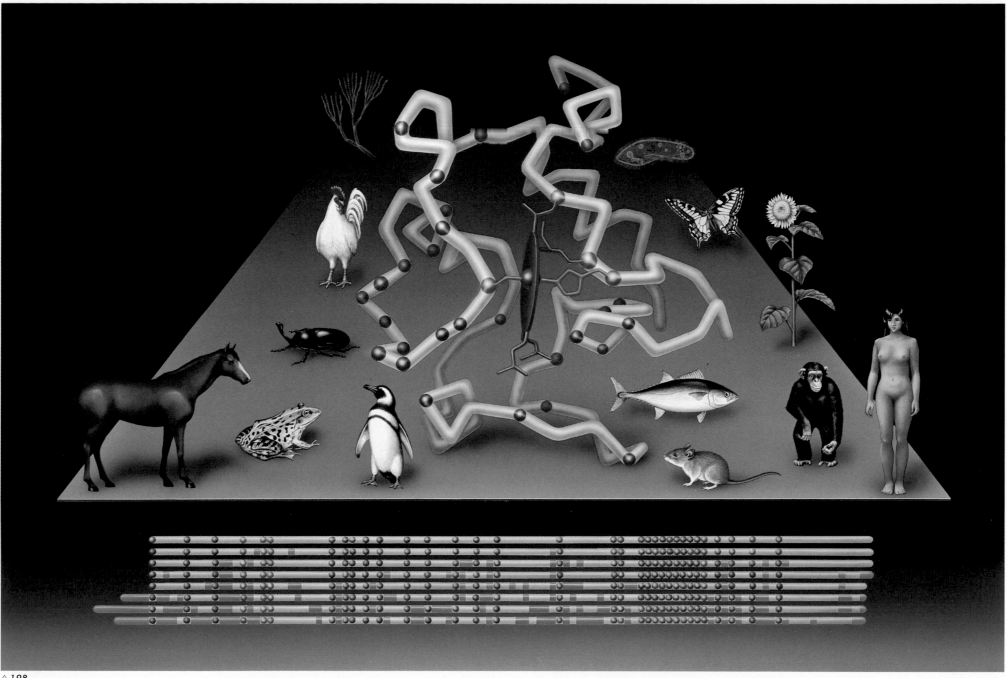

NEWTON 198.

JAPAN 1.
ILLUSTRATOR: ETSUKO TAKAHASHI 2.
SYSTEMATICAL GRAPHS 3.
NEWTON MAGAZINE 4.
EVOLUTION OF LIFE BY SEARCHING MOLECULES/©KYOIKUSHA NEWTON 5.

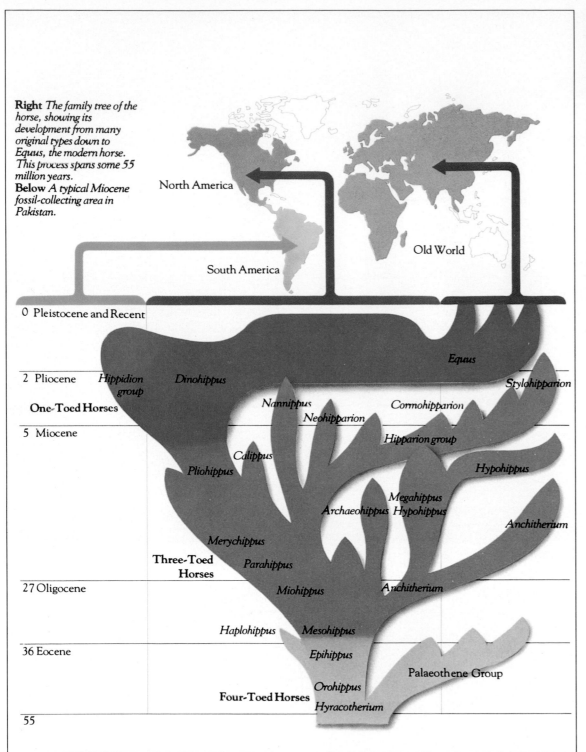

Right *The family tree of the horse, showing its development from many original types down to Equus, the modern horse. This process spans some 55 million years.*
Below *A typical Miocene fossil-collecting area in Pakistan.*

North America

South America

Old World

0 Pleistocene and Recent

Equus

2 Pliocene   *Hippidion group*   *Dinohippus*   *Stylohipparion*

One-Toed Horses

Nannippus   *Cormohipparion*
Neohipparion

5 Miocene

Hipparion group

Calippus

Hypohippus

Pliohippus

Megahippus
Archaeohippus Hypohippus

Anchitherium

Merychippus

Three-Toed Horses   *Parahippus*

Miohippus   *Anchitherium*

27 Oligocene

Haplohippus   *Mesohippus*

36 Eocene

Epihippus

Palaeothene Group

Orohippus

Four-Toed Horses   *Hyracotherium*

55

△199

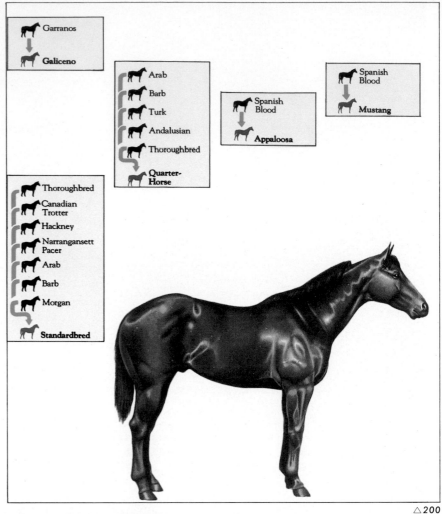

Garranos → Galiceno

Arab
Barb
Turk
Andalusian
Thoroughbred
Quarter-Horse

Spanish Blood → **Appaloosa**

Spanish Blood → **Mustang**

Thoroughbred
Canadian Trotter
Hackney
Narrangansett Pacer
Arab
Barb
Morgan
Standardbred

△200

QED PUBLISHING LTD. 199~201.

U.K. 1.
QED PUBLISHING LTD. 2.
SYSTEMATICAL GRAPHS 3.
BOOK."THE BOOK OF THE HORSE" 4.
HORSE EVOLUTION 5.

NEWTON 202.

JAPAN 1.
ILLUSTRATOR:MINORU KOBAYASHI 2.
SYSTEMATICAL GRAPHS 3.
NEWTON MAGAZINE 4.
ⒸKYOIKUSHA NEWTON 5.
EVOLUTION CHART OF IMMUNITY SYSTEM

Features: good-tempered, active.
Use: light draught, riding.

Jutland

- Ancient Stock
- Yorkshire Coach Horse
- Cleveland Bay
- Suffolk Punch
- **Jutland**

Coldblood
Origin: Jutland Is.
Height: 15.3 hands.
Colour: chestnut or roan.
Physique: massive, compact horse; plain head and short, feathered legs.
Features: good-tempered.
Use: draught.

Danish Sport Horse

- Hanoverian
- Native Halfbred
- Thoroughbred
- Trakehner
- Polish
- Anglo-Norman
- **Danish Sports Horse**

Warmblood
Origin: Denmark – developed by crossing various breeds from Northern Europe with locally bred mares
Height: 16.1 hands
Colour: all colours
Physique: varies, middleweight build
Use: general riding

Knabstrup

- Flaebehoppen
- Fredericksborg
- **Knabstrup**

Warmblood
Height: 15.3 hands.
Colour: spotted, Appaloosa patterns on roan base.
Physique: similar to but lighter than the Fredericksborg.
Use: circus.

Fjord

- Asiatic Wild Horse
- **Norwegian Fjord Pony**

Pony
Height: 14 hands.
Colour: dun, cream or yellow with dorsal stripe and upright black and silver mane.
Physique: small head, strong, short neck and powerful, compact body.
Use: work in the mountains; agriculture, transport, riding and driving.

Døle

- Danish Cold Blood
- Thoroughbred
- Trotter
- **Døle**

Warmblood
Height: 15 hands.
Colour: black, brown or bay.
Physique: two types; heavy draught – similar to the Dale; pony type – upright shoulder, deep girth, short legs with good bone and little feather.
Features: tough, versatile.
Use: agricultural work, riding and driving.

Døle Trotter

- Trotter
- Døle
- **Døle Trotter**

Warmblood
Height: 15 hands.
Colour: black, brown or bay.
Physique: lighter version of Døle with no feather.
Use: trotting races.

Finnish

- Indigenous Forest pony
- Finnish Draught
- **Finnish**
- Finnish Universal

Coldblood
Height: 15.2 hands.
Colour: chestnut, bay and brown.
Physique: short neck, upright shoulder, deep, strong legs, light feather.
Features: tough, long-lived, even-tempered and fast.
Use: timber hauling, agriculture and trotting races.

ICELAND

Iceland Pony

- Pony
- Irish Blood
- **Iceland Pony**

Pony
Height: 12.2 hands.
Colour: grey, dun.
Physique: stocky, compact body, full mane and tail.
Features: independent, tough and able to amble.
Use: mining, pack and communications.

△201

△202

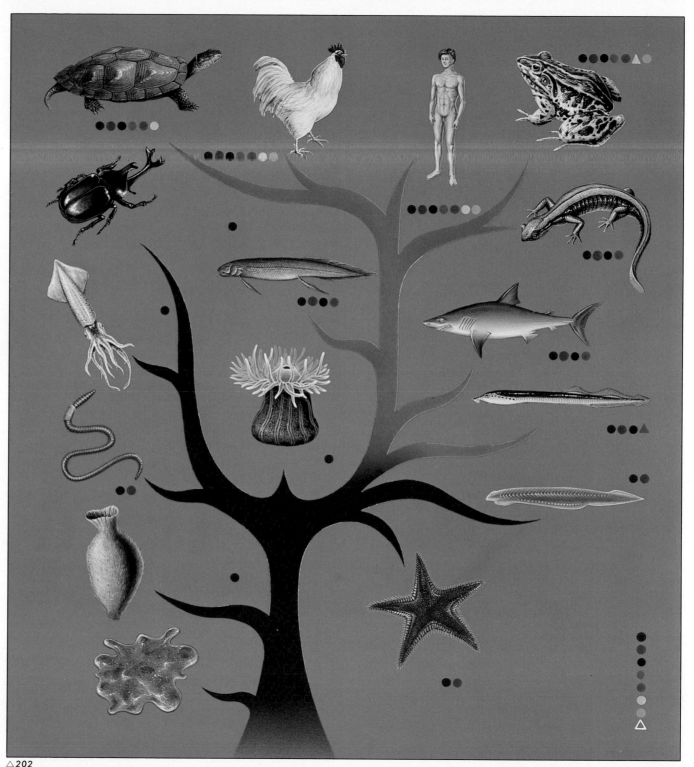

ITALY

Italian Heavy Draught

Breton
Italian Heavy Draught

Coldblood
Origin: Italy.
Height: 15.2 hands.
Colour: sorrel or roan.
Physique: fine, long head, shortish neck, flat back.
Features: fast, strong.
Use: meat and agricultural.

Salerno

Neapolitan
Salerno

Warmblood
Origin: Maremma and Salerno.
Height: 16 hands.
Colour: solid colours.
Physique: large, refined head.
Use: riding.

Murghese

Oriental
Murghese

Warmblood
Height: 15.2 hands.
Physique: Oriental features but heavier frame.
Features: versatile.
Use: dual-purpose horse

---

for agricultural work or riding.

Avelignese

Oriental
Halflinger
Avelignese

Pony
Origin: Alps and Appennines.
Height: 14 hands.
Colour: chestnut.
Physique: heavy-frame.
Features: sure-footed.
Use: pack, agricultural.

Calabrese

Neapolitan
Calabrese

Warmblood
Origin: Calabria.
Colour: solid colours.
Physique: middleweight, short-coupled riding horse.
Use: riding.

GREECE

Skyros

Tarpan
Skyros

Pony
Origin: Island of Skyros.

Height: 10 hands.
Colour: dun, brown or grey.
Physique: light of bone, upright shoulder and often cow-hocked.
Use: pack, carrying water, agricultural work and riding.

Peneia

Oriental
Native Stock
Peneia

Pony
Origin: Peneia, Peloponnese.
Height: 10 to 14 hands.
Colour: most colours.
Physique: Oriental.
Features: frugal, hardy.
Use: pack and agricultural

Pindos

Oriental
Ancient Stock
Pindos

Pony
Origin: Mountains of Thessaly and Epirus.
Height: 12.1 hands.
Colour: grey or dark.
Physique: tough.
Use: riding and light agricultural work.

SPAIN

Andalusian

Garrano
Noriker
Barb
Arab
Andalusian

Warmblood
Origin: Andalusia.
Height: 16 hands.
Physique: largish head, almost convex profile, strong, arched neck.
Features: intelligent and athletic.
Use: high school and general.

Hispano Anglo-Arab

Hispano Arab
Thoroughbred
Hispano Anglo-Arab

Warmblood
Origin: Estramadura and Andalusia.
Height: 15.3 hands.
Colour: bay, chestnut or grey.
Use: competitions, riding and testing young bulls.

TURKEY

Karacabey

Nonius
Native Stock
Karacabey

Warmblood
Height: 16 hands.
Colour: solid colours.
Physique: tough.
Use: riding, light draught, agricultural work, cavalry and pack.

MAJORCA

Balearic

Pony
Height:
Colour: bay or brown.
Physique: fine head, usually Roman nose.
Features: good-tempered.
Use: agricultural work and driving.

PORTUGAL

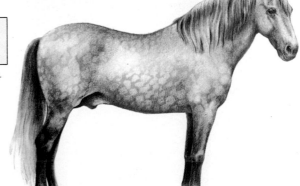
Skyros

Italian Heavy Draught

Altér Real

Lusitano

Salerno

Andalusian

Sorraia

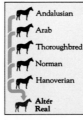

Tarpan
Sorraia

Pony
Origin: River Sorraia district.
Height: 13 hands.
Colour: dun with a dorsal stripe and stripes on legs.
Physique: primitive appearance, long head, straight profile, long ears.
Features: tough and frugal.
Use: runs wild.

Altér Real

Warmblood
Origin: Alentejo province.
Height: 15.2 hands.

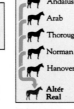

Andalusian
Arab
Thoroughbred
Norman
Hanoverian
Altér Real

Colour: chestnut, bay or piebald.
Physique: smallish head with straight profile.
Features: spirited.
Use: riding.

Garrano (Minho)

Pony
Origin: Garranho do

Arab
Garrano

Minho, Traz dos Montes.
Height: 11 hands.
Colour: dark chestnut.
Physique: light frame.
Features: strong.
Use: riding and pack.

Lusitano

Warmblood
Origin: Southern and Central Portugal.
Height: 15.1 hands.
Colour: grey.
Physique: small head, small ears, large eyes, thick neck.
Features: frugal.
Use: bullring.

ARABIAN PENINSULA

Arab

Asiatic Wild Stock → Arab

Thoroughbred
Height: 14.3 hands
Colour: bay, chestnut (original colours), grey.
Physique: small tapering head, concave face, broad forehead, large, dark eyes, small ears, arched neck.
Features: fast, free floating action, stamina toughness.
Use: improving other breeds, riding

EGYPT

Egyptian Arab
Thoroughbred
Height: 14.3 hands.
Colour: grey.
Physique: two types; the Kuhaylan is more rangey than the short coupled Siglavy.
Features: speed
Use: racing, general riding and breeding.

IRAN

Caspian Pony
Pony
Origin: Iran
Height: 10–11.2 hands
Colour: grey, brown, bay, chestnut
Physique: Arab-type head, fine boned
Features: sure footed
Use: transport, riding

Pahlavan
Warmblood
Origin: Iran
Height: 15.2–16 hands
Colour: solid colours
Physique: strong, elegant
Features: developed by crossing Plateau Persian

with Arab and Thoroughbred
Use: riding

Plateau Persian → Thoroughbred → Arab → **Pahlavan**

Persian Arab

Tarpan → **Persian Arab**

Thoroughbred
Height: 15 hands
Colour: grey or bay.
Physique: elegant, compact body, otherwise as Arab.
Features: possibly older than the desert Arab.
Use: similar to the Arab.

Plateau Persian

Arab
Shiragazi
Quashquai
Darashouri
Basseri
Bahhtiari
Jaf
→ **Plateau Persian**

Warmblood
Origin: Central Persian Plateau.
Height: 15 hands.
Colour: grey, bay or chestnut.
Physique: Arab features, but this varies as this breed is an amalgamation.
Features: good action, strong and sure-footed.
Use: riding.

Turkoman (Turkmen)

Mongols' Horse
Scythians' Horse
→ **Turkoman**

Warmblood
Height: 15.2 hands.
Colour: solid colours.
Physique: narrow chest, light but tough frame.
Features: floating action, speed and endurance.
Use: foundation stock for other breeds, riding, cavalry and racing.

Barb

European Wild Stock → **Barb**

Warmblood
Height: 14.2 hands.
Colour: bay, brown chestnut, black and grey.
Physique: long head, straight profile, sloping shoulder, low set tail and long strong legs.
Features: frugal and tough.
Use: improving other breeds, riding and transport.

ALGERIA & MOROCCO

SOUTH AFRICA

Basuto

Arab
Barb
Thoroughbred
Persian
→ **Basuto**

Pony
Height: 14.2 hands
Colour: chestnut, bay, brown and grey.
Physique: quality head, longish neck and back, strong, straightish shoulder, short legs and hard hooves.
Features: sure-footed, tough with great stamina.
Use: racing, polo and riding.

Arab

Barb

Persian Arab

Caspian

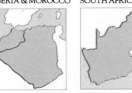

Basuto

△204

203,204. QED PUBLISHING LTD.   *1. U.K.*   *2. QED PUBLISHING LTD.*   *3. FORMATION OF TABLES AND CHARTS*   *4. BOOK, "THE BOOK OF THE HORSE"*   *5. BREED CHARACTERISTICS*

83

△205

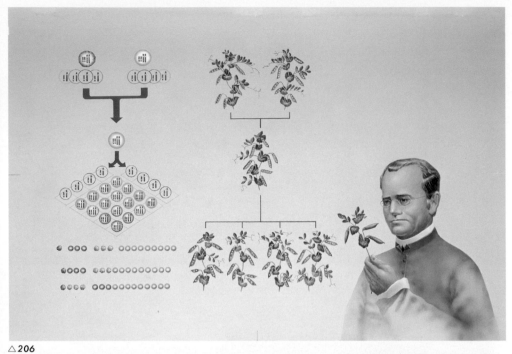

△206

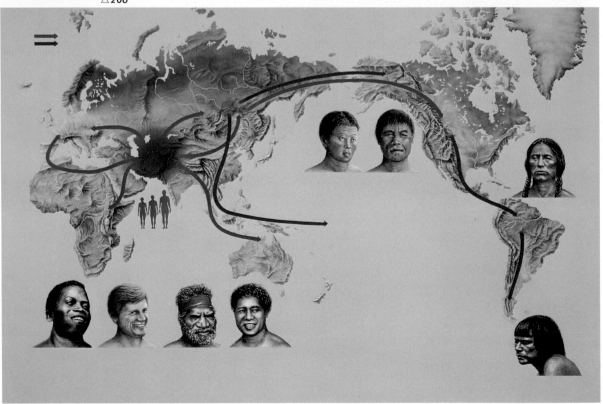

△207

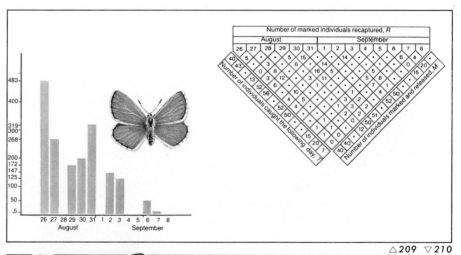

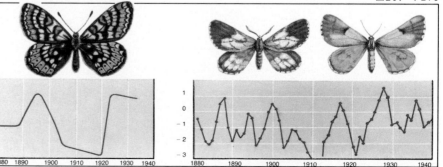

ARNOLDO MONDADORI EDITORE, S.P.A. 208~210.

ITALY 1.
ARNOLDO MONDADORI EDITORE, S.P.A. 2.
SYSTEMATICAL GRAPHS 3.
BOOK, "THE WORLD OF BUTTERFLIES" 4.

PPRR   pprr   P
♂   ♀

PR

PpRr   PpRr   F$_1$
♂   ♀

PR   1 PPRR   PR

2 PPRr   3 PPRr

Pr   4 PpRR   10 PPrr   5 PpRR   Pr

pR   6 PpRr   7 PpRr   8 PpRr   9 PpRr   pR

pr   11 Pprr   13 ppRR   12 Pprr   pr

14 ppRr   15 ppRr

16 pprr

F$_2$

△208

Number of marked individuals recaptured, R

August | September

483
400
319
300
268
200
172
147
125
100
50
.5

26 27 28 29 30 31 1 2 3 4 5 6 7 8
August — September

△209 ▽210

1880 1890 1900 1910 1920 1930 1940

1880 1890 1900 1910 1920 1930 1940

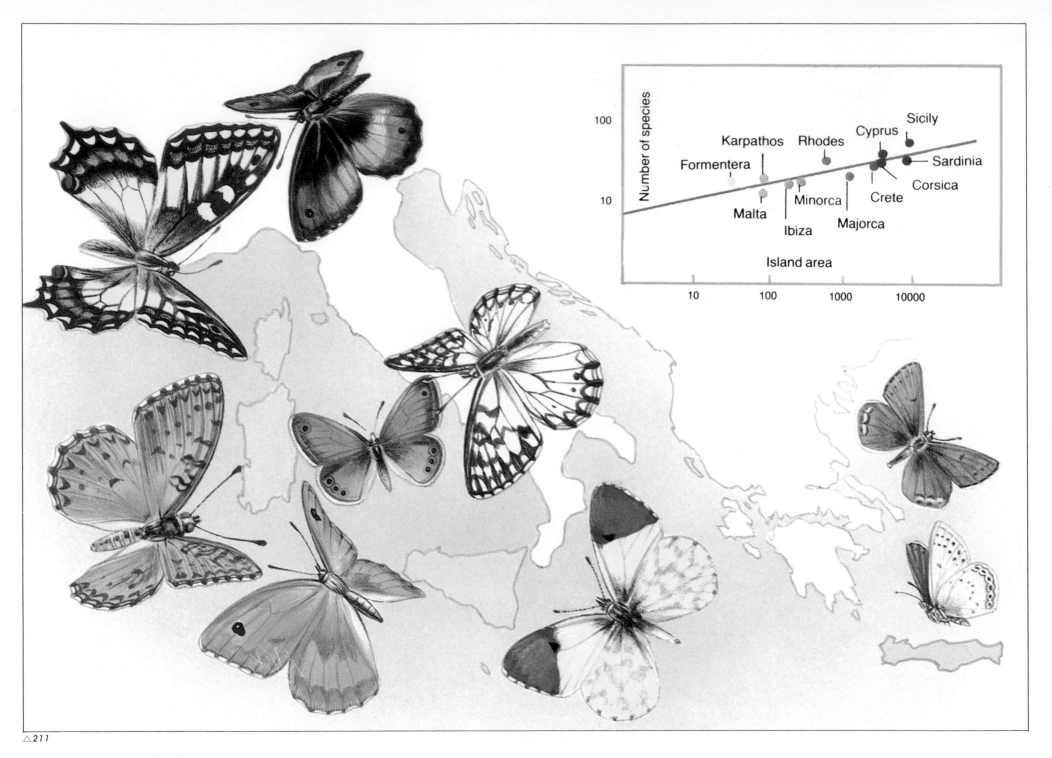

Number of species

100

10

Formentera

Karpathos   Rhodes   Cyprus   Sicily

Malta   Minorca   Crete   Sardinia

Ibiza   Majorca   Corsica

Island area

10   100   1000   10000

△211

211. ARNOLDO MONDADORI EDITORE, S.P.A.   *1. ITALY   2. ARNOLDO MONDADORI EDITORE S.P.A.   3. SYSTEMATICAL GRAPHS   4. BOOK, "THE WORLD OF BUTTERFLIES"   5. SPECIES COUNT

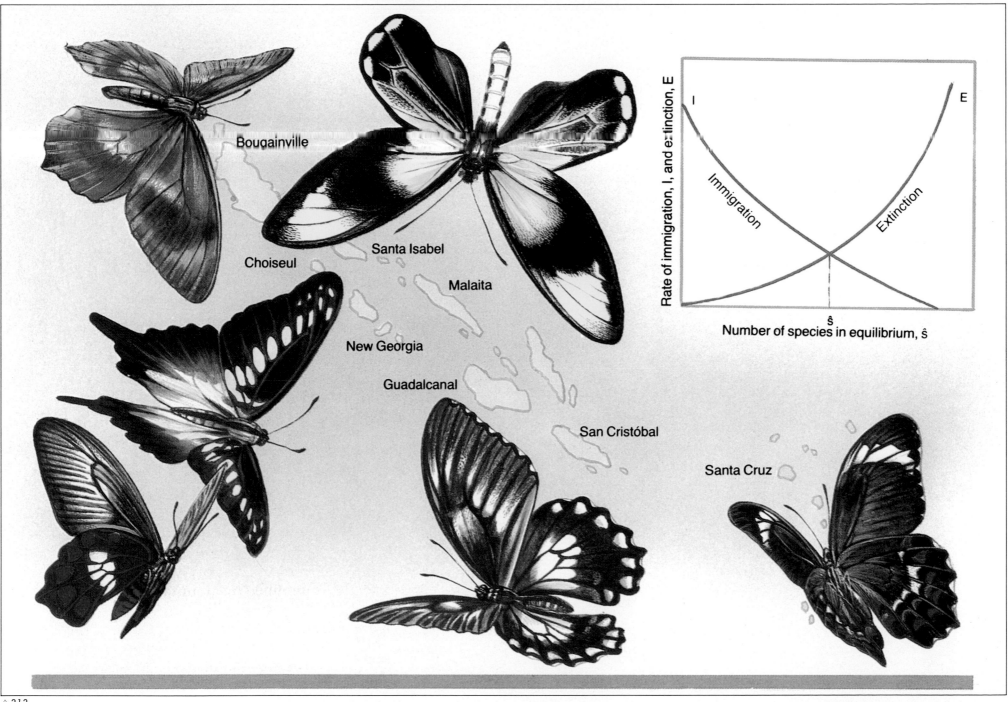

Bougainville

Santa Isabel

Choiseul

Malaita

New Georgia

Guadalcanal

San Cristóbal

Santa Cruz

Rate of immigration, I, and extinction, E

I

E

Immigration

Extinction

ŝ

Number of species in equilibrium, ŝ

ARNOLDO MONDADORI EDITORE, S.P.A. 212.

BOOK, "THE WORLD OF BUTTERFLIES" 4. ITALY 1.
RATES OF IMMIGRATION AND EXTINCTION 5. ARNOLDO MONDADORI EDITORE, S.P.A. 2.
SYSTEMATICAL GRAPHS 3.

ZEUGLOPTERA

DACHNONYPHA

MONOTRYSIA (A)

MONOTRYSIA (B)

DITRYSIA

1 Micropterigoidea
2 Eriocranioidea
3 Hepialoidea
4 Nepticuloidea
5 Incurvarioidea
6 Cossoidea
7 Tineaoidea
8 Tortricoidea
9 Hyponomeutoidea
10 Gelechioidea
11 Copromorphoidea
12 Castnioidea
13 Zygaenoidea
14 Pyraloidea
15 Pterophoroidea
16 Hesperioidea
17 Papilionoidea
18 Geometrioidea
19 Bombycoidea
20 Calliduloidea
21 Sphingoidea
22 Notodontoidea
23 Noctuoidea

△213

213. ARNOLDO MONDADORI EDITORE, S.P.A.

1. ITALY
2. ARNOLDO MONDADORI EDITORE, S.P.A.
3. SYSTEMATICAL GRAPHS
4. BOOK, "THE WORLD OF BUTTERFLIES"

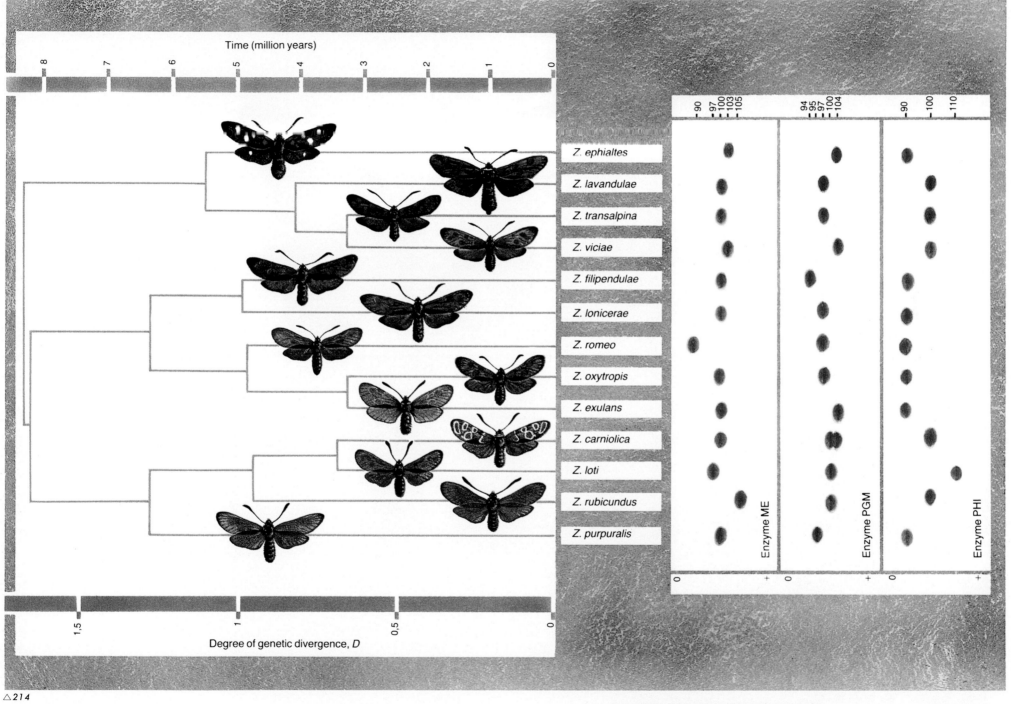

Time (million years)

Degree of genetic divergence, D

Z. ephialtes
Z. lavandulae
Z. transalpina
Z. viciae
Z. filipendulae
Z. lonicerae
Z. romeo
Z. oxytropis
Z. exulans
Z. carniolica
Z. loti
Z. rubicundus
Z. purpuralis

Enzyme ME
Enzyme PGM
Enzyme PHI

△214

214. ARNOLDO MONDADORI EDITORE, S.P.A.

1. ITALY
2. ARNOLDO MONDADORI EDITORE S.P.A.
3. SYSTEMATICAL GRAPHS
4. BOOK, "THE WORLD OF BUTTERFLIES"

ARNOLDO MONDADORI EDITORE, S.P.A. 215, 216.

ITALY 1.
ARNOLDO MONDADORI EDITORE, S.P.A. 2.
SYSTEMATICAL GRAPHS 3.
BOOK, "THE WORLD OF BUTTERFLIES" 4.
MIGRATION PATTERNS 5.

△215 ▽216

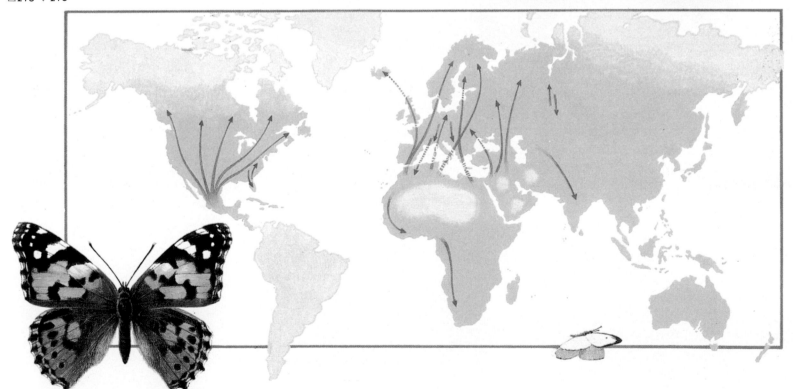

ARNOLDO MONDADORI EDITORE, S.P.A. 217, 218.

ITALY 1.
ARNOLDO MONDADORI EDITORE, S.P.A. 2.
SYSTEMATICAL GRAPHS 3.
BOOK, "THE WORLD OF BUTTERFLIES" 4.

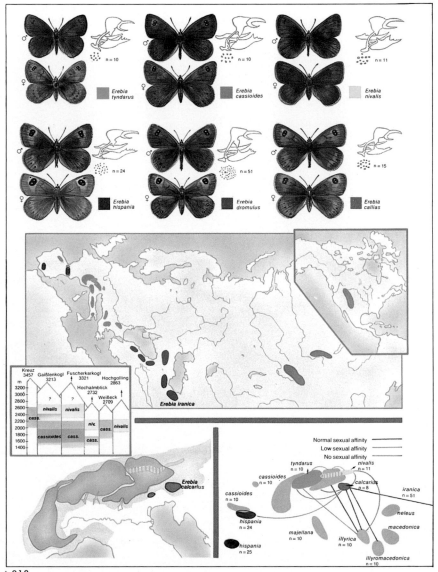

△217 △218

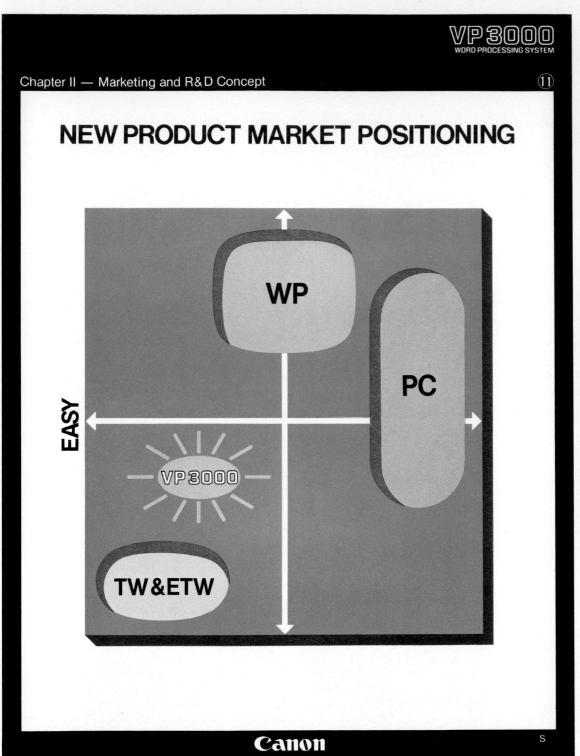

VP 3000 WORD PROCESSING SYSTEM

NEW PRODUCT MARKET POSITIONING

EASY

WP

PC

VP3000

TW&ETW

Canon S

△219

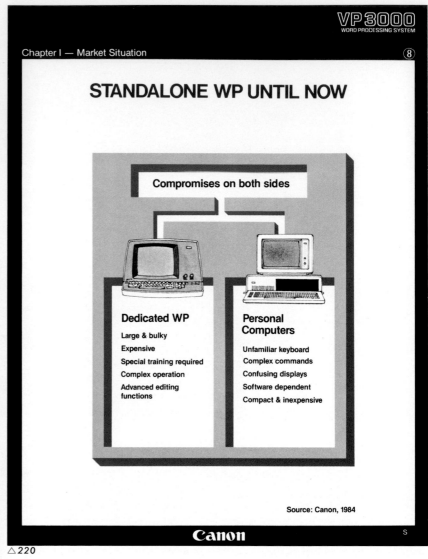

VP 3000 WORD PROCESSING SYSTEM

STANDALONE WP UNTIL NOW

Compromises on both sides

Dedicated WP

Large & bulky

Expensive

Special training required

Complex operation

Advanced editing functions

Personal Computers

Unfamiliar keyboard

Complex commands

Confusing displays

Software dependent

Compact & inexpensive

Source: Canon, 1984

Canon S

△220

219,220. HAKUHODO INC./DIAGRAMS INC.

1. JAPAN
2. HAKUHODO INC./DIAGRAMS INC.
*   ART DIRECTOR: TAKASHI KITAMURA*
*   MASAYOSHI MORIOKA*
*   DESIGNER: TSUTOMU OKAMOTO*
*   REIKO HAYASHI*
*   RYÔCHI TAYA*
*   NORIKO YURI*
3. FLOW CHARTS
4. PAMPHLET
5. CANON INC.

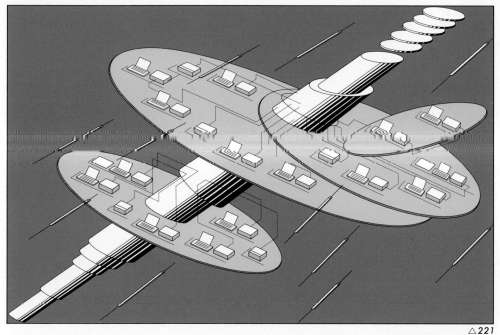

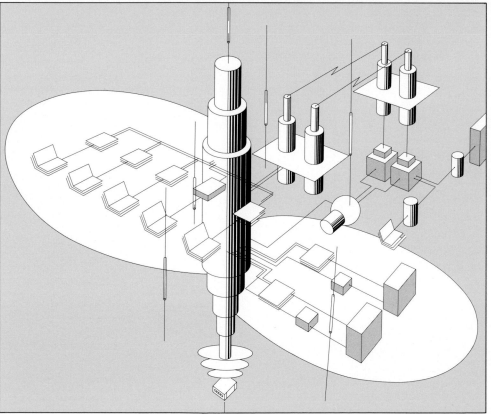

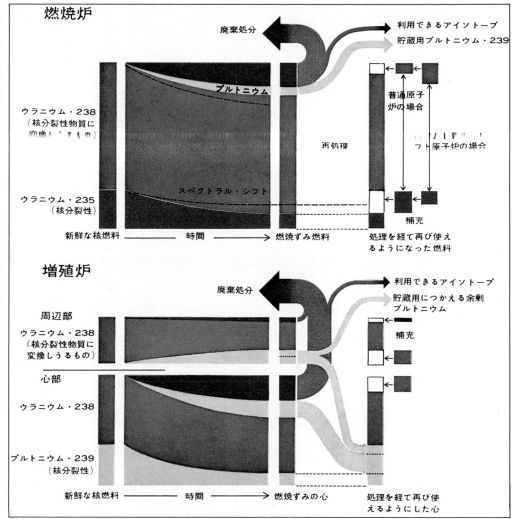

221, 222. HAKUHODO INC./DIAGRAMS INC.

1. JAPAN
2. HAKUHODO INC./DIAGRAMS INC.
   ART DIRECTOR: KAI NAKAGAWA
   DESIGNER: TSUTOMU OKAMOTO
   　　　　　RYŌCHI TAYA
   　　　　　REIKO HAYASHI
   　　　　　NORIKO YURI
3. FLOW CHARTS
5. COMPUTER OFFICE AUTOMATION SYSTEM

223. KOICHIRO INAGAKI

1. JAPAN
2. INAGAKI ASSOCIATES
3. FLOW CHARTS
4. PRESIDENT MAGAZINE
5. NUCLEAR REACTOR
   AND INCINERATOR

Osnovna organizacijska shema delovne skupnosti Gospodarske banke Ljubljana

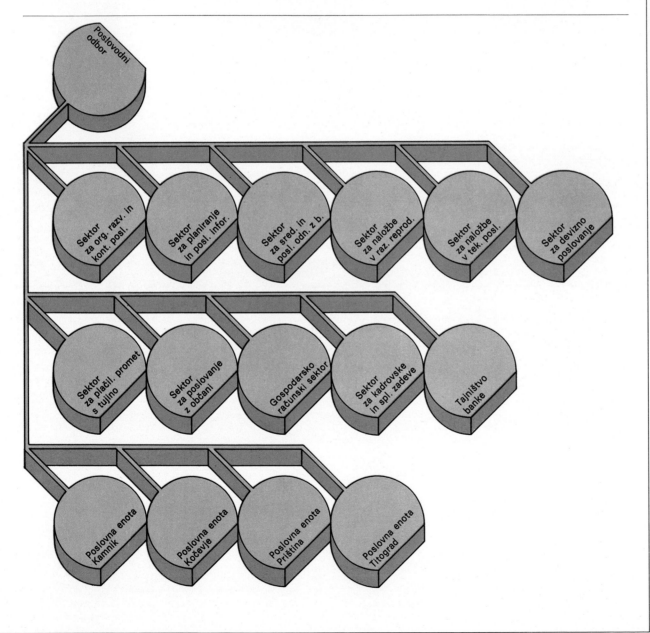

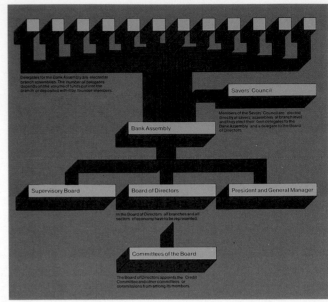

△225

224,225. PETER SKALAR

1. YUGOSLAVIA
3. SYSTEMATICAL GRAPHS

SUDARSHAN DHEER 226.

△224

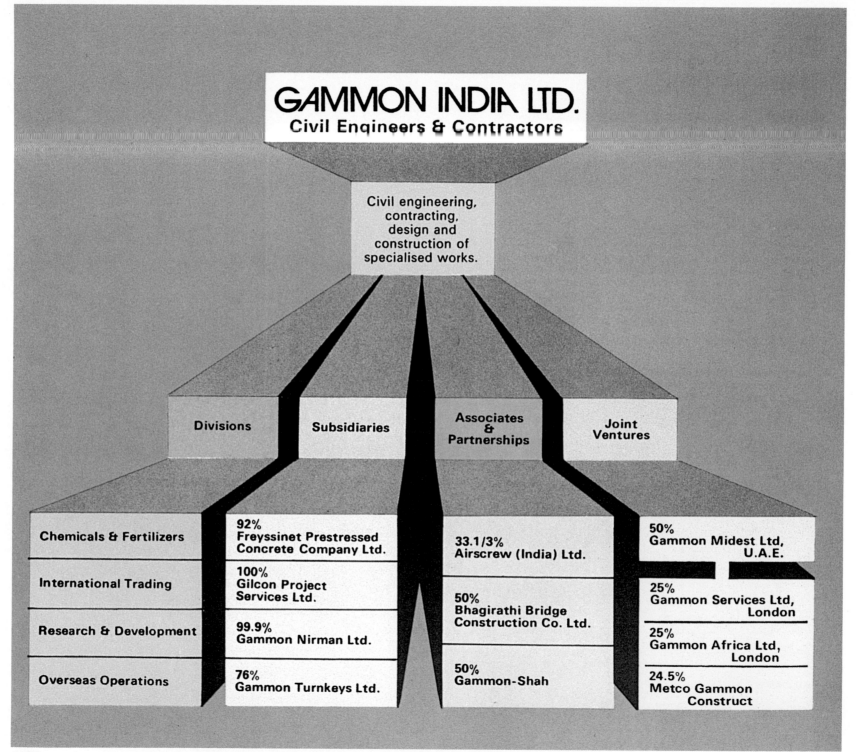

Experience

Dames & Moore has provided consultation to clients in the earth and environmental sciences for more than 40 years. Since the passage of RCRA and subsequent regulations, approximately 600 projects involving waste-related activities have been completed for clients located in 48 of the 50 states. The services performed range from siting and permitting of hazardous waste management facilities to closure assistance and expert testimony.

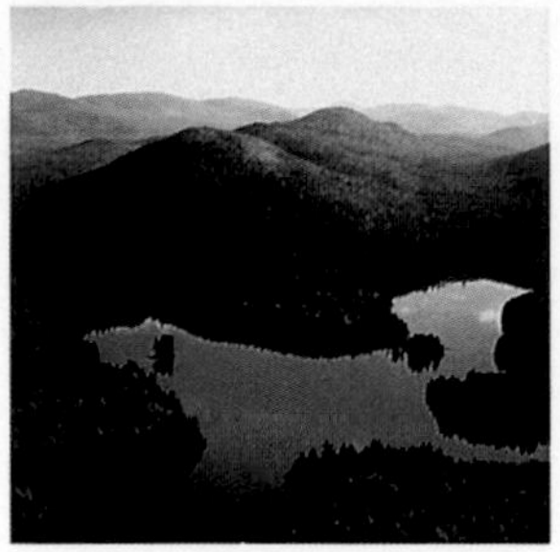

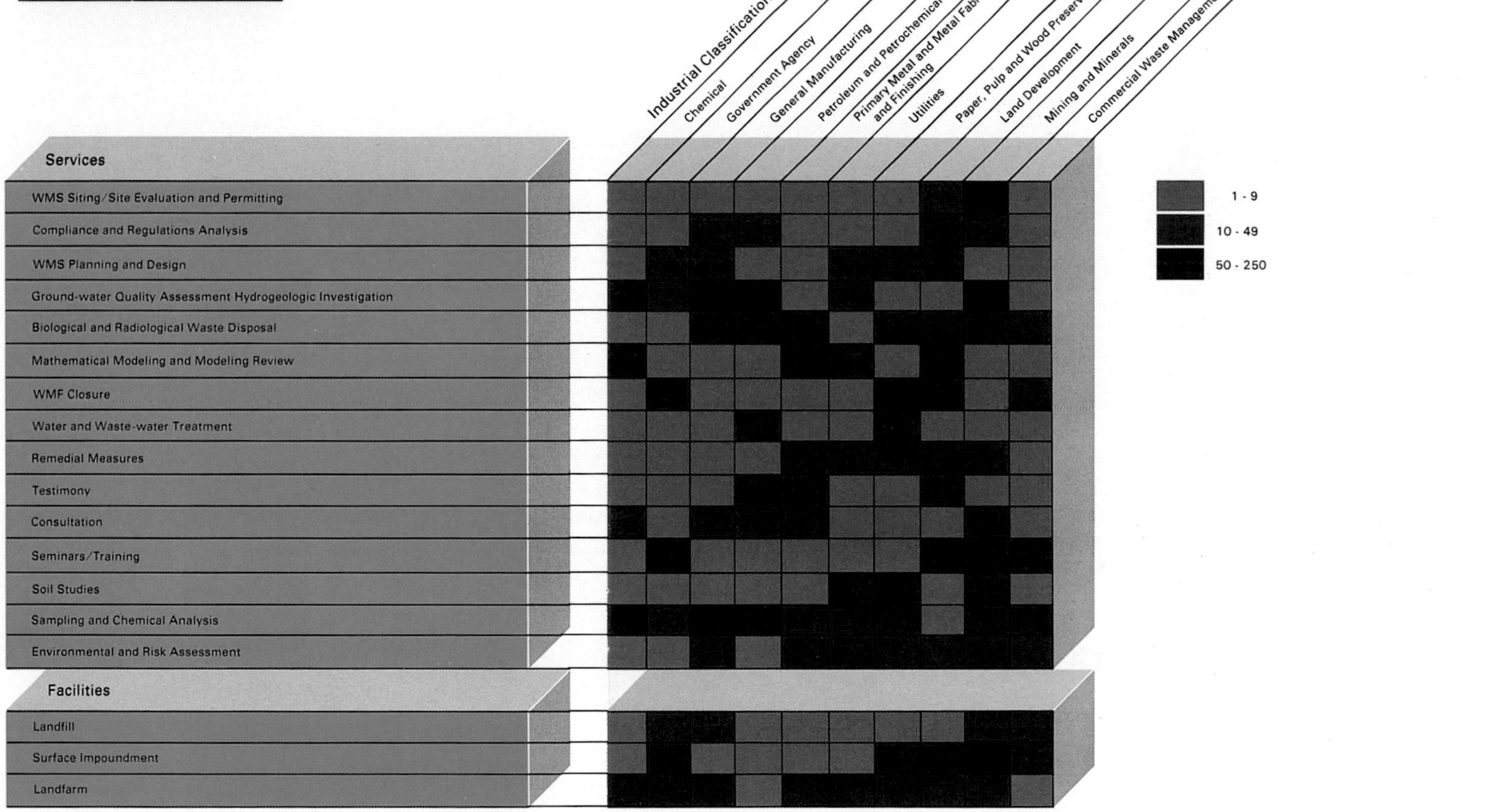

△227

227. BILL BROWN

1. U.S.A.
2. BILL BROWN & ASSOCIATES
   ART DIRECTOR: BILL BROWN
   DESIGNER: SHOJI TERAISHI
3. SYSTEMATICAL GRAPHS
4. CATALOGUE
5. DAMES & MOORE
   WASTE MANAGEMENT FACILITIES AND SERVICES

Implementation of solutions to waste management problems may require remedial actions, facility modification or closure of a facility. Dames & Moore's experience in each assists the client in the implementation of these solutions.

For immediate response situations, Dames & Moore's technical staff provides on-site assessment of contamination problems and of mitigation activities. The staff is also available to coordinate remedial activities with regulatory personnel. For remedial activities in situations where the impact on the environment or public health is less immediate, Dames & Moore's involvement can include all the steps discussed previously as well as on-site inspections, monitoring and management assistance.

Dames & Moore provides a variety of construction-related services, including preparation of bid lists, evaluation of bids, contractor selection, scheduling, construction inspection (both resident and nonresident), materials testing and preparation of drawings. Overall construction management services are also available.

In many instances, closure of a waste management facility is the best alternative. Identification of suitable closure techniques is essential for holding down costs while assuring post-closure reliability of the site.

Dames & Moore has prepared comprehensive closure and post-closure plans for a variety of industrial concerns and can certify that all applicable federal and state regulations have been satisfied while minimizing post-closure maintenance problems. In addition, the firm can provide construction-related services for closure activities.

Dames & Moore can develop an extensive array of remedial actions, together with cost estimates and the relative advantages and disadvantages of each.

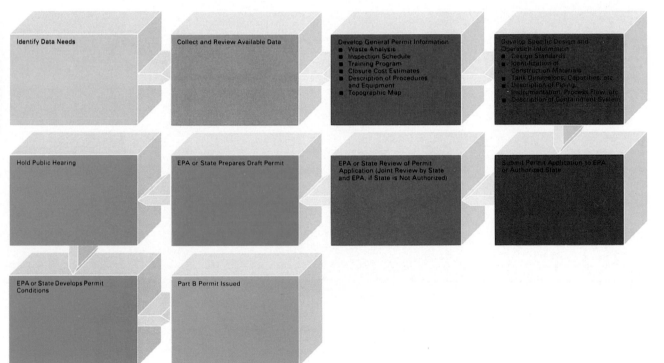

Identify Data Needs

Collect and Review Available Data

Develop General Permit Information
- Waste Analysis
- Inspection Schedule
- Training Program
- Closure Cost Estimates
- Description of Procedures and Equipment
- Topographic Map

Develop Specific Design and Operation Information
- Design Standards
- Identification of Construction Materials
- Tank Dimensions, Capacities, etc.
- Description of Piping, Instrumentation, Process Flow, etc.
- Description of Containment System

Hold Public Hearing

EPA or State Prepares Draft Permit

EPA or State Review of Permit Application (Joint Review by State and EPA, if State is Not Authorized)

Submit Permit Application to EPA or Authorized State

EPA or State Develops Permit Conditions

Part B Permit Issued

△228

BILL BROWN 228.

U.S.A. 1.
BILL BROWN & ASSOCIATES 2.
ART DIRECTOR: BILL BROWN
DESIGNER: SHOJI TERAISHI
SYSTEMATICAL GRAPHS 3.
CATALOGUE 4.
DAMES & MORE/WASTE MANAGEMENT ASSISTANCE 5.

日本の自然暦

DATA JAPAN 1
Nature in Japan

日本の自然暦

DATA JAPAN 2
Nature in Japan

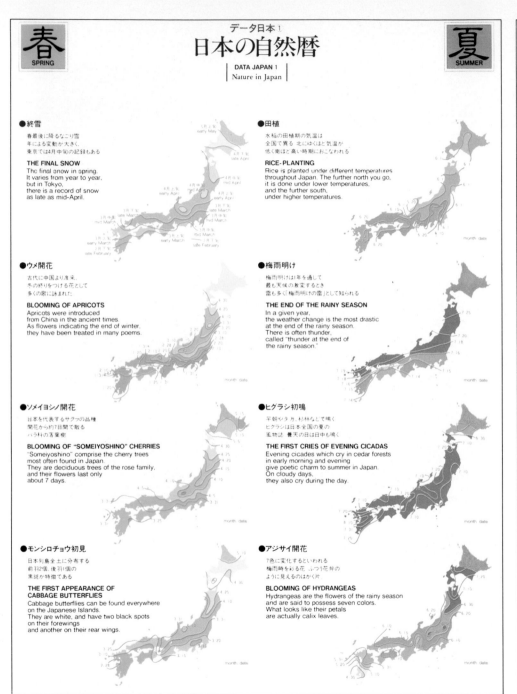

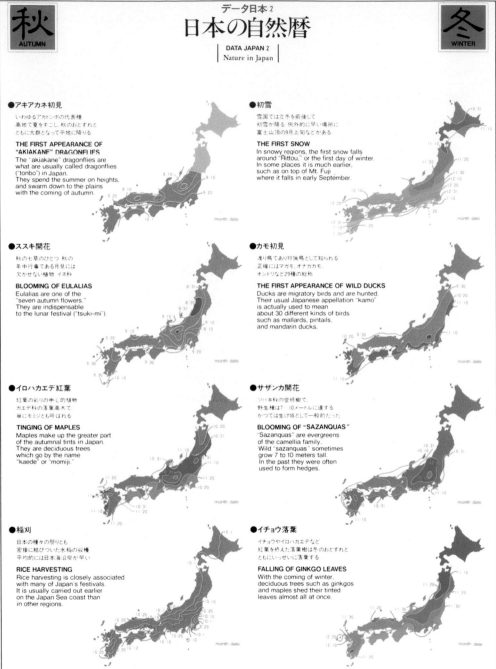

●終雪

春最後に降るなごり雪
年による変動が大きく、
東京では4月中旬の記録もある

THE FINAL SNOW
The final snow in spring.
It varies from year to year,
but in Tokyo,
there is a record of snow
as late as mid-April.

●田植

水稲の田植期の気温は
全国で異る 北にゆくほど気温が
低く南ほど暖い時期におこなわれる

RICE-PLANTING
Rice is planted under different temperatures
throughout Japan. The further north you go,
it is done under lower temperatures,
and the further south,
under higher temperatures.

●ウメ開花

古代に中国より渡来、
冬の殿りをつける花として
多くの歌に詠まれた

BLOOMING OF APRICOTS
Apricots were introduced
from China in the ancient times.
As flowers indicating the end of winter,
they have been treated in many poems.

●梅雨明け

梅雨明けは1年を通して
最も天候の激変するとき
雷も多く「梅雨明けの雷」として知られる

THE END OF THE RAINY SEASON
In a given year,
the weather change is the most drastic
at the end of the rainy season.
There is often thunder,
called "thunder at the end of
the rainy season."

●ソメイヨシノ開花

日本を代表するサクラの品種
開花から約7日間で散る
バラ科の落葉樹

BLOOMING OF "SOMEIYOSHINO" CHERRIES
"Someiyoshino" comprise the cherry trees
most often found in Japan.
They are deciduous trees of the rose family,
and their flowers last only
about 7 days.

●ヒグラシ初鳴

早朝やゆう方、杉林などで鳴く
ヒグラシは日本全国の夏の
風物誌 曇天の日は日中も鳴く

THE FIRST CRIES OF EVENING CICADAS
Evening cicadas which cry in cedar forests
in early morning and evening
give poetic charm to summer in Japan.
On cloudy days,
they also cry during the day.

●モンシロチョウ初見

日本列島全土に分布する
前羽2個、後羽1個の
黒斑が特徴である

**THE FIRST APPEARANCE OF
CABBAGE BUTTERFLIES**
Cabbage butterflies can be found everywhere
on the Japanese Islands.
They are white, and have two black spots
on their forewings
and another on their rear wings.

●アジサイ開花

7色に変化するといわれる
梅雨時を彩る花。ふつう花弁の
ように見えるのはがく片

BLOOMING OF HYDRANGEAS
Hydrangeas are the flowers of the rainy season
and are said to possess seven colors.
What looks like their petals
are actually calix leaves.

●アキアカネ初見

いわゆるアカトンボの代表種
高地で夏をすごし、秋のおとずれと
ともに大群となって平地に降りる

**THE FIRST APPEARANCE OF
"AKIAKANE" DRAGONFLIES**
The "akiakane" dragonflies are
what are usually called dragonflies
("tonbo") in Japan.
They spend the summer on heights,
and swarm down to the plains
with the coming of autumn.

●初雪

雪国では立冬を前後して
初の雪が降る 例外的に早い場所に
富士山頂の9月上旬などがある

THE FIRST SNOW
In snowy regions, the first snow falls
around "Rittou," or the first day of winter.
In some places it is much earlier,
such as on top of Mt. Fuji
where it falls in early September.

●ススキ開花

秋の七草のひとつ 秋の
年中行事である月見には
欠かせない植物 イネ科

BLOOMING OF EULALIAS
Eulalias are one of the
"seven autumn flowers."
They are indispensable
to the lunar festival ("tsuki-mi").

●カモ初見

渡り鳥であり狩猟鳥として知られる
正確にはマガモ、オナガカモ、
オンドリなど29種の総称

THE FIRST APPEARANCE OF WILD DUCKS
Ducks are migratory birds and are hunted.
Their usual Japanese appellation "kamo"
is actually used to mean
about 30 different kinds of birds
such as mallards, pintails,
and mandarin ducks.

●イロハカエデ紅葉

紅葉の彩りの中心的植物
カエデ科の落葉高木で、
単にモミジとも呼ばれる

TINGING OF MAPLES
Maples make up the greater part
of the autumnal tints in Japan.
They are deciduous trees
which go by the name
"kaede" or "momiji."

●サザンカ開花

ツバキ科の常緑樹で、
野生種は7～10メートルに達する
かつては生け垣として一般的だった

BLOOMING OF "SAZANQUAS"
"Sazanquas" are evergreens
of the camellia family.
Wild "sazanquas" sometimes
grow 7 to 10 meters tall.
In the past they were often
used to form hedges.

●稲刈

日本の種々の祭りとも
密接に結びついた水稲の収穫
平均的には日本海沿岸が早い

RICE HARVESTING
Rice harvesting is closely associated
with many of Japan's festivals.
It is usually carried out earlier
on the Japan Sea coast than
in other regions.

●イチョウ落葉

イチョウやイロハカエデなど
紅葉を終えた落葉樹は冬のおとずれと
ともにいっせいに落葉する

FALLING OF GINKGO LEAVES
With the coming of winter,
deciduous trees such as ginkgos
and maples shed their tinted
leaves almost all at once.

△229　△230

229,230. CAN

1. JAPAN
2. CAN
3. VISUAL GRAPHS OR FUNCTIONS/PROGRESSIONS
4. PICTORIAL INFORMATION FOR HOTEL GUEST
5. IMPERIAL HOTEL/NATURE IN JAPAN

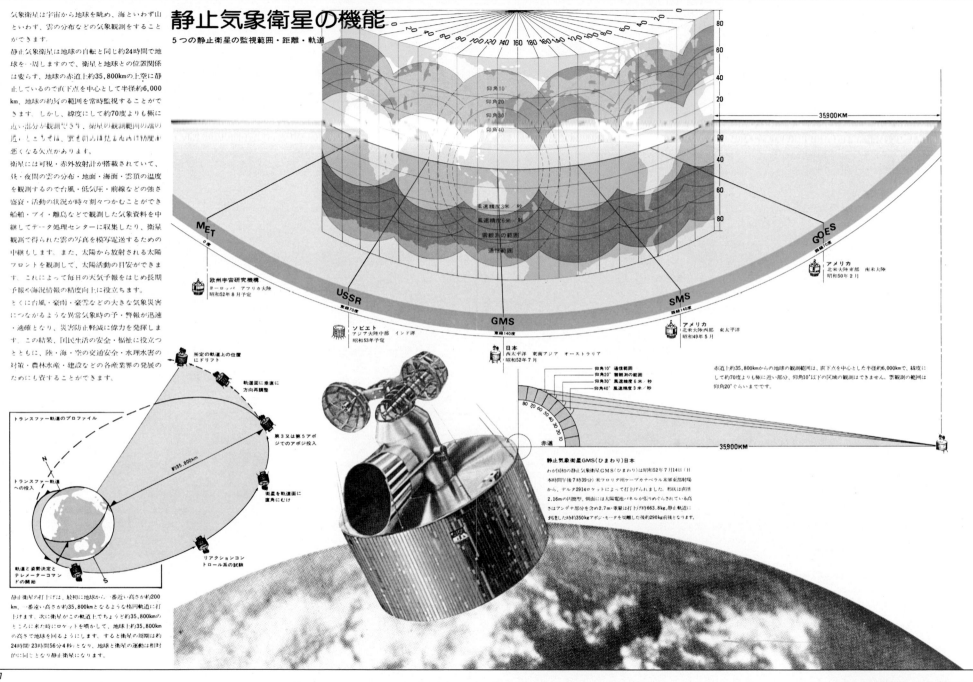

静止気象衛星の機能

5つの静止衛星の監視範囲・距離・軌道

気象衛星は宇宙から地球を眺め、海といわず山といわず、雲の分布などの気象観測をすることができます。

静止気象衛星は地球の自転と同じ約24時間で地球を一周しますので、衛星と地球との位置関係は変らず、地球の赤道上約35,800kmの上空に静止しているので直下点を中心として半径約6,000km、地球の約1/4の範囲を常時監視することができます。しかし、緯度にして約70度よりも極に近い部分が観測できず、衛星より観測範囲の端の近いところでは、雲も斜めに見えるため精度が悪くなる欠点があります。

衛星には可視・赤外放射計が搭載されていて、昼・夜間の雲の分布・地面・海面・雲頂の温度を観測するので台風・低気圧・前線などの強さ盛衰・活動の状況が時々刻々つかむことができ、船舶・ブイ・離島などで観測した気象資料を中継してデータ処理センターに収集したり、衛星観測で得られた雲の写真を模写電送するための中継もします。また、太陽から放射される太陽フロントを観測して、太陽活動の目安ができます。これによって毎日の天気予報をはじめ長期予報や海況情報の精度向上に役立ちます。

とくに台風・豪雨・豪雪などの大きな気象災害につながるような異常気象時の予・警報が迅速・適確となり、災害防止軽減に偉力を発揮します。この結果、国民生活の安全・福祉に役立つとともに、陸・海・空の交通安全・水理水害の対策・農林水産・建設などの各産業界の発展のためにも資することができます。

MET 欧州宇宙研究機構 ヨーロッパ アフリカ大陸 昭和52年8月予定 0度

USSR ソビエト アジア大陸中部 インド洋 昭和53年予定 東経70度

GMS 日本 西太平洋 東南アジア オーストラリア 昭和52年7月 東経140度

SMS アメリカ 北米大陸西部 東太平洋 昭和49年5月 西経140度

GOES アメリカ 北米大陸東部 南米大陸 昭和50年2月 西経70度

35,900KM

仰角10° 通信範囲
仰角20° 警報観測の範囲
仰角30° 風速精度5米/秒
仰角40° 風速精度3米/秒

赤道上約35,800kmからの地球の観測範囲は、直下点を中心とした半径約6,000kmで、緯度にして約70度よりも極に近い部分、仰角10°以下の区域の観測はできません。雲観測の範囲は仰角20°ぐらいまでです。

トランスファー軌道のプロファイル

所定の軌道上の位置にドリフト
軌道面に垂直に方向再調整
第3又は第5アポジでのアポジ挿入
衛星を軌道面に直角にむける
リアクションコントロール系の試験
軌道と姿勢決定とテレメーターコマンドの開始

約35,800km

静止衛星の打上げは、最初に地球から一番近い高さが約200km、一番遠い高さが約35,800kmとなるような楕円軌道に打上げます。次に衛星がこの軌道上で丁度約35,800kmのところに来た時にロケットを噴かして、地球上約35,800kmの高さで地球を回るようにします。すると衛星の周期は約24時間23時間56分4秒となり、地球と衛星の運動は相対的に同じとなり静止衛星になります。

静止気象衛星GMS(ひまわり)日本

わが国初の静止気象衛星GMS(ひまわり)は昭和52年7月14日(日本時間午後7時39分)米フロリダ州ケープカナベラル米軍基地射場から、デルタ2914ロケットによって打上げられました。形状は直径2.16mの円筒型、側面には太陽電池パネルが張りめぐらされている高さはアンテナ部分を含め2.7m・重量は打上げ時約663.8kg、静止軌道に到達した時約350kgアポジ・モーターを切離した後約290kg前後となります。

△231

231. TSUTOMU OKAMOTO

PAMPHLET 4.
THE METEOROLOGICAL AGENCY 5.
FUNCTION OF STATIONARY WEATHER SATELLITE

JAPAN 1.
DIAGRAMS INC. 2.
VISUAL GRAPHS OR FUNCTIONS/PROGRESSIONS 3.

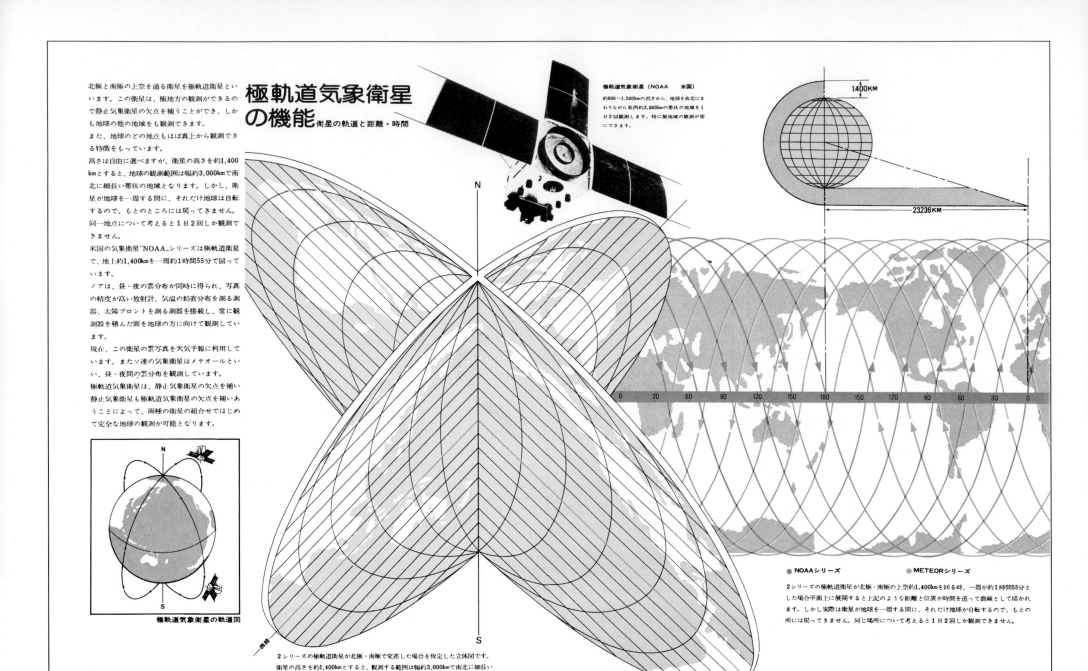

北極と南極の上空を通る衛星を極軌道衛星といいます。この衛星は、極地方の観測ができるので静止気象衛星の欠点を補うことができ、しかも地球の他の地域をも観測できます。

また、地球のどの地点もほぼ真上から観測できる特徴をもっています。

高さは自由に選べますが、衛星の高さを約1,400kmとすると、地球の観測範囲は幅約3,000kmで南北に細長い帯状の地域となります。しかし、衛星が地球を一周する間に、それだけ地球は自転するので、もとのところには戻ってきません。同一地点について考えると1日2回しか観測できません。

米国の気象衛星"NOAA"シリーズは極軌道衛星で、地上約1,400kmを一周約1時間55分で回っています。

ノアは、昼・夜の雲分布が同時に得られ、写真の精度が高い放射計、気温の鉛直分布を測る測器、太陽プロトンを測る測器を搭載し、常に観測器を積んだ面を地球の方に向けて観測しています。

現在、この衛星の雲写真を天気予報に利用しています。またソ連の気象衛星はメテオールといい、昼・夜間の雲分布を観測しています。

極軌道気象衛星は、静止気象衛星の欠点を補い静止気象衛星も極軌道気象衛星の欠点を補いあうことによって、両種の衛星の組合せではじめて完全な地球の観測が可能となります。

極軌道気象衛星の軌道図

極軌道気象衛星の機能
衛星の軌道と距離・時間

極軌道気象衛星（NOAA　米国）

約800〜1,500kmの高さから、地球を南北にまわりながら東西約3,000kmの帯状の地域を1日2回観測します。特に極地域の観測が密にできます。

1400KM

23236KM

2シリーズの極軌道衛星が北極・南極の上空約1,400kmで交差した場合を仮定した立体図です。衛星の高さを約1,400kmとすると、観測する範囲は幅約3,000kmで南北に細長い帯状になります。1周を約1時間55分とした時の1日の周期を表わしたものです。

● NOAAシリーズ　　　　● METEORシリーズ

2シリーズの極軌道衛星が北極・南極の上空約1,400kmを回る時、一周が約1時間55分とした場合平面上に展開すると上記のような距離と位置が時間を追って曲線として描かれます。しかし実際は衛星が地球を一周する間に、それだけ地球が自転するので、もとの所には戻ってきません。同じ場所について考えると1日2回しか観測できません。

△232

232. DIAGRAMS INC.

REIKO HAYASHI

1. JAPAN
2. DIAGRAMS INC.
   ART DIRECTOR: TSUTOMU OKAMOTO
   DESIGNER: NORIKO YURI
3. VISUAL GRAPHS OR FUNCTIONS/PROGRESSIONS
4. PAMPHLET
5. THE METEOROLOGICAL AGENCY
   FUNCTION OF ORBITING WEATHER SATELLITE

世界気象衛星組織

5つの静止衛星と2シリーズの極軌道衛星の分布

昭和32年に人工衛星スプートニクの打上げが成功して以来、衛星技術は気象や通信の分野に応用されるようになりました。エッサ・ノアなどの気象衛星が打上げられ、気象観測や雲の写真の解析という新しい分野が開拓され、電子計算機の進歩とあいまって、気象業務の発展が期待されるようになりました。

国連の専門機関の一つである世界気象機関（WMO）では、気象衛星を効果的に配置して、宇宙から地球全域を観測し、電子計算機をフルに活用して気象業務を近代化し、これによって、天気予報の精度を向上させるために世界気象監視（WWW）計画を推進しています。WWW計画の中で最も重要なものとして、静止気象衛星や極軌道気象衛星をうまく組合せて地球を観測する世界気象衛星系があります。

世界気象衛星系は、5個の静止気象衛星と2シリーズの極軌道気象衛星からできています。これらにより、宇宙開発の進歩は著しく将来の予想を期待することができます。

より精度の高い観測が実施されることはもちろんのこと、マイクロウェーブを使用したり、赤外線を応用した測定を利用して水蒸気分布、降雨域の分布・雨の強さの検出ができるようになります。その他に融水・融雪の時期を予知することにより洪水予報が有効にでき、さらに波浪・流水・海流の状況、海洋汚染の状態、プランクトンの量的検出もできるようになるでしょう

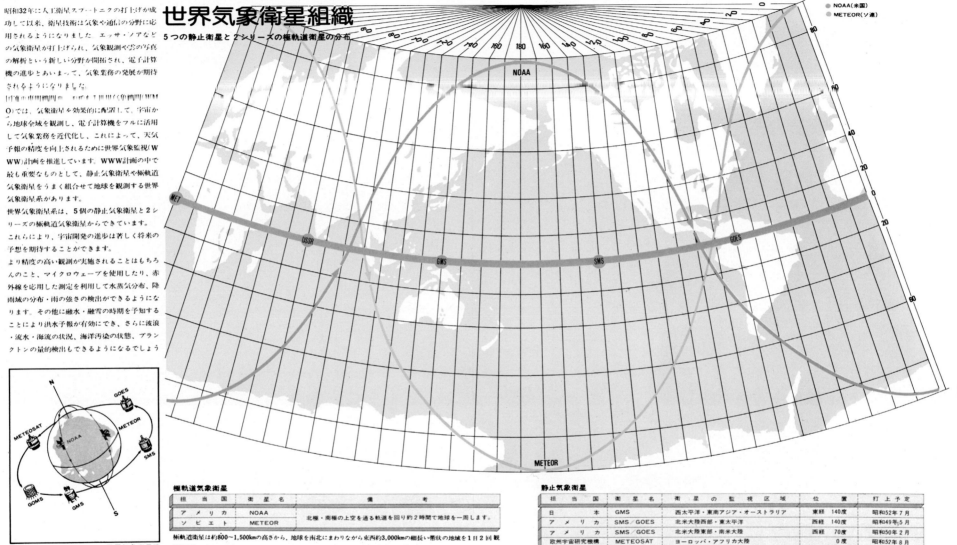

● NOAA（米国）
● METEOR（ソ連）

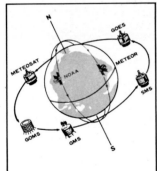

世界気象衛星系

極軌道気象衛星

担　当　国	衛星名	備　　　　　　考
アメリカ	NOAA	北極・南極の上空を通る軌道を回り約2時間で地球を一周します。
ソビエト	METEOR	

極軌道衛星は約800〜1,500kmの高さから、地球を南北にまわりながら東西約3,000kmの細長い帯状の地域を1日2回観測します。また、地球のどの地点もほぼ真上から観測することができる特徴をもっています。

静止気象衛星

担　当　国	衛星名	衛　星　の　監　視　区　域	位　置	打上予定
日　本	GMS	西太平洋・東南アジア・オーストラリア	東経 140度	昭和52年7月
アメリカ	SMS／GOES	北米大陸西部・東太平洋	西経 140度	昭和49年5月
アメリカ	SMS／GOES	北米大陸東部・南太大陸	西経 70度	昭和50年2月
欧州宇宙研究機構	METEOSAT	ヨーロッパ・アフリカ大陸	0度	昭和52年8月
ソビエト	GOMS	アジア大陸中部・インド洋	東経 70度	昭和53年

静止気象衛星は赤道上約35,800kmに打上げられ、地球の同一地点を常時観測することができその範囲は衛星の直下点を中心とした半径約6,000kmです。この衛星は、台風、低気圧などの動きを常時監視できる特徴をもっています。

TSUTOMU OKAMOTO 233.

THE METEOROLOGICAL AGENCY 5.　　　VISUAL GRAPHS OR FUNCTIONS/PROGRESSIONS 3.　　　JAPAN 1.
CONSTITUTION OF WORLDWIDE WEATHER SATELLITES　　　PAMPHLET 4.　　　DIAGRAMS INC. 2.

101

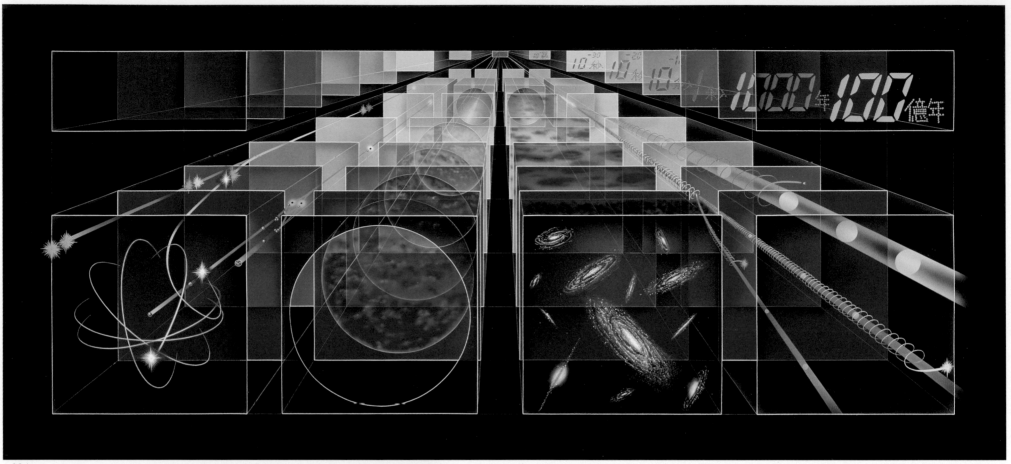

234,235. NEWTON

1. *JAPAN*
2. *ILLUSTRATOR:ICHIMATSU MEGURO(234)*
   ILLUSTRATOR:KEN SAWADA(235)
3. *VISUAL GRAPHS OR FUNCTIONS/PROGRESSIONS*
4. *NEWTON MAGAZINE*
5. *©KYOIKUSHA NEWTON*
   CHRONOLOGICAL TABLE OF SPACE(234)
   CONCENTRATION OF OXYGEN AND THE SPEED
   AT WHICH SUBSTANCES BURN(235)

236. NEWTON

1. *JAPAN*
2. *ILLUSTRATOR:KAZUHO ITOH*
3. *VISUAL GRAPHS OR FUNCTIONS/PROGRESSIONS*
4. *NEWTON MAGAZINE*
5. *©KYOIKUSHA NEWTON*
   FALLING MOTION

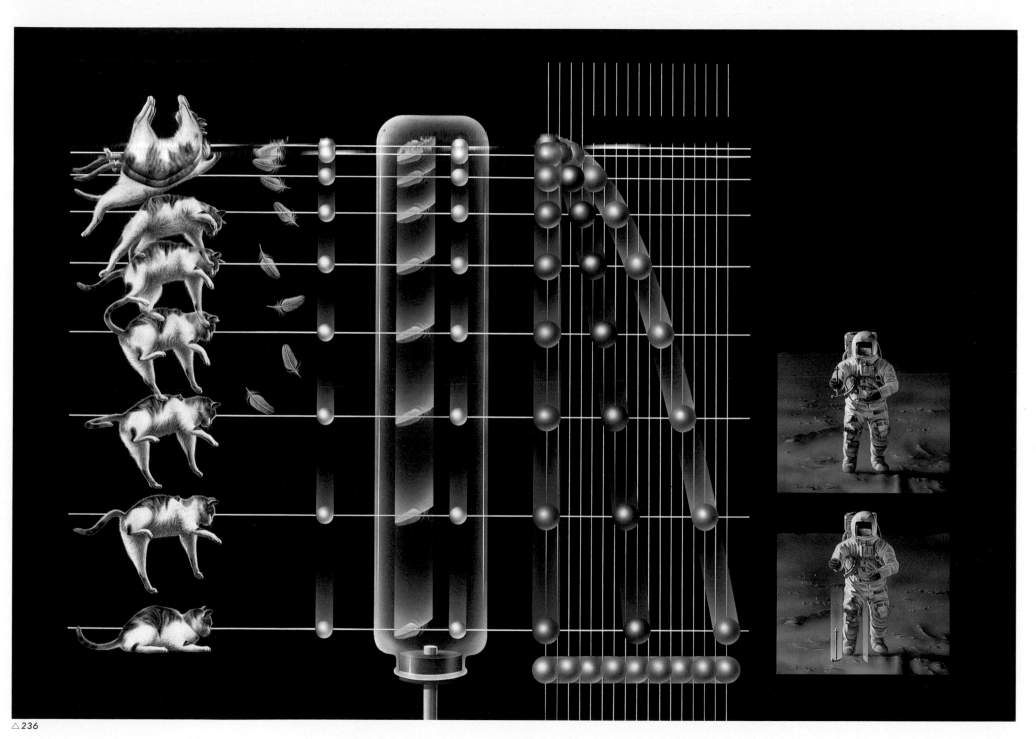

△237

Kazuaki Iwasaki 903 R.

KAZUAKI IWASAKI 237.

JAPAN 1.
COSMOS ORIGIN LTD. 2.
VISUAL GRAPHS OR FUNCTIONS/PROGRESSIONS 3.
"THE SOLAR SYSTEM 9 PLANETS CHART" FOR A PICTORIAL BOOK 4.
OBUNSHA PRESS 5.

△ 238   ▽ 239

238,239. KAZUAKI IWASAKI

1. JAPAN
2. COSMOS ORIGIN LTD.
3. VISUAL GRAPHS OR FUNCTIONS/PROGRESSIONS
4. EXHIBIT AT THE CITY OF TOYAMA
     CULTURE CENTER (238)
   EXHIBIT AT THE NATIONAL
     SCIENCE MUSEUM (239)
5. THE BIRTH PROCESS OF THE SOLAR SYSTEM (238)
   THE SUN AND THE VAN ALLEN BELT (239)

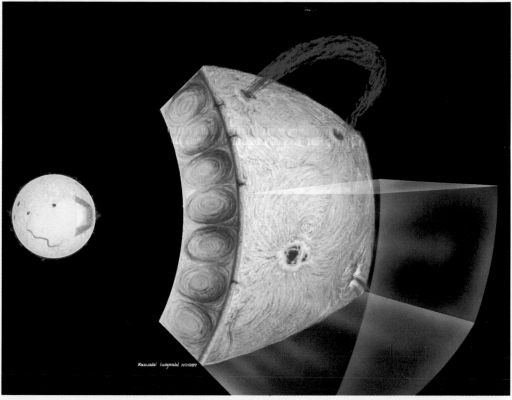

△240

△241 ▽242

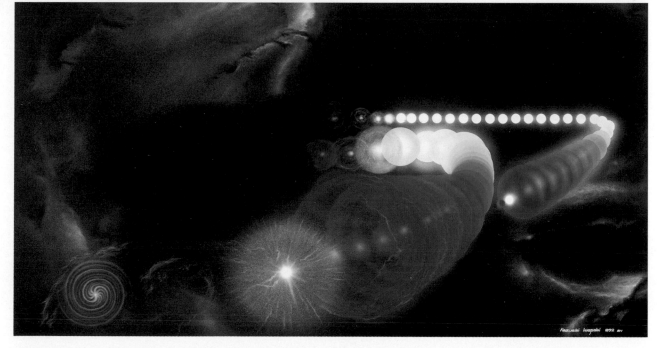

240~242. KAZUAKI IWASAKI

1. JAPAN
2. COSMOS ORIGIN LTD.
3. VISUAL GRAPHS OR FUNCTIONS/PROGRESSIONS
4. PICTORIAL BOOK
5. OBUNSHA PRESS (240, 242)
   GAKKEN CO. LTD. (241)
   THE SOLAR SYSTEM ORBIT CHART (240)
   THE SURFACE STRUCTURE OF THE SUN (241)
   A WHOLE LIFE OF A FIXED STAR (242)

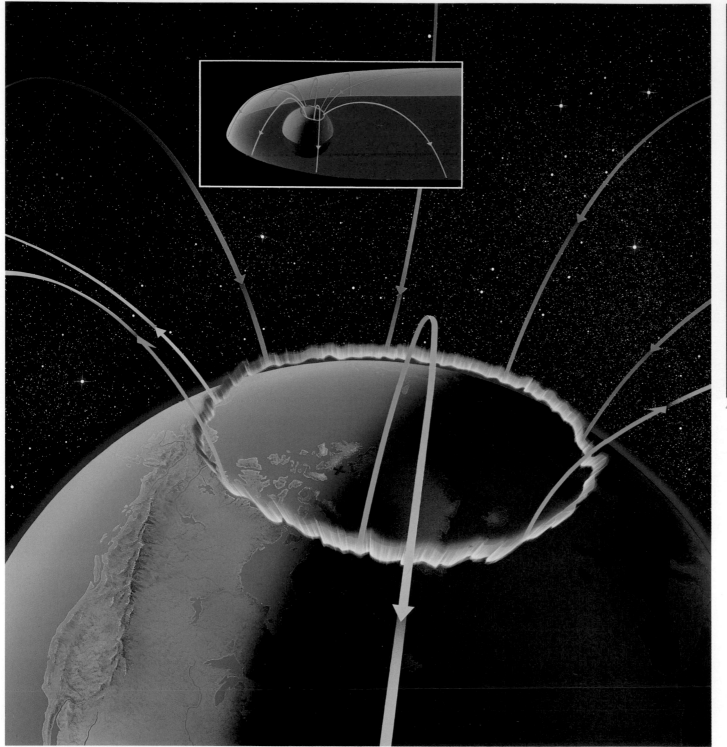

△243

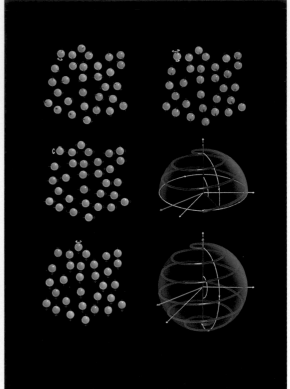

△244

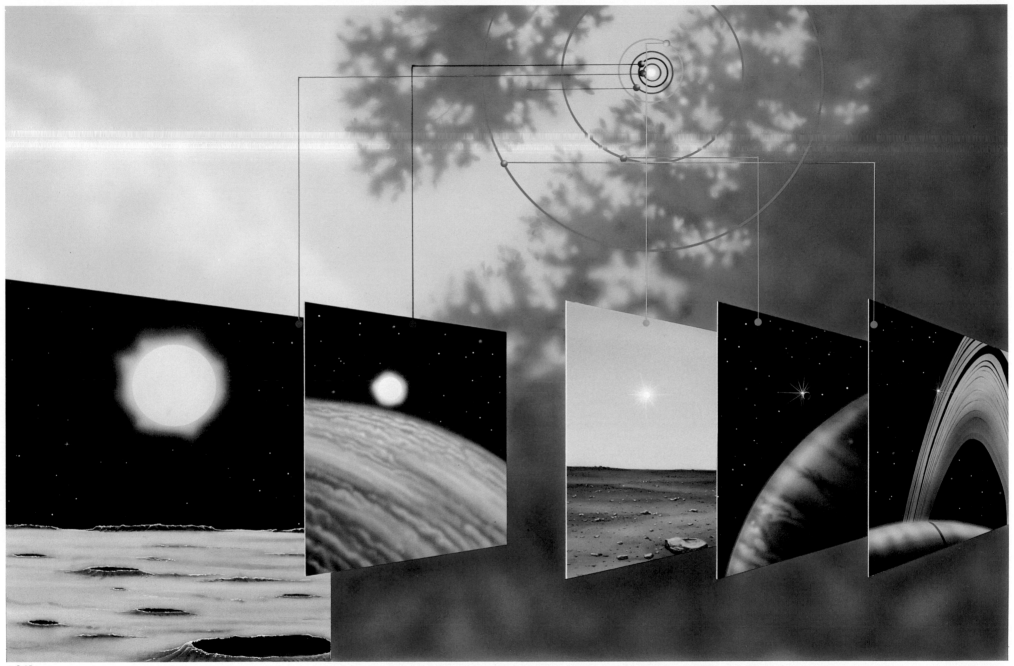

△245

NEWTON 245.

JAPAN 1.
ILLUSTRATOR: YUYA KANAI 2.
TIME TABLES 3.
NEWTON MAGAZINE 4.
©KYOIKUSHA NEWTON/DISTANT AND NEAR STARS 5.

NEWTON 246, 247.

JAPAN 1.
ILLUSTRATOR: HITOSHI ASANO (246) 2.
ILLUSTRATOR: TOMOHISA MONMA (247)
TIME TABLES 3.
NEWTON MAGAZINE 4.
©KYOIKUSHA NEWTON 5.
THE FIRST TRIAL FLIGHT OF SPACE SHUTTLE (246)
THE MOVEMENT OF SPACE SHUTTLE (247)

△246 ▽247

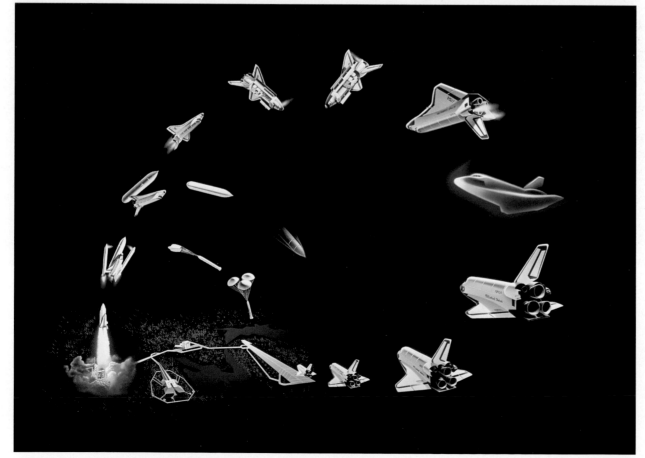

The body

The shoulder runs from the withers – the bony prominence dividing the neck from the back and the highest part of the dorsal spine – down to the point of the shoulder. The shoulder itself should be long and sloping, especially at the upper end. An upright shoulder reduces endurance, as the horse has to do more work to cover the ground, and it cannot help to reduce concussion, which instead is passed on to the rider, making the horse uncomfortable to ride. This is particu-l... lj...1 ...lf...l...l.....l...llll.....l......ll.

The breast lies to the frame of the shoulder between the forelegs. It should be broad and muscular; narrow-breasted horses are weak and lack stamina. The underside of the neck should be concave and not unduly muscular.

The jaws run down to the muzzle. Well-defined, slightly distended nostrils and a large, generous eye are a sign of quality and good breeding. So are alert, well-pricked ears, which should not be too large. Between them lies the poll, leading to the top of neck, the crest, which runs down to the withers and back. The back consists of about eleven of the eighteen dorsal vertebrae, as well as the arches of the corresponding ribs. Behind it lie the loins, which should be strong and well-muscled. These extend to the croup, or rump, which runs down to the tail and its underside, the dock.

Standing behind the horse, the points of the hip ... ... projecting outwards on either side of the backbone, above the flanks. This outwards projection means that they can easily be injured.

Just below the loins, a triangular depression, known as the 'hollow of the flank', is located. This is the highest point of the flank, which stretches downwards from the lumbar spine. The condition of the flank often acts as a guide to the health of the horse; if the horse is sick, it may well be 'tucked up' or distended.

Teeth and age

Age in the horse is determined by examining the six incisors (grinding teeth). The two central incisors are cut when a foal is ten days old and are followed within a month or six weeks by the lateral incisors. The corner incisors follow between six and nine months, to complete the horse's full set of milk teeth.

Walk

The trot (below) is an active, two-time pace, the legs moving in diagonal pairs with a moment of suspension. The rider rises in the saddle for one stride, then sits again.

The walk (right) is the slowest pace of the horse. The animal moves one leg after another in the sequence, left fore, right hind, right fore, left hind, in a regular four-time rhythm.

Trot

Canter

The canter (above) is a three-time pace. The horse moves with long, even strides, leading with either foreleg. The right foreleg sequence is left hind, left diagonal (right hind and left fore), right fore, followed by a moment of suspension.

Gallop

The gallop (left) is a fast canter, which speeds into a four-time pace – the horse's fastest. The right fore sequence is left hind, right hind, left fore and right fore. The moment of suspension, with all legs in the air, is much longer than in the canter.

△248

QED PUBLISHING LTD. 248.

ENGLAND 1.
QED PUBLISHING LTD. 2.
TIME TABLES 3.
BOOK, "THE BOOK OF THE HORSE" 4.
HORSE PACES 5.

U.S.A. 1.
VISUAL GRAPHS OR FUNCTIONS/PROGRESSIONS 3.
NEW YORK TIMES NEWSPAPER (249) 4.
TIME MAGAZINE (250)
CHASE MANHATTAN BANK (U.S.A.) (251) 5.

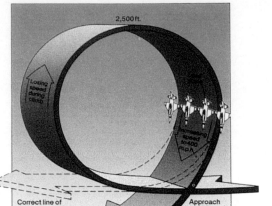

△250

△249

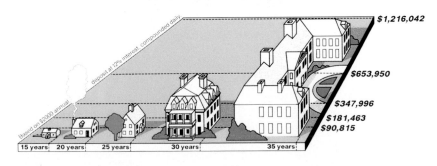

HOW CHASE IRA's BUILD A $2000 TAX SHELTER INTO A MILLION-DOLLAR ESTATE.

△251

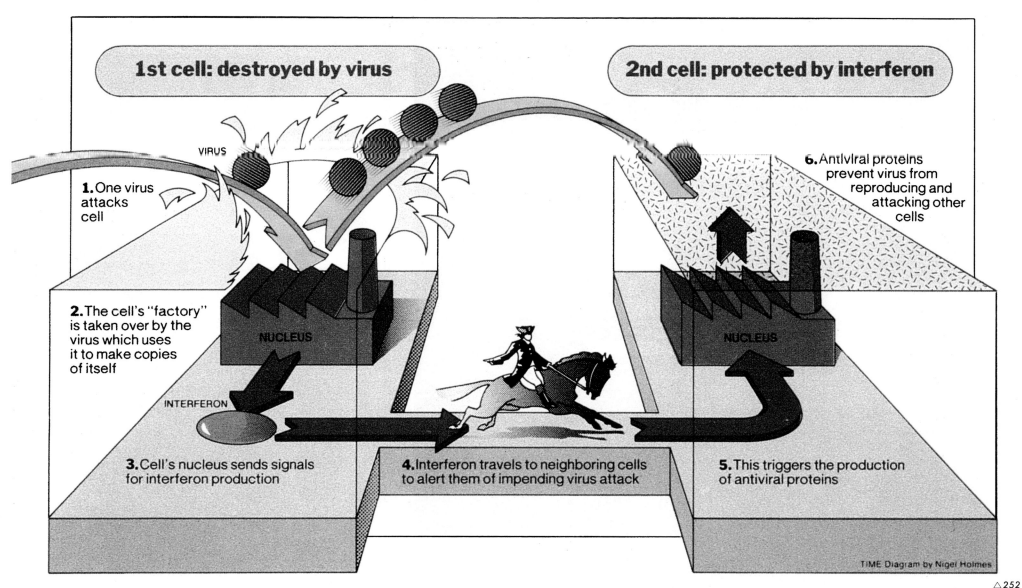

1st cell: destroyed by virus

2nd cell: protected by interferon

VIRUS

1. One virus attacks cell

6. Antiviral proteins prevent virus from reproducing and attacking other cells

2. The cell's "factory" is taken over by the virus which uses it to make copies of itself

NUCLEUS

NUCLEUS

INTERFERON

3. Cell's nucleus sends signals for interferon production

4. Interferon travels to neighboring cells to alert them of impending virus attack

5. This triggers the production of antiviral proteins

TIME Diagram by Nigel Holmes

△252

252. NIGEL HOLMES

1. U.S.A.
3. TIME TABLES
4. TIME MAGAZINE
5. INTERFERON

113

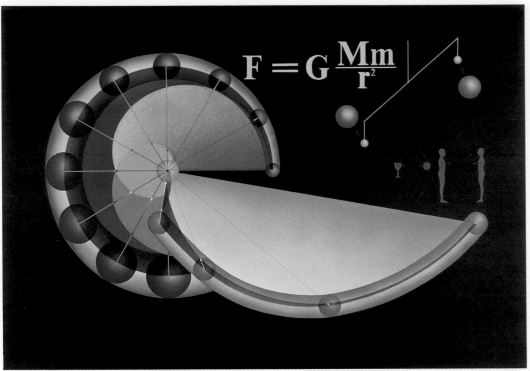

$$F = G\frac{Mm}{r^2}$$

△266 ▽267

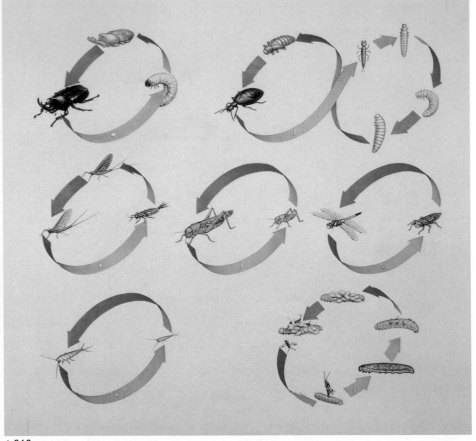

△268

NEWTON 266~268.

JAPAN 1.
ILLUSTRATOR: ETSUKO TAKAHASHI (266) 2.
ILLUSTRATOR: ETSUKO TAKAHASHI (267)
ILLUSTRATOR: AKINORI YOSHITANI (268)
VISUAL GRAPHS OR FUNCTIONS/PROGRESSIONS 3.
NEWTON MAGAZINE 4.
ⒸKYOIKUSHA NEWTON 5.
THE LAW OF UNIVERSAL GRAVITATION $F=G\frac{Mm}{r^2}$ (266)
CATCHING ELECTROMAGNETIC WAVES FROM SPACE (267)
METAMORPHOSES OF INSECTS (268)

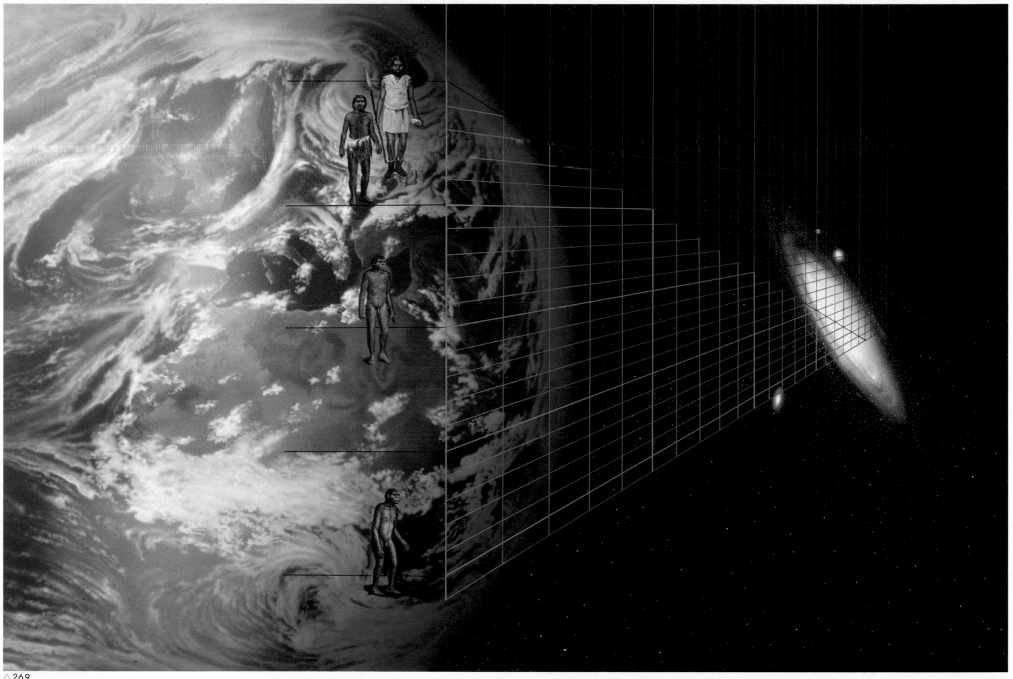

△269

NEWTON MAGAZINE 4.
©KYOIKUSHA NEWTON 5.
THE LIGHT FROM ANDROMEDA NEBULA
REACHES THE EARTH IN 2,100,000 YEARS.

JAPAN 1.
ILLUSTRATOR: MIKIO OKAMOTO 2.
VISUAL GRAPHS OR FUNCTIONS/PROGRESSIONS 3.

△270

△271

△272

NEWTON 273.

1. JAPAN
2. ILLUSTRATOR: KEN SAWADA
3. FLOW CHARTS
4. NEWTON MAGAZINE
5. ©KYOIKUSHA NEWTON
TRANSFERRING SOUND INTO LIGHT (ANALOGUE-DIGITAL TRANSFER)

270~272. NEWTON

1. JAPAN
2. ILLUSTRATOR: MIKIO OKAMOTO (270)
   ILLUSTRATOR: EMIKO FUJIMARU (271)
   ILLUSTRATOR: ETSUKO TAKAHASHI (272)
3. VISUAL GRAPHS OR FUNCTIONS/PROGRESSIONS
4. NEWTON MAGAZINE
5. ©KYOIKUSHA NEWTON
   SUMMER IN JAPAN VISITED BY THE RAINY SEASON AND TYPHOONS (270)
   TIDAL WAVES CAUSED BY SUBMARINE EARTHQUAKES (271)
   BRIGHTNESS OF STARS AND THEIR DISTANCES FROM THE EARTH MEASURED BY THE LIGHT (272)

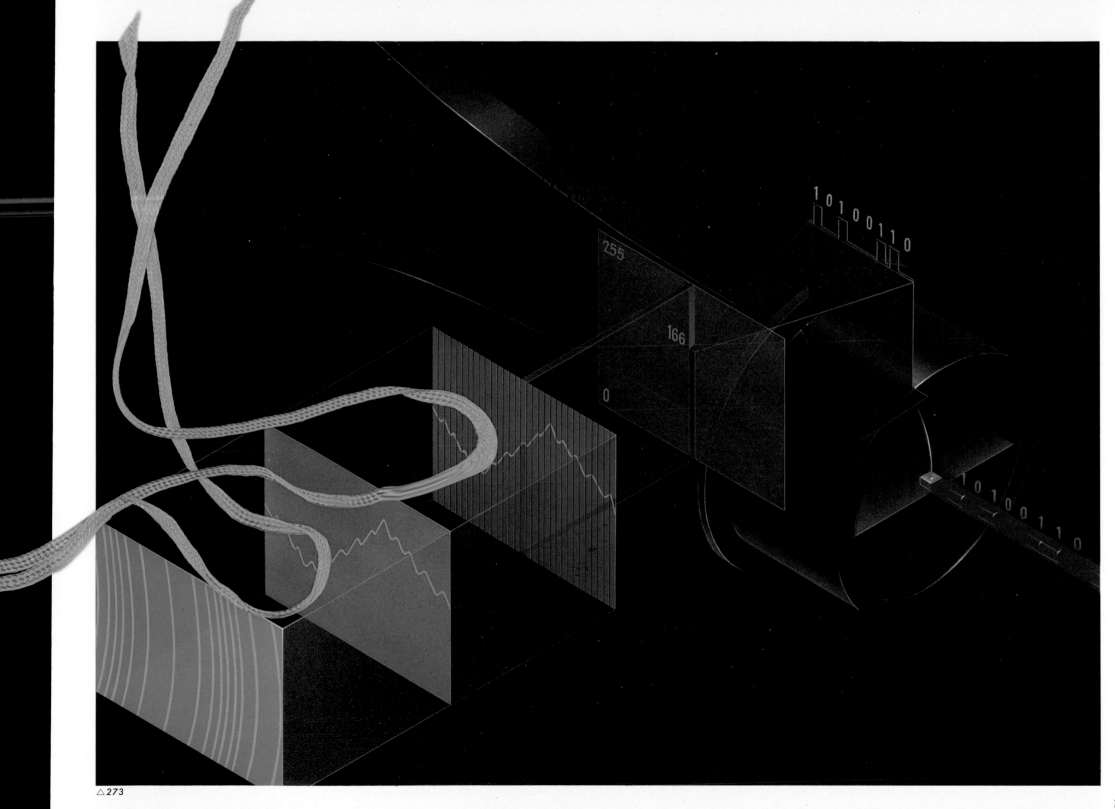

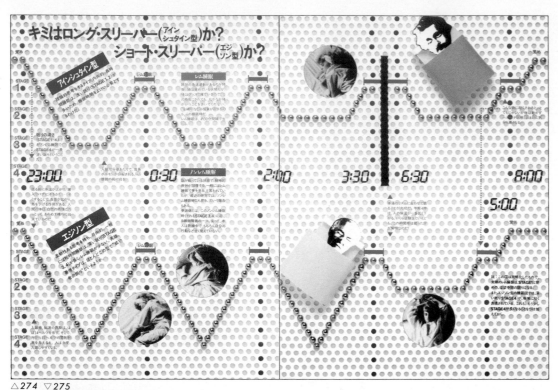

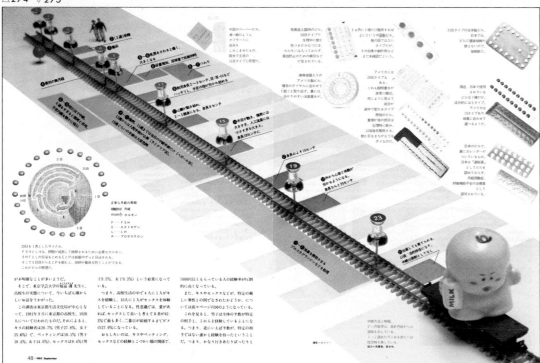

تحسين معدات الصيد وأساليبه

الشبكة الخيشومية التقليدية

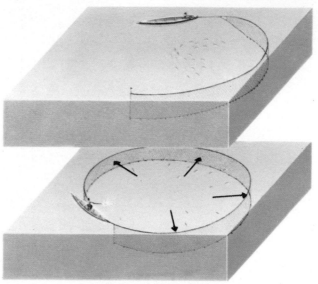

الشبكة الجديدة العا'مة ذات الكيس

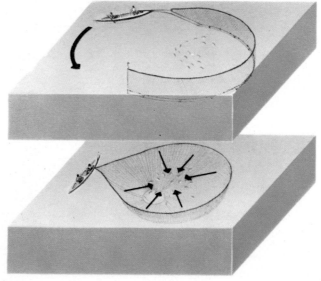

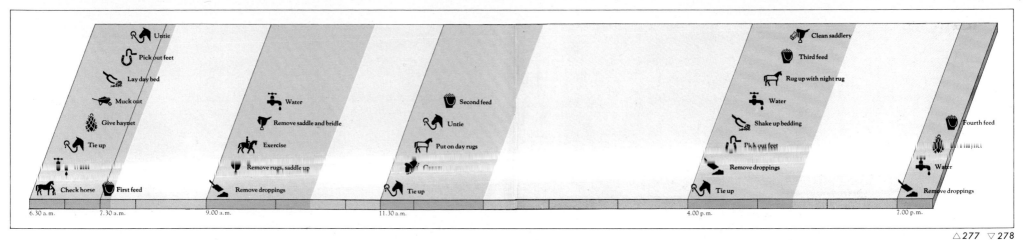

△ 277 ▽ 278

QED PUBLISHING LTD. 277,278.

274,275. TOHRU HIRAYOSHI

276. THE DIAGRAM GROUP

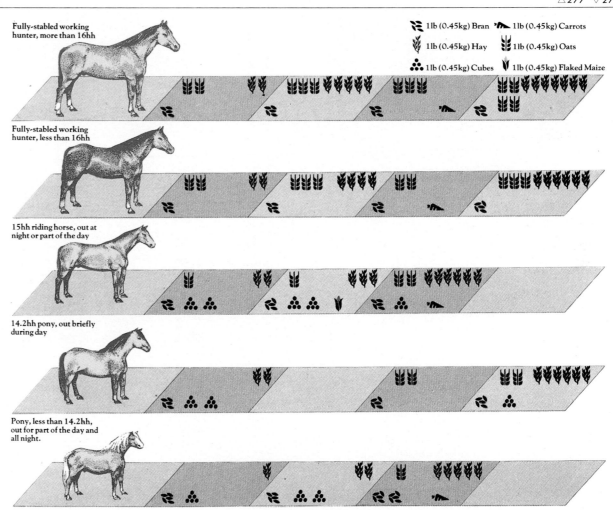

Fully-stabled working hunter, more than 16hh

Fully-stabled working hunter, less than 16hh

15hh riding horse, out at night or part of the day

14.2hh pony, out briefly during day

Pony, less than 14.2hh, out for part of the day and all night.

1lb (0.45kg) Bran   1lb (0.45kg) Carrots
1lb (0.45kg) Hay   1lb (0.45kg) Oats
1lb (0.45kg) Cubes   1lb (0.45kg) Flaked Maize

診療所（医院）建築　　構成：西山 和夫

基本動作 1こま16cm

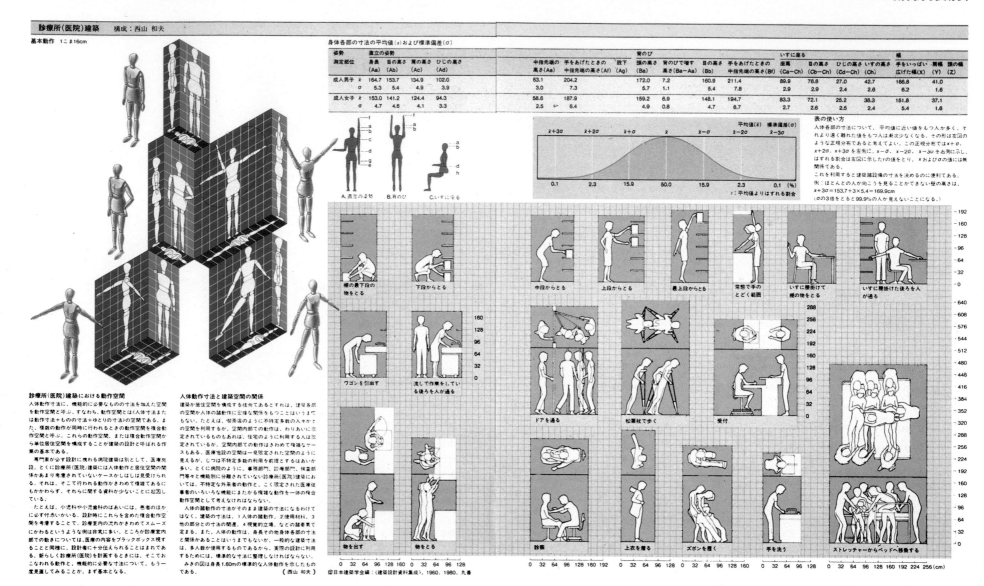

身体各部の寸法の平均値(x̄)および標準偏差(σ)

279. TERUYUKI KUNITO

1. JAPAN
2. VISUAL TECHNOLOGY SYSTEMS
   PRODUCE: TOPPAN IDEA CENTER
   ART DIRECTOR: TERUYUKI KUNITO AND 12 OTHERS

DESIGNER: TOSHITSUGU HIRAMATSU AND 55 OTHERS
ILLUSTRTAOR: TOMOYUKI NARASHIMA AND 37 OTHERS
3. VISUAL GRAPHS OR FUNCTIONS/PROGRESSIONS
4. ENCYCLOPEDIA

5. KODANSHA
PLAN FOR HEALTH CENTERS WHICH WILL ACCOMODATE
PATIENTS' SPECIAL NEEDS (255)

percold hydrogen—chilled the O-rings.

Meantime, the search for physical evidence continued. The recovery operation centered on the right SRB, believed to be on the ocean floor 30 miles off the Florida coast. The Times interest in NASA management procedures was evident early in the week during hearings in Washington. But at that point, there was no indication that the investigators harbored any serious doubts about the space agency's performance. Indeed, the commission gave a particularly rough grilling to Richard C. Cook, an analyst in NASA's budget office who wrote a memo last July warning that O-ring problems could result in disaster—a warning discounted at the time due to Cook's lack of technical experience. "There is little question that flight safety has been and is still being compromised by potential failure of the seals," Cook had written. "Failure during launch would certainly be catastrophic."

In the wake of Cook's testimony, NASA released hundreds of pages of documents relating to the O-ring controversy. Twenty-four times in tests and prior flights, some erosion of O-rings had occurred. Engineers at NASA's Marshall Space Flight center in Huntsville, Ala., and at SRB manufacturer Morton Thiokol Inc. had been working to solve the problem. Thiokol proposed 40 different alternatives, ranging from aluminum or rope in the O-ring gaps to reinforcement of the seal with the same insulation used to protect the steel SRB casing.

An ominous puff of smoke: *Liftoff clue*

tion of the odds and concluded that the chance of an SRB disaster was real if not overwhelming: 1 in 35.

With public attention riveted on its every move, the space agency's handling of the Challenger tragedy tarnished its carefully cultivated image. NASA initially would not even release such facts as the temperature at Kennedy Space Center at launch time. By last week NASA had relented, issuing documents and a detailed time line of the flight of Challenger. Still, the revelations caused dismay in some corners of NASA itself. For instance, film clips of two earlier shuttle missions seemed to show some unexpected flames around the bases of the SRB's, eerily similar to those in portions of Challenger's liftoff.

Another teacher: Even before NASA had determined why teacher Christa McAuliffe and the other six Challenger astronauts had died, and even before it could say what action would be needed to prevent a similar catastrophe, the agency announced that it would send another teacher up in the shuttle, probably Barbara Morgan of McCall, Idaho, McAuliffe's backup. It was a surprising public-relations lapse for the historically sure-footed agency, reinforcing the impression that NASA is up in the air about what to do next. If Rogers's surprise announcement Saturday was any guide, NASA will have to spend the coming months defending itself.

WILLIAM D. MARBACH with MARY HAGER
in Washington, VINCE COPPOLA
in Cape Canaveral and bureau reports

Given NASA's impressive safety record, why did the shuttle flights continue after the O-ring hazard became clear? Officials said they thought the seals would hold and that chances of some sort of catastrophe involving the SRB were slim. But not everyone was a believer. Consultants to the U.S. Air Force disputed NASA's calcula-

A Flaw From the Beginning?

With several theories to consider, investigators focused on Challenger's booster-rocket seals

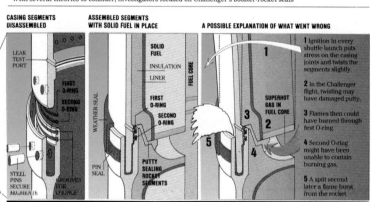

CASING SEGMENTS DISASSEMBLED

LEAK TEST PORT
FIRST O-RING
SECOND O-RING
STEEL PINS SECURE SEGMENTS
GROOVES FOR O-RINGS

ASSEMBLED SEGMENTS WITH SOLID FUEL IN PLACE

SOLID FUEL
INSULATION
LINER
FIRST O-RING
SECOND O-RING
PUTTY SEALING ROCKET SEGMENTS
WEATHER SEAL
FUEL CORE
PIN SEAL

A POSSIBLE EXPLANATION OF WHAT WENT WRONG

SUPERHOT GAS IN FUEL CORE

1 Ignition in every shuttle launch puts stress on the casing joints and twists the segments slightly.

2 In the Challenger flight, twisting may have damaged putty.

3 Flames then could have burned through first O-ring.

4 Second O-ring might have been unable to contain burning gas.

5 A split second later a flame burst from the rocket.

JB OHLSSON—NEWSWEEK

AREA OF DETAIL

NEWSWEEK: FEBRUARY 24, 1986 **59**

△280

△281

Zeroing In on the O Rings

Revelations about Challenger *confront the presidential panel*

Even the celebrities on the blue-ribbon commission charged with investigating the explosion of space shuttle *Challenger* were upstaged last week by a steady stream of disclosures. First, the New York *Times* revealed that NASA internal documents had long ago warned about problems with the crucial O rings, the two giant synthetic-rubber washers that seal each joint between the booster-rocket segments. Next, an article in *Aviation Week & Space Technology* spelled out in extraordinary detail how the starboard booster had caused *Challenger's* external liquid-fuel tank to explode. Then, NASA released pictures showing a mysterious puff of black smoke apparently emerging from the booster at lift-off. The 13-member panel, which includes former Secretary of State William Rogers, Nobel Laureate Physicist Richard Feynman and Astronauts Neil Armstrong and Sally Ride, seemed to have its hands full just keeping up with the new information.

The O rings, already suspect, were spotlighted early in the week when the *Times* printed details of memos leaked by an unnamed solid-fuel rocket expert. One document, written last July by Richard Cook, an agency budget analyst, noted that booster O rings had shown signs of charring on previous missions and could lead to a "catastrophic" situation.

Panel Chairman Rogers reacted defensively to the *Times* scoop. At a commission hearing, he asked Cook rhetorically: "Do you think your engineering experience based on the short time you've been at NASA improved your ability to pass judgment on what others had decided?" Cook, who has no engineering experience, seemed stunned and did not reply to the question but forcefully defended the facts in his memo. Two days later, he told the press that NASA engineers had "whispered" in his ear that because of the O-ring problems they "held their breaths" during every shuttle launch. In other testimony, one of NASA's booster experts, Lawrence Mulloy, conceded that damage to the rings had occurred previously. In the 171 joints from spent booster segments that NASA has examined, he said, six primary rings showed signs of erosion.

The week's most tantalizing story, in *Aviation Week,* reported that the jet of flame from the side of *Challenger's* right booster had either melted or wrenched loose the struts that held the booster to the lower end of the external tank. The booster then pivoted on its still intact upper-attachment fitting and crashed its nose into

CHAIN OF DISASTER?

Nose cap
Main parachutes
Recovery beacon
Forward attachment site
Igniter
Solid-fuel segments

Casing
O rings
Pin
Retainer band
Putty

The explosion may have been triggered by a leak in the joint where two segments of the booster are connected. This leak may have destroyed the struts holding the rocket to the lower end of the external tank.

External tank
Solid-rocket booster
Orbiter

The lower portion of the booster may have rotated outward, causing its nose to crush the top of the external tank.

Hollow core
Aft attachment struts
Aft skirt
Nozzle

TIME Diagram by Joe Lertola

the tank wall. The escaping liquid oxygen and liquid hydrogen ignited, causing the fatal explosion. At week's end NASA had not commented on the report.

Nearly everyone, including the space agency, seemed to be zeroing in on a failure of the right booster rocket, probably at its bottom joint, as the event that initiated the tragedy. The puff of black smoke seen in the NASA photographs and videotape lends support to theories that an O ring was at fault. According to a flight "time-line" compiled by NASA and released at week's end the smoke first appeared .445 seconds after booster ignition. It swirled between the rocket and the external tank, near where the fatal burnthrough seems to have occurred. One

Feynman

TERRY ASHE

solid-rocket specialist noted that because the puff was dark, it probably did not result from combustion of the booster's solid fuel, which produces light-colored smoke. More likely, it came from the burning O ring or the putty placed inside the rings to protect the seal.

What might have caused an O ring in the right booster to fail? Panelist Feynman demonstrated one possibility at the public hearing by conducting a simple experiment in front of the TV cameras. He placed a small section of a ring in a C-clamp and submerged it in a cup of ice water. Then, removing the section and releasing it from the clamp, he concluded, "The resilience is very much reduced when the temperature is reduced." That fact may be significant, because the booster joints that the O rings are supposed to seal shift under the enormous stresses of launch. If the rings are not resilient, they may not seat properly in their grooves, leaving gaps through which the hot gases can escape. Thus, Feynman asked, would the low temperature (38°F) at *Challenger's* lift-off have increased the chance of failure?

NASA's Mulloy conceded that the rings start to lose their resiliency at a temperature of 50°F. But despite some reservations expressed the day before the tragedy by booster manufacturer Morton Thiokol, Mulloy said, NASA technicians had concluded (and Thiokol experts concurred) that the seals would work. Mulloy later volunteered that even if the primary O ring failed, the backup ring "would seat as it has done in the past, even under those temperature conditions."

Mulloy's statement seemed at odds with a 1982 NASA report. The document concluded that because of shifting motions in the boosters 'at launch, the secondary O rings might not seat properly. But NASA decided that the shuttle could keep flying without an assured backup, knowing that the consequences of failure, in the agency's own words, could be "loss of mission, vehicle and crew."

At week's end, as NASA continued to maintain a stiff upper lip about both the rocket's defects and the shuttle's future, Rogers issued a terse but devastating statement: he had advised the President that after only one week of hearings, the commission "has found that the process [of decision making leading up to Challenger's launch] may have been flawed." As a result, NASA was being asked to exclude those of its personnel involved in the launch from any further role on the investigating teams. **—By Jamie Murphy.**
Reported by Jay Branegan/Washington and Jerry Hannifin/Cape Canaveral

18

Acnil
Corporate
Identity

Schema
di orario estivo
linea locale

GIULIO CITTATO 282.

ITALY 1.
FORMATION OF TABLES AND CHARTS 3.
TIME SCHEDULE BOATS 4.
ACTV 5.
GUIDE TO VENICE TRANSPORTATION SYSTEM

↓ ❶ Linea locale · Local line / Lokallinie / Ligne locale · P.Roma/Lido · 200 lire

↓ ❶ Linea locale · Local line / Lokallinie / Ligne locale · Lido/P.Roma · 200 lire

△282

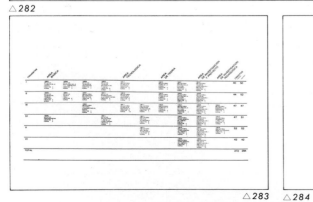

△283

△284

ROBERTO LOPEZ 283, 284.

MEXICO 1.
TABLES AND CHARTS 3.
DIAGRAM FOR A MASTER DEGREE PROGRAM 4.
UNIVERSIDAD AUTONOMA METROPOLITANA 5.

EXCEL PROGRAM CROSS REFERENCE

EXAR	XL¹	XL²	XL³	XL⁴	XL⁵	XL⁶	EXAR STANDARD EXCEL PROCESS
Fairchild		Level 2	Level 5	Level 4	Level 6		XR performs temp cycle instead of thermal shock
Motorola	Level 2	Level 1	Level 3	Level 1	Level 2	Level 3	XR does not perform D.C. tests at 100°C
National		Π I	▲+			Λ I	
Signetics		Supr II Level A	Supr II Level B				XR performs temp cycle instead of thermal shock
Texas Instr.	Pep II	Pep I	Pep III			Pep IV	
Raytheon	A+1		A+2		A+3		

MARKING EXAMPLE

```
XR2206XY
8136        XLZ
Data Code
```

→ X—Grade Designation
   C—Commercial

→ Y—Package Type
   P—Plastic
   N—Ceramic

→ Z—Screening Level
   1 through 6

△285

Tools / Use

Tools	Project Management	Software Development	Hardware Development
Hierarchical File Structure	▓	▢	
Protected File Structure	▓	▢	
Software Version Control	▓	▢	▓
Software Generation Utility	▓	▢	
Line Printer Spooling	▓	▢	
Distributed Job Control	▓	▢	
File Archival	▓		
Time/Date Stamp	▓	▢	
Electronic Mail	▓	▢	
High Level Languages		▢	
HLL Debugger (PSCOPE)		▢	
Assemblers		▢	▓
Screen Oriented Editors		▢	
Link/Locate Utilities		▢	
In-Circuit Emulators		▢	▓
PROM Programmers			▓

△286

285, 286. YASUSHI OKITA

1. U.S.A.
2. YASHI OKITA DESIGN
3. TABLES AND CHARTS
4. BROCHURE
5. EXAR INTEGRATED SYSTEMS, INC. (285)
   INTEL CORPORATION (286)

287. MARCELO VARELA/LAURA LAZZERETTI

1. ARGENTINA
2. ESTUDIO HACHE S.R.L.
3. TABLES AND CHARTS
4. BOOKLET
5. CIBA-GEIGY DE ARGENTINA S.A.
   MEDICAL DIAGNOSIS CHART

DIAGNOSTICOS CIBA-GEIGY
DOLOR DE OIDO

Dr. Diego A. Querol
Médico del Servicio de Otología
del Hospital de Clínicas José de San Martín

		Antecedentes o anamnesis	Dolor	Supuración	Hipoacusia	Síndrome vestibular	Otoscopia
Otitis externa		Rascado de oído Maniobra instrumental Piletas de natación	+ (Aumenta al palpar el pabellón)	Escasa, no mucosa	Sí se oblitera el conducto por edema, sino No	−	Inflamación piel del conducto auditivo externo Inflamación pabellón auricular
Otitis media aguda		Proceso agudo vías areas superiores (Rinitis, faringitis,etc)	+	SI (perforada) (abundante) o No (congestiva)	SI	Posible	Tímpano congestivo Perforación puntiforme
Mastoiditis		Proceso agudo vías areas superiores (Rinitis, faringitis)	+ + Mastoideo		SI	Posible	Tímpano congestivo Caida pared postero superior del conducto
Aerotitis		Descenso en avión u otro cambio brusco de presión (buceo) Con dolor	+	NO	SI	Posible	Tímpano congestivo Pequeños hematomas
Otalgias	Odontógena	Odontológica (Caries, 3er. molar, etc.)	+	NO	NO	NO	Normal
	Disfunción articulación témporo-mandibular	Craqueo articulación Hábito de masticar (chicles, etc.)	+ En puntada	NO	NO	NO	Normal

△287

129

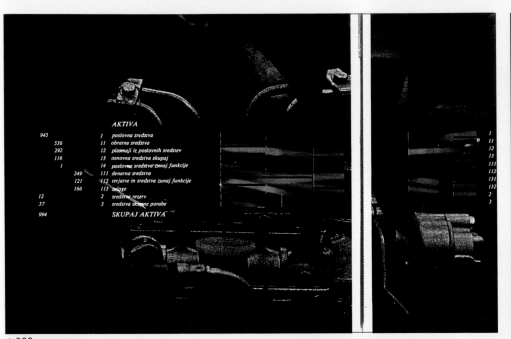

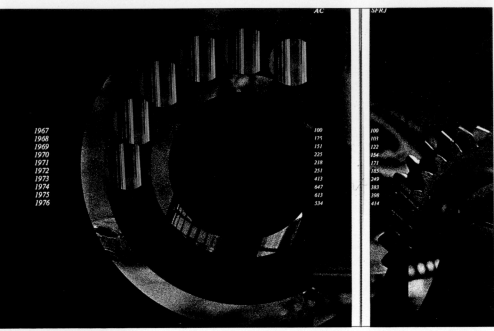

	AKTIVA		AC	SFRJ
945	1 poslovna sredstva	1		
536	11 obratna sredstva	11		
292	12 plasmaji iz poslovnih sredstev	12		
116	13 osnovna sredstva skupaj	13		
1	14 poslovna sredstva zunaj funkcije	111		
249	111 denarna sredstva	112		
121	112 terjatve in sredstva zunaj funkcije	131		
166	113 zaloge	132		
12	2 sredstva rezerv	2		
37	3 sredstva skupne porabe	3		
994	SKUPAJ AKTIVA			

	AC	SFRJ
1967	100	100
1968	175	103
1969	151	122
1970	225	154
1971	218	171
1972	251	185
1973	413	249
1974	647	383
1975	613	398
1976	534	414

△288 △289

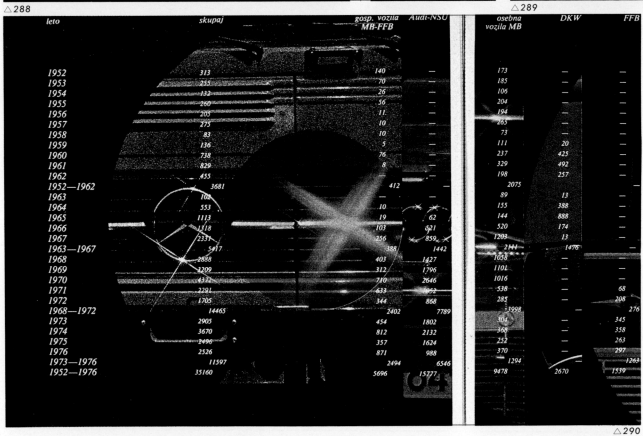

leto	skupaj	gosp. vozila MB-FFB	Audi-NSU	osebna vozila MB	DKW	FFB
1952	313	140	—	173	—	—
1953	255	70	—	185	—	—
1954	132	26	—	106	—	—
1955	260	56	—	204	—	—
1956	205	11	—	194	—	—
1957	275	10	—	265	—	—
1958	83	10	—	73	—	—
1959	136	5	—	111	20	—
1960	738	76	—	237	425	—
1961	829	8	—	329	492	—
1962	455	—	—	198	257	—
1952—1962	3681	412	—	2075	—	—
1963	102	—	—	89	13	—
1964	553	10	—	155	388	—
1965	1113	19	62	144	888	—
1966	1318	103	521	520	174	—
1967	2331	256	859	1203	13	—
1963—1967	5417	388	1442	2111	1476	—
1968	2888	403	1427	1058	—	—
1969	3209	312	1796	1101	—	—
1970	4372	710	2646	1016	—	—
1971	2291	633	1052	538	—	68
1972	1705	344	868	285	—	208
1968—1972	14465	2402	7789	3998	—	276
1973	2905	454	1802	304	—	345
1974	3670	812	2132	368	—	358
1975	2496	357	1624	252	—	263
1976	2526	871	988	370	—	297
1973—1976	11597	2494	6546	1294	—	1263
1952—1976	35160	5696	15777	9478	2670	1539

△290

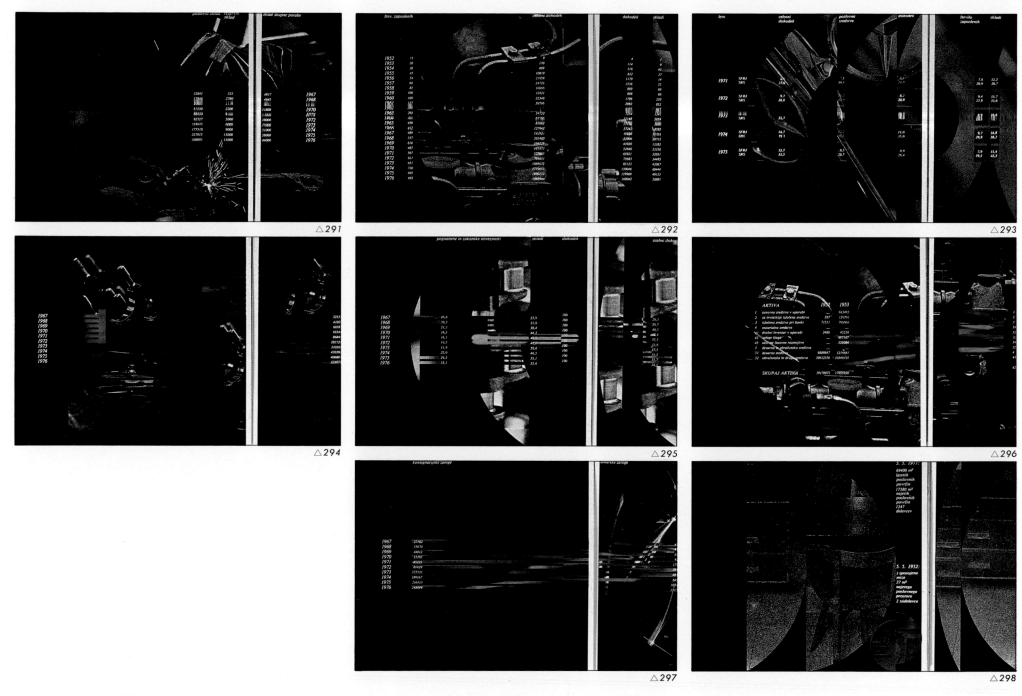

288~298. NINO KOVACEVIC

1. YUGOSLAVIA
3. FORMATION OF TABLES AND CHARTS
4. AUTOCOMMERCE 25 YEARS REPORT
5. AUTO STATISTICS AND BRAND COMPARISONS (288~290)

299~301. UKEI TOMORI

1. JAPAN
3. MAPS
5. EXHIBITED IN SANPO-CHO,
   IBARAGI ETHNOLOGICAL MUSEUM (299)
   NEWTON
   NEW CALENDONIA ISLAND (300)
   SHOGAKUKAN PUBLISHING CO, LTD
   SHIMANTO RIVER IN SHIKOKU, JAPAN (301)

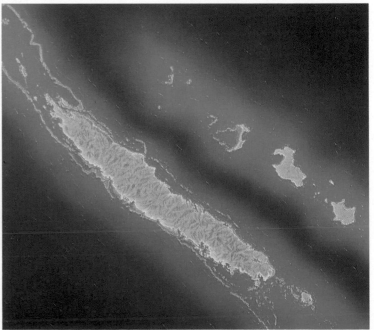

△299   △300

△ 303

302. MINORU TOMODA

1. JAPAN
2. TOMODA MINORU ILLUSTRATION OFFICE
3. MAPS
4. NEWTON MAGAZINE
5. KYOIKUSHA
   THE AEGEAN SEA

NEWTON 303.

JAPAN 1.

MAPS 3.

NEWTON MAGAZINE 4.

ⒸKYOIKUSHA NEWTON 5.

TOPOGRAPHICAL MAP OF LAND AND SEABED

135

△304

304. UKEI TOMORI

1. JAPAN
3. MAPS
4. MAP OF JAPAN
5. HITACHI LTD.
   MAP OF JAPANESE ISLANDS AND
   THEIR RELATIONSHIP TO THE OCEAN FLOOR

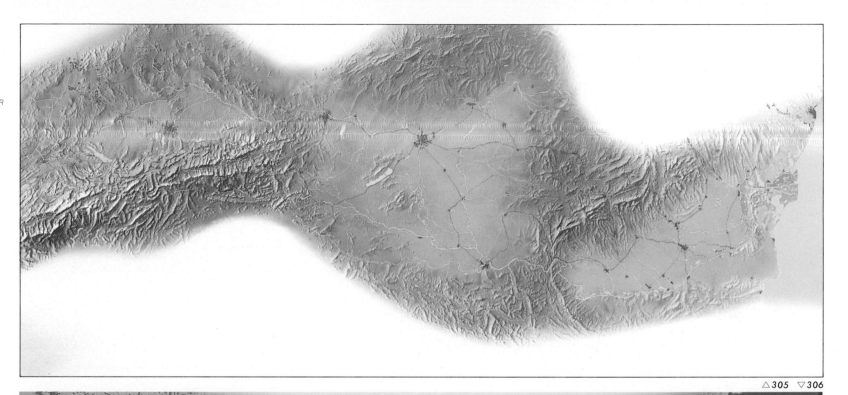

△305 ▽306

305, 306. MINORU TOMODA

1. JAPAN
2. TOMODA MINORU ILLUSTRATION OFFICE
3. MAPS
4. NEWTON MAGAZINE
5. KYOIKUSHA
   THE DANUBE VALLEY (305)
   THE FIVE LAKES, ST. LAURENCE RIVER (306)

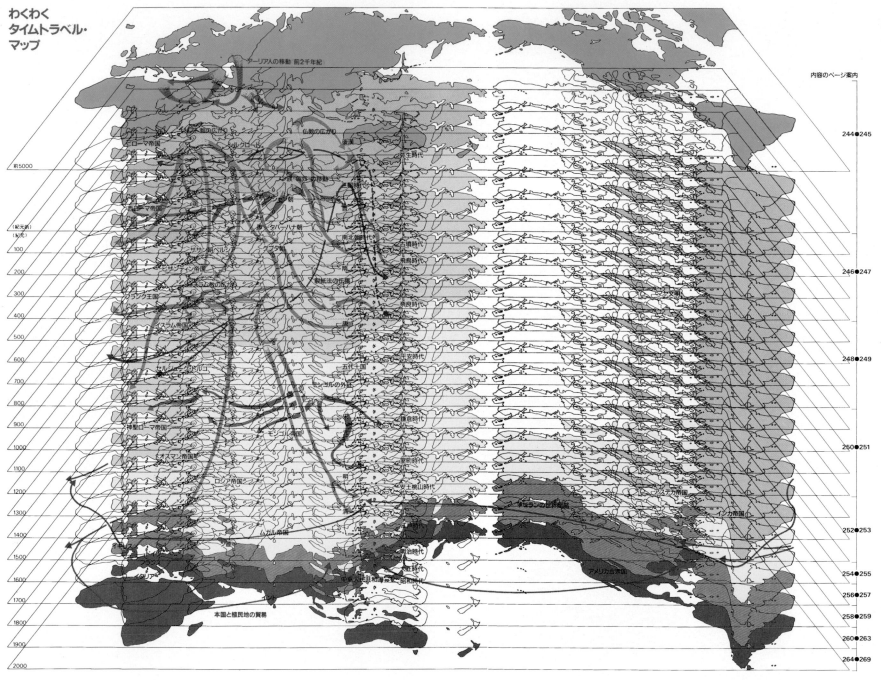

わくわく
タイムトラベル・
マップ

ターリア人の移動 前2千年紀

前5000

(紀元前)
(紀元後)
100
200
300
400
500
600
700
800
900
1000
1100
1200
1300
1400
1500
1600
1700
1800
1900
2000

ローマ帝国
西ローマ帝国
ビザンティン帝国
フランク王国
イスラム帝国
神聖ローマ帝国
オスマン帝国
ロシア帝国（シベリア）
ムガル帝国
イタリア

仏教の広がり
シルクロード
ゲルマン人の移動
製紙法の伝播
モンゴルの外圧
モンゴル帝国

後漢
サータバーハナ朝
サーサーン朝ペルシア
グプタ朝
南北朝時代

弥生時代
古墳時代
飛鳥時代
奈良時代
平安時代
五代十国
明
清
鎌倉時代
室町時代
安土桃山時代
江戸時代
明治時代
大正時代
中華人民共和国・昭和時代

アステカ帝国
テオティワカンの世界観
マヤ文明
インカ帝国
アメリカ合衆国

本国と植民地の貿易

内容のページ案内

244●245

246●247

248●249

250●251

252●253

254●255

256●257

258●259

260●263

264●269

大年表は こんな内容

時代色、豊富な図版、
工夫された文字部分、
世界史の流れが
ビジュアルに
整理されて理解できる

● 中学・高校教科書の内容を網羅した
● 現代史の部分の記述をくわしくした
● 本年表では前5000年から現代までを原始・古代・中世・近世・近代・現代と区別し、そしてそれぞれの時代の色をきめ、年表上でその時代色をフルに活用した。（見開き左右の色帯を参照、世界の時代区分はヨーロッパを基準とした）
● 図版はすべて資料からかき起こし、時代色を使用した、上段にはその時代の風俗画と時代を代表する「美女」を配置した
● 中央の帯で色の濃い部分は、日本・朝鮮・中国で文化が栄えた時期をしめす
● 他に工夫したものに見開き左右下の地図、文字色をかえた重要事項の説明、引用文、付録「年代対応表・年号表・国名県名対照表・年代のあらわし方と暦のいろいろ・ユニカディア歴史図版索引・国名略記」などがある
● この年表の時代区分―時代を区分する方法は歴史観や時代区分の目的の違いによってさまざまある。本年表は原始・古代・中世・近世・近代・現代と区分する方法を用いた。各年代のとり方も各種あるが便宜的に一つにしぼった（3巻285ページ時代区分の項目参照）

時代色

原始
古代
中世
近世
近代
現代

この地図について

❶ 紀元1年から2000年までを100年毎に区切り、21枚の世界地図を重ねた（一番上には紀元前5000年の地図を1枚重ねた）
❷ 世界を大きく6地域と日本に分け各地域を時代色でぬり分けた
❸ アジアは、その全体を中国の時代区分法で統一した
❹ 北アメリカ・アフリカ・オーストラリアの植民地時代以前は時代色を使わなかった
❺ 植民地時代の地域はその本国の時代色に準じた
❻ テーマを限って、地域と時間をこえる文化の流れを地図上に矢印で示した

△307

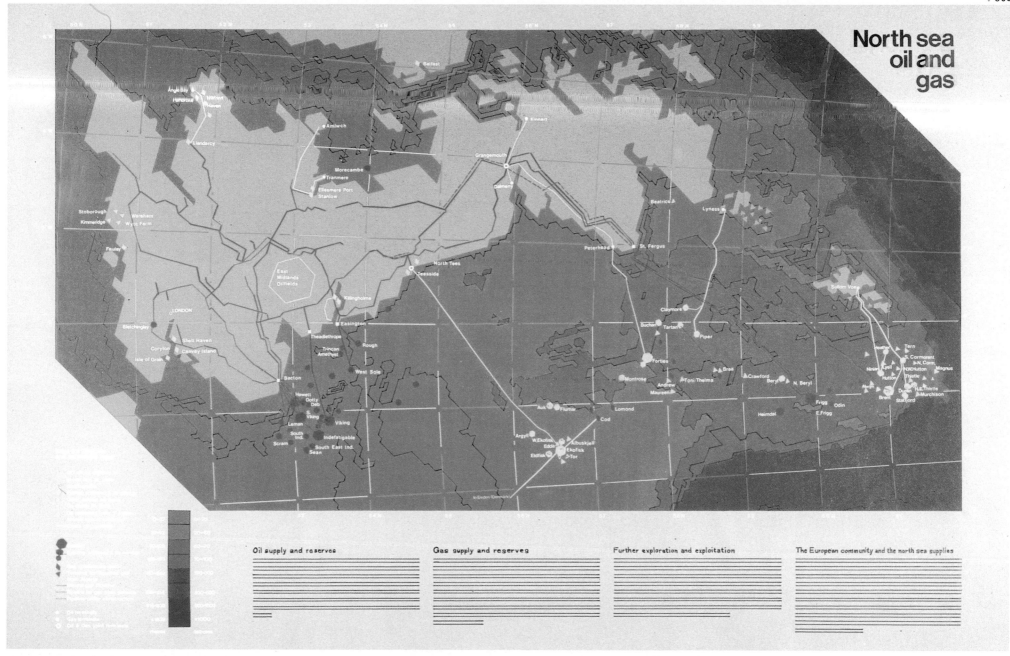

North sea oil and gas

307. YUKIHIRO UNNO/TAKEHIKO OKADA/ISAO KONAKA

1. JAPAN
3. DECORATIVE MAPS
4. ENCYCLOPEDIA, "UNICADIA"
5. KODANSHA
   TIME TRAVEL CHART

EITETSU NOZAWA 308.

U.K. 1.
FREELANCE AT EDITORIAL DESIGN CONSULTANTS LTD. 2.
MAPS 3.
POSTER 4.
NORTH SEA OIL AND GAS 5.
OIL AND GAS SUPPLIES

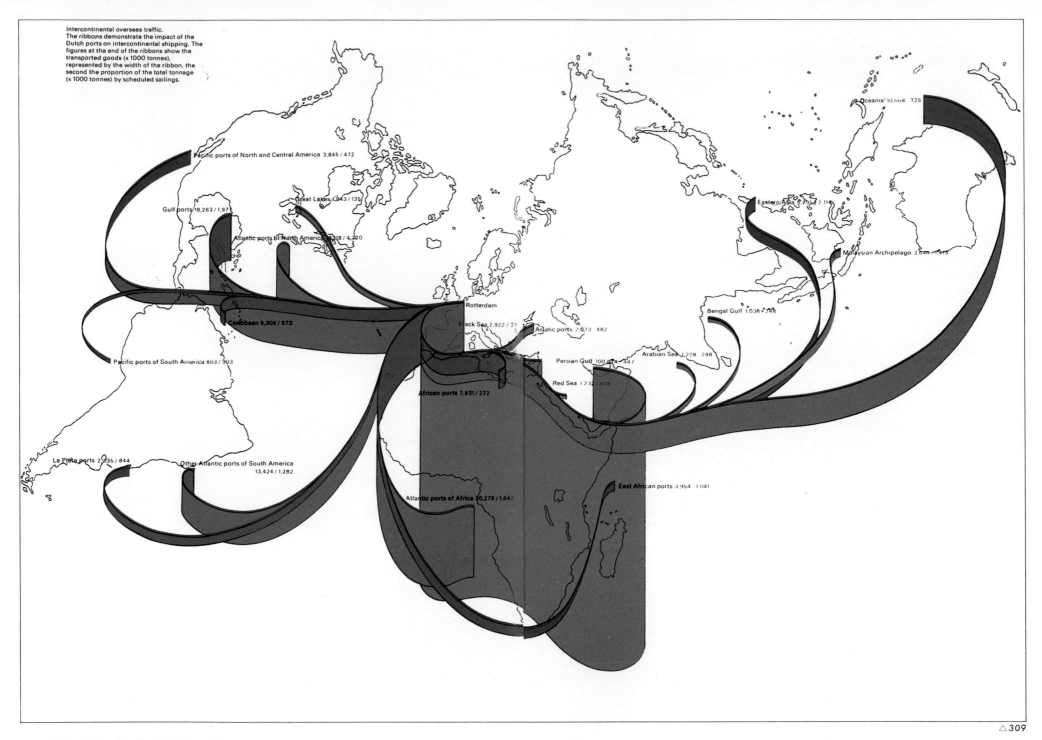

Intercontinental overseas traffic.
The ribbons demonstrate the impact of the
Dutch ports on intercontinental shipping. The
figures at the end of the ribbons show the
transported goods (x 1000 tonnes),
represented by the width of the ribbon, the
second the proportion of the total tonnage
(x 1000 tonnes) by scheduled sailings.

Pacific ports of North and Central America 3,845 / 472

Gulf ports 18,263 / 1,971

Great Lakes 4,343 / 135

Atlantic ports of North America 2,018 / 4,320

Oceania 10,668 / 725

Eastern Asia 2,795 / 2,11

Malaysian Archipelago 3,646 / 1,413

Rotterdam

Caribbean 6,309 / 573

Black Sea 2,922 / 39

Asiatic ports 2,073 / 482

Bengal Gulf 1,038 / 249

Pacific ports of South America 803 / 903

Persian Gulf 100,074 / 347

Arabian Sea 1,228 / 248

Red Sea 1,732 / 408

African ports 7,931 / 272

La Plata ports 2,735 / 844

Other Atlantic ports of South America
13,424 / 1,282

East African ports 3,954 / 1,041

Atlantic ports of Africa 30,279 / 1,642

△309

309. BENNO WISSING/JOHN STEGMEYER

1. U.S.A.
2. THE WISSING GENGLER GROUP, INC.
3. MAPS
4. BOOK ON THE PORT OF ROTTERDAM DEVELOPMENT POTENTIAL
5. THE IMPACT OF DUTCH PORTS ON INTERCONTINENTAL SHIPPING

140

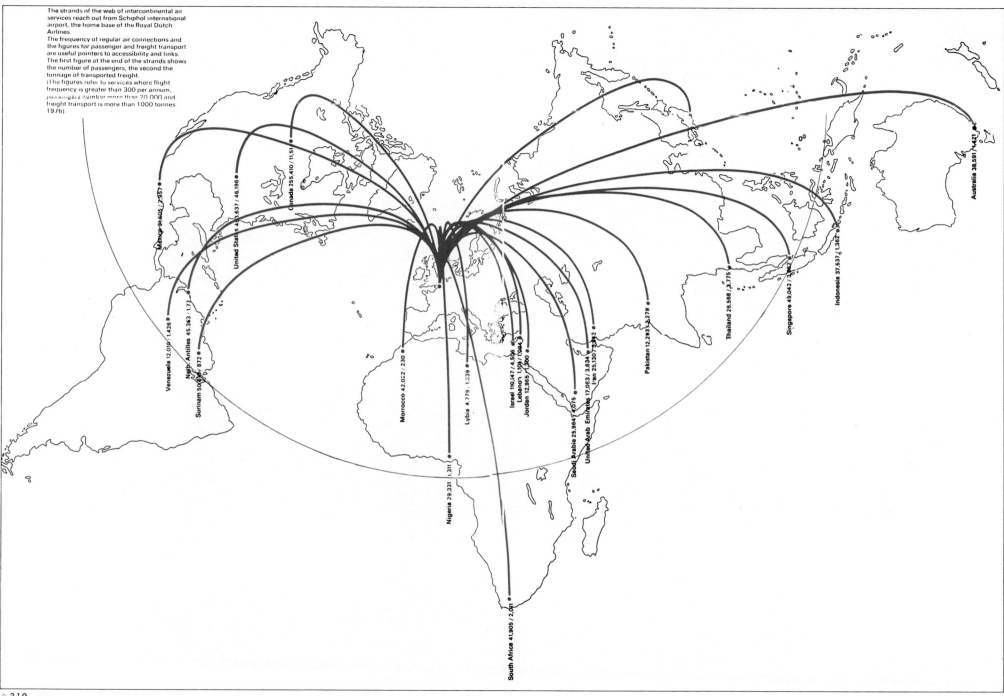

The strands of the web of intercontinental air
services reach out from Schiphol international
airport, the home base of the Royal Dutch
Airlines.
The frequency of regular air connections and
the figures for passenger and freight transport
are useful pointers to accessibility and links.
The first figure at the end of the strands shows
the number of passengers, the second the
tonnage of transported freight.
(The figures refer to services where flight
frequency is greater than 300 per annum,
passengers number more than 20.000 and
freight transport is more than 1000 tonnes
1976).

Mexico 31.505 / 2.957
United States 443.637 / 46.196
Canada 255.410 / 11.51
Venezuela 12.019 / 1.426
Neth. Antilles 45.363 / 1.73
Surinam 50.016 / 872
Morrocco 42.022 / 230
Lybia 4.779 / 1.239
Israel 110.147 / 4.596
Lebanon 1.091 / 1.084
Jordan 12.965 / 1.200
Saudi Arabia 25.964 / 4.075
United Arab Emirates 17.053 / 3.634
Iran 25.130 / 3.343
Pakistan 12.283 / 2.279
Nigeria 29.331 / 1.311
South Africa 41.905 / 2.061
Thailand 26.568 / 2.775
Singapore 49.042 / 6.22
Indonesia 37.537 / 1.362
Australia 38.591 / 1.421

△310

BENNO WISSING/JOHN STEGMEYER 310.

INTER CONTINENTAL AIR SERVICES FROM SCHIPHOL INTERNATIONAL AIRPORT 5.

MAPS 3.   U.S.A. 1.
BOOK ON THE PORT OF ROTTERDAM DEVELOPMENT POTENTIAL 4.   THE WISSING GENGLER GROUP. INC. 2.

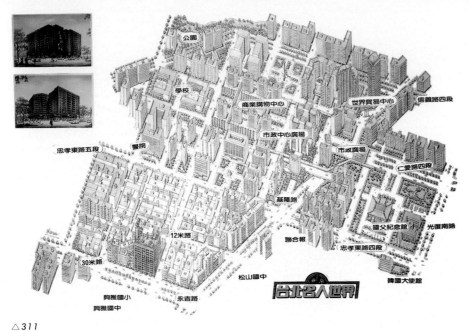

△311

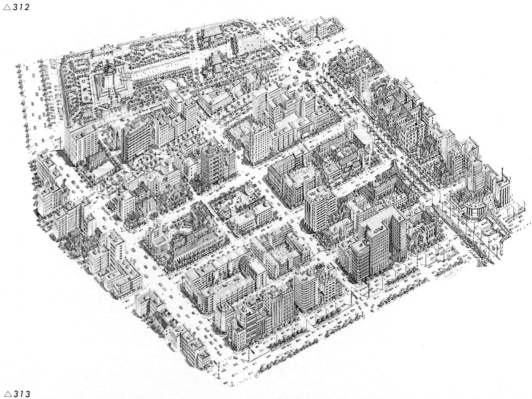

△312

△313

311～313. HWONG KINGDER

1. TAIWAN R.O.C.
3. DECORATIVE MAPS
4. PAMPHLET
5. CITY DEVELOPMENT AND BUILDING LOCATION CHARTS (311～313)

314, 315. HWONG KINGDER

1. TAIWAN R.O.C.
3. DECORATIVE MAPS
4. PAMPHLET
5. BUILDING LOCATION CHARTS

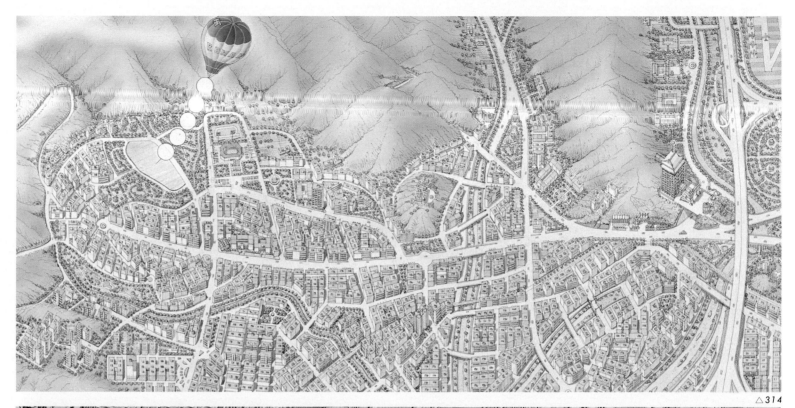

△314

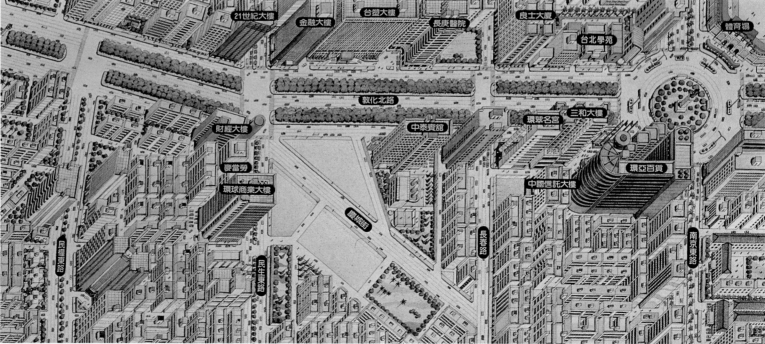

△315

143

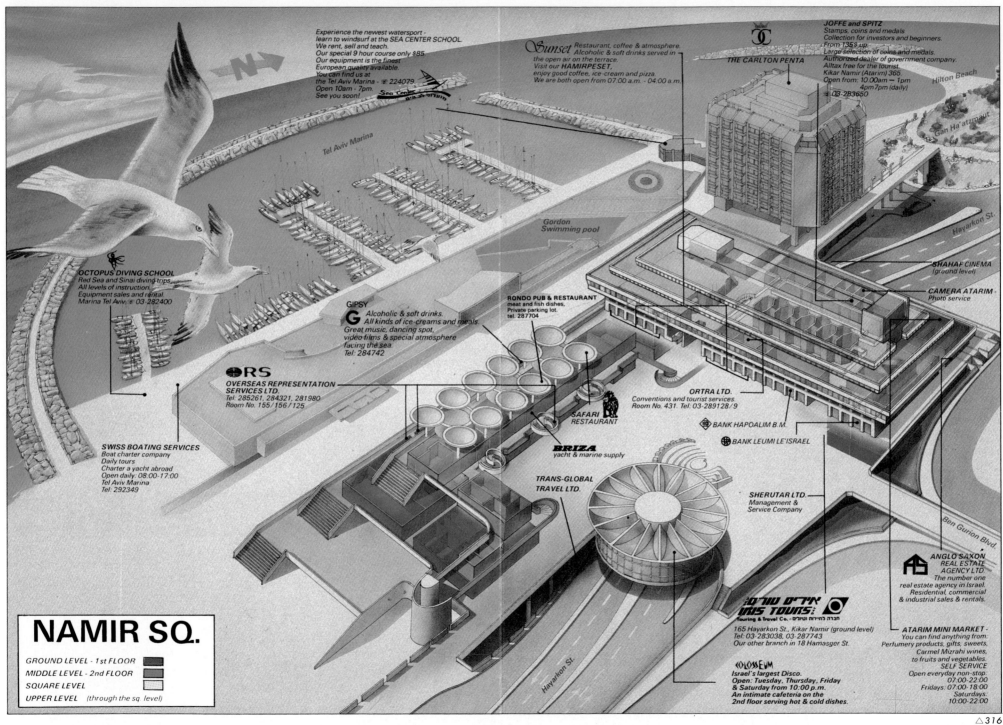

Experience the newest watersport -
learn to windsurf at the SEA CENTER SCHOOL.
We rent, sell and teach.
Our special 9 hour course only $85.
Our equipment is the finest
European quality available.
You can find us at
the Tel Aviv Marina - ☎ 224079
Open 10am - 7pm.
See you soon! **Sea Center**

Sunset Restaurant, coffee & atmosphere.
Alcoholic & soft drinks served in
the open air on the terrace.
Visit our **HAMIRPESET**,
enjoy good coffee, ice-cream and pizza.
We are both open from 07:00 a.m. - 04:00 a.m.

JOFFE and SPITZ
Stamps, coins and medals
Collection for investors and beginners.
From 135$ up.
Large selection of coins and medals.
Authorized dealer of government company.
Alltax free for the tourist.
Kikar Namir (Atarim) 365.
Open from: 10.00am — 1pm
4pm7pm (daily)
☎ 03-2B3650

THE CARLTON PENTA

Hilton Beach

Gan Ha'atzmaut

Tel Aviv Marina

Gordon Swimming pool

Hayarkon St.

OCTOPUS DIVING SCHOOL
Red Sea and Sinai diving trips.
All levels of instruction.
Equipment sales and rental.
Marina Tel Aviv. ☎ 03-282400

GIPSY
G Alcoholic & soft drinks.
All kinds of ice-creams and meals.
Great music, dancing spot,
video films & special atmosphere
facing the sea.
Tel: 284742

RONDO PUB & RESTAURANT
meat and fish dishes,
Private parking lot.
tel. 287704

SHAHAF CINEMA
(ground level)

CAMERA ATARIM -
Photo service

○RS
**OVERSEAS REPRESENTATION
SERVICES LTD.**
Tel: 285261, 284321, 281980
Room No. 155/156/125

**SAFARI
RESTAURANT**

ORTRA LTD.
Conventions and tourist services.
Room No. 431. Tel: 03-289128/9

◈ **BANK HAPOALIM B.M.**

SWISS BOATING SERVICES
Boat charter company
Daily tours
Charter a yacht abroad
Open daily: 08:00-17:00
Tel Aviv Marina
Tel: 292349

BRIZA
yacht & marine supply

**TRANS-GLOBAL
TRAVEL LTD.**

⊕ **BANK LEUMI LE'ISRAEL**

SHERUTAR LTD.
Management &
Service Company

Ben Gurion Blvd.

**ANGLO SAXON
REAL ESTATE
AGENCY LTD.**
The number one
real estate agency in Israel.
Residential, commercial
& industrial sales & rentals.

אירים טורס:
IRIS TOURS ◉
Touring & Travel Co. - וטיולים
165 Hayarkon St., Kikar Namir (ground level)
Tel: 03-283038, 03-287743
Our other branch in 18 Hamasger St.

COLOSSEVM
Israel's largest Disco.
Open: Tuesday, Thursday, Friday
& Saturday from 10:00 p.m.
An intimate cafeteria on the
2nd floor serving hot & cold dishes.

ATARIM MINI MARKET -
You can find anything from:
Perfumery products, gifts, sweets,
Carmel Mizrahi wines,
to fruits and vegetables.
SELF SERVICE
Open everyday non-stop:
07:00-22:00
Fridays: 07:00-18:00
Saturdays:
10:00-22:00

Hayarkon St.

NAMIR SQ.

GROUND LEVEL - 1st FLOOR
MIDDLE LEVEL - 2nd FLOOR
SQUARE LEVEL
UPPER LEVEL *(through the sq. level)*

△316

144

316. SHLOMO COHEN

1. ISRAEL   3. DECORATIVE MAPS
2. POINTOUT LTD.   4. TOURIST MAP PUBLISHED BY POINTOUT

ROLF CIGLER/HARALD CIGLER 317.

DECORATIVE MAPS 3.   SWITZERLAND 1.
ECOLOGY-ILLUSTRATION FOR RINGIER PUBLISHERS 85 4.   ATELIER CIGLER. 2.

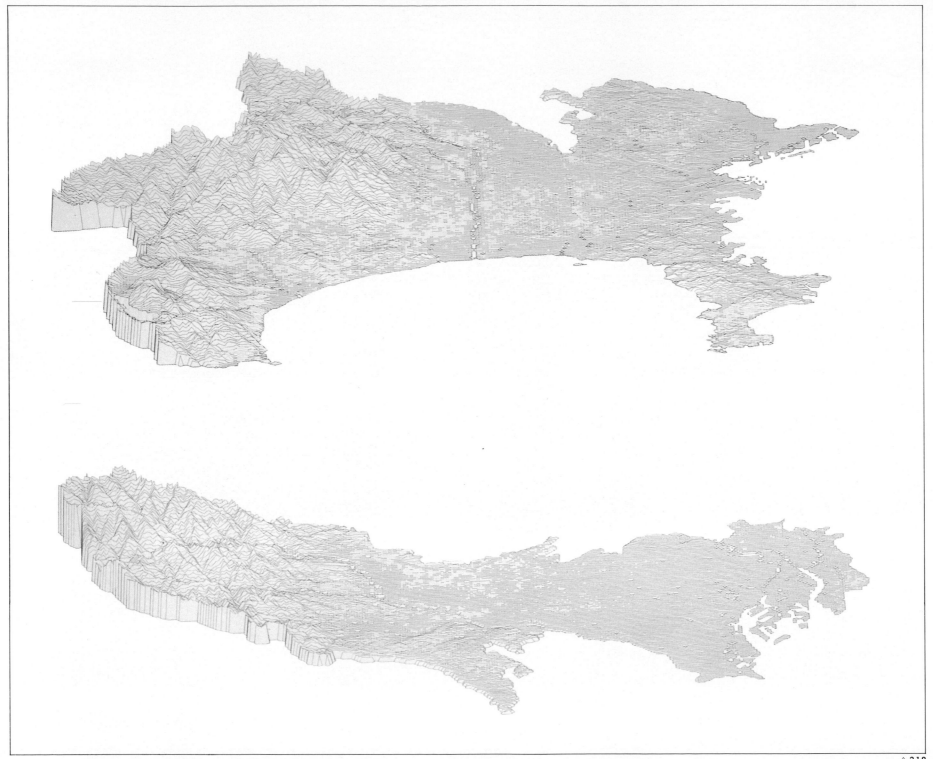

△318

1. JAPAN
2. NIPPON GRAPHIC MAP CORP., LTD. ©CARTOGRAPHER H. SUZAKI
3. MAPS
4. GRAPHIC MAP
5. CENTRAL TOKYO

DECORATIVE MAPS 3.
GRAPHIC MAP 4.
KORAKUEN AMUSEMENT PARK 5.
RIDE LOCATION MAP

JAPAN 1.
NIPPON GRAPHIC MAP CORP., LTD. 2.
©CARTOGRAPHER H. SUZAKI

EXPO'85

テーマ：人間・居住・環境と科学技術　期間：昭和60年3月17日—9月16日　場所：茨城県筑波研究学園都市

科学万博 ▲つくば'85

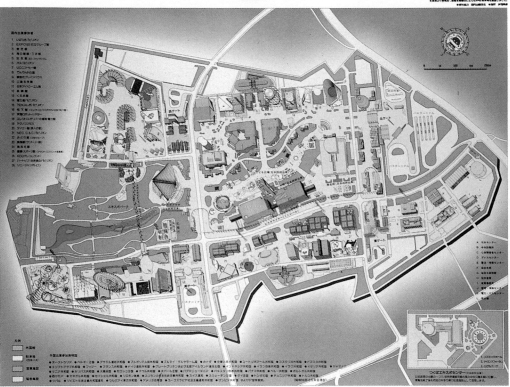

1985

	MON TUE WED THU FRI SAT	MON TUE WED THU FRI SAT	MON TUE WED THU FRI SAT	MON TUE WED THU FRI SAT	MON TUE WED THU FRI SAT
1 JANUARY	1 2 3 4 5	6 7 8 9 10 11 12	13 14 15 16 17 18 19	20 21 22 23 24 25 26	27 28 29 30 31
2 FEBRUARY	1 2	3 4 5 6 7 8 9	10 11 12 13 14 15 16	17 18 19 20 21 22 23	24 25 26 27 28
3 MARCH	1 2	3 4 5 6 7 8 9	10 11 12 13 14 15 16	17 18 19 20 21 22 23	24 25 26 27 28 29 30 31
4 APRIL	1 2 3 4 5 6	7 8 9 10 11 12 13	14 15 16 17 18 19 20	21 22 23 24 25 26 27	28 29 30
5 MAY	1 2 3 4	5 6 7 8 9 10 11	12 13 14 15 16 17 18	19 20 21 22 23 24 25	26 27 28 29 30 31
6 JUNE	1	2 3 4 5 6 7 8	9 10 11 12 13 14 15	16 17 18 19 20 21 22	23 24 25 26 27 28 29 30
7 JULY	1 2 3 4 5 6	7 8 9 10 11 12 13	14 15 16 17 18 19 20	21 22 23 24 25 26 27	28 29 30 31
8 AUGUST	1 2 3	4 5 6 7 8 9 10	11 12 13 14 15 16 17	18 19 20 21 22 23 24	25 26 27 28 29 30 31
9 SEPTEMBER	1 2 3 4 5 6 7	8 9 10 11 12 13 14	15 16 17 18 19 20 21	22 23 24 25 26 27 28	29 30
10 OCTOBER	1 2 3 4 5	6 7 8 9 10 11 12	13 14 15 16 17 18 19	20 21 22 23 24 25 26	27 28 29 30 31
11 NOVEMBER	1 2	3 4 5 6 7 8 9	10 11 12 13 14 15 16	17 18 19 20 21 22 23	24 25 26 27 28 29 30
12 DECEMBER	1 2 3 4 5 6 7	8 9 10 11 12 13 14	15 16 17 18 19 20 21	22 23 24 25 26 27 28	29 30 31

このカレンダーは、筑輪公共企業の補助を受けて制作しました。　　　　　財団法人 国際科学技術博覧会協会

△320

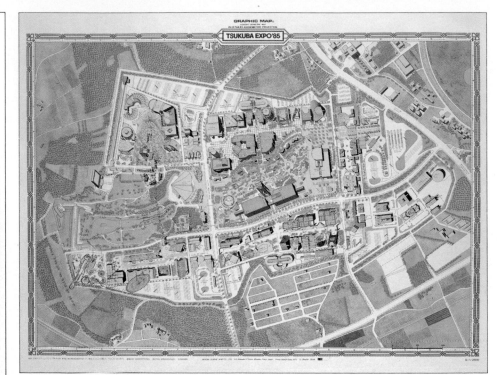

△321

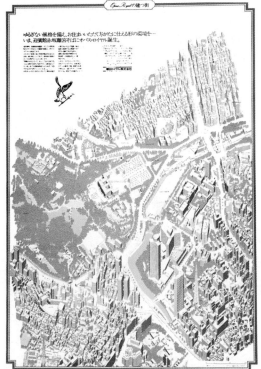

△322

320～322. NIPPON GRAPHIC MAP CORP., LTD.

1. JAPAN
2. NIPPON GRAPHIC MAP CORP., LTD.
   ⓒCARTOGRAPHER H. SUZAKI
3. MAPS
4. TSUKUBA EXPO '85 (320, 321)
5. A BIRD'S-EYE VIEW OF A CITY IN TOKYO (322)

EXPO '85

テーマ：人間・居住・環境と科学技術　期間：昭和60年3月17日〜9月16日　場所：茨城県筑波研究学園都市

科学万博  つくば'85

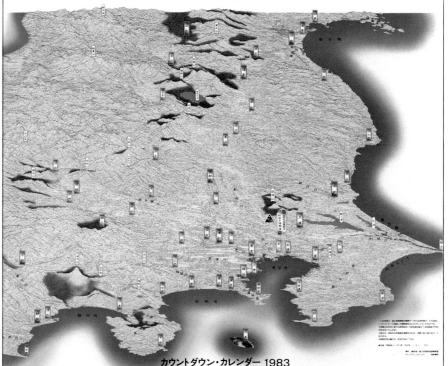

カウントダウン・カレンダー 1983

△323

EXPO '85

テーマ：人間・居住・環境と科学技術　期間：昭和60年3月17日〜9月16日　場所：茨城県筑波研究学園都市

科学万博 つくば'85

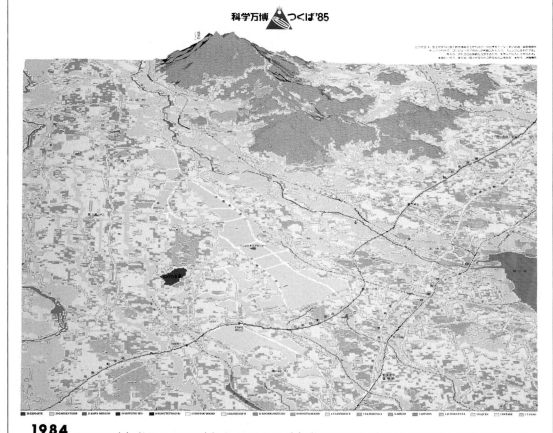

1984

△324

323, 324. NIPPON GRAPHIC MAP CORP., LTD.

1. JAPAN
2. NIPPON GRAPHIC MAP CORP., LTD.　©CARTOGRAPHER H. SUZAKI
3. MAPS
4. TSUKUBA EXPO '85
5. EXPO '85 MAP AND CALENDAR (324)

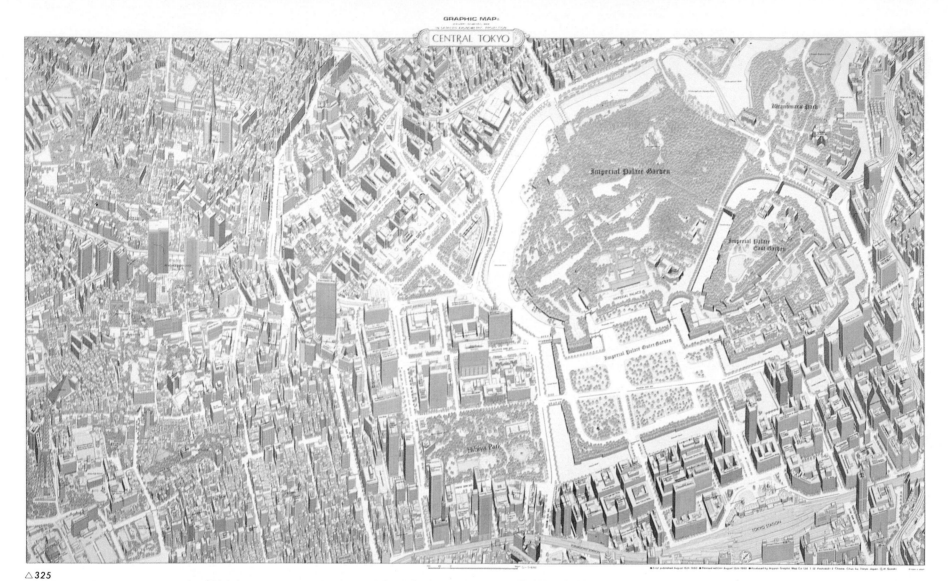

△ 325

△ 326

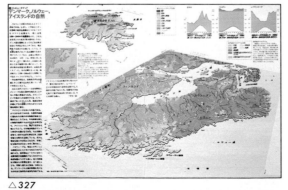

△ 327

325～327. NIPPON GRAPHIC MAP CORP., LTD.

1. JAPAN
2. NIPPON GRAPHIC MAP CORP., LTD. ©CARTOGRAPHER H. SUZAKI
3. MAPS
5. CENTRAL TOKYO (325)
   TERRAIN OF SWEDEN AND FINLAND (326)
   TERRAIN OF DENMARK, NORWAY, AND ICELAND (327)

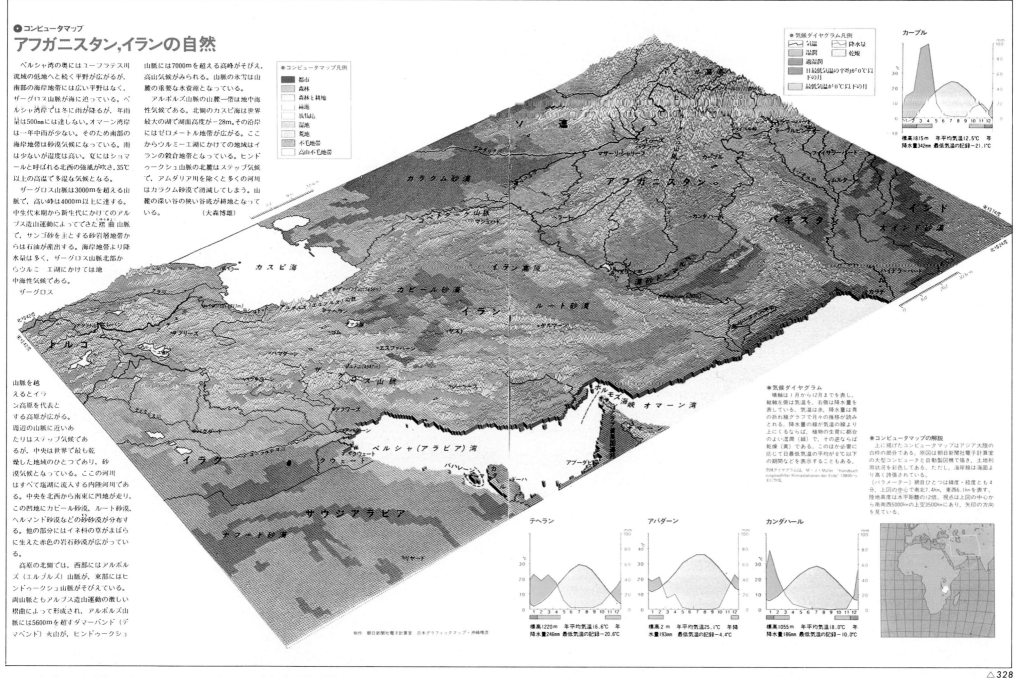

アフガニスタン,イランの自然

ペルシャ湾の奥にはユーフラテス川流域の低地へと続く平野が広がるが、南部の海岸地帯には広い平野はなく、ザーグロス山脈が海に迫っている。ペルシャ湾岸では冬に雨が降るが、年雨量は500mmには達しない。オマーン湾岸は一年中雨が少ない。そのため南部の海岸地帯は砂漠気候になっている。雨は少ないが湿度は高い。夏にはショマールと呼ばれる北西の強風が吹き、35℃以上の高温で多湿な気候となる。

ザーグロス山脈は3000mを超える山脈で、高い峰は4000m以上に達する。中生代末期から新生代にかけてのアルプス造山運動によってできた褶曲山脈で、サンゴ砂を主とする砂岩層地帯からは石油が産出する。海岸地帯より降水量は多く、ザーグロス山脈北部からウルミー工湖にかけては地中海性気候である。

ザーグロス山脈には7000mを超える高峰がそびえ、高山気候がみられる。山脈の氷雪は山麓の重要な水資源となっている。

アルボルズ山脈の山麓一帯は地中海性気候である。北側のカスピ海は世界最大の湖で湖面高度が−28m。その沿岸にはゼロメートル地帯が広がる。ここからウルミー工湖にかけての地域はイランの穀倉地帯となっている。ヒンドゥークシュ山脈の北側はステップ気候で、アムダリア川を除くと多くの河川はカラクム砂漠で消滅してしまう。山麓の深い谷の狭い谷底が耕地となっている。

（大森博雄）

山脈を越えるとイラン高原を代表とする高原が広がる。周辺の山脈に近いあたりはステップ気候であるが、中央は世界で最も乾燥した地域のひとつであり、砂漠気候となっている。ここの河川はすべて塩湖に流入する内陸河川である。中央を北西から南東に凹地が走り、この凹地にカビール砂漠、ルート砂漠、ヘルマンド砂漠などの砂岩砂漠が分布する。他の部分にはイネ科の草がまばらに生えた赤色の岩石砂漠が広がっている。

高原の北側では、西部にはアルボルズ（エルブルズ）山脈が、東部にはヒンドゥークシュ山脈がそびえている。両山脈ともアルプス造山運動の激しい褶曲によって形成され、アルボルズ山脈には5600mを超すダマーバンド（デマベンド）火山が、ヒンドゥークシュ

● コンピュータマップ凡例
- 都市
- 森林
- 森林と耕地
- 耕地
- 荒れ地
- 湿地
- 荒地
- 不毛地帯
- 高山不毛地帯

● 気候ダイヤグラム凡例
- 気温
- 降水量
- 湿潤
- 乾燥
- 過湿潤
- 日最低気温の平均が「0℃以下の月」
- 最低気温が「0℃以下の月」

カーブル
標高1815m　年平均気温12.5℃　年降水量342mm　最低気温の記録−21.1℃

テヘラン
標高1220m　年平均気温16.6℃　年降水量246mm　最低気温の記録−20.6℃

アバダーン
標高2m　年平均気温25.1℃　年降水量193mm　最低気温の記録−4.4℃

カンダハール
標高1055m　年平均気温18.0℃　年降水量186mm　最低気温の記録−10.0℃

● 気候ダイヤグラム
横軸は1月から12月までを表し、縦軸左側は気温を、右側は降水量を表している。気温は赤、降水量は青の折れ線グラフで月々の推移が読みとれる。降水量の線が気温の線より上にくるならば、植物の生育に都合のよい湿潤（緑）で、その逆ならば乾燥（黄）である。このほか必要に応じて日最低気温の平均が0℃以下の期間などを表示することもある。

気候ダイヤグラムは、M・J・Müller "Handbuch ausgewählter Klimastationen der Erde" 1980から作成。

● コンピュータマップの解説
上に掲げたコンピュータマップはアジア大陸の白枠の部分である。原図は朝日新聞社電子計算室の大型コンピュータと自動製図機で描き、土地利用状況を色彩してある。ただし、海岸線は海面より高く誇張されている。

（パラメーター）網目ひとつは緯度・経度とも4分、上図の中心で南北7.4km、東西6.1kmを表す。陸地高度は水平距離の12倍。視点は上図中心から南南西5000kmの上空3500kmにあり、矢印の方向を見ている。

制作 朝日新聞社電子計算室　日本グラフィックマップ・共崎埼原

328. NIPPON GRAPHIC MAP CORP., LTD.

1. JAPAN
2. NIPPON GRAPHIC MAP CORP., LTD.　©CARTOGRAPHER H. SUZAKI
3. MAPS
5. TERRAIN OF AFGHANISTAN AND IRAN

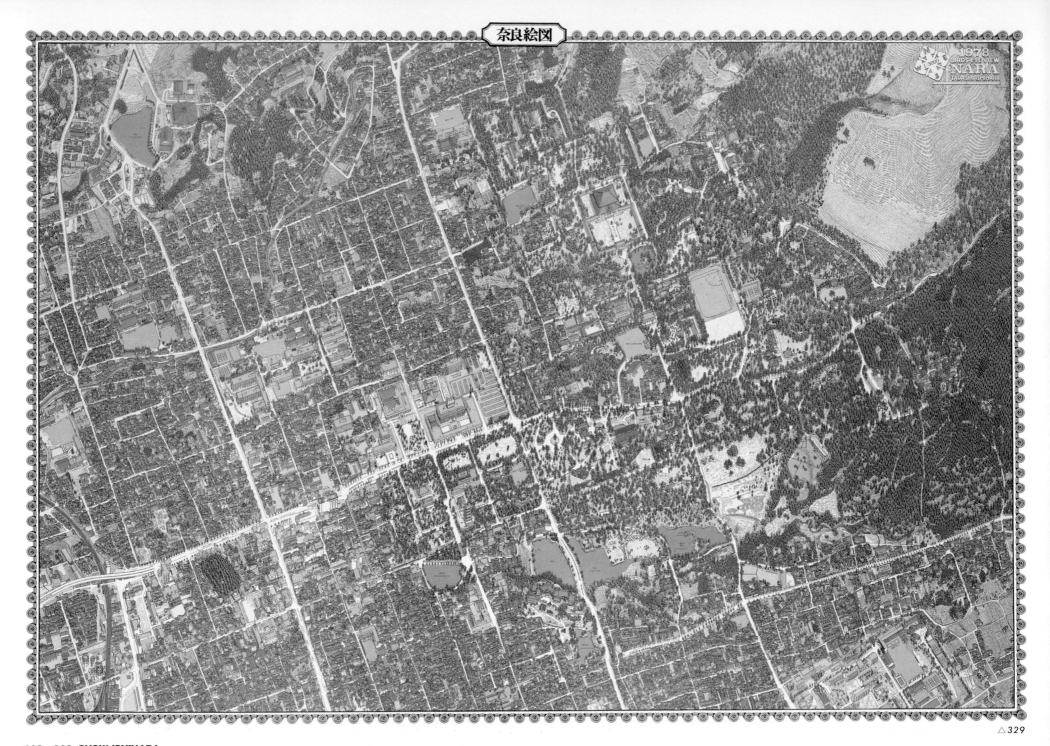

△329

329～332. SHOW ISHIHARA

1. JAPAN

3. MAPS (BIRD'S-EYE)

4. POSTER

5. MAP OF NARA, JAPAN (329)

　TODAIJI TEMPLE AND GROUNDS (330)

　KYOTO, JAPAN (331-332)

同志社大学
DOSHISHA
UNIV.

KYOTO OLD IMPERIAL PALACE

NATIONAL GARDEN

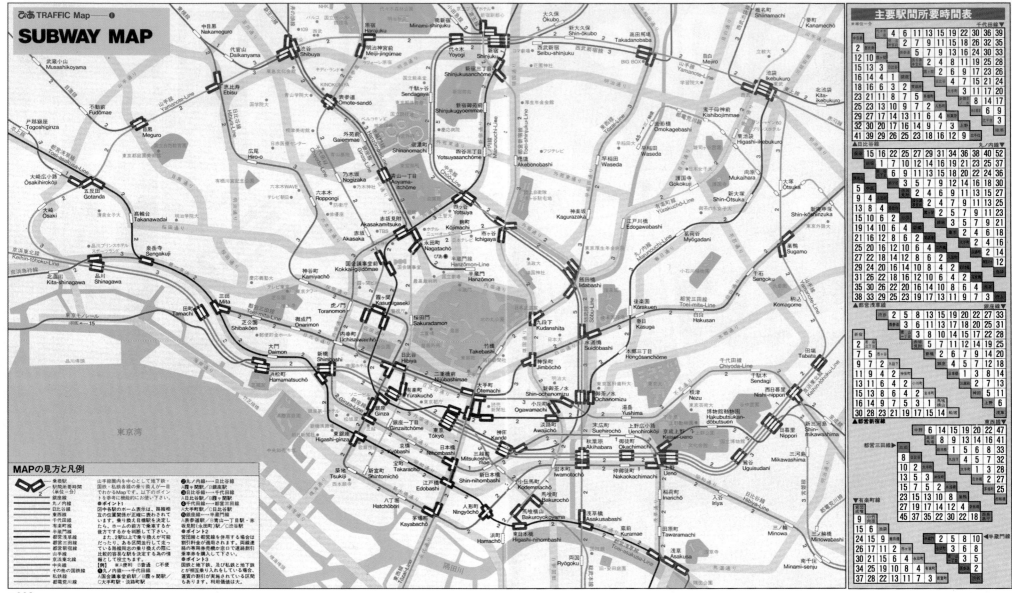

△333

333. MORISHITA CO., LTD.

1. JAPAN
2. MORISHITA CO., LTD.
   NOBUO MORISHITA/ART DIRECTION, DESIGN
   CAORI ISHIKAWA/DESIGN
   TAKAMOTO ISHII
   HIROSHI KIYONO
   HIROYUKI KIMURA/DESIGN
   YUKO ISHIKAWA/DESIGN

3. DECORATIVE MAPS
4. MAGAZINE "PIA MAP"
5. PIA CO., LTD.
   HOURS BETWEEN STATIONS (UNIT : MINUTES)

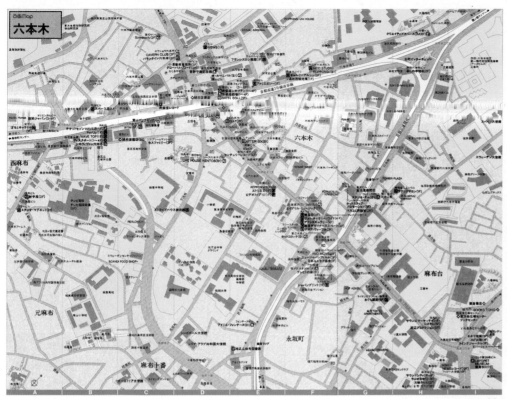

△334

△335

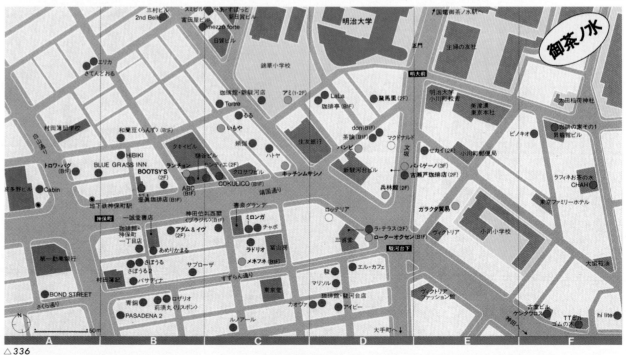

△336

334〜336. MORISHITA CO., LTD.

1. JAPAN
2. MORISHITA CO., LTD.
   NOBUO MORISHITA/ART DIRECTION, DESIGN
   CAORI ISHIKAWA/DESIGN
   TAKAMOTO ISHII
   HIROSHI KIYONO
   HIROYUKI KIMURA/DESIGN
3. DECORATIVE MAPS
4. MAGAZINE "PIA MAP"
5. PIA CO., LTD.
   YUKO ISHIKAWA/DESIGN
   MAP OF ROPPONGI, TOKYO (334)
   MAP OF GINZA, TOKYO (335)
   MAP OF OCHANOMIZU, TOKYO (336)

秩父宮ラグビー場

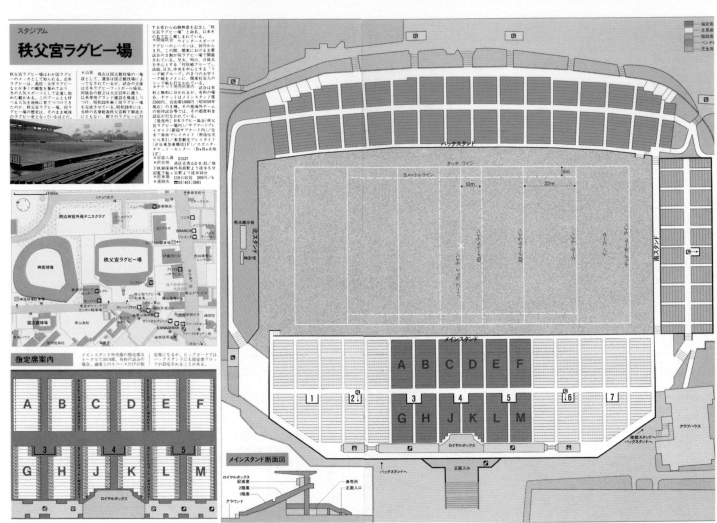

バックスタンド

5メートルライン　タッチ・ライン

10m　22m　5m

用器標示器

北スタンド　時計塔

南スタンド

ハーフ・ウェイ・ライン　10メートル・ライン　22メートル・ライン　ゴール・ライン

メインスタンド

| A | B | C | D | E | F |

1　2　3　4　5　6　7

| G | H | J | K | L | M |

ロイヤルボックス

開閉スタンドへ　バックスタンドへ

クラブハウス

バックスタンドへ　正面入口　正面入口へ

指定席案内

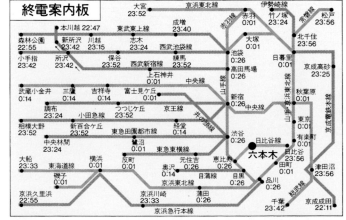

| A | B | C | D | E | F |

3　4　5

| G | H | J | K | L | M |

ロイヤルボックス

メインスタンド断面図

ロイヤルボックス記者席　前売所　正面入口

2階席　1階席　グラウンド

△337

品川プリンスホテル アイスアリーナ 東伏見アイスアリーナ

品川プリンスホテルアイスアリーナ

その他の施設案内

スイミングセンター

アイスショー開催時

エンド・フェース・オフ・サークル　アイスリンク　センター・サークル　フェース・オフ・スポット

ディフェンディング・ゾーン　ニュートラル・ゾーン　ディフェンディング・ゾーン　ブルー・ライン

本部席

ロイヤルボックス

△338

337〜340. MORISHITA CO., LTD.

1. JAPAN
2. MORISHITA CO., LTD.
   NOBUO MORISHITA
   CAORI ISHIKAWA
   TAKAMOTO ISHII
   HIROSHI KIYONO
   HIROYUKI KIMURA
   YUKO ISHIKAWA
3. DECORATIVE MAPS
4. MAGAZINE "PIA MAP"
5. PIA CO., LTD.
   RUGBY GROUND (337)
   SKATING RINK (338)
   TIME TABLE FOR THE LAST TRAINS (339)
   INTERRELATION OF PRICE AND
   DISTANCE IN TAXI FARE CALCULATION (340)

終電案内板

△339

タクシーMAP

六本木

△340

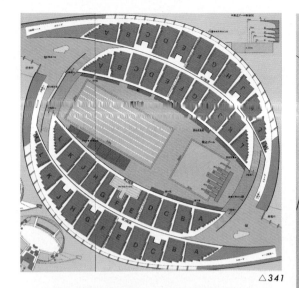

△341

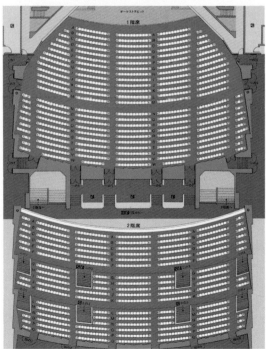

△342　△343

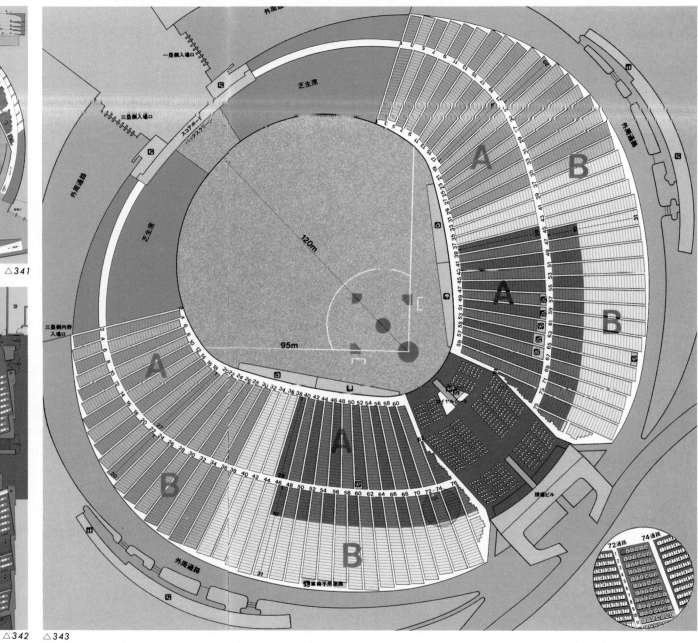

MORISHITA CO., LTD. 341〜343.

JAPAN 1.

MORISHITA CO., LTD. 2.

DECORATIVE MAPS 3. NOBUO MORISHITA/DESIGN

MAGAZINE "PIA MAP" 4. CAORI ISHIKAWA/DESIGN

5. PIA CO., LTD. 5. TAKAMOTO ISHII

SWIMMING POOL (341) HIROSHI KIYONO

THEATER (342) HIROYUKI KIMURA

BASEBALL GROUND (343) YUKO ISHIKAWA

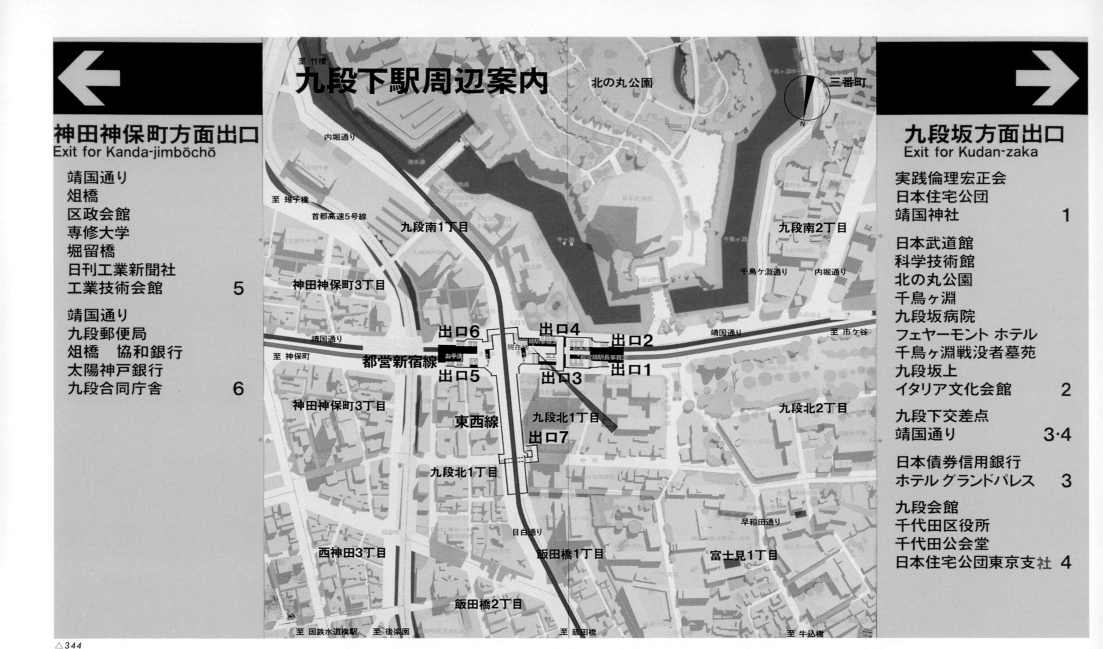

九段下駅周辺案内

北の丸公園
三番町
N

神田神保町方面出口
Exit for Kanda-jimbōchō

靖国通り
俎橋
区政会館
専修大学
堀留橋
日刊工業新聞社
工業技術会館　　　5

靖国通り
九段郵便局
俎橋　協和銀行
太陽神戸銀行
九段合同庁舎　　　6

九段坂方面出口
Exit for Kudan-zaka

実践倫理宏正会
日本住宅公団
靖国神社　　　　　1

日本武道館
科学技術館
北の丸公園
千鳥ヶ淵
九段坂病院
フェヤーモント ホテル
千鳥ヶ淵戦没者墓苑
九段坂上
イタリア文化会館　　2

九段下交差点
靖国通り　　　　3・4

日本債券信用銀行
ホテル グランドパレス　3

九段会館
千代田区役所
千代田公会堂
日本住宅公団東京支社　4

△344

344. REI INDUSTRIAL DESIGNERS INC.

1. JAPAN
2. REI INDUSTRIAL DESIGNERS INC.
3. DECORATIVE MAPS
4. RAILWAY STATION MAP
5. TEITO RAPID TRANSIT AUTHORITY

△345

△346

△347

△348

345～348. REI INDUSTRIAL DESIGNERS INC.

1. JAPAN
2. REI INDUSTRIAL DESIGNERS INC.
3. DECORATIVE MAPS
4. SUBWAY SIGN SYSTEM (345, 346)
   RE-DEVELOPMENT AREA SIGN PLANNING (347, 348)
5. TEITO RAPID TRANSIT AUTHORITY (345, 346)
   MORI BUILDING CO., LTD. (347, 348)
   MAP AROUND THE STATION IN TOKYO (345)
   SUBWAY MAP (346)

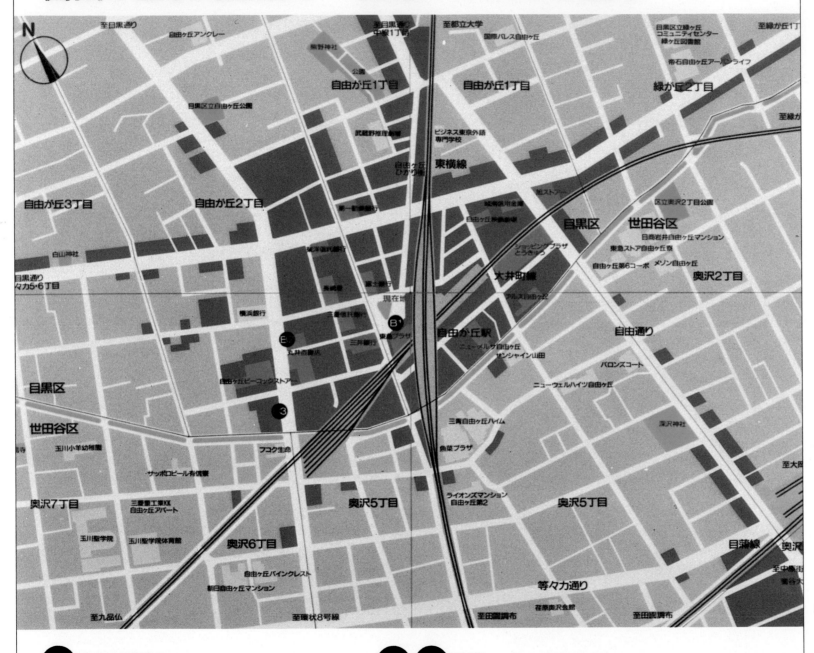

自由が丘駅周辺案内・🚌 バスのりば案内

REI INDUSTRIAL DESIGNERS INC. 349.

JAPAN 1.
REI INDUSTRIAL DESIGNERS INC. 2.
DECORATIVE MAPS 3.
MAP AROUND THE RAILWAY STATION 4.
TOKYU CORPORATION 5.

REI INDUSTRIAL DESIGNERS INC. 350, 351.

JAPAN 1.
REI INDUSTRIAL DESIGNERS INC. 2.
DECORATIVE MAPS 3.
RAILWAY POSTERS 4.
TOKYU CORPORATION 5.
FARE TABLE (350)
RAILWAY ROUTE MAP (351)

B1 自由が丘コーチ 自由が丘駅ー駒沢営業所 **B2** **B3** 渋11 渋谷駅ー田園調布駅

△349

162

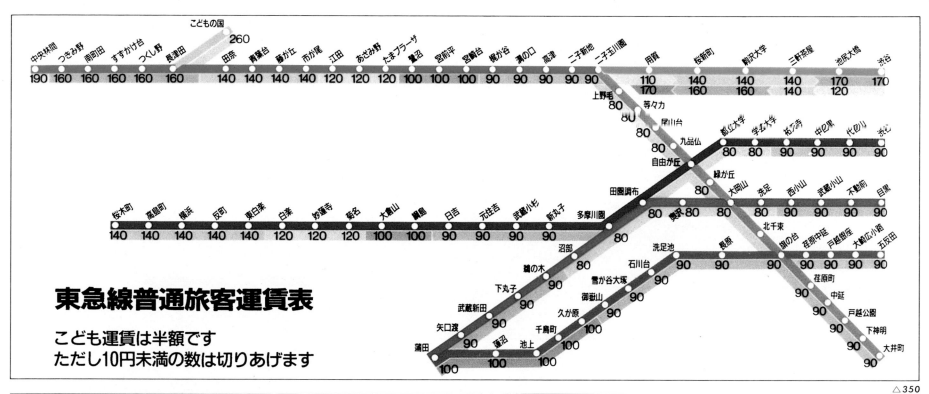

東急線普通旅客運賃表

こども運賃は半額です
ただし10円未満の数は切りあげます

△350

東急線路線案内

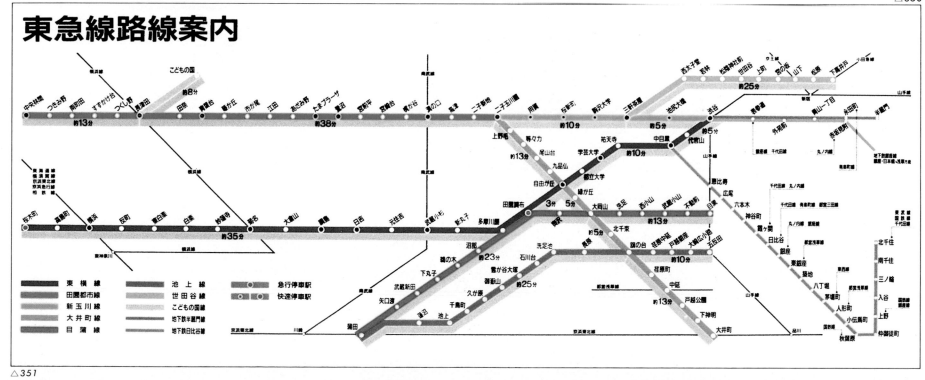

東横線	池上線	急行停車駅
田園都市線	世田谷線	快速停車駅
新玉川線	こどもの国線	
大井町線	地下鉄半蔵門線	
目蒲線	地下鉄日比谷線	

△351

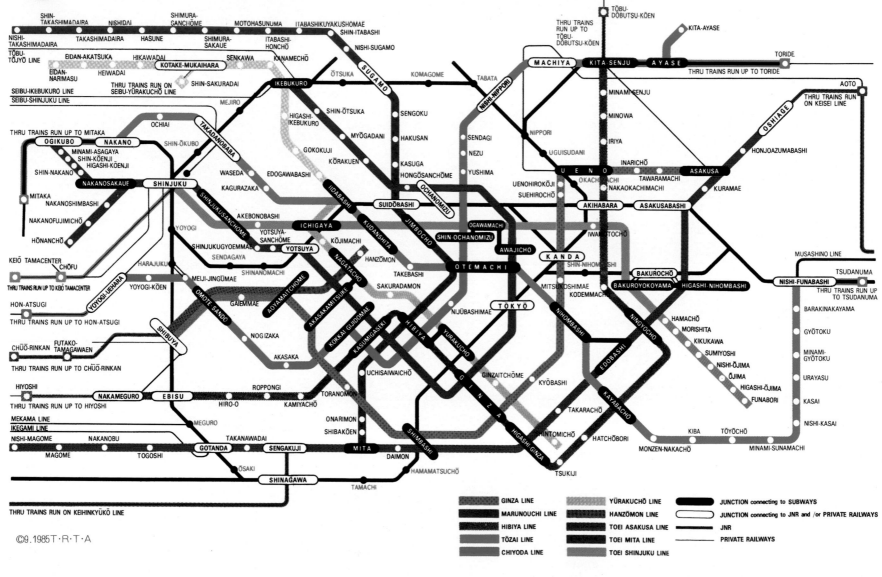

SUBWAYS IN TŌKYŌ TEITO RAPID TRANSIT AUTHORITY

©9.1985 T·R·T·A

GINZA LINE	YŪRAKUCHŌ LINE	JUNCTION connecting to SUBWAYS
MARUNOUCHI LINE	HANZŌMON LINE	JUNCTION connecting to JNR and /or PRIVATE RAILWAYS
HIBIYA LINE	TOEI ASAKUSA LINE	JNR
TŌZAI LINE	TOEI MITA LINE	PRIVATE RAILWAYS
CHIYODA LINE	TOEI SHINJUKU LINE	

△352

352, 353. HIDEYA KAWAKITA

1. JAPAN
2. JAPAN BELIER ART CENTER INC.
3. DECORATIVE MAPS
4. TOKYO SUBWAY MAPS
5. TEITO RAPID TRANSIT AUTHORITY
ENGLISH SUBWAY GUIDE (352) JAPANESE SUBWAY GUIDE (353)

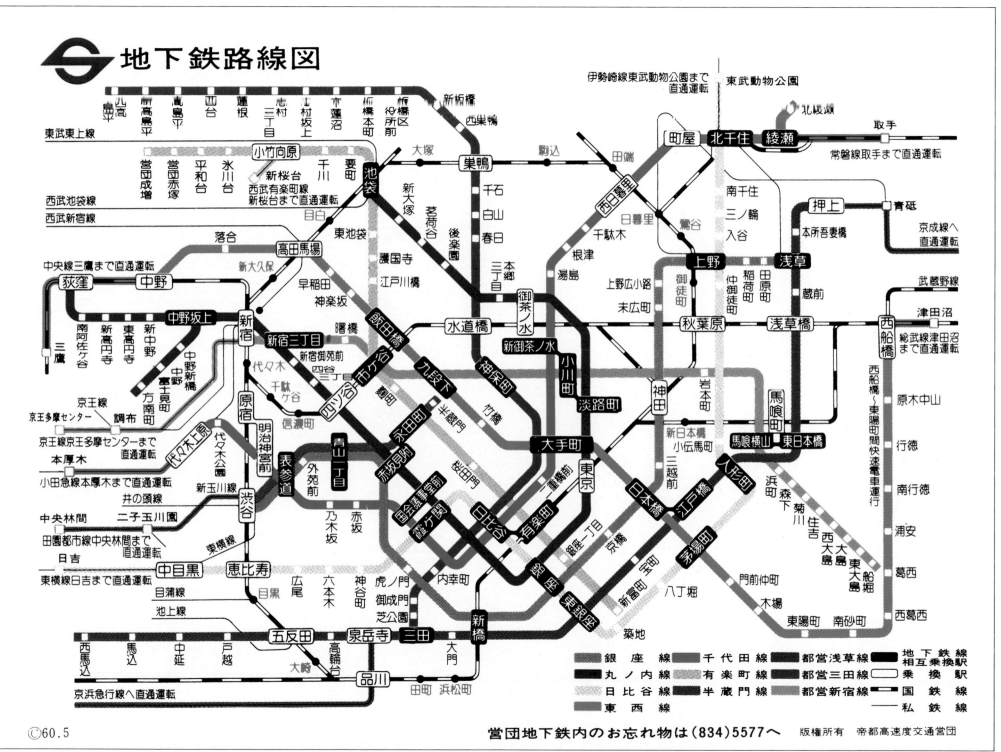

地下鉄路線図

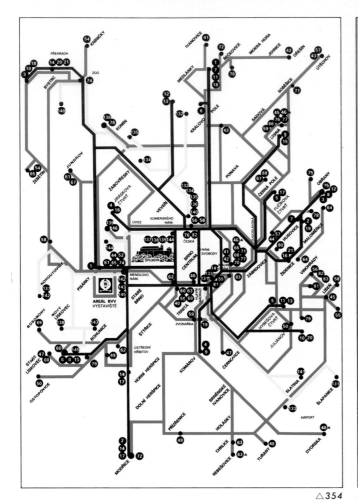

△354

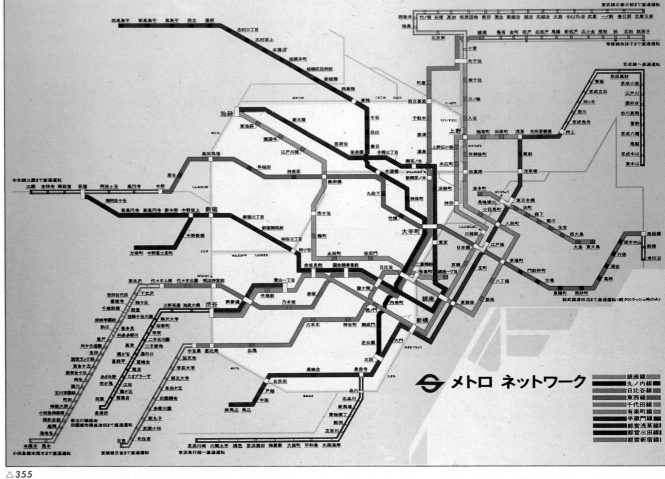

△355

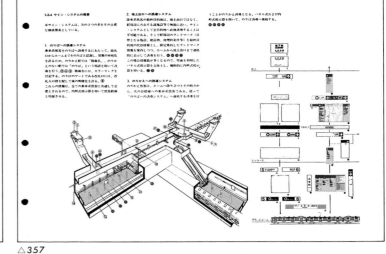

△356

△357

354. JAN RAJLICH JR.

1. CZECHOSLOVAKIA
3. DECORATIVE MAPS
4. BVV
   TRADE FAIRS AND EXHIBITIONS, BRNO, CZECHOSLOVAKIA 1985

355~357. REI INDUSTRIAL DESIGNERS INC.

1. JAPAN
2. REI INDUSTRIAL DESIGNERS INC.
3. DECORATIVE MAPS
4. METRO NETWORK (355)
   RAILWAY STATION MAP (356)
   SIGN SYSTEM EXPLANATORY CHART (357)
5. TEITO RAPID TRANSIT AUTHORITY

1. ITALY
3. DECORATIVE MAPS
4. MAP FOR BOAT LINES VENICE (358)
   BROCHURE (359)
   MAP FOR TELEPHONE IN VENICE (360)

5. ACTV VENICE TRANSPORT SYSTEM (358)
   CILA ARCHITECTURAL FIRM (359)
   SIP; ITALIAN PHONE COMPANY (360)

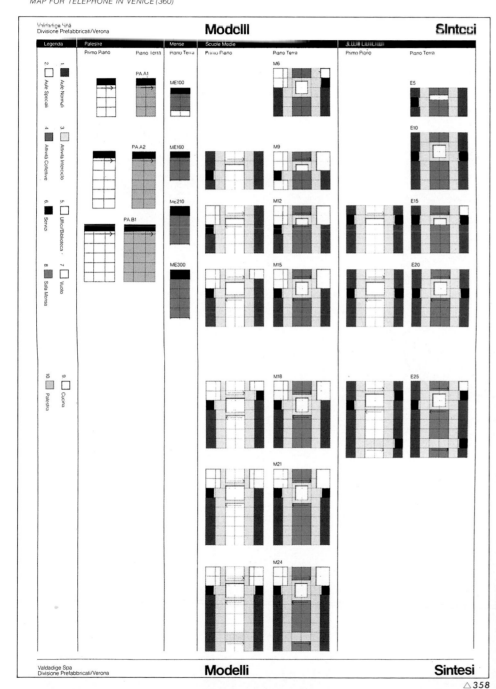

△358

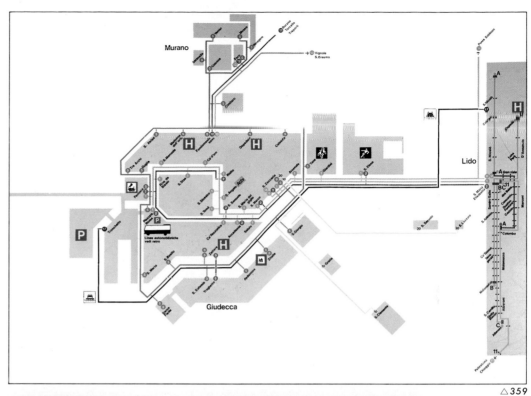

△359

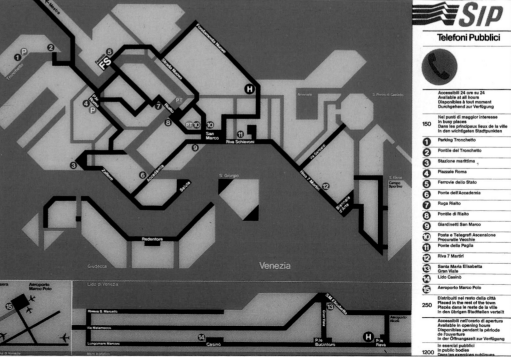

△360

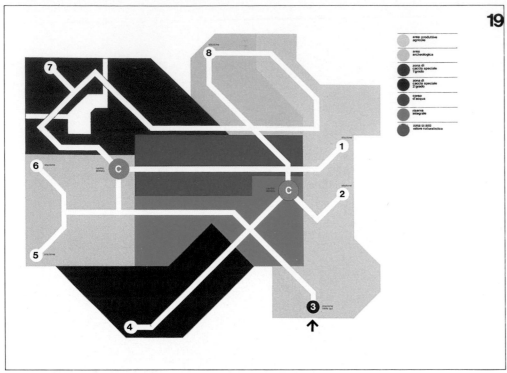

△361 ▽362

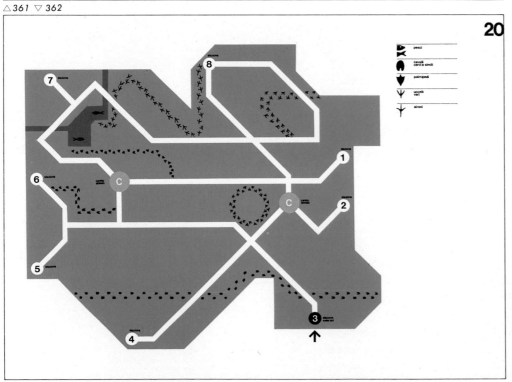

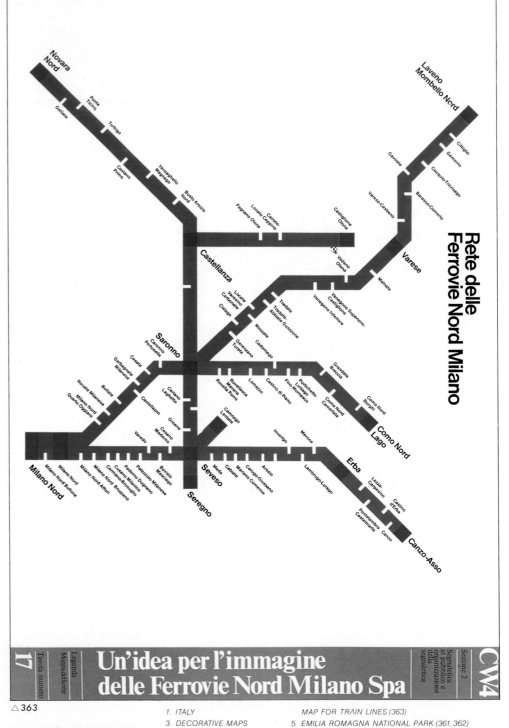

Rete delle Ferrovie Nord Milano

Un'idea per l'immagine delle Ferrovie Nord Milano Spa

△363

361~363. GIULIO CITTATO

1. ITALY
3. DECORATIVE MAPS
4. PARK MAP (361, 362)

MAP FOR TRAIN LINES (363)
5. EMILIA ROMAGNA NATIONAL PARK (361, 362)
FERROVIE NORD MILAND MAP (363)

17   Acnil
Corporate
Identity   Segnaletica

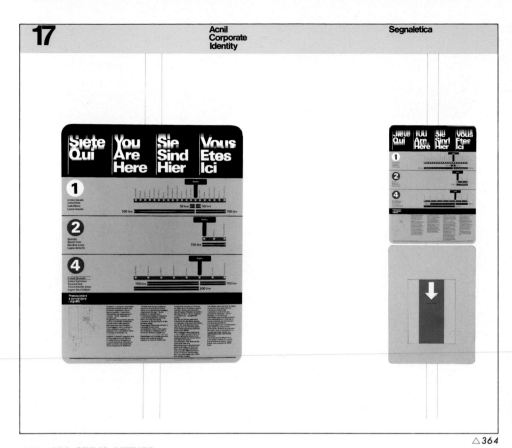

△364

364～366. GIULIO CITTATO

1. ITALY
3. DECORATIVE MAPS
4. INFORMATION FOR TOURISTS (364)
   MAP FOR BOAT LINES IN VENICE (365, 366)
5. ACTV VENICE TRANSPORT SYSTEM

15   Acnil
Corporate
Identity   Mappa
Linee
Interne

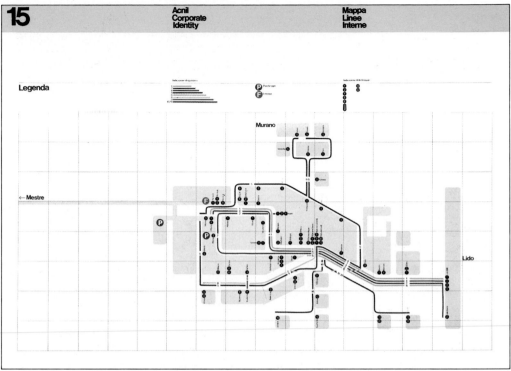

△365

16   Aonil
Corporate
Identity   Mappa
Linee
Foranee

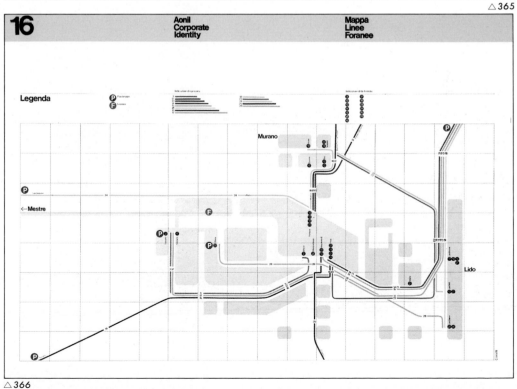

△366

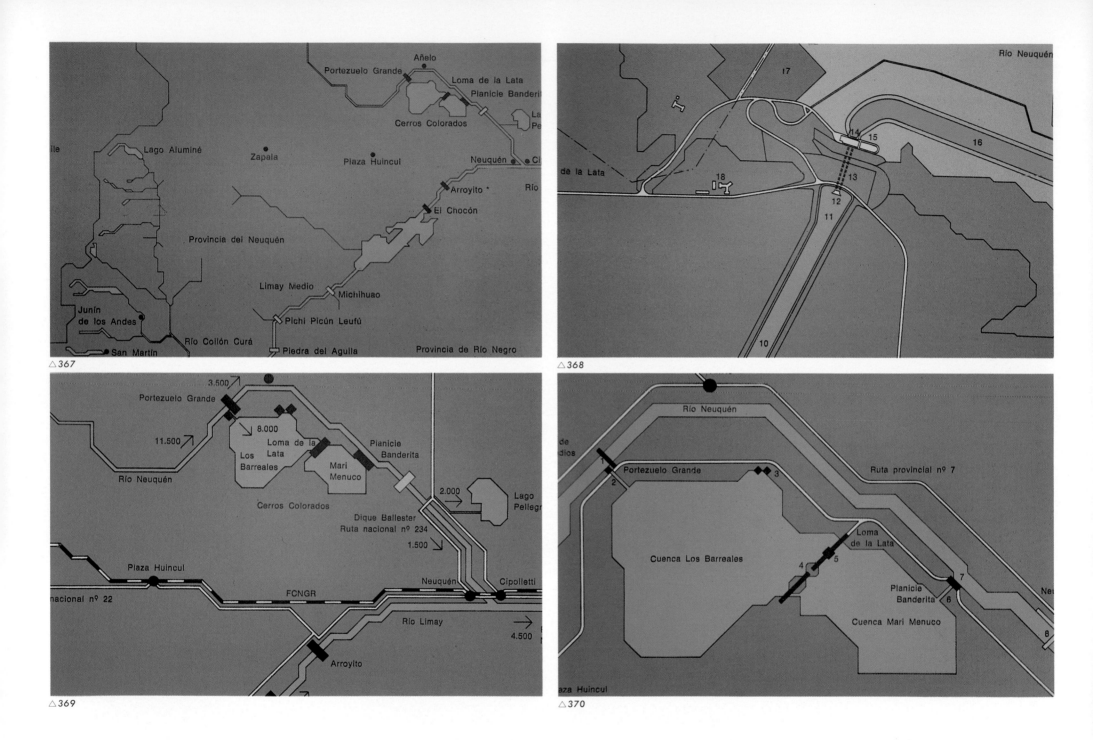

△367

△368

△369

△370

367~370. PEDROZA GUSTAVO

1. ARGENTINA
3. DECORATIVE MAPS

371, 372. RICHARD FREDERICK DAHN

1. U.S.A.
2. DESIGN COLLABORATIVE/SEATTLE
3. MAPS
5. ILLUSTRATION FOR A DESIGN STUDY OF
   THE WEST SEATTLE FREEWAY DONE
   BY ARTHUR BRICKSON

373. ANDRZEJ J. OLEJNICZAK

1. U.S.A.
2. O & J DESIGN INC.
3. MAPS
5. CROSS & BROWN
   MANHATTAN OFFICE SPACE AVAILABILITY SURVEY

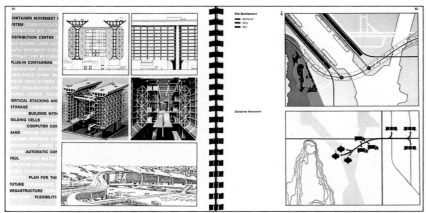

△371

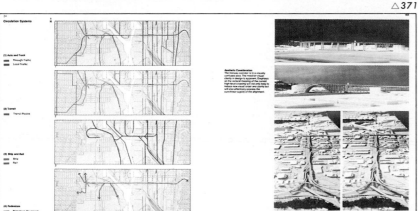

△372   △373

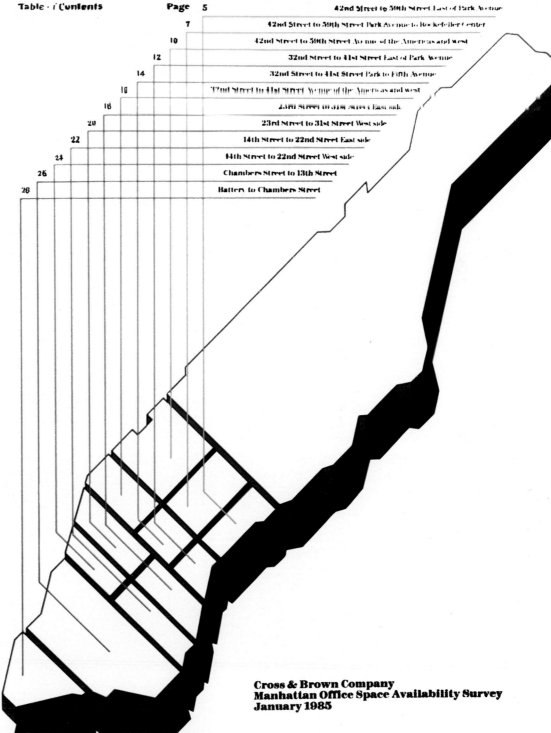

**Cross & Brown Company
Manhattan Office Space Availability Survey
January 1985**

171

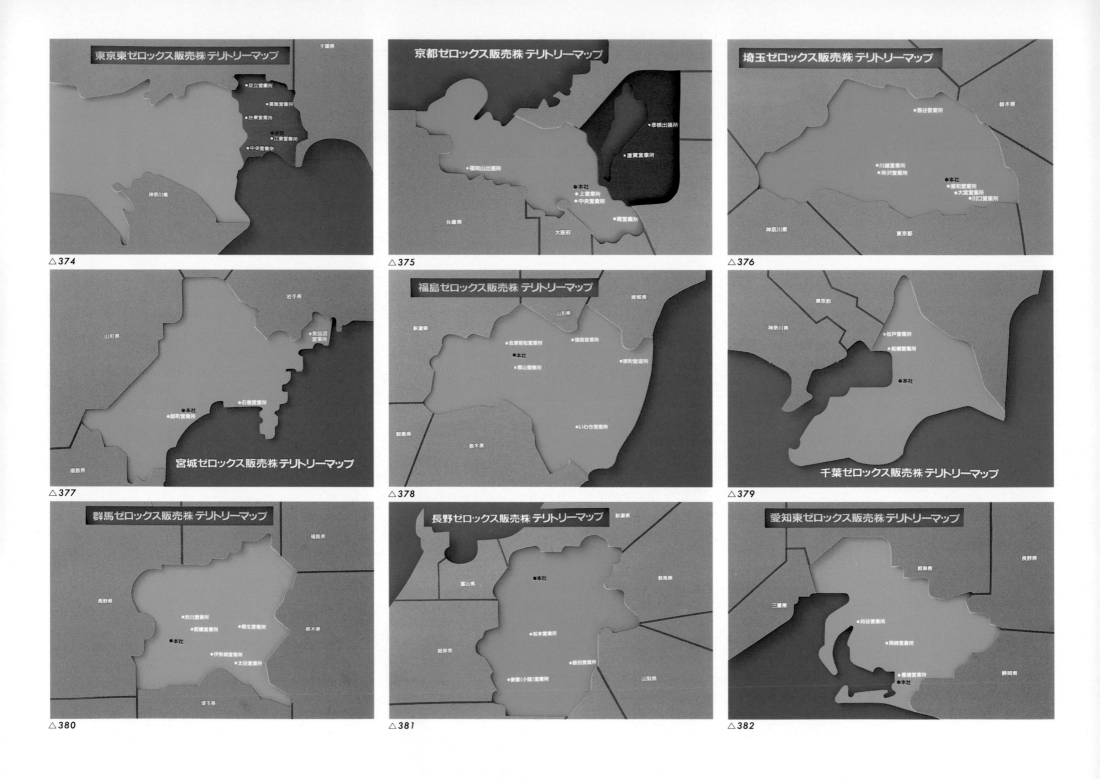

△374

△375

△376

△377

△378

△379

△380

△381

△382

172

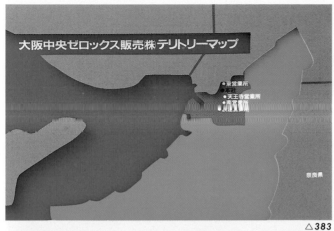

大阪中央ゼロックス販売㈱ テリトリーマップ

△383

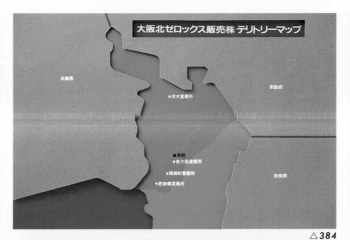

大阪北ゼロックス販売㈱ テリトリーマップ

△384

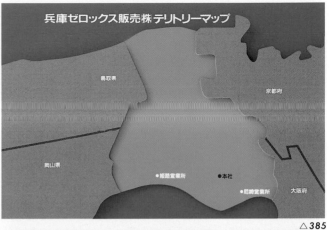

兵庫ゼロックス販売㈱ テリトリーマップ

△385

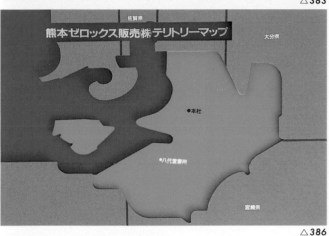

熊本ゼロックス販売㈱ テリトリーマップ

△386

岡山ゼロックス販売㈱ テリトリーマップ

△387

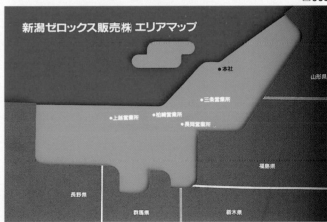

新潟ゼロックス販売㈱ エリアマップ

△388

374～390. TSUTOMU OKAMOTO

1. JAPAN
2. DIAGRAMS INC.
3. DECORATIVE MAPS
4. TERRITORY MAP
5. FUJI XEROX CO., LTD.
   MAPS OF JAPANESE PREFECTURES
   WITH OFFICE LOCATIONS
   (RED: MAIN OFFICES)
   (WHITE: BRANCHES) (374～390)

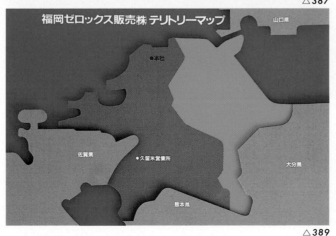

福岡ゼロックス販売㈱ テリトリーマップ

△389

新潟ゼロックス販売㈱ テリトリーマップ

△390

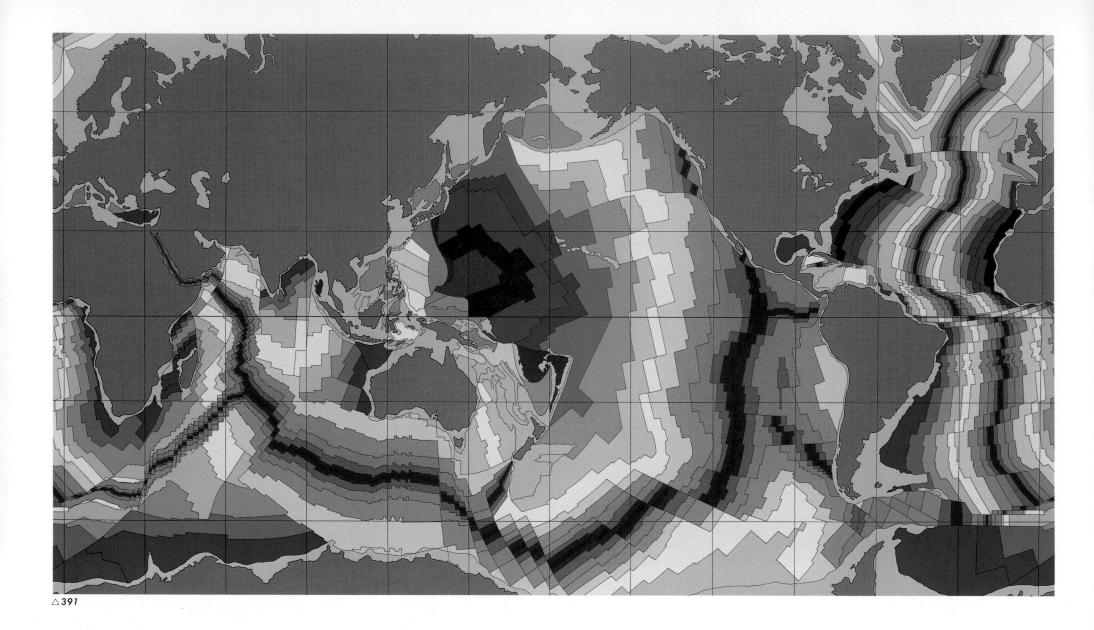

△391

391. NEWTON

1. JAPAN
2. ILLUSTRATOR: ETSUKO TAKAHASHI, ART KŌBŌ
3. DECORATIVE MAPS
4. NEWTON MAGAZINE
5. ⓒKYOIKUSHA NEWTON
   THE EXPANDING OCEAN

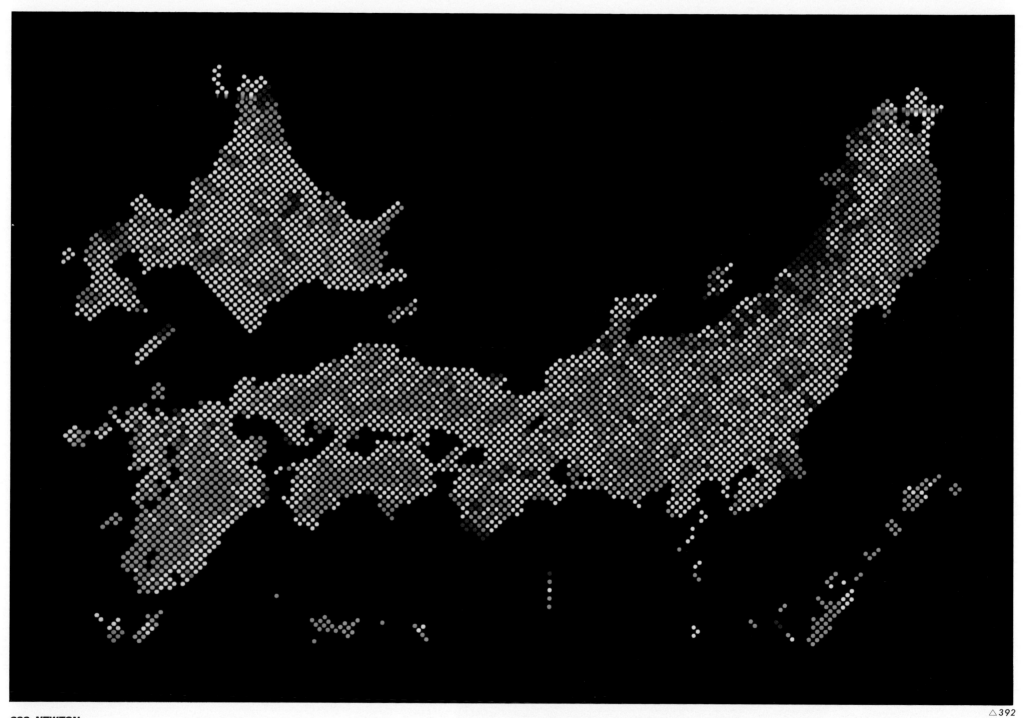

392. NEWTON

1. JAPAN
2. ILLUSTRATOR: ETSUKO TAKAHASHI
3. DECORATIVE MAPS

4. NEWTON MAGAZINE
5. ©KYOIKUSHA NEWTON
   DEATH RATE BY STOMACH CANCER (IN CITIES, TOWNS, VILLAGES)

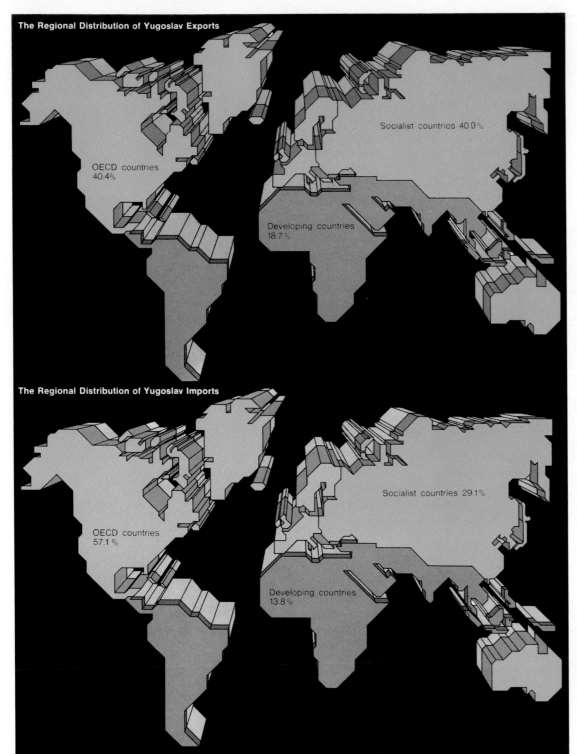

The Regional Distribution of Yugoslav Exports

Socialist countries 40.0%

OECD countries 40.4%

Developing countries 18.7%

The Regional Distribution of Yugoslav Imports

Socialist countries 29.1%

OECD countries 57.1%

Developing countries 13.8%

393, 394. PETER SKALAR

1. YUGOSLAVIA
3. COMPARATIVE STATISTICS
5. REGIONAL DISTRIBUTION OF YUGOSLAV EXPORTS (393)
   FOREIGN OFFICE DIRECTORY (394)

Representative Offices Abroad

Abidjan
B. P. 1433
Telephone: 32 39 92
Telex: 745
Director: Anton Petkovšek

Beirut
P. O. Box 13/5232
Gefinor Center, Bloc C-304
Telephone: 346 543/4
Telex: 20 722
Director: Ivan Rudolf

Berlin (GDR)
Warschauer Strasse 8/VI
Telephone: 5 89 15 18
Telex: 112 425
Director: Franc Slapnik

Budapest
Dózsa György utca 92 a
Telephone: 221 454
Telex: 22 63 43
Director: Vilijem Hakl

Caracas
Edificio BECO-Chacaito
Apartado 68901 Altamira
Telephone: 72 09 50
Telex: 2 34 57
Director: Egon Prinčič

Frankfurt/Main
Kaiserstrasse 11/III
Telephone: 280 269
Telex: 416 810
Director: Ivan Simončič

London
7 Birchin Lane, 6th Floor
Telephone: 626-8848/9
Telex: 888394
Director: Marjan Kandus

Milan
Corsia dei Servi 11
Telephone: 700 908
Telex: 32594
Director: Rudolf Selič

Moscow
Mosfilmovskaja 42
Telephone: 147 84 03
Telex: 7554
Representative: Franc Ferkolj

Nairobi
P. O. Box 73773
Telephone: 331 368
Telex: 22005

New York
The Seagram Building
Suite 3502
375 Park Avenue
Telephone: 752 1243
Telex: 666729
Director: Jože Tepina

Paris
31, avenue des Champs
Elysées
Telephone: 225 12 58
Telex: 660863
Director: Anton Lavtar

Prague
Lazarska 5
Telephone: 29 11 07
Telex: 121386
Director: Viktor Meglič

Rio de Janeiro
Apartado 604
Av. Ataulfo de Paiva
Telephone: 274 1743, 333 8344
Telex: 031 1562
Representative: Bogdan Šalej

Warsaw
Swietokrzyska 36 m 15
Telephone: 201253
Telex: 815423
Representative: Vukota Samardžić

Representative Office in Yugoslavia

Beograd
29. novembra 1/III
Telephone: 334 173
Telex: 12989
Director: Miroslav Prelić

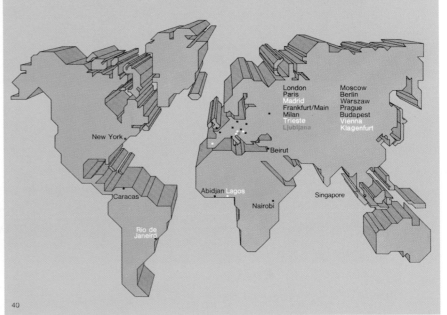

London
Paris
Madrid
Frankfurt/Main
Milan
Trieste
Ljubljana

Moscow
Berlin
Warszaw
Prague
Budapest
Vienna
Klagenfurt

New York

Beirut

Caracas

Abidjan Lagos

Nairobi

Singapore

Rio de Janeiro

40

176

△393 △394

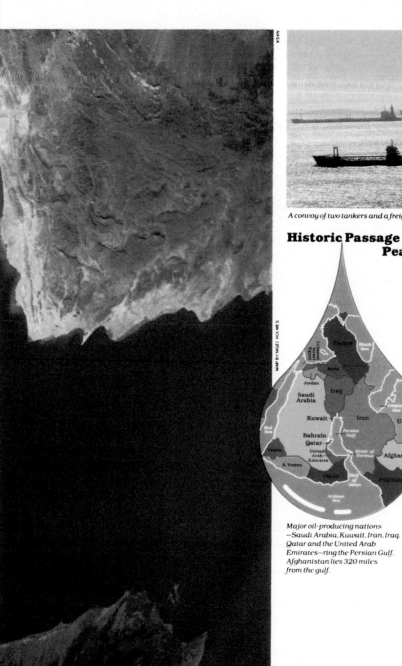

Persian Gulf is at left and the Gulf of Oman at right.

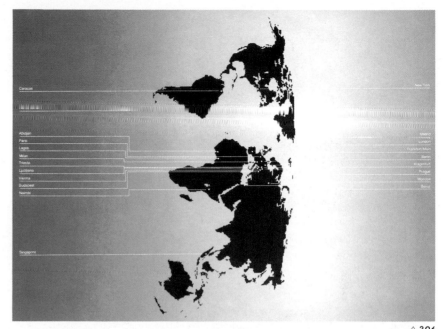

NASA

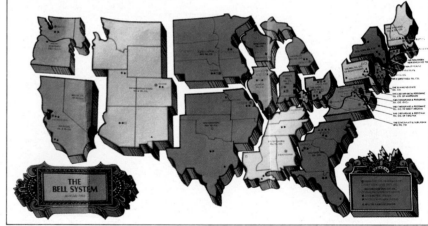

A convoy of two tankers and a freighter heads for the open sea.

MAPS BY NIGEL HOLMES

Historic Passage for Frankincense, Pearls and Black Gold

From Kuwait and Iraq, from Bahrain and Saudi Arabia and Iran, from the United Arab Emirates along what buccaneers knew as the Pirate Coast, giant tankers steam out of the Persian Gulf, freighted with the oil that fuels the fires of the non-Communist world. Historically the ships that have voyaged outbound through the Strait of Hormuz have borne frankincense, pearls and red ocher, as control of the trade lanes passed from the Portuguese in the 16th century to the Dutch and then the British. But in this century the outbound traffic carries black gold. The 77 tankers that pass through the strait on an average day carry enough fuel to provide every American with nearly a pint of gasoline per hour. The countries on the gulf's borders hold 56 percent of the world's proven reserves. The statistics that spell out the Japanese and Western nations' dependence are staggering: the U.S. gets a third of its imported crude from the gulf, Western Europe gets 61 percent and Japan, 73 percent. In fact, if Japan's supply were to be cut off, one expert believes, the Japanese economy would wither in a month. The U.S.S.R., by contrast, is virtually self-sufficient in oil, a fact that suggests the recent Soviet muscle-flexing in the gulf may be intended to underline the terrible fragility of the West's oil lifeline. Sultan Qaboos bin Said, the pro-Western ruler of Oman, has stated that he fears the Soviet presence in the gulf, coupled with its recent thrust into Afghanistan, may be part of "an overall plan to encircle the Arabian Peninsula and cut the oil routes."

Major oil-producing nations —Saudi Arabia, Kuwait, Iran, Iraq, Qatar and the United Arab Emirates—ring the Persian Gulf. Afghanistan lies 320 miles from the gulf.

27

△396

△397

△398

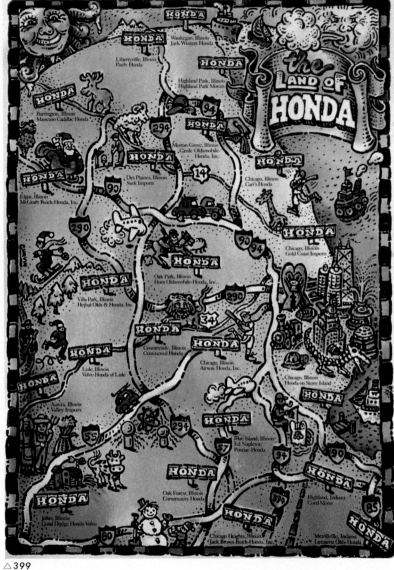

△399

398. SOREN THAAE

1. DENMARK
2. 3-D ILLUSTRATIONS
3. DECORATIVE MAPS
5. DANISH STATE RAILWAYS
   TOURIST MAP OF FOOD
   AND LODGING LOCATIONS

ABE GURVIN 399.

U.S.A. 1.
ABE GURVIN ILLUSTRATION & DESIGN 2.
DECORATIVE MAPS 3.
MAP OF CHICAGO HONDA DEALERS 4.
HONDA MOTOR CO. 5.

178

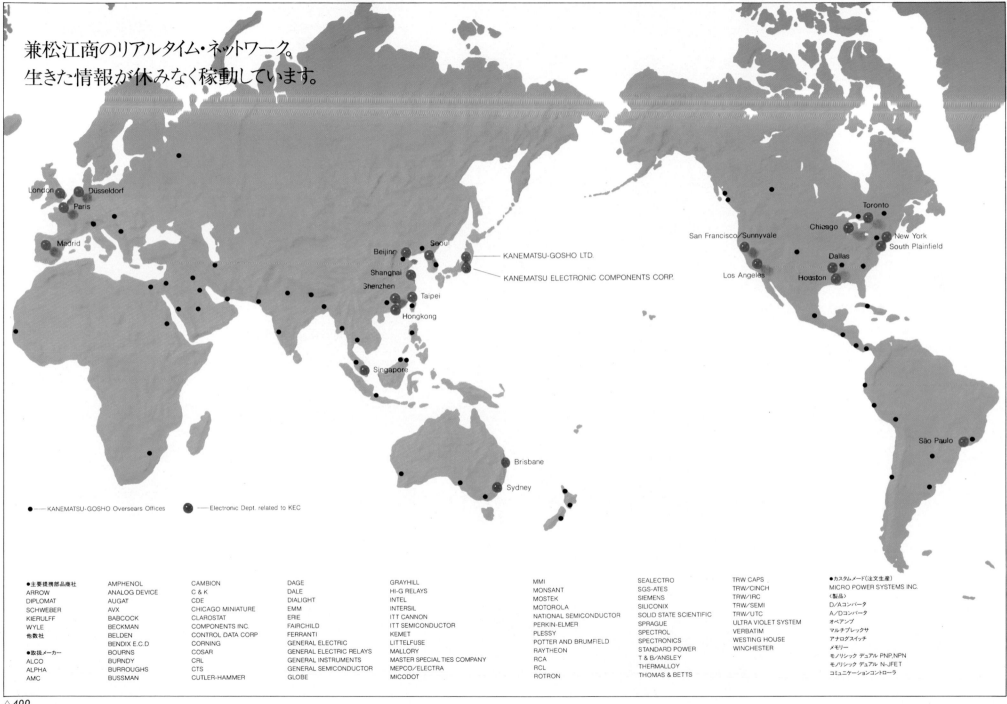

兼松江商のリアルタイム・ネットワーク。
生きた情報が休みなく稼動しています。

London　Düsseldorf
Paris
Madrid

Beijing　Seoul
Shanghai　KANEMATSU-GOSHO LTD.
Shenzhen　KANEMATSU ELECTRONIC COMPONENTS CORP.
Taipei
Hongkong

Singapore

Brisbane
Sydney

San Francisco/Sunnyvale
Chicago　Toronto
New York
South Plainfield
Dallas
Los Angeles　Houston

São Paulo

● —KANEMATSU-GOSHO Oversears Offices　● —Electronic Dept. related to KEC

●主要提携部品商社							●カスタムメード(注文生産)
ARROW	AMPHENOL	CAMBION	DAGE	GRAYHILL	MMI	SEALECTRO	MICRO POWER SYSTEMS INC.
DIPLOMAT	ANALOG DEVICE	C & K	DALE	HI-G RELAYS	MONSANT	SGS-ATES	TRW CAPS
SCHWEBER	AUGAT	CDE	DIALIGHT	INTEL	MOSTEK	SIEMENS	TRW/CINCH
KIERULFF	AVX	CHICAGO MINIATURE	EMM	INTERSIL	MOTOROLA	SILICONIX	TRW/IRC
WYLE	BABCOCK	CLAROSTAT	ERIE	ITT CANNON	NATIONAL SEMICONDUCTOR	SOLID STATE SCIENTIFIC	TRW/SEMI
他数社	BECKMAN	COMPONENTS INC.	FAIRCHILD	ITT SEMICONDUCTOR	PERKIN-ELMER	SPRAGUE	TRW/UTC
	BELDEN	CONTROL DATA CORP	FERRANTI	KEMET	PLESSY	SPECTROL	ULTRA VIOLET SYSTEM
●取扱メーカー	BENDIX E.C.D	CORNING	GENERAL ELECTRIC	LITTELFUSE	POTTER AND BRUMFIELD	SPECTRONICS	VERBATIM
ALCO	BOURNS	COSAR	GENERAL ELECTRIC RELAYS	MALLORY	RAYTHEON	STANDARD POWER	WESTING HOUSE
ALPHA	BURNDY	CRL	GENERAL INSTRUMENTS	MASTER SPECIALTIES COMPANY	RCA	T & B/ANSLEY	WINCHESTER
AMC	BURROUGHS	CTS	GENERAL SEMICONDUCTOR	MEPCO/ELECTRA	RCL	THERMALLOY	
	BUSSMAN	CUTLER-HAMMER	GLOBE	MICODOT	ROTRON	THOMAS & BETTS	

〈製品〉
D/Aコンバータ
A/Dコンバータ
オペアンプ
マルチプレックサ
アナログスイッチ
メモリー
モノリシック デュアル PNP,NPN
モノリシック デュアル N-JFET
コミュニケーションコントローラ

△400

HIROSHI KOJITANI 400.

KANEMATSU ELECTRONIC COMPONENTS CORP. 5.　COMPARATIVE STATISTICS 3.　JAPAN 1.
REAL TIME NETWORK OF KANEMATSU-GOSHO　COMPANY PAMPHLET 4.

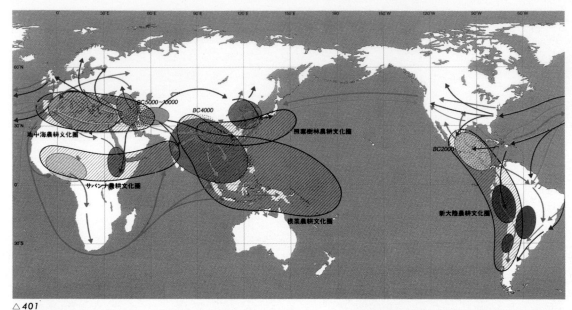

△401

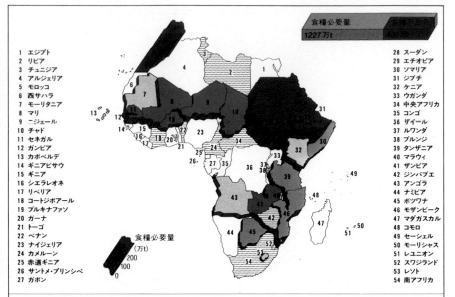

図9 食糧不足に直面している国

食糧不足分(1985年2月)

| 0 | 1 | 5 | 10 | 50(万t) | 以上 |

▨▨ 1981年に1人当たり食糧生産指数
100以上で食糧自給国

FAO『FOOD SITUATION IN AFRICAN COUNTRIES AFFECTED BY EMERGENCIES, Special report, February 1985』
FAO『Production Year Book』(1981)より

　この図は1985年2月にFAO(国連食糧農業機関)が発表した報告書に基づいている。それぞれの国の食糧必要量から，その国が海外から買い付けた量と外国からの援助量を差し引いたものが食糧不足分である。人口が少ないのに不足分が多い国が目立つ。ブルキナファソ，チャド，マリ，ニジェールなどで，いずれもサハラ砂漠に面した国々である。干ばつによる国土の砂漠化が70年代初頭から悩みの種であった。なお，干ばつ直前の1981年の食糧自給国13カ国も示した。

△403

食糧必要量
1227万t

食糧必要量
(万t)
200
100
0

1 エジプト
2 リビア
3 チュニジア
4 アルジェリア
5 モロッコ
6 西サハラ
7 モーリタニア
8 マリ
9 ニジェール
10 チャド
11 セネガル
12 ガンビア
13 カボベルデ
14 ギニアビサウ
15 ギニア
16 シエラレオネ
17 リベリア
18 コートジボアール
19 ブルキナファソ
20 ガーナ
21 トーゴ
22 ベナン
23 ナイジェリア
24 カメルーン
25 赤道ギニア
26 サントメ・プリンシペ
27 ガボン

28 スーダン
29 エチオピア
30 ソマリア
31 ジブチ
32 ケニア
33 ウガンダ
34 中央アフリカ
35 コンゴ
36 ザイール
37 ルワンダ
38 ブルンジ
39 タンザニア
40 マラウィ
41 ザンビア
42 ジンバブエ
43 アンゴラ
44 ナミビア
45 ボツワナ
46 モザンビーク
47 マダガスカル
48 コモロ
49 セーシェル
50 モーリシャス
51 レユニオン
52 スワジランド
53 レソト
54 南アフリカ

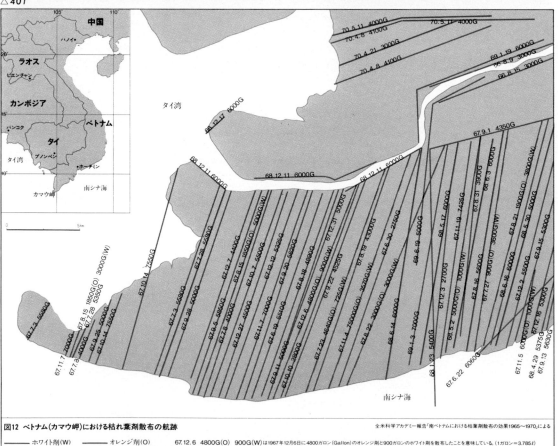

図12 ベトナム(カマウ岬)における枯れ葉剤散布の航跡

全米科学アカデミー報告『南ベトナムにおける枯葉剤散布の効果1965〜1970』による

―― ホワイト剤(W)　―― オレンジ剤(O)　67.12.6 4800G(O) 900G(W)は1967年12月6日に4800ガロン(Gallon)のオレンジ剤と900ガロンのホワイト剤を散布したことを意味している。(1ガロン=3.785ℓ)

△402

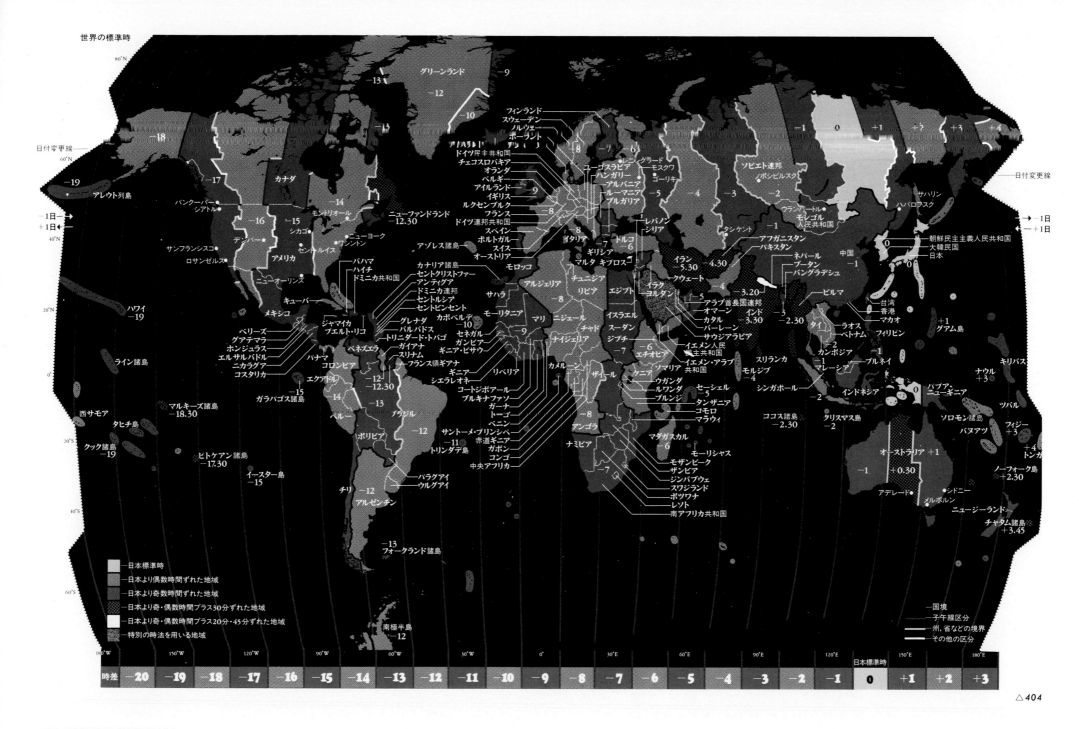

世界の標準時

404. YOSHIAKI SHIRAMASA

1. JAPAN

2. MAPS

5. STANDARD TIME IN THE WORLD

181

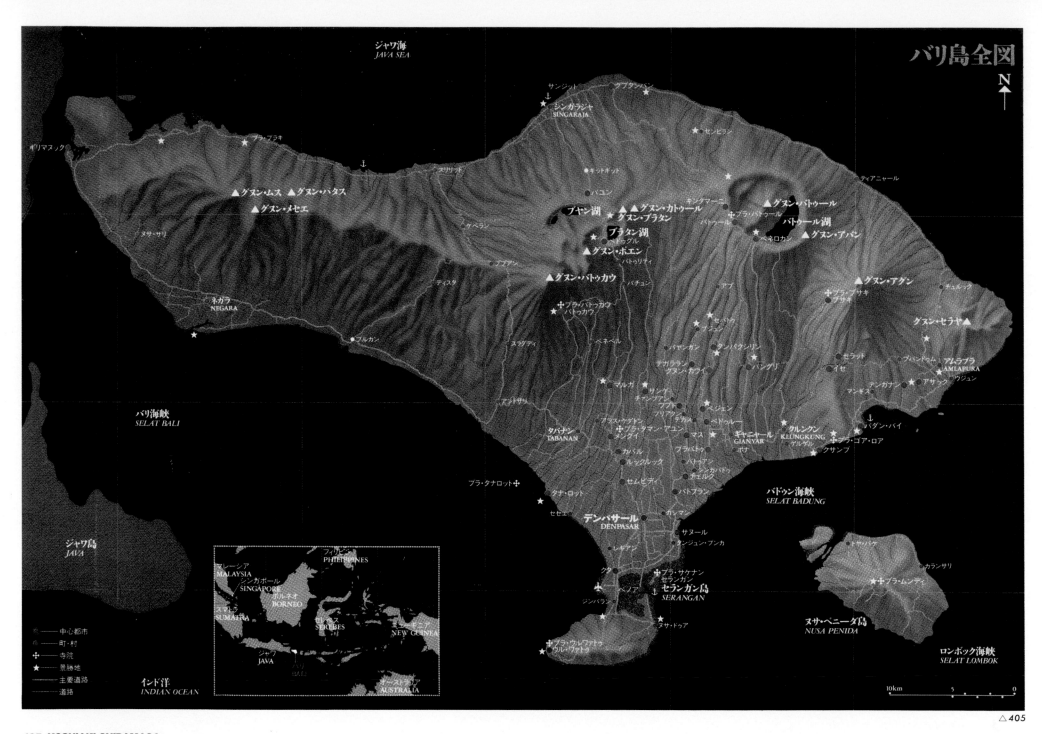

バリ島全図

N

ジャワ海
JAVA SEA

サンジット クブタンバハン
⚓ シンガラジャ
SINGARAJA
★ センビラン
ギリマヌック
ブラ・プラキ
ティアニャール
スリリット
キットギット
▲ グヌン・ムス ▲ グヌン・ハタス
バユン
▲ グヌン・バトゥール
ヌサ・サリ
▲ グヌン・メセエ
キンタマーニ
▲ グヌン・カトゥール
ブヤン湖 ★ ▲ ✠ ブラ・バトゥール
バトゥール湖
ケベラン
▲ グヌン・ブラタン
バトゥール
ブラタン湖
ベネロカン ▲ グヌン・アバン
バトゥグル
ブブアン
▲ グヌン・ボエン
ディスタ
バトゥリティ
▲ グヌン・バトゥカウ
バチュン
▲ グヌン・アグン
アブ
ネガラ
NEGARA
✠ ブラ・ブサキ
ブサキ
チュルック
✠ ブラ・バトゥカウ
バトゥカウ
グヌン・セラヤ ▲
ブルカン
ベネベル
セバトゥ
ブジュン
スラダティ
パヤンガン
タンパクシリン
セラット
ブハンドゥム アムラプラ
AMLAPURA
テガララン
グヌン・カワイ
バングリ
イセ
アントサリ
マルガ
テンガナン
アサック ウジュン
マンギス
シンガ
チャンプアン
ウブド
パリアタン テラガ
ペジェン
バリ海峡
SELAT BALI
ペドゥルー
アラス・ケダトン
✠ ブラ・タマン・アユン
メングイ
マス
★ クルンクン
KLUNGKUNG
ゲルゲル
⚓ パダン・バイ
タバナン
TABANAN
カパル
ブラバトゥ
ギャニャール
GIANYAR
ボナ
✠ ブラ・ゴア・ロア
ルックルック
バトゥアン
シンガパドゥ
チェルク
クサンプ
セムビディ
バトブラン
バドゥン海峡
SELAT BADUNG
ブラ・タナロット ✠
タナ・ロット
★
セセ
カラン
デンパサール
DENPASAR
サヌール
タンジュン・ブンカ
ジャワ島
JAVA
レギアン
クタ ✠ ブラ・サケナン
セランガン
ベノア
セランガン島
SERANGAN
ジンバラン
ヌサ・ドゥア
トヤパク
カランサリ
✠ ブラ・ムンディ
ヌサ・ペニーダ島
NUSA PENIDA
✠ ブラ・ウルワツ
ウル・ワツ
ロンボック海峡
SELAT LOMBOK

フィリピン
PHILIPPINES
マレーシア
MALAYSIA
シンガポール
SINGAPORE
ボルネオ
BORNEO
スマトラ
SUMATRA
セレベス
SEREBES
ニューギニア
NEW GUINEA
ジャワ
JAVA
バリ
BALI
オーストラリア
AUSTRALIA

インド洋
INDIAN OCEAN

◎──中心都市
◎──町・村
✠──寺院
★──景勝地
────主要道路
────道路

10km   5   0

△405

405. YQSHIAKI SHIRAMASA

1. JAPAN
3. MAPS   5. MAP OF BAIL ISLAND

182

406. YOSHIAKI SHIRAMASA

1. JAPAN

3. MAPS

5. MAP OF JAPAN'S POSITION
   ON THE EARTH'S SURFACE

△406

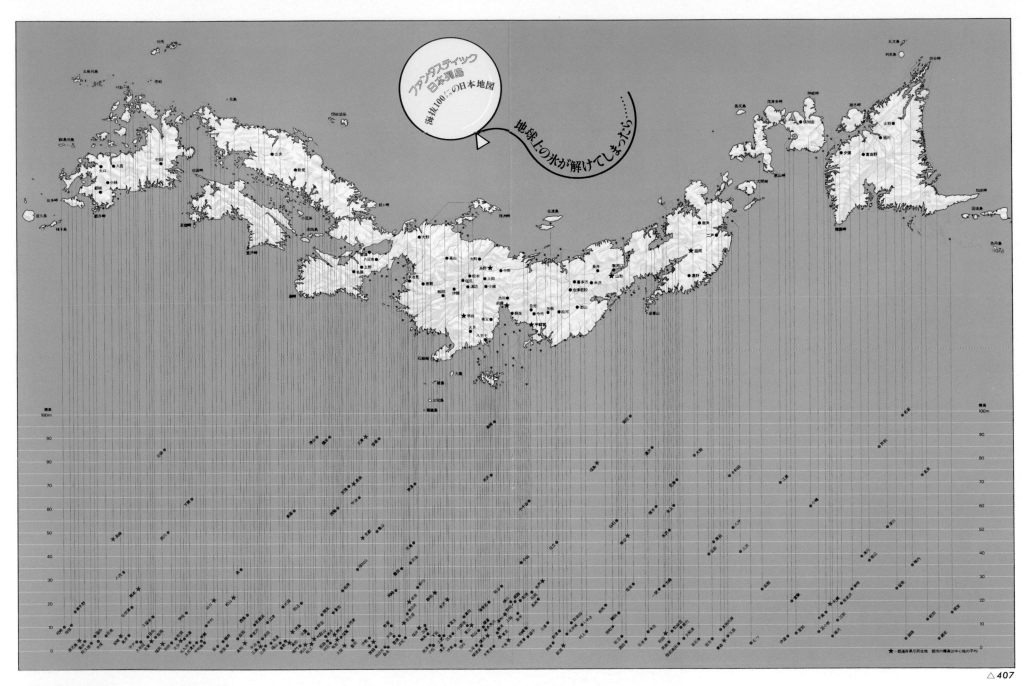

407. MORISHITA CO., LTD.

1. JAPAN
2. MORISHITA CO., LTD.
   NOBUO MORISHITA/DESIGN
   GAORI ISHIKAWA
   TAKAMOTO ISHII

HIROSHI KIYONO
HIROYUKI KIMURA
YUKO ISHIKAWA

3. MAPS
4. MAGAZINE "SAWAYAKA"
5. DIAMOND INC.
   PROBABLE EFFECT OF ICE MELTING ON JAPAN

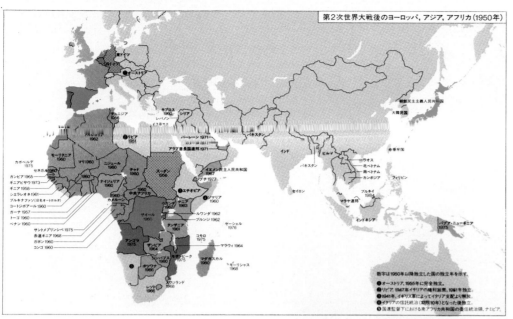

第2次世界大戦後のヨーロッパ, アジア, アフリカ(1950年)

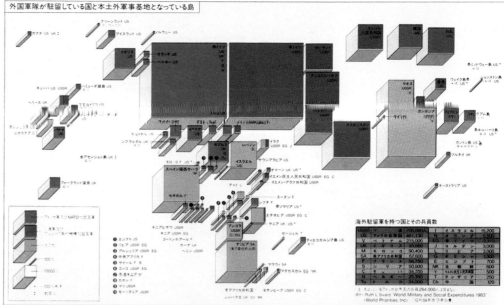

外国軍隊が駐留している国と本土外軍事基地となっている島

△408 △409

408～411. MORISHITA CO., LTD.

1. JAPAN
2. MORISHITA CO., LTD.
   NOBUO MORISHITA
   CAORI ISHIKAWA
   TAKAMOTO ISHII
   HIROSHI KIYONO
   HIROYUKI KIMURA
   YUKO ISHIKAWA
3. MAPS
4. WEEKLY MAGAZINE "ASAHI HYAKKA"
5. ASAHI SHIMBUN SHA
   NEW BOUNDARIES OF AFRICAN, EUROPEAN,
   AND ASIAN COUNTRIES AFTER WWII (408)
   NUMBER OF ARMIES COMMISSIONED AS
   AIDS TO FOREIGN COUNTRIES (409)

ソ連のみたアメリカの核による包囲

"Whence the Threat to Peace" (ソ連国防省, 1982年刊) より

アメリカのみたソ連の核攻撃力

"Soviet Military Power 1984" (アメリカ合衆国国防総省) より

△410 △411

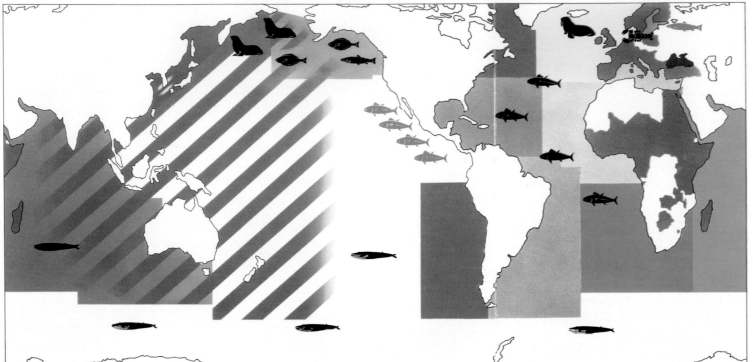

أجهزة تابعة للمنظمة

CARPAS	اللجنة الاستشارية الإقليمية لمصايد جنوب غرب الأطلنطي
CECAF	مجلس مصايد شرق وسط المحيط الأطلنطي
CIFA	لجنة مصايد الأسماك الداخلية في أفريقيا
EIFAC	المجلس الاستشاري لمصايد الأسماك الداخلية الأوروبية
GFCM	المجلس العام لمصايد البحر الأبيض المتوسط
IOFC	مجلس مصايد المحيط الهندي
IPFC	مجلس مصايد المحيطين الهندي والهادي
WECAFC	مجلس مصايد غرب وسط المحيط الأطلنطي

أجهزة مستقلة

IBSFC	المجلس الدولي لمصايد بحر البلطيق
ICNAF	المجلس الدولي لمصايد شمال غرب المحيط الأطلنطي
ICSEAF	المجلس الدولي لمصايد جنوب شرق المحيط الأطلنطي
INPFC	المجلس الدولي لمصايد شمال المحيط الهادي
JKFC	مجلس المصايد المشترك بين اليابان وجمهورية كوريا
JSFC	المجلس الياباني – السوفيتي لمصايد شمال غرب المحيط الهادي
MCBSF	المجلس المشترك لمصايد البحر الأسود
NEAFC	مجلس مصايد شمال شرق المحيط الأطلنطي
PCSP	اللجنة الدائمة لمؤتمر استعمال الموارد البحرية وصيانتها في جنوب المحيط الهادي

اللجنة الدائمة للسلمون في بحر البلطيق
المجلس الأمريكي للتونة الاستوائية
المجلس الدولي لصيانة التونة بالأطلنطي
المجلس الدولي لأسماك الهاليبوت بالمحيط الهادي
المجلس الدولي لمصايد السلمون بالمحيط الهادي
المجلس الدولي لصيد الحيتان
مجلس مصايد فقمة الفراء بشمال المحيط الهادي
مجلس صيد الفقمة بشمال شرق المحيط الاطلنطي
مجلس المحاريات لمنطقة سكاجراك – كاتيجات

أنشئت الأجهزة الدولية للمصايد بغرض إيجاد حل لمشاكل إدارة الموارد الحية وصيانتها ، وإذا كانت هذه الأجهزة لم تثبت نجاحها دائما إلا أنها زادت إدراك أعضائها بضرورة ممارسة رقابة مشددة على المصايد في العالم .

أسماك القاع	الأسماك السياحة الشاطئية	التونة	الكركند والكركند الشوكي	السرطان	الجمبري ...الخ	الرخويات	الحيتان

استغلال كثيف
استغلال معتدل
استغلال غيركاف أوبسيط

---

٧ – تنمية المصايد في أندونيسيا

تسويق الأسماك وتوزيعها في جاوة

حصر تسهيلات تسويق الأسماك — التسهيلات التسويقية المقترحة

مزادات
غرف ومخازن التبريد
مصانع الثلج
سيارات نقل الأسماك
أسواق السمك
مراكز إنزال محاصيل الأسماك

تم حصر تسهيلات تسويق الأسماك بالتفصيل (أنظر الشكل الأيسر) في جاوة بغرض اقتراح التحسينات (أنظر الشكل الأيمن) اللازمة لزيادة فعالية استعمال كميات الأسماك الموجودة .

تقع كثير من مناطق انتاج الأسماك الرئيسية في أندونيسيا على مسافة بعيدة من مراكز الاستهلاك . فمقاطعة جاوة التي تمثل ٦٧ ٪ من السكان وتستهلك كمية تقرب من ٧٠ ٪ من اجمالي الانتاج السمكي لا تنتج إلا ٢٠ ٪ . ومن هذه الكمية . ويؤدى تداول الأسماك على ظهر سفن الصيد إلى سرعة تلف المحصول ، كما يؤثر نقص وسائل التخزين والنقل والطرق في توزيع الأسماك ذات النوعية الجيدة ، سواء كانت طازجة أو مجمدة ، داخل البلاد . وفي كثير من الأحيان تملح الأسماك أو تجفف أو تدخن بطريقة بدائية لحفظها وتوزيعها .

وفي هذه الظروف ينبغي إعادة النظر في جميع الأنشطة ابتداء من صيد الأسماك وحتى بيعها النهائي في الأسواق . ويجب أن يكون الهدف زيادة قيمة المحصول واستقرارها للصيادين وتحسين عرض الأسماك ونوعيتها للمستهلكين . ومن شأن تحسين شبكات التسويق والتوزيع زيادة الكميات المعروضة من الأسماك بالإقلال من التالف والأساليب غير الفعالة دون حاجة لزيادة المحصول نفسه .

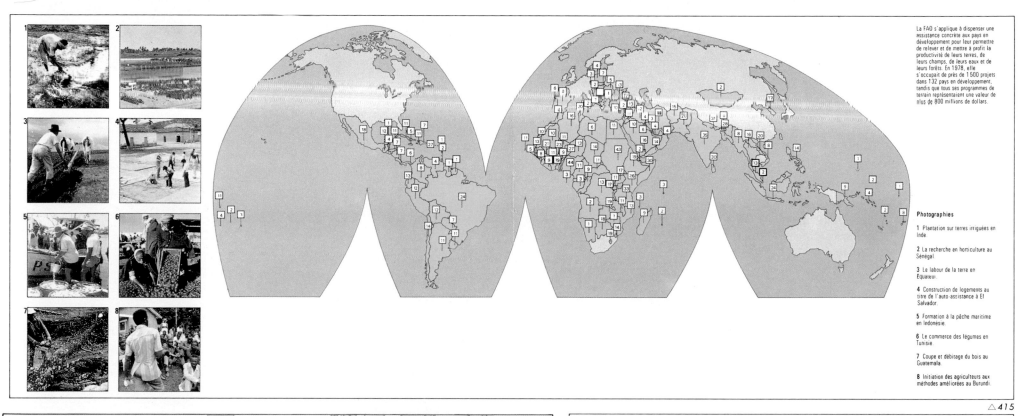

La FAO s'applique à dispenser une assistance concrète aux pays en développement pour leur permettre de relever et de mettre à profit la productivité de leurs terres, de leurs champs, de leurs eaux et de leurs forêts. En 1978, elle s'occupait de près de 1 500 projets dans 132 pays en développement, tandis que tous ses programmes de terrain représentaient une valeur de plus de 800 millions de dollars.

Photographies

1 Plantation sur terres irriguées en Inde.

2 La recherche en horticulture au Sénégal.

3 Le labour de la terre en Équateur.

4 Construction de logements au titre de l'auto-assistance à El Salvador.

5 Formation à la pêche maritime en Indonésie.

6 Le commerce des légumes en Tunisie.

7 Coupe et débitage du bois au Guatemala.

8 Initiation des agriculteurs aux méthodes améliorées au Burundi.

△415

Organes FAO des pêches

△416

	CARPAS	Commission consultative régionale des pêches pour l'Atlantique Sud-Ouest
	COPACE	Comité des pêches pour l'Atlantique Centre-Est
	CPCA	Comité des pêches continentales pour l'Afrique
	CECPI	Commission européenne consultative pour les pêches dans les eaux intérieures
	CGPM	Conseil général des pêches pour la Méditerranée
	CPOI	Commission des pêches pour l'océan Indien
	CIPP	Conseil indo-pacifique des pêches
	COPACO	Commission FAO des pêches pour l'Atlantique Centre-Ouest
	COPESCAL	Commission des pêches intérieures pour l'Amérique latine

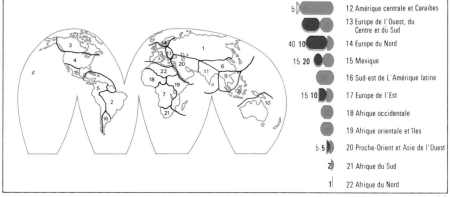

5 — 12 Amérique centrale et Caraïbes

13 Europe de l'Ouest, du Centre et du Sud

40 10 — 14 Europe du Nord

15 20 — 15 Mexique

16 Sud-est de L'Amérique latine

15 10 — 17 Europe de l'Est

18 Afrique occidentale

19 Afrique orientale et îles

5 5 — 20 Proche-Orient et Asie de l'Ouest

2 — 21 Afrique du Sud

1 — 22 Afrique du Nord

△417

412~417. THE DIAGRAM GROUP

1. U.K.
2. COMPUTER GRAPHICS-COMPARATIVE STATISTICS
3. MAPS
4. BOOK
5. FISHING AREAS/WORLD HUNGER (412~414)
FAO IN AFRICA (415~417)

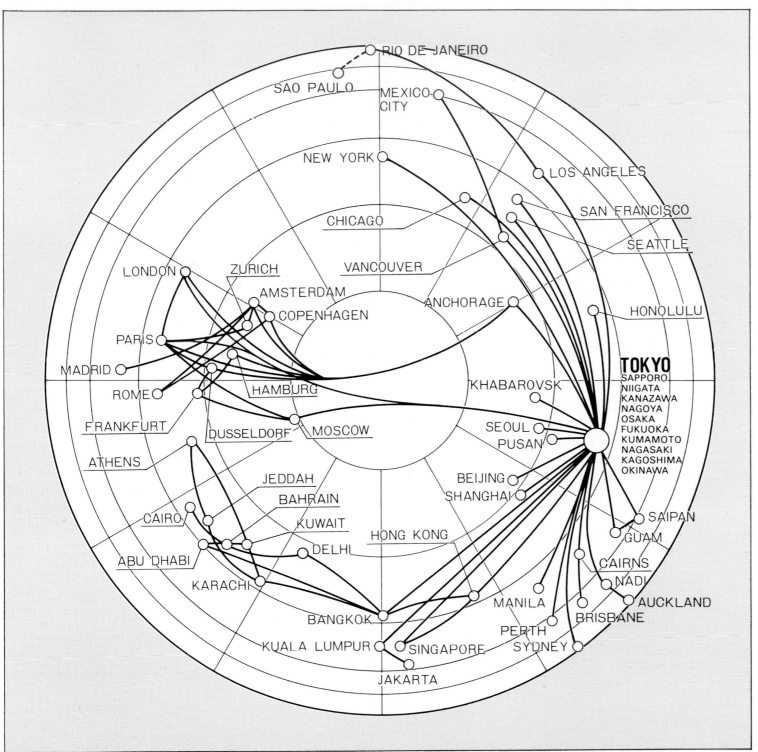

RIO DE JANEIRO
SAO PAULO
MEXICO CITY
NEW YORK
LOS ANGELES
CHICAGO
SAN FRANCISCO
SEATTLE
VANCOUVER
LONDON
ZURICH
AMSTERDAM
ANCHORAGE
COPENHAGEN
HONOLULU
PARIS
MADRID
ROME
HAMBURG
KHABAROVSK
TOKYO
SAPPORO
NIIGATA
KANAZAWA
NAGOYA
OSAKA
FUKUOKA
KUMAMOTO
NAGASAKI
KAGOSHIMA
OKINAWA
FRANKFURT
DUSSELDORF
MOSCOW
SEOUL
PUSAN
ATHENS
JEDDAH
BEIJING
SHANGHAI
BAHRAIN
CAIRO
KUWAIT
SAIPAN
GUAM
ABU DHABI
DELHI
HONG KONG
CAIRNS
NADI
KARACHI
AUCKLAND
MANILA
BRISBANE
BANGKOK
PERTH
KUALA LUMPUR
SINGAPORE
SYDNEY
JAKARTA

△418

△419

418～420. JAPAN AIR LINES CO., LTD.

1. JAPAN
2. JAPAN AIR LINES CO., LTD.
3. DECORATIVE MAPS
5. INTERNATIONAL ROUTES AND TOKYO CONNECTIONS

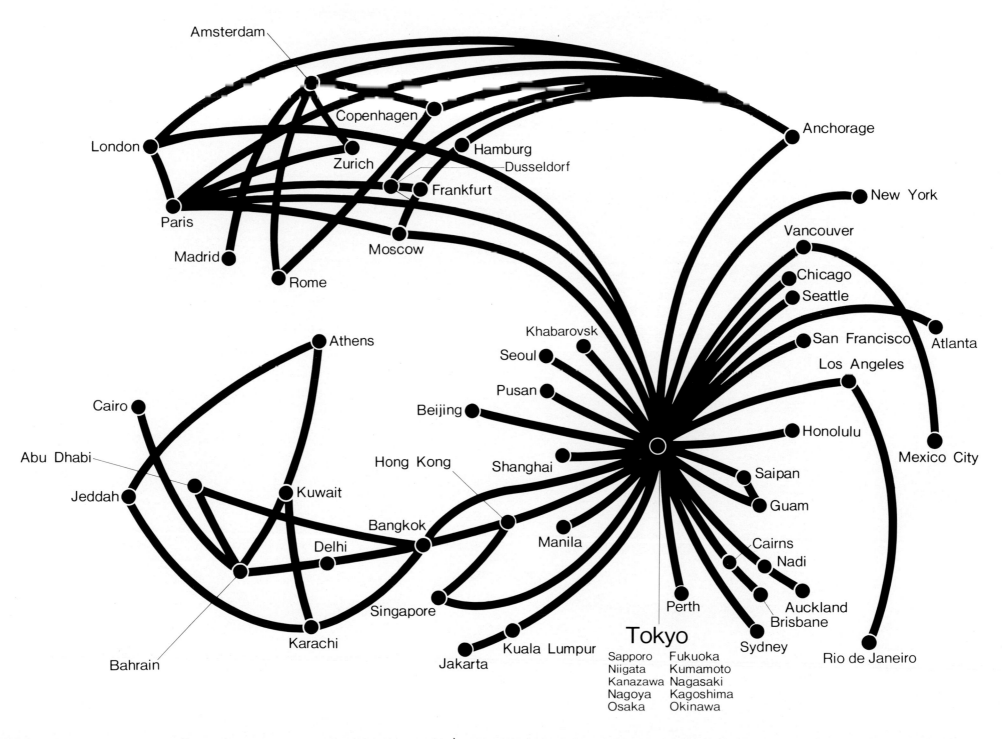

Amsterdam
Copenhagen
London
Hamburg
Zurich
Dusseldorf
Frankfurt
Paris
Moscow
Madrid
Rome
Anchorage
New York
Vancouver
Chicago
Seattle
San Francisco
Atlanta
Los Angeles
Khabarovsk
Seoul
Honolulu
Pusan
Beijing
Mexico City
Hong Kong
Shanghai
Saipan
Athens
Guam
Cairo
Abu Dhabi
Kuwait
Jeddah
Bangkok
Cairns
Nadi
Delhi
Manila
Singapore
Auckland
Karachi
Perth
Brisbane
Bahrain
Jakarta
Kuala Lumpur
Sydney
Rio de Janeiro

Tokyo
Sapporo Fukuoka
Niigata Kumamoto
Kanazawa Nagasaki
Nagoya Kagoshima
Osaka Okinawa

△420

189

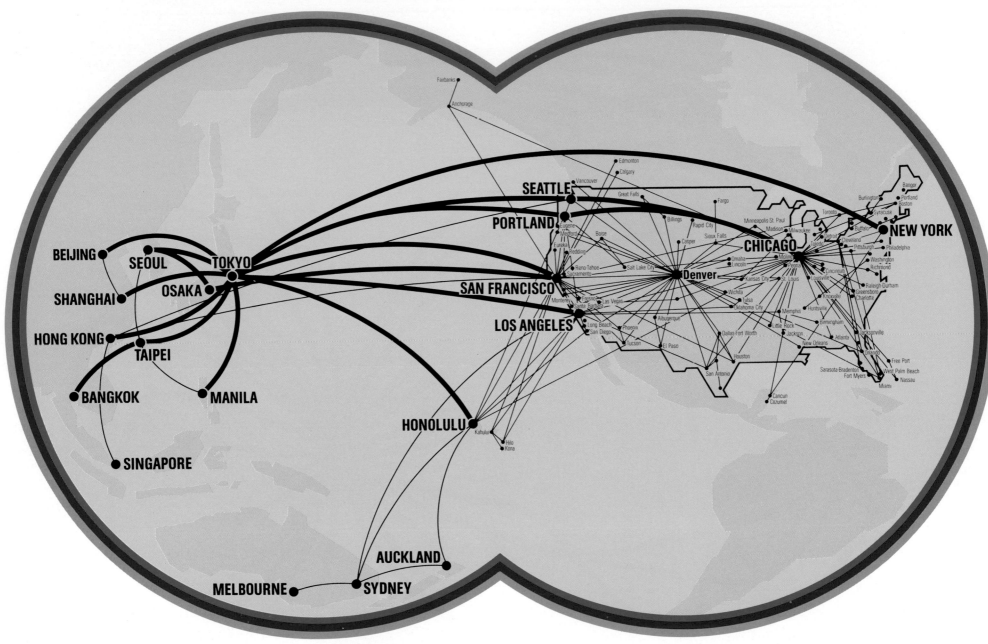

△421

421,422. HIROSHI ISOKAWA

1. JAPAN
2. DENTSU INCORPORATED
3. DECORATIVE MAPS
5. UNITED AIRLINES
   EAST ASIAN ROUTES

190

△423

△424

△425

△426　△427

423~427. GK GRAPHICS

1. JAPAN
2. GK GRAPHICS
3. PICTORIAL DIAGRAMS
4. TSUKUBA EXPO '85 SIGN PLANNING
5. PRODUCTION YEAR : 1985
   PRODUCTION AREA : TOKYO
   PRODUCERS : GK SEKKEI ASSOCIATES / GK GRAPHICS
   CLIENT : INTERNATIONAL SCIENCE TECHNIQUE EXPO ASSOCIATION
   RIGHTS RESERVED BY : GK GRAPHICS
   PHOTOGRAPHER : TAKESHI NAKASA

GK GRAPHICS 428~430.

1. JAPAN
2. GK GRAPHICS
3. PICTORIAL DIAGRAMS
4. TSUKUBA EXPO '85 SIGN PLANNING
5. PRODUCTION YEAR : 1985
   PRODUCTION AREA : TOKYO
   PRODUCERS : GK SEKKEI ASSOCIATES/GK GRAPHICS
   CLIENT : INTERNATIONAL SCIENCE TECHNIQUE EXPO ASSOCIATION
   RIGHTS RESERVED BY : GK GRAPHICS
   PHOTOGRAPHER : TAKESHI NAKASA

△429

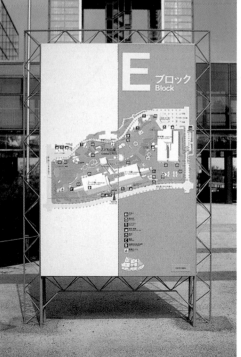

△428　△430

193

△431　△432

431,432. GK GRAPHICS

1. JAPAN
2. GK GRAPHICS
3. PICTORIAL DIAGRAMS
4. TSUKUBA EXPO '85 SIGN PLANNING
5. PRODUCTION YEAR : 1985
   PRODUCTION AREA : TOKYO
   PRODUCERS : GK SEKKEI ASSOCIATES / GK GRAPHICS
   CLIENT : INTERNATIONAL SCIENCE TECHNIQUE EXPO ASSOCIATION
   RIGHTS RESERVED BY : GK GRAPHICS
   PHOTOGRAPHER : TAKESHI NAKASA

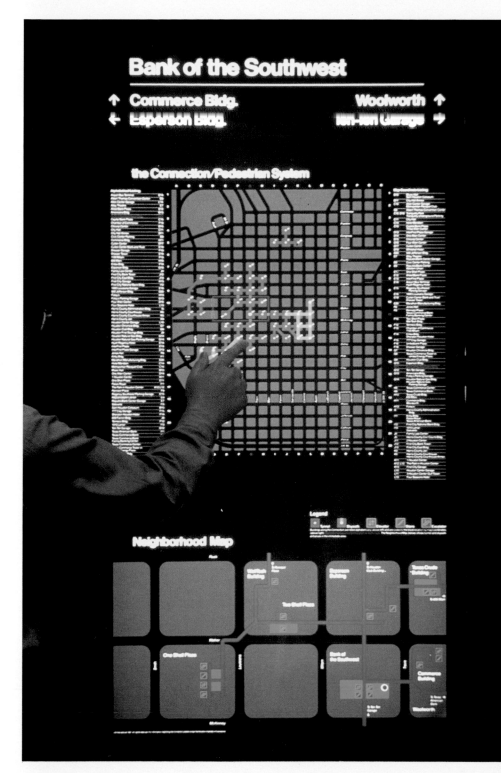

△ 433

△ 434

△ 435

433~435. FRANK F. DOUGLAS

1. U.S.A.
2. 3D/INTERNATIONAL
3. DECORATIVE MAPS
4. THE HOUSTON AD HOC TUNNEL COMMITTEE
5. 29 INFORMATION LOCATIONS IN THE DOWNTOWN HOUSTON
   TUNNEL SYSTEM (433)

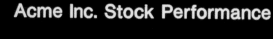

Acme Inc. Stock Performance

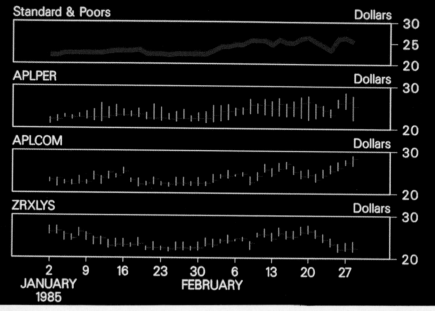

Standard & Poors — Dollars 30 25 20

APLPER — Dollars 30 20

APLCOM — Dollars 30 20

ZRXLYS — Dollars 30 20

2 9 16 23 30 6 13 20 27
JANUARY   FEBRUARY
1985

△ 436

Federal Government Deficit
Seasonally adjusted annual rates

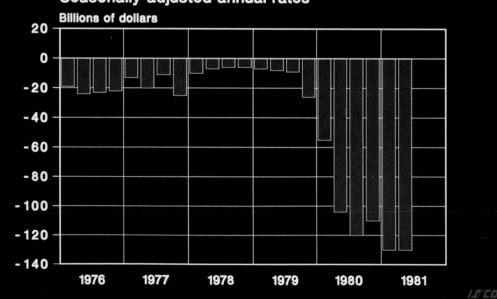

Billions of dollars

20 0 -20 -40 -60 -80 -100 -120 -140

1976   1977   1978   1979   1980   1981

20 LARGEST U.S. PETROLEUM REFINING COMPANIES

		1983 Sales ($ Billions)
▦	Exxon	88.6
▦	Mobil	54.6
▦	Texaco	40
▦	Standard Oil (Indiana)	27.6
▦	Standard Oil of California	27.3
▦	Gulf Oil	26.6
▦	Atlantic Richfield	25.1
▦	Shell Oil	19.7
	U.S. Steel	16.9
▦	Phillips Petroleum	15.2
▦	Sun	14.7
▦	Tenneco	14.4
▦	Getty Oil	11.6
▦	Standard Oil (Ohio)	11.6
▦	Unocal	10.1
	Amerada Hess	8.4
▦	Union Pacific	8.4
	Ashland Oil	7.9
	Coastal	6
	Charter	5.6

▦   ISSCO Customer

△ 437   △ 438

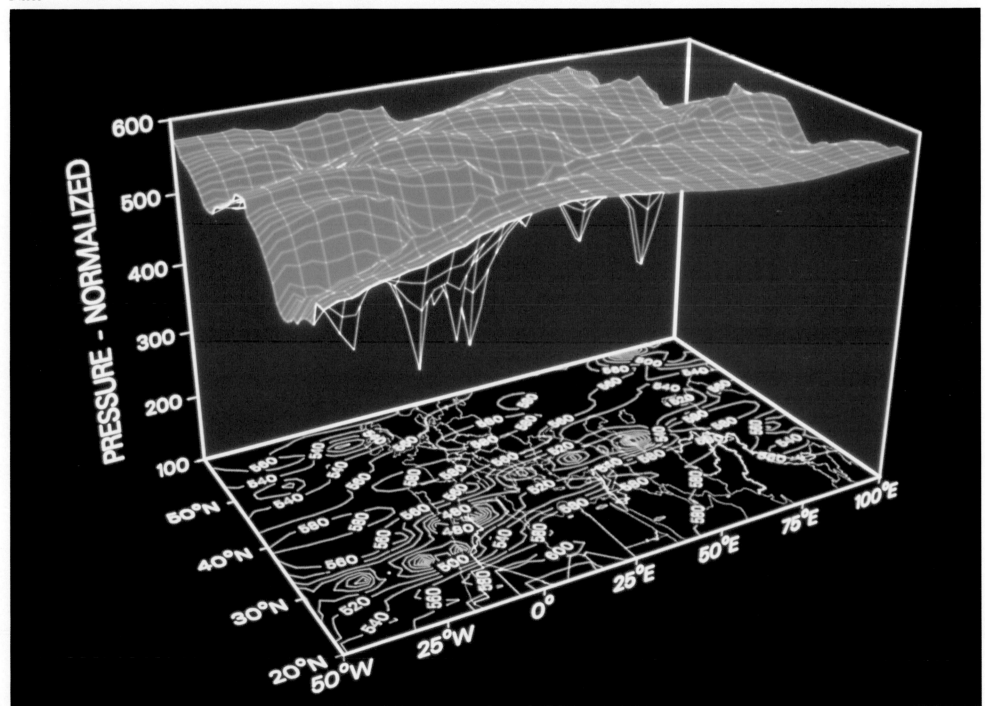

△439

△440

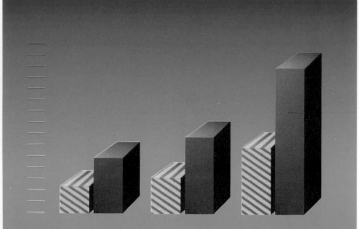

△441

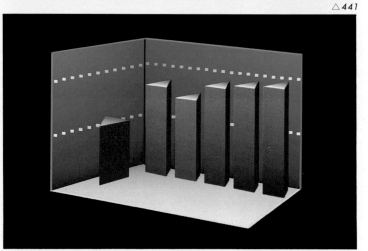

△442

△443

440~443. TIM ALT/KENNETH R. WEISS

1. U.S.A.
2. DIGITAL ART
3. COMPUTER GRAPHICS-COMPARATIVE STATISTICS
5. PWS PUBLISHERS (440)
   ABERT, NEWHOFF + BURR (441,442)
   UNPUBLISHED (443)

1. JAPAN
2. DIAGRAM VISUAL INFORMATION LTD. (D.V.I.)
3. NEC CORP.
5. POPULATION DENSITY DIAGRAMS. EACH EMPHASIZING DIFFERENT RESULTS

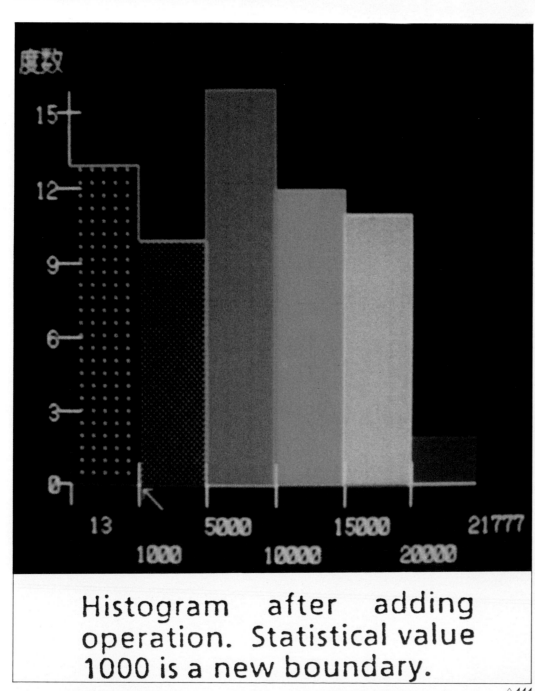

Histogram after adding operation. Statistical value 1000 is a new boundary.

△444

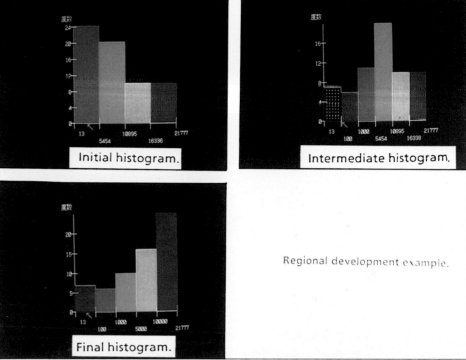

Initial histogram.

Intermediate histogram.

Final histogram.

Regional development example.

△445 ▽446

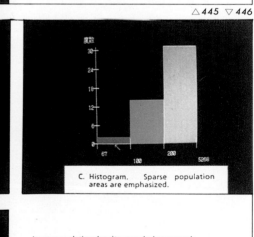

A. Histogram. Dense population areas are emphasized.

C. Histogram. Sparse population areas are emphasized.

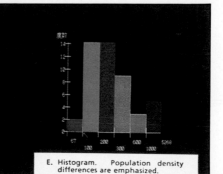

E. Histogram. Population density differences are emphasized.

Japan population density map design example.

Assumed designers' intensions are;
(1) Emphasizing dense population areas.
(2) Emphasizing sparse population areas.
(3) Emphasizing population density differences between

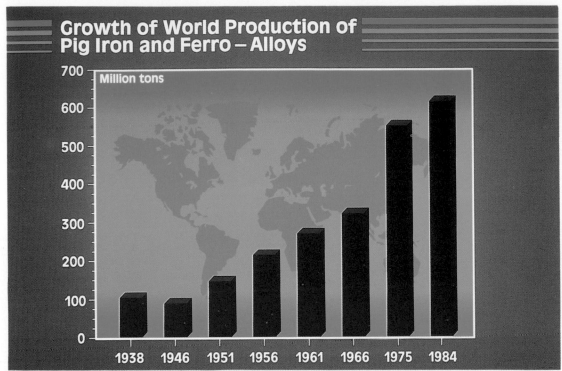

Growth of World Production of Pig Iron and Ferro – Alloys

Million tons

700
600
500
400
300
200
100
0

1938 1946 1951 1956 1961 1966 1975 1984

△447

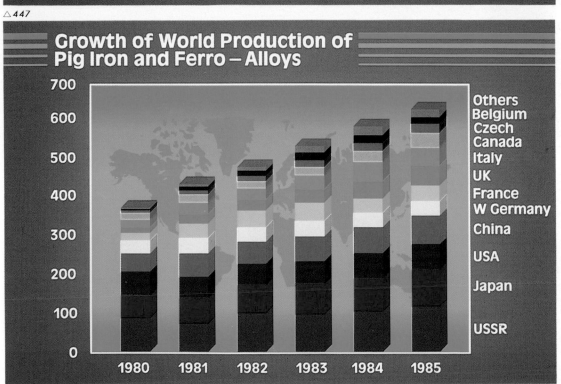

Growth of World Production of Pig Iron and Ferro – Alloys

700
600
500
400
300
200
100
0

1980 1981 1982 1983 1984 1985

Others
Belgium
Czech
Canada
Italy
UK
France
W Germany
China
USA
Japan
USSR

△448

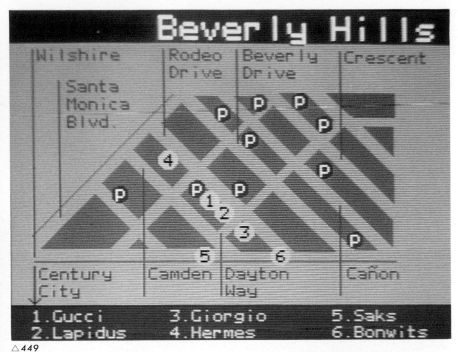

△449

GREGORY THOMAS 449.

U.S.A. 1.
CBS TELEVISION NETWORK 2.
COMPUTER GRAPHICS-COMPARATIVE STATISTICS 3.
CBS EXTRAVISION 4.
LOCATION MAP OF MAJOR STORES IN BEVERLY HILLS 5.

447,448. C-THUR GRAPHICS LIMITED

1. U.K.
2. NATIONAL SOUND REPRODUCERS LTD.
3. COMPUTER GRAPHICS-COMPARATIVE STATISTICS

TERUTOSHI TADA 450.

JAPAN 1.
NIPPON UNIVAC INFORMATION SYSTEMS KAISHA. LTD. 2.
COMPUTER GRAPHICS-COMPARATIVE STATISTICS 3.

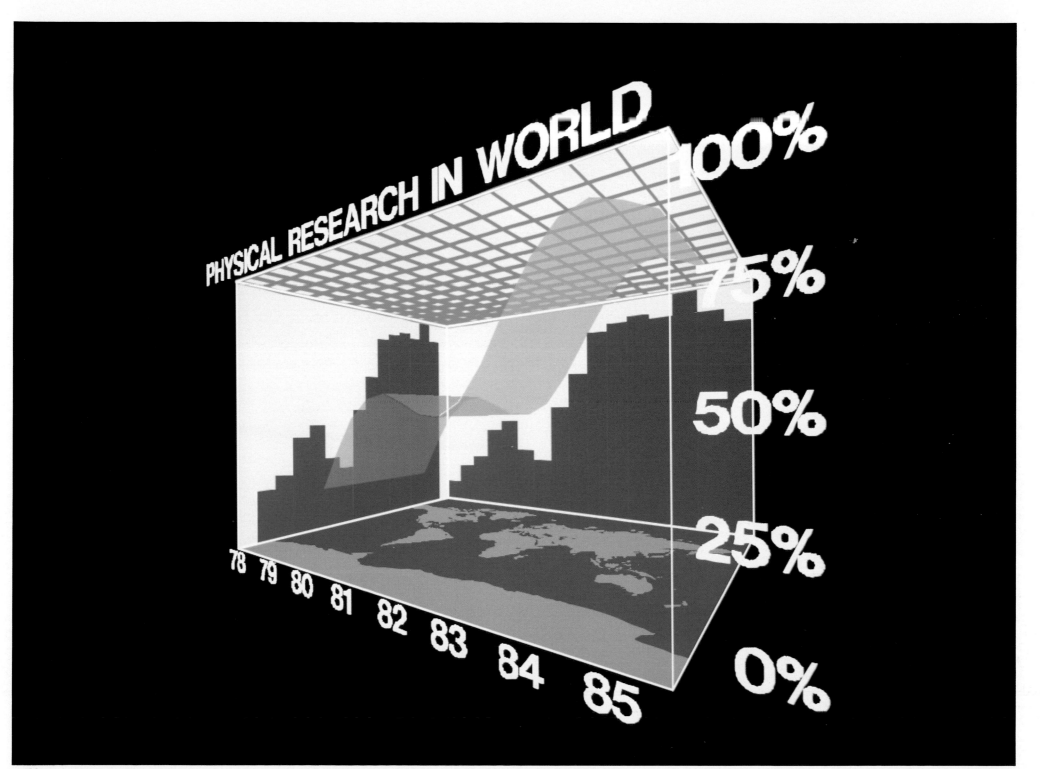

△451

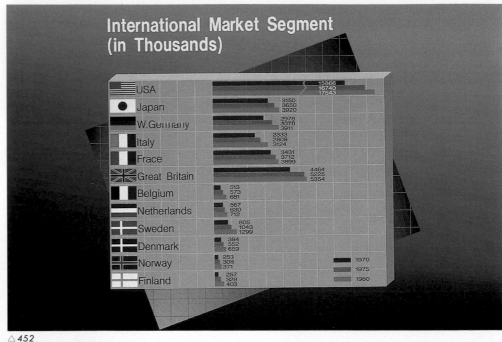

△452

△453

NISSHO ELECTRONICS 451~456.

JAPAN 1.
NISSHO ELECTRONICS 2.
COMPUTER GRAPHICS-COMPARATIVE STATISTICS 3.
PRODUCED BY DICOMED CORP (451, 452, 454, 455, 456) 4.

TIM ALT/KENNETH R. WEISS 457.

U.S.A. 1.
DIGITAL ART 2.
COMPUTER GRAPHICS-COMPARATIVE STATISTICS 3.
ABERT, NEWHOFF + BURR 5.

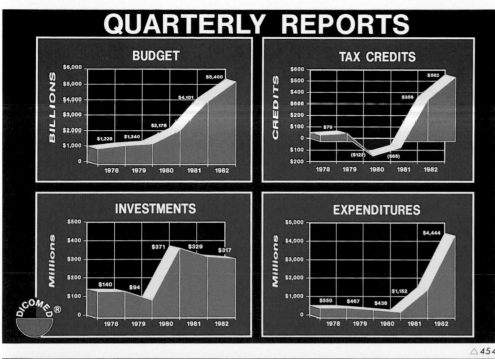

△454

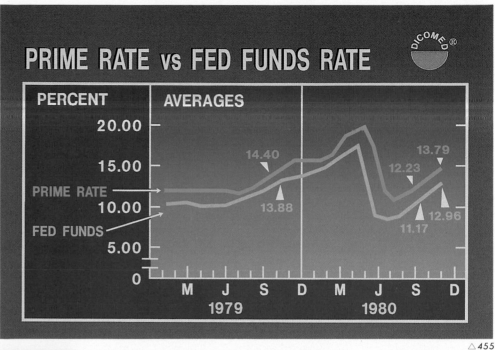

△455

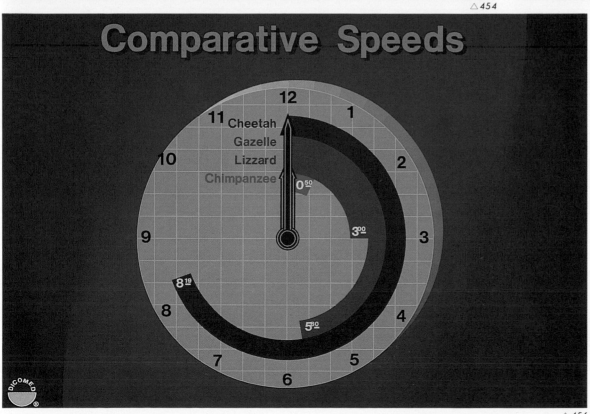

△456

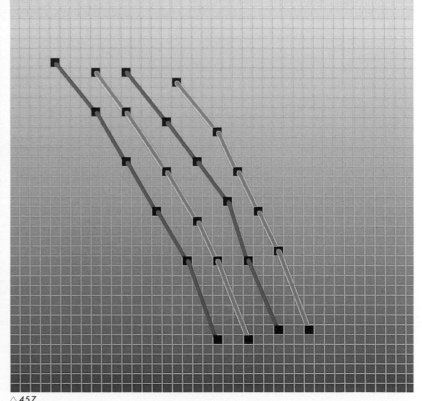

△457

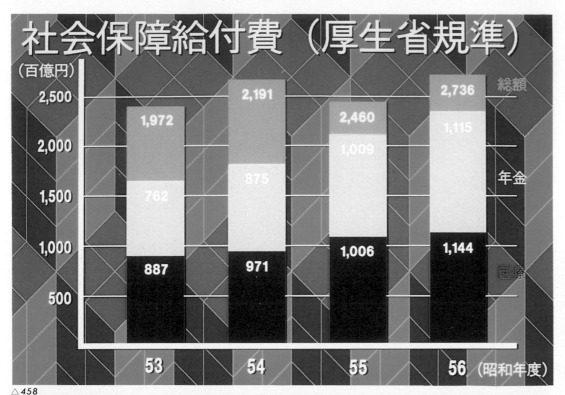

社会保障給付費（厚生省規準）

（百億円）

	53	54	55	56 （昭和年度）
総額	1,972	2,191	2,460	2,736
年金			1,009	1,115
	762	875		
医療	887	971	1,006	1,144

△458

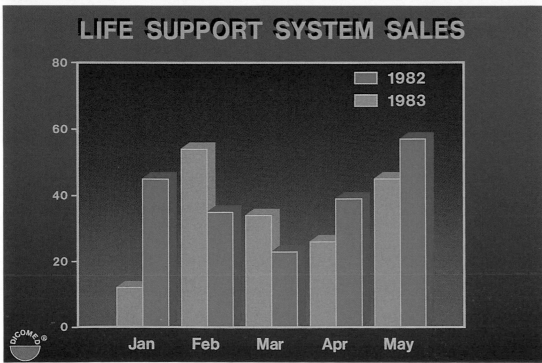

LIFE SUPPORT SYSTEM SALES

1982
1983

Jan Feb Mar Apr May

△459

458,459. NISSHO ELECTRONICS　　　　　**TIM ALT/KENNETH R. WEISS 460.**

1. JAPAN
2. NISSHO ELECTRONICS
3. COMPUTER GRAPHICS-COMPARATIVE STATISTICS
4. PRODUCED BY DICOMED CORP (459)

U.S.A. 1.
DIGITAL ART 2.
COMPUTER GRAPHICS-SEGMENT CHARTS 3.
AMERON CORP. 5.

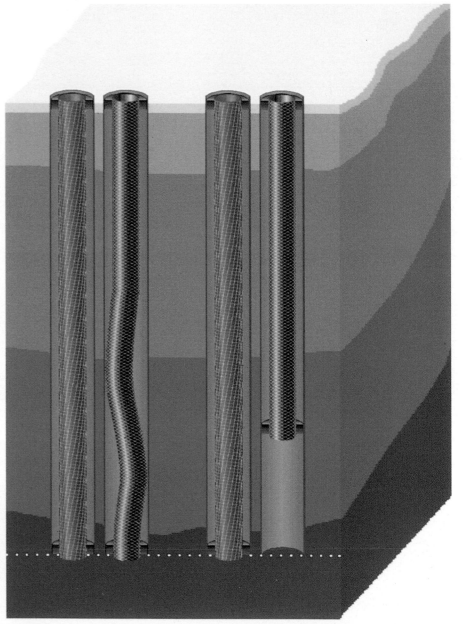

△460

1. JAPAN
2. NISSHO ELECTRONICS
3. COMPUTER GRAPHICS—COMPARATIVE STATISTICS (461,463,464)
          —FLOW MOVEMENTS (462)
5. SOCIAL EDUCATION EXPENSES (461)
   COMPARISON OF SLIDE-PREPARATION METHODS (462)
   OCCUPATIONS PREFERRED BY STUDENTS (463)

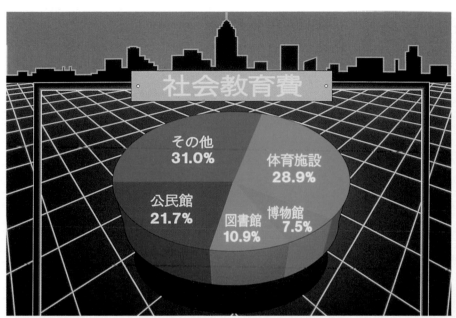

△461

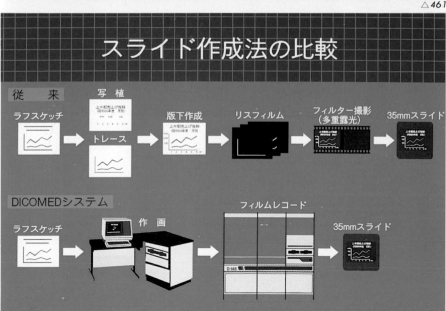

△462   △464

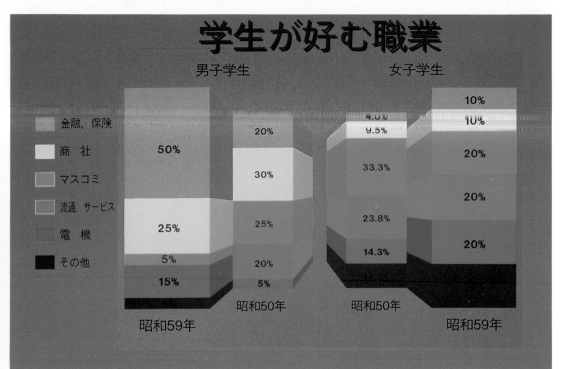

△463

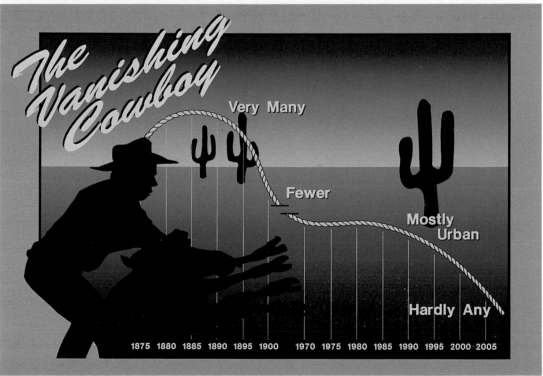

Stores Opened
Through 1981

△ 465

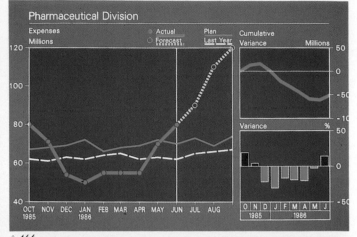

Pharmaceutical Division

△ 466

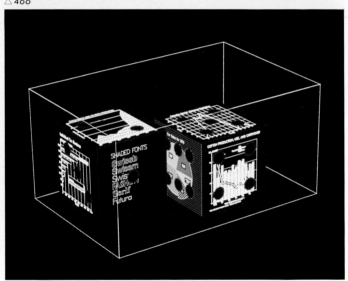

△ 467

465~467. PETER BOOT

1. U.S.A.

2. ISSCO

3. COMPUTER GRAPHICS-COMPATIVE STATISTICS

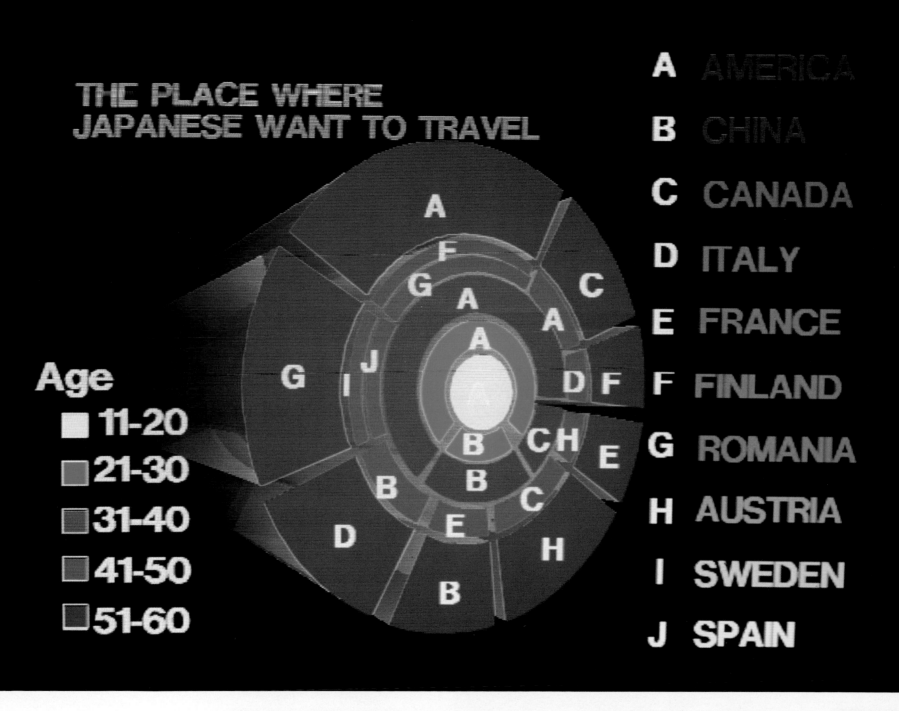

THE PLACE WHERE
JAPANESE WANT TO TRAVEL

A AMERICA
B CHINA
C CANADA
D ITALY
E FRANCE
F FINLAND
G ROMANIA
H AUSTRIA
I SWEDEN
J SPAIN

Age
■ 11-20
■ 21-30
■ 31-40
■ 41-50
■ 51-60

NIPPON UNIVAC INFORMATION SYSTEMS KAISHA. LTD. 2.
COMPUTER GRAPHICS-COMPARATIVE STATISTICS 3.

YASUNORI IWAMOTO 468.
JAPAN 1.

△469

△470

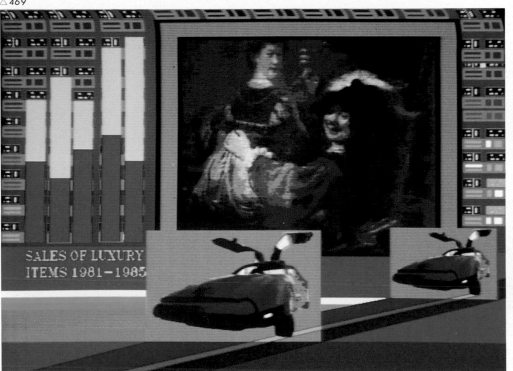

SALES OF LUXURY ITEMS 1981-1985

△471

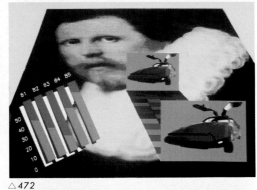

△472

△473

SAUL BERNSTEIN 469~473.

U.S.A. 1.
COMPUTER GRAPHICS-COMPARATIVE STATISTICS 3.
LUXURY ITEMS SALES REPORT 1980-85 5.

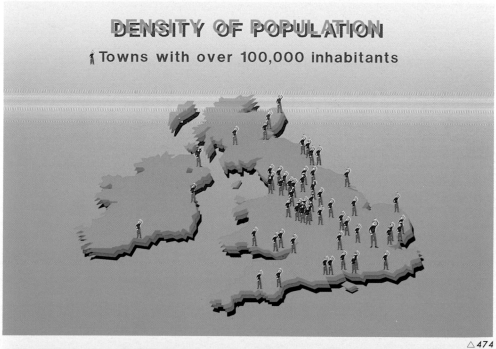

DENSITY OF POPULATION

↑ Towns with over 100,000 inhabitants

△474

C-THUR GRAPHICS LTD. 474.

U.K. 1.
NATIONAL SOUND REPRODUCERS LTD. 2.
COMPUTER GRAPHICS-DECORATIVE MAPS 3.

TEXNAI CGL. 475,476.

JAPAN 1.
TEXNAI INC. 2.
COMPUTER GRAPHICS-DECORATIVE MAPS 3.
CATALOGUE 4.
YOSHIDA IND., INC. 5.
THREE DIMENSIONAL WORLD MAP, GENERATED BY A RAY-TRACING SYSTEM (475)

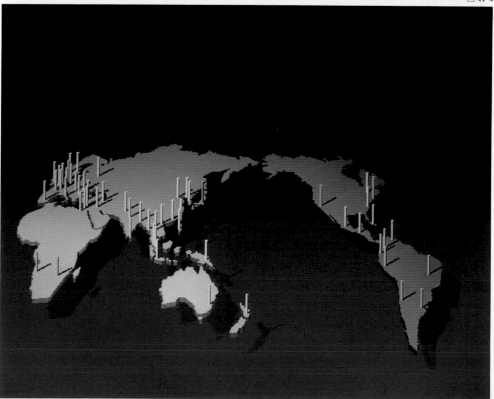

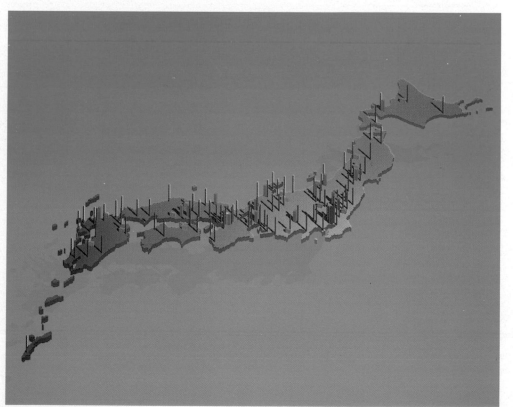

△475   △476

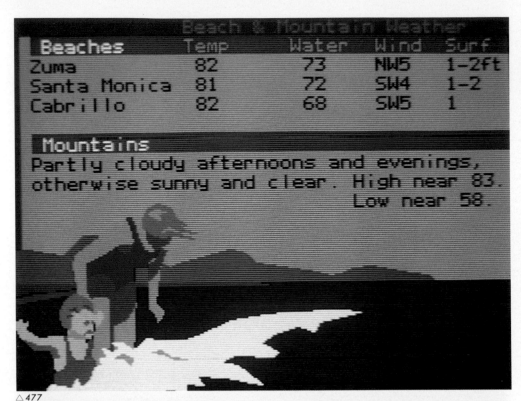

Beach & Mountain Weather

Beaches	Temp	Water	Wind	Surf
Zuma	82	73	NW5	1-2ft
Santa Monica	81	72	SW4	1-2
Cabrillo	82	68	SW5	1

Mountains
Partly cloudy afternoons and evenings, otherwise sunny and clear. High near 83. Low near 58.

△477

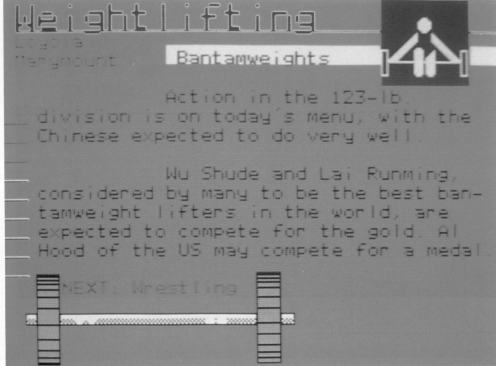

Weightlifting

Bantamweights

Action in the 123-lb. division is on today's menu, with the Chinese expected to do very well.

Wu Shude and Lai Runming, considered by many to be the best bantamweight lifters in the world, are expected to compete for the gold. Al Hood of the US may compete for a medal.

NEXT: Wrestling

△478

HISPANIC LA

66. Calendario de Eventos
67. Noticias y servicios en la comunidad
68. Deportes

△479

GREGORY THOMAS 477～479,480,481,483.

U.S.A. 1.
CBS TELEVISION NETWORK 2.
DESIGN DIRECTOR : GREGORY THOMAS
ARTIST : DON LINDSEY (479,481)
COMPUTER GRAPHICS-TABLES AND CHARTS 3.
1984 OLYMPICS (478,481) 4.
1984 ELECTIONS (480)
CBS EXTRAVISION 5.

TERUTOSHI TABA 482.

JAPAN 1.
NIPPON UNIVAC INFORMATION SYSTEMS KAISHA 2.
COMPUTER GRAPHICS-FORMATION OF TABLES AND CHARTS 3.
T-SHIRT MEASUREMENTS 5.

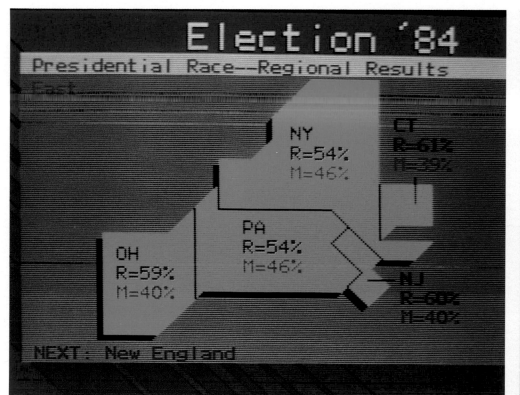

Election '84

Presidential Race--Regional Results

East

NY
R=54%
M=46%

CT
R=61%
M=39%

PA
R=54%
M=46%

OH
R=59%
M=40%

NJ
R=60%
M=40%

NEXT: New England

△480

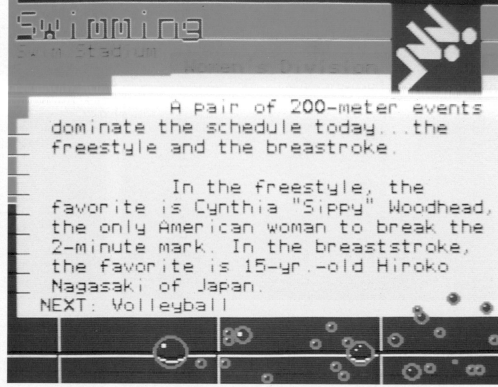

Swimming

Swim Stadium

Women's Division

A pair of 200-meter events dominate the schedule today...the freestyle and the breaststroke.

In the freestyle, the favorite is Cynthia "Sippy" Woodhead, the only American woman to break the 2-minute mark. In the breaststroke, the favorite is 15-yr.-old Hiroko Nagasaki of Japan.
NEXT: Volleyball

△481

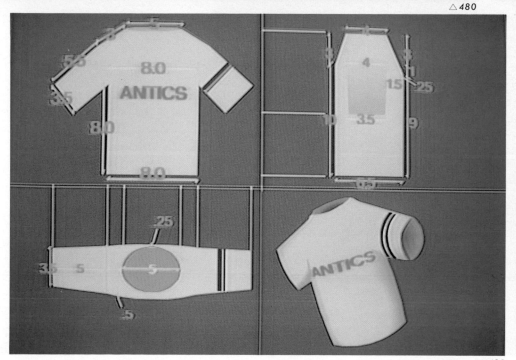

ANTICS

8.0

8.0

8.0

8.0

4

15 25

35

25

5

5

5

ANTICS

△482 △483

p47

Nightclubs

Ft.Lauderdale

One-Up Lounge   566-9961
3001 E.Orland Park Blvd.
Hours: 8pm-2am. Band
starts 9pm, "Rainy Days."

Pier Top Lounge, Pier 66 Hotel 525-6666
2301 SE 17th Street. Open until 1:30pm.
Band starts 9:20pm, "Sunburst."

September   563-4331
2975 N.Federal Hwy. Hours: 6:45pm-2am.
Band: "September's" $5 cover.
More nightclubs: NEXT

America's
Storyteller

Kodak

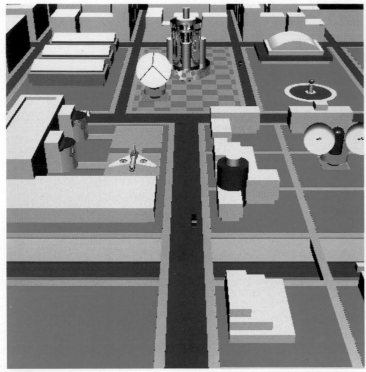

△498

△499

△500

TEXNAI CGL 498～501.

JAPAN 1.
TEXNAI INC. 2.
COMPUTER GRAPHICS-DECORATIVE MAPS 3.
NEWSPAPER (498) 4.
CATALOGUE (499)
PUBLIC RELATIONS PUBLICATION (500)
MAGAZINE (500)
JIJI COMMUNICATIONS 5.
TOWN IN THE 21ST CENTURY (498)
PANGBORN DESIGN
THREE DIMENSIONAL MAP OF MICHIGAN (499)
ISEHARA CITY (JAPAN)
NEW CITY PLAN (500)
(ALL WERE CREATED WITH A RAY-TRACING SYSTEM)
YAMAKEI INC.
THREE DIMENSIONAL MAP OF THE JAPANESE ALPS

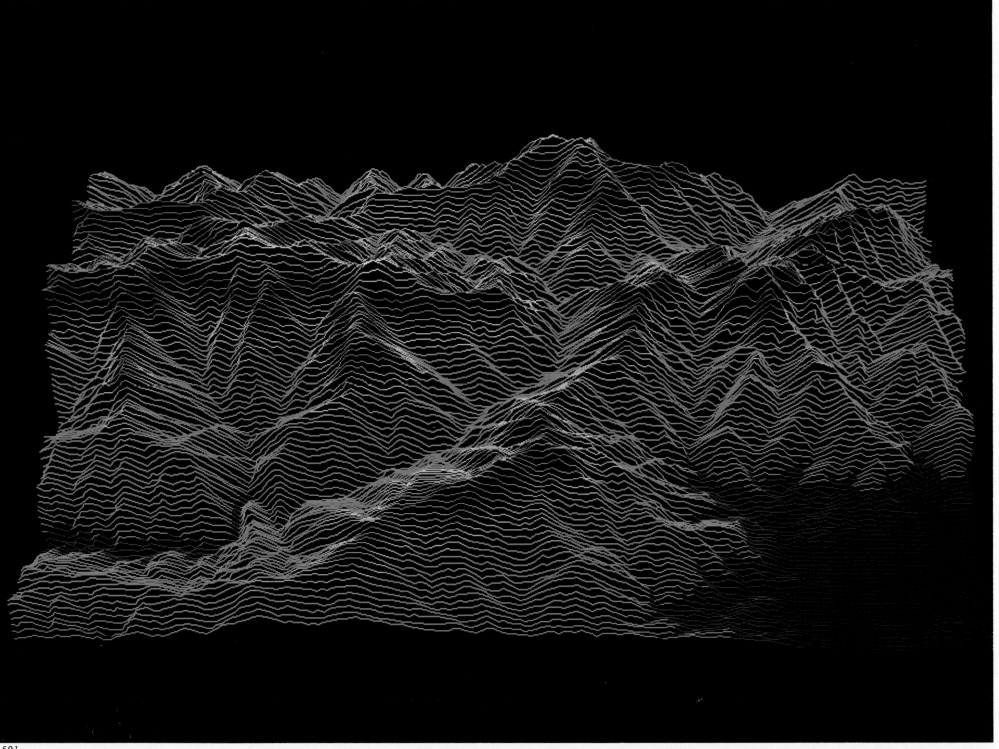

△501

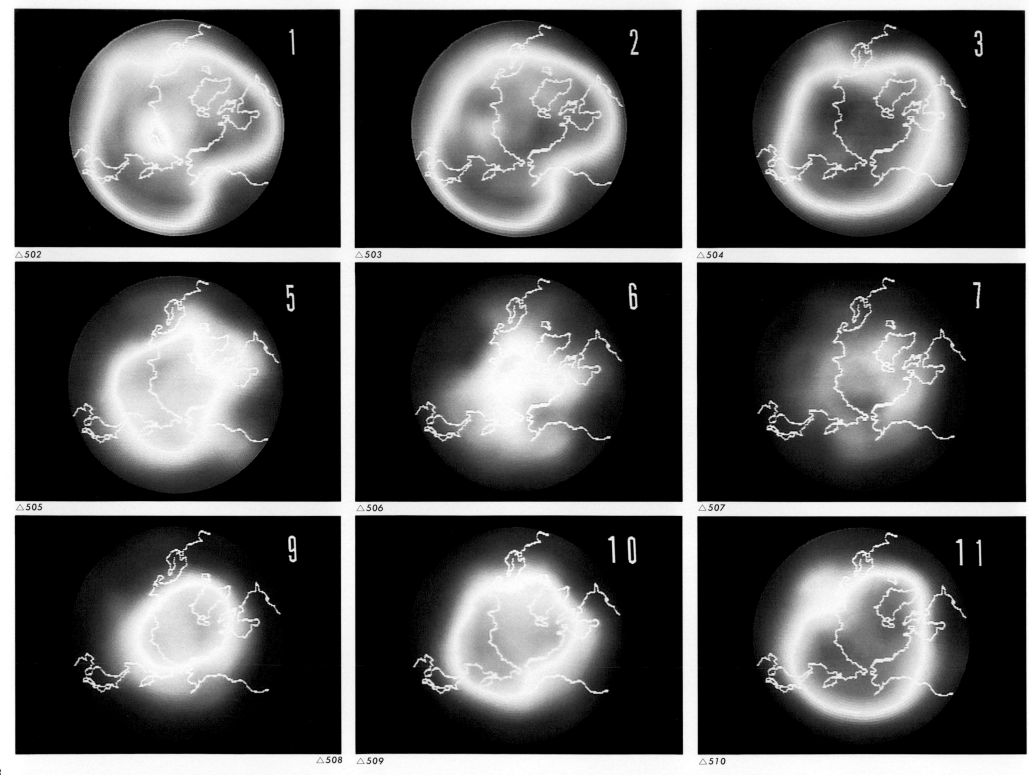

△502 △503 △504 △505 △506 △507 △508 △509 △510

218

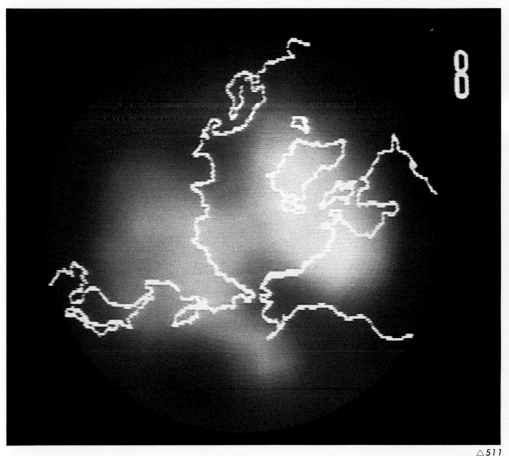

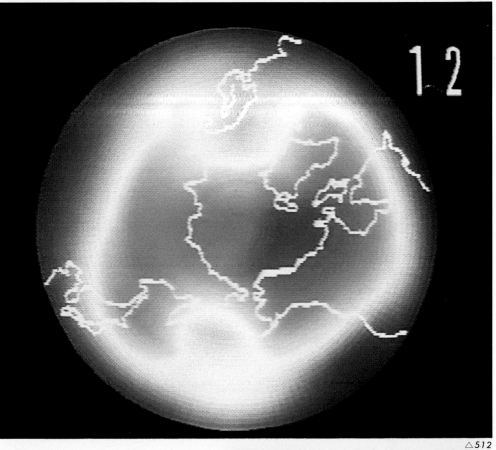

△511

△512

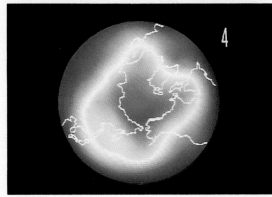

502~512. NHK (JAPAN BROADCASTING CORP.)

1. JAPAN
2. NHK (JAPAN BROADCASTING CORP.)
3. COMPUTER GRAPHICS
5. APPLIANCE OF COMPUTER GRAPHICS TO THE PRODUCTION OF TV PROGRAMS
COMPUTER GRAPHICS ARE NOW BEING USED IN THE
PRODUCTION OF TV PROGRAMS TO EXPRESS REALITY
AND SOLIDITY. IN PRODUCING A PROGRAM, IT IS
IMPORTANT NOT ONLY TO CREATE A SENSE OF REALITY
BUT ALSO TO EXPRESS THE CONCEPT AND PURPOSE
NEEDED BY THE CG IMAGE PROGRAM. IN THIS SENSE,
VISUALLY SIMPLE AND CLEAR DESIGNS BECOME A
NECESSITY.

"UNUSUAL WEATHER"
TEMPERATURE CHANGES IN THE WEATHER OF 1977 ARE
COMBINED IN THIS TIME-LAPSE DIAGRAM WITH
AN ANIMATED DIAGRAM OF THE EARTH SHOWN FROM
ABOVE THE NORTH POLE. THE NUMBERS INDICATE
MONTHS, RED INDICATES HIGH TEMPERATURES, AND
BLUE INDICATES LOW TEMPERATURES.

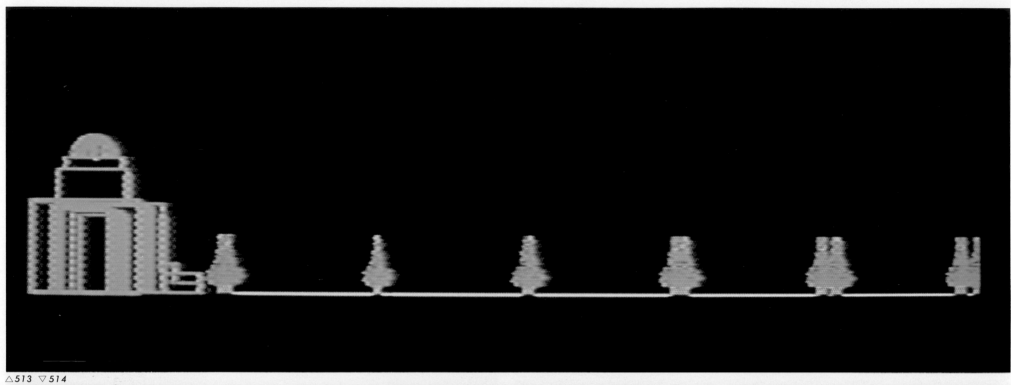

△513 ▽514

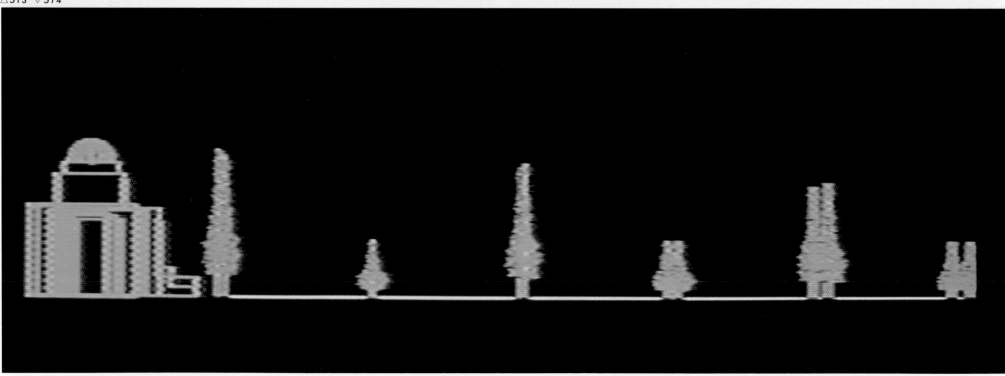

513~517. NHK (JAPAN BROADCASTING CORP.)

1. JAPAN
2. NHK (JAPAN BROADCASTING CORP.)
3. COMPUTER GRAPHICS
5. "PERSPECTIVES"
   KAIGA-KAN (AN ART MUSEUM) IS SHOWN IN ORDER TO ILLUSTRATE THE
   VISUAL EFFECT OF TREES PLANTED ALONG AN ENTRANCE DRIVE. EQUIVALENT
   TREE HEIGHTS DRAW ATTENTION TO THE STRUCTURE (513, 515, 517), AND
   UNEQUIVALENT HEIGHTS ARE DISTRACTING (514, 516).

△515

△516

△517

221

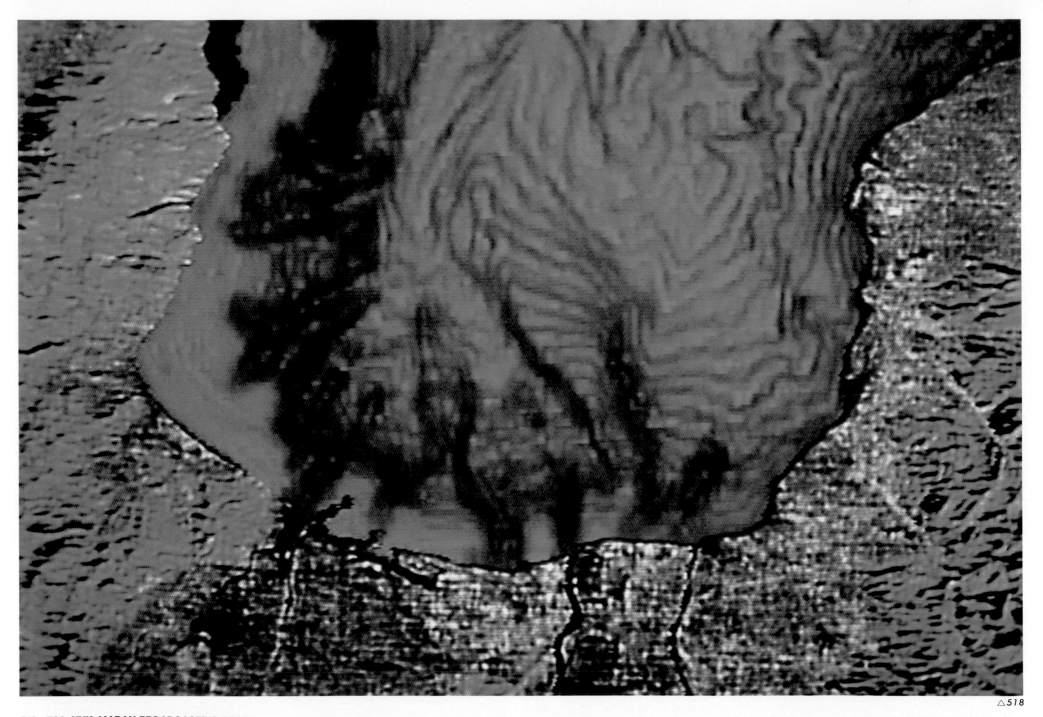

△518

518~522. NHK (JAPAN BROADCASTING CORP.)

1. JAPAN
2. NHK (JAPAN BROADCASTING CORP.)
3. COMPUTER GRAPHICS

5. "TOYAMA BAY, SEARCHING THE MYSTERIOUS OCEAN"
THIS ANIMATION SHOWS CONDITIONS UNDER THE OCEAN
OF TOYAMA BAY, WHICH IS KNOWN FOR ITS MYSTERIOUS

FLOOD TIDE, MIRAGES, AND THE WORLD'S OLDEST
BURIED FOREST. D-1 IS A COMBINATION OF LANDSATT'S
IMAGE OF THE EARTH'S SURFACE AND THE BOTTOM

OF THE OCEAN WHICH WAS CREATED BY C.G. DEPTH
IS TEN TIMES THE ACTUAL SIZE.

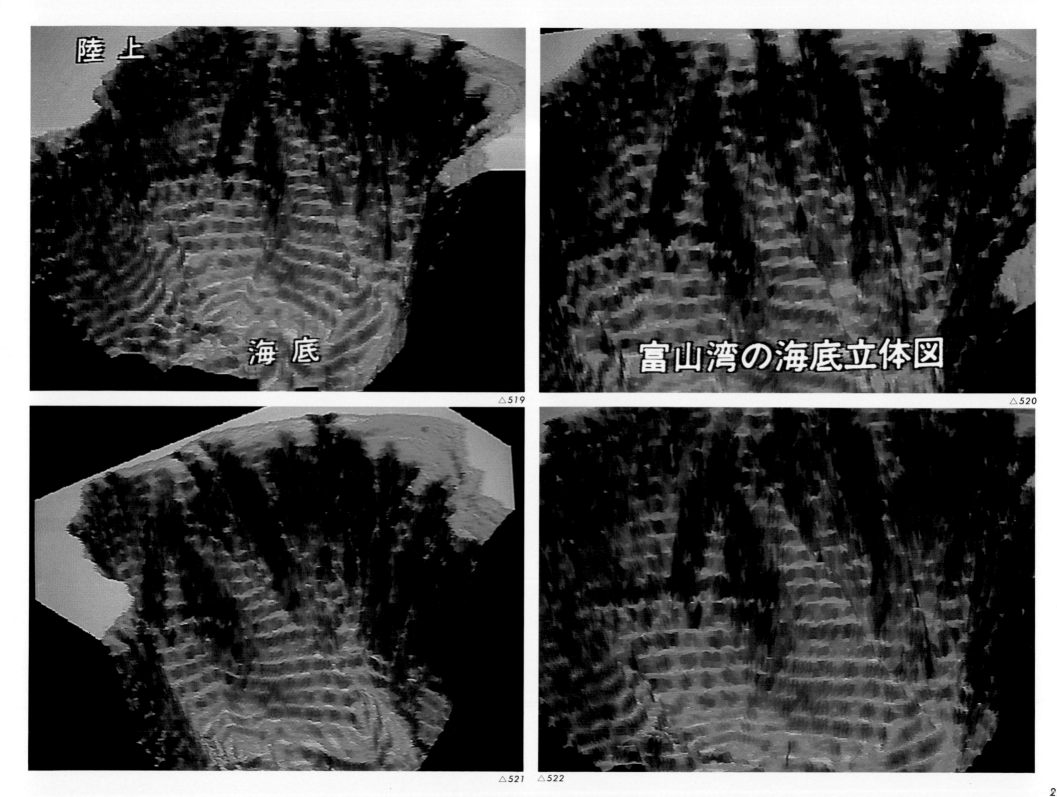

陸上

海底

富山湾の海底立体図

△519

△520

△521 △522

523~526. NHK (JAPAN BROADCASTING CORP.)

1. JAPAN
2. NHK (JAPAN BROADCASTING CORP.)
3. COMPUTER GRAPHICS
5. "IF THE HIMALAYA MOUNTAINS DID NOT EXIST"
   THE INFLUENCE OF THE DISTANT HIMALAYAS ON THE
   WEATHER PATTERNS OF JAPAN IS SHOWN BY THE DIRECTION
   AND VELOCITY OF THE WIND IN ANIMATED FORM.
   IF THE HIMALAYAS DID NOT EXIST, JAPAN'S WEATHER
   WOULD BE MUCH CALMER THAN THE PRESENT
   WEATHER.

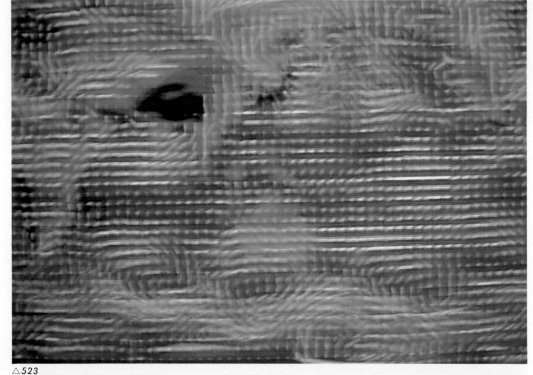

△523

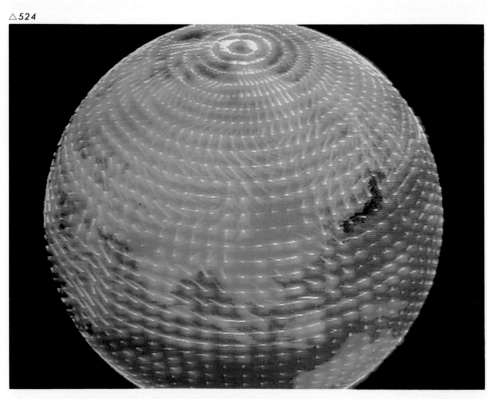

△524

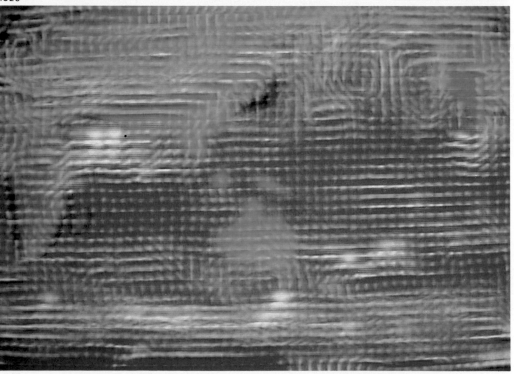

△525

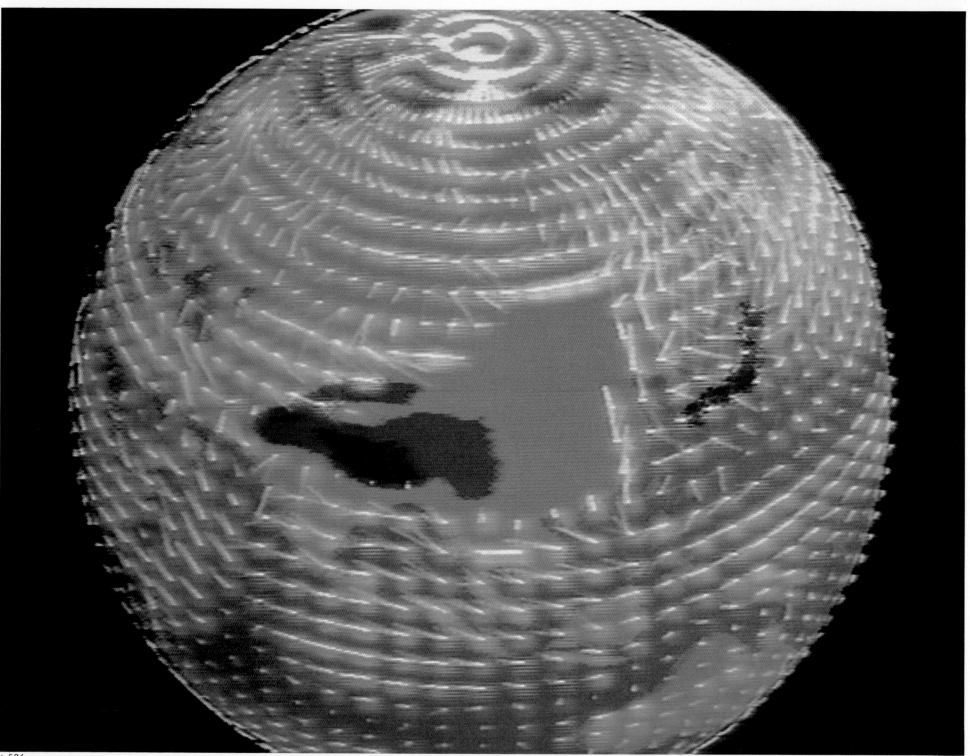

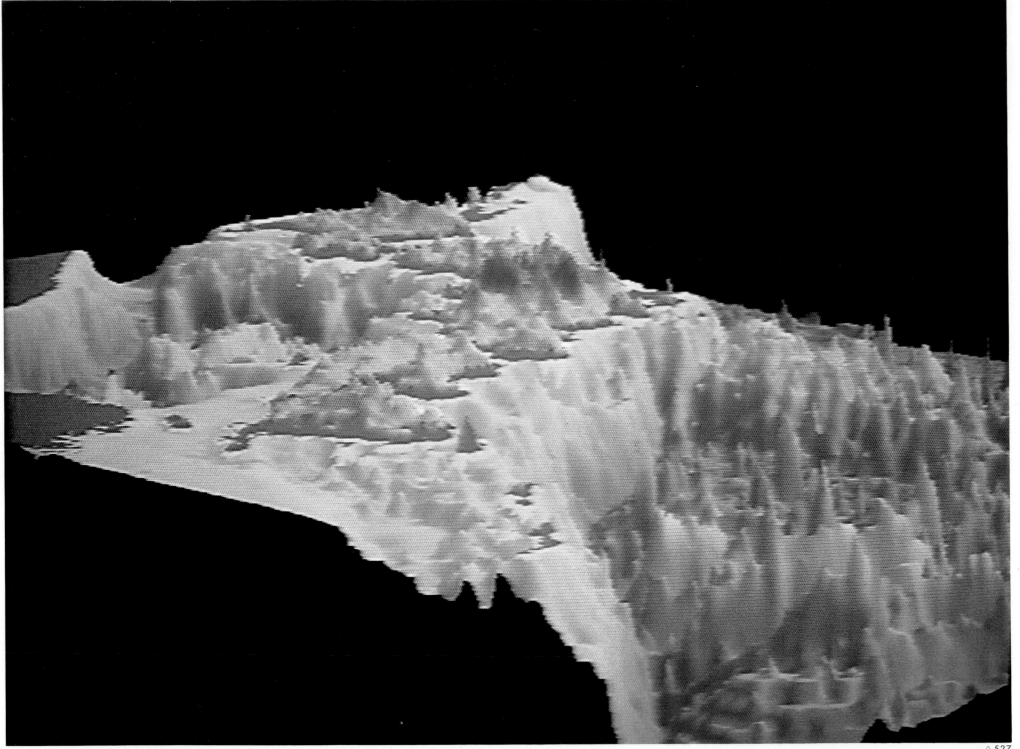

△527

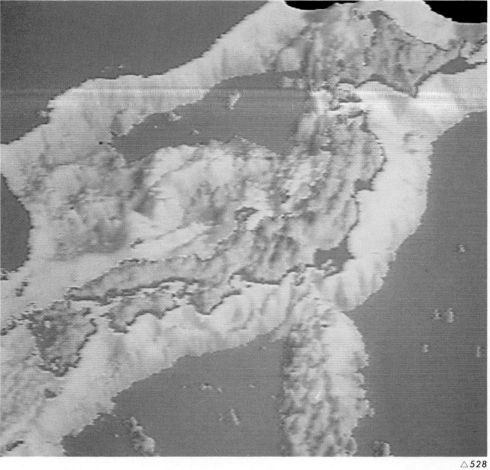

△528

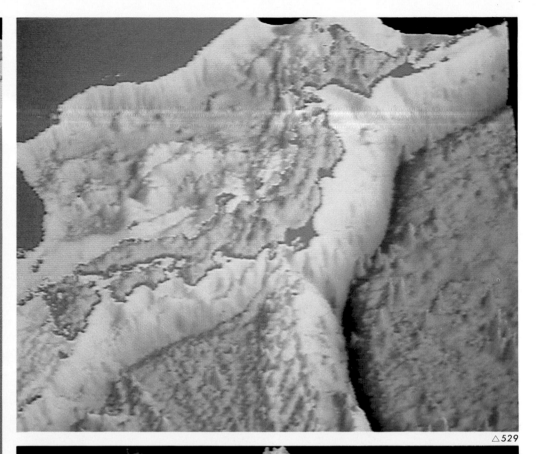

△529

△530

527~535. NHK (JAPAN BROADCASTING CORP.)

1. JAPAN
2. NHK (JAPAN BROADCASTING CORP.)
3. COMPUTER GRAPHICS
5. "MAP OF THE JAPANESE ARCHIPELAGO"
   ANIMATION SHOWS THE JAPANESE ARCHIPELAGE WHICH
   IS VIEWED FROM A POSITION ABOVE THE ISLAND.
   IN THIS DIAGRAM, THE SURFACE OF THE OCEAN
   GRADUALLY LOWERS FROM ITS ORIGINAL HEIGHT
   AND STATE UNDER THE OCEAN AS THE VIEW-POINT
   CHANGES.

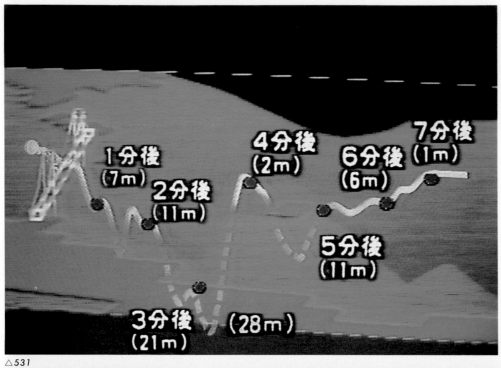

△531

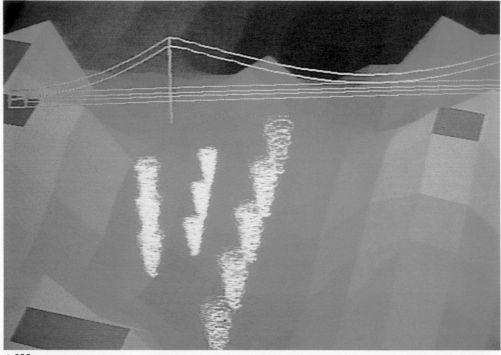

△532

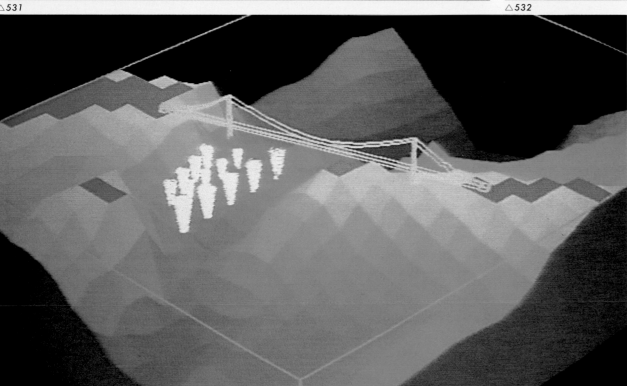

△533

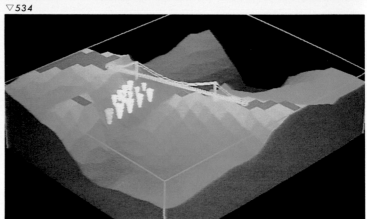

▽534

531～535 NHK (JAPAN BROADCASTING CORP.)

1. JAPAN
2. NHK (JAPAN BROADCASTING CORP.)
3. COMPUTER GRAPHICS
5. "NARUTO'S (A PLACE IN JAPAN) WHIRLPOOLS"
   THE RELATION BETWEEN THE OCCURENCE OF OCEAN'S WHIRL TO THE NARUTO'S
   TERRAIN, SHOWN BY ANIMATION. E-1 SHOWS A BUOY DROPPED FROM THE
   "OHNARUTO BRIDGE" BEING PULLED INSIDE THE WHIRLPOOL AND CARRIED AWAY,
   WITH ITS TIME LAPSE.

△535

△536

△537

536,537. TIM ALT/KENNETH R. WEISS

1. U.S.A.
2. DIGITAL ART
3. COMPUTER GRAPHICS-FORMATION OF TABLES AND CHARTS
4. GAME CHART (536)
5. ALUARTZ GROUP (536)
   OMNINET (537)

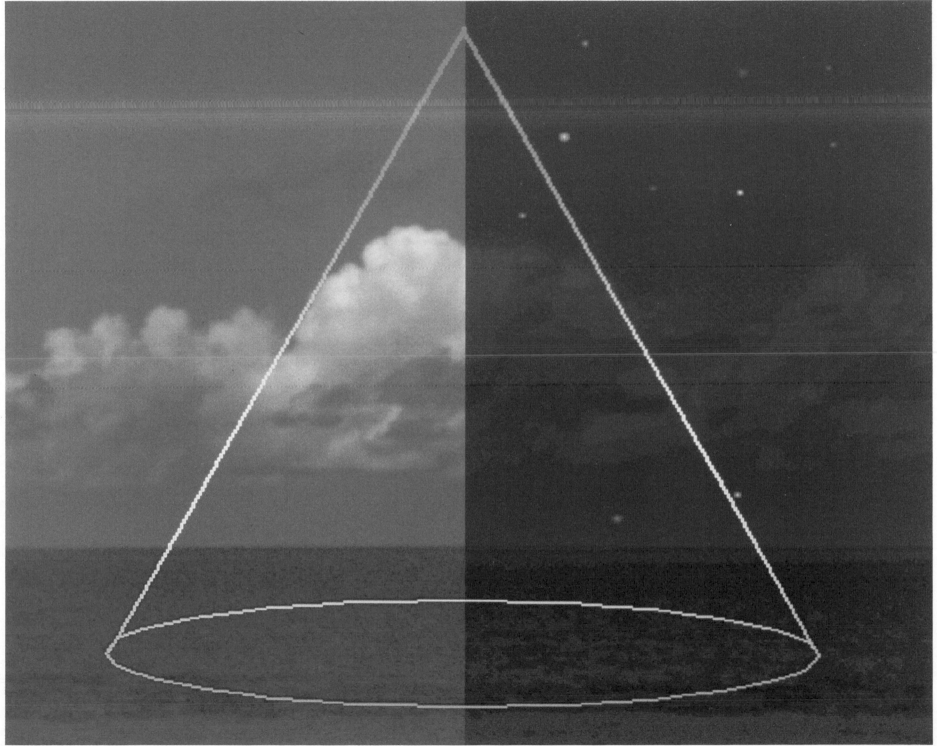

△539

231

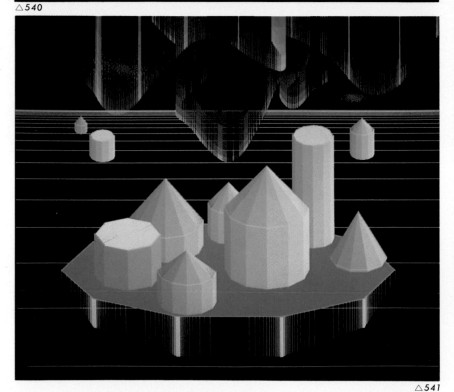

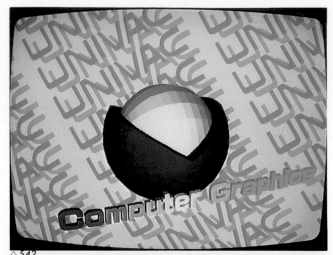

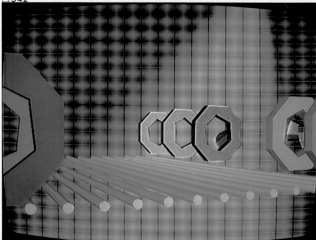

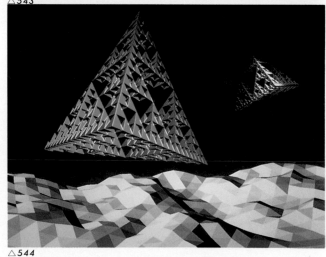

JAPAN RADIO CO. 540,541,544.

JAPAN 1.
COMPUTER GRAPHICS-CREATIVE DIAGRAMS 3.

HIDEMARU SATO 542,543.

JAPAN 1.
NIPPON UNIVAC INFORMATION SYSTEMS KAISHA. LTD. 2.
COMPUTER GRAPHICS-CREATIVE DIAGRAMS 3.
ANTICS PROJECT 4.

△540

△542

△543

△541

△544

TIM ALT/KENNETH R. WEISS 538,539.

U.S.A. 1.
DIGITAL ART 2.
COMPUTER GRAPHICS-CREATIVE DIAGRAMS 3.
SCOTT. GRIFFITHS DESIGN ASSOCIATES 5.

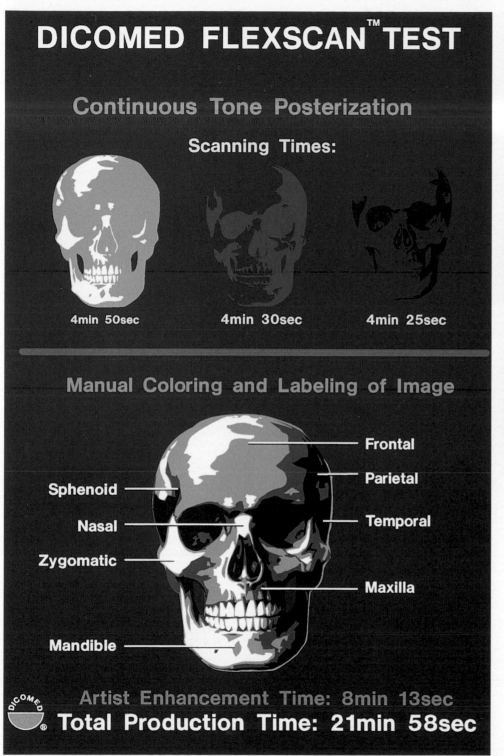

DICOMED FLEXSCAN™ TEST

Continuous Tone Posterization

Scanning Times:

4min 50sec   4min 30sec   4min 25sec

Manual Coloring and Labeling of Image

Sphenoid

Nasal

Zygomatic

Frontal

Parietal

Temporal

Maxilla

Mandible

Artist Enhancement Time: 8min 13sec

Total Production Time: 21min 58sec

△545

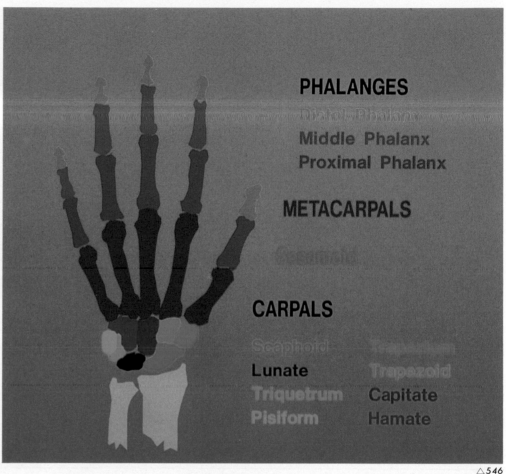

PHALANGES

Distal Phalanx

Middle Phalanx

Proximal Phalanx

METACARPALS

Sesamoid

CARPALS

Scaphoid   Trapezium

Lunate   Trapezoid

Triquetrum   Capitate

Pisiform   Hamate

△546

NISSHO ELECTRONICS 545, 546.

JAPAN 1.
NISSHO ELECTRONICS 2.
COMPUTER GRAPHICS-DISSECTIONS; EXPLANATORY GRAPHS 3.
PRODUCED BY DICOMED 4.

△547

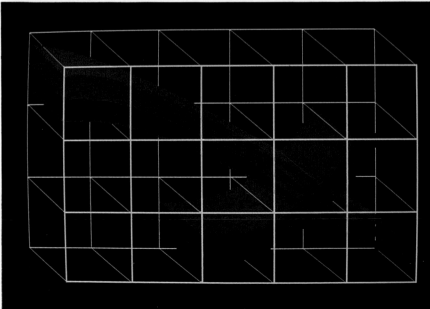

△548

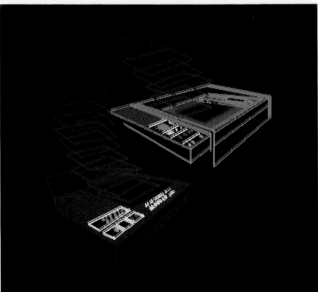

547～551. JERRY RUSSELL BLANK

1. U.S.A.
2. THE BLANK COMPANY
3. COMPUTER GRAPHICS-PICTORIAL DIAGRAMS
4. BECHTAL BRIEFS/MAGAZINE (547)
   BIO RAD PHARMACEUTICALS/MAGAZINE (548)
   KRUEGER CORP./MAGAZINE (549,550)
   MICROCOMMUNICATIONS/MAGAZINE (551)
5. EDITORIAL ILLUSTRATION (547,551)
   ADVERTISEMENT (548)
   ARTICLE ILLUSTRATION (549,550)

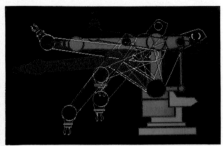

△549

△550

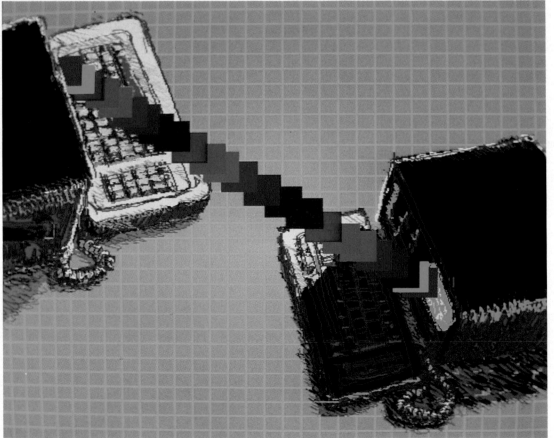

△551

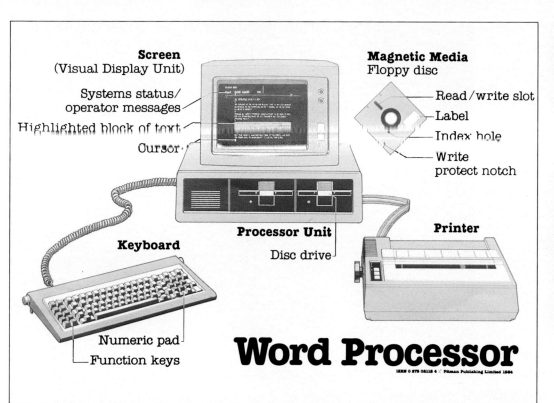

Word Processor

Screen
(Visual Display Unit)

Systems status/
operator messages

Highlighted block of text

Cursor

Keyboard

Numeric pad

Function keys

Processor Unit

Disc drive

Magnetic Media
Floppy disc

Read/write slot

Label

Index hole

Write
protect notch

Printer

ISBN 0 273 02115 4 © Pitman Publishing Limited 1984

△552

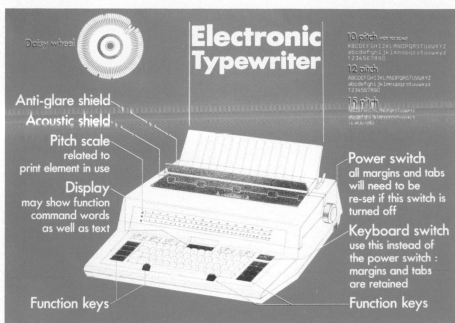

Daisy wheel

Electronic Typewriter

10 pitch NOT TO SCALE
ABCDEFGHIJKLMNOPQRSTUVWXYZ
abcdefghijklmnopqrstuvwxyz
1234567890

12 pitch
ABCDEFGHIJKLMNOPQRSTUVWXYZ
abcdefghijklmnopqrstuvwxyz
1234567890

15 pitch
ABCDEFGHIJKLMNOPQRSTUVWXYZ
abcdefghijklmnopqrstuvwxyz
1234567890

Anti-glare shield

Acoustic shield

Pitch scale
related to
print element in use

Display
may show function
command words
as well as text

Function keys

Power switch
all margins and tabs
will need to be
re-set if this switch is
turned off

Keyboard switch
use this instead of
the power switch :
margins and tabs
are retained

Function keys

△554

Keyboard

Row 4	1 2 3 4 5 6 7 8 9 0
Row 3	Q W E R T Y U I O P
Row 2	A S D F G H J K L ;
Row 1	Z X C V B N M , .
	SPACE BAR

A S D F   SPACE BAR   J K L ;

△553

EITETSU NOZAWA 552~554.

U.K. 1.
FREELANCE AT EDITORIAL DESIGN CONSULTANTS LTD. 2.
DISSECTIONS ; EXPLANATORY GRAPHS 3.
PITMAN PUBLISHING LTD. 5.

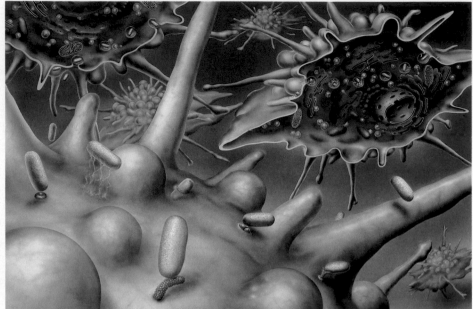

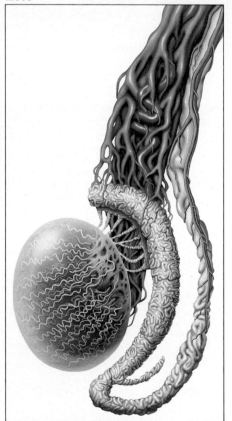

△556

△555   △557

Y.D.I. 555～557.

JAPAN 1.
Y.D.I. 2.
DISSECTIONS ; EXPLANATORY GRAPHS 3.

△558

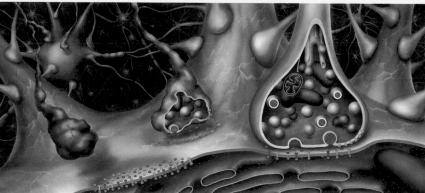

△559

Y.D.I. 558〜560.

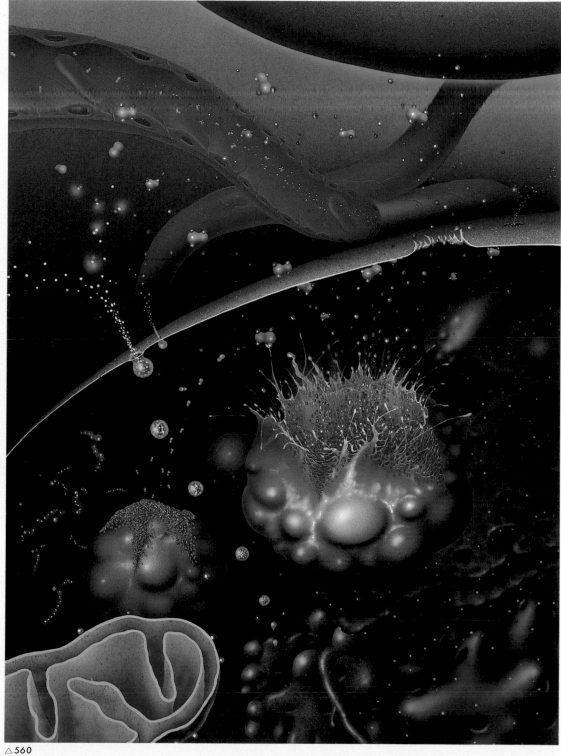

△560

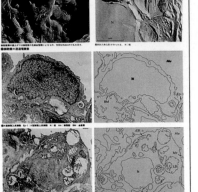
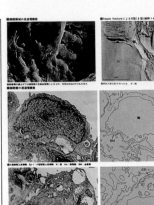
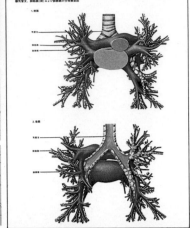

TERUYUKI KUNITO. 561~565.

JAPAN 1.
VISUAL TECHNOLOGY SYSTEMS 2.
PRODUCER : TOPPAN IDEA CENTER
ART DIRECTOR : TERUYUKI KUNITO AND 12 OTHERS
DESIGNER: TOSHITSUGU HIRAMATSU AND 55 OTHERS
ILLUSTRATOR : TOMOYUKI NARASHIMA AND 37 OTHERS
DISSECTIONS ; EXPLANATORY GRAPHS 3.
ENCYCLOPEDIA 4.
KODANSHA 5.

△561   △562   △563   △564

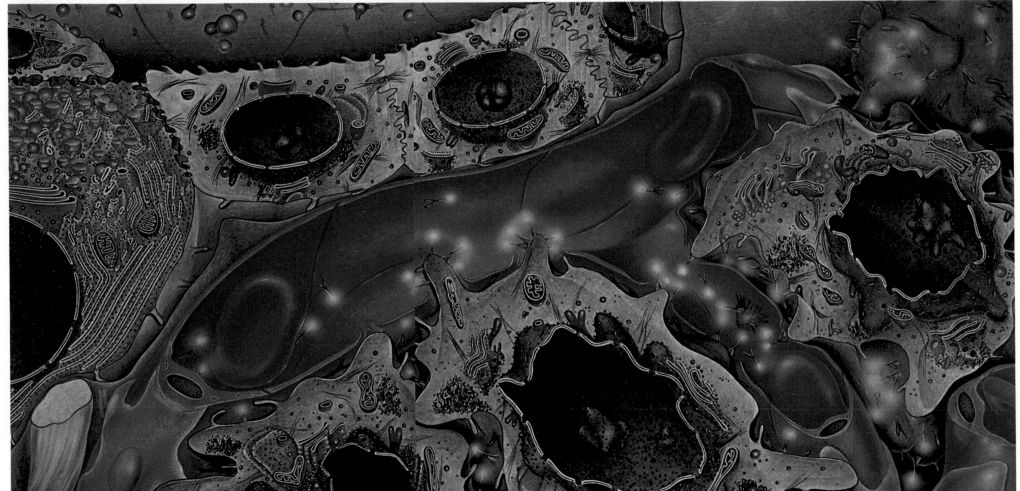

△565

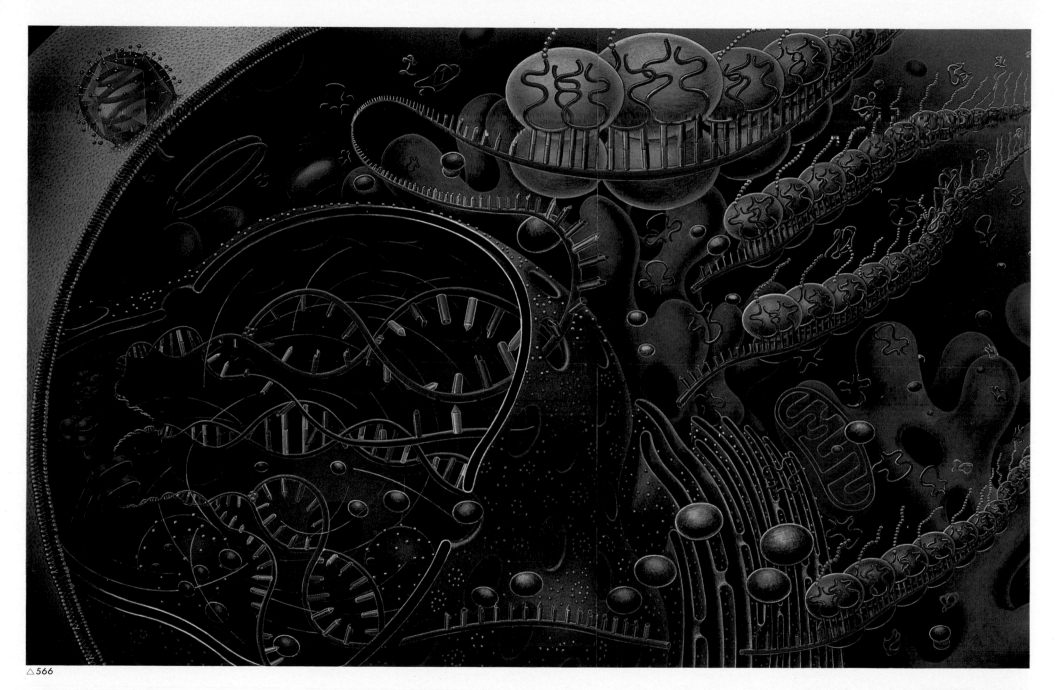

△566

TERUYUKI KUNITO 566.

JAPAN 1.
VISUAL TECHNOLOGY SYSTEMS 2.
PRODUCER : TOPPAN IDEA CENTER
ART DIRECTOR : TERUYUKI KUNITO AND 12 OTHERS
ENCYCLOPEDIA 4.   DESIGNER : TOSHITSUGU HIRAMATSU AND 55 OTHERS
KODANSHA 5.   ILLUSTRATOR : TOMOYUKI NARASHIMA AND 37 OTHERS

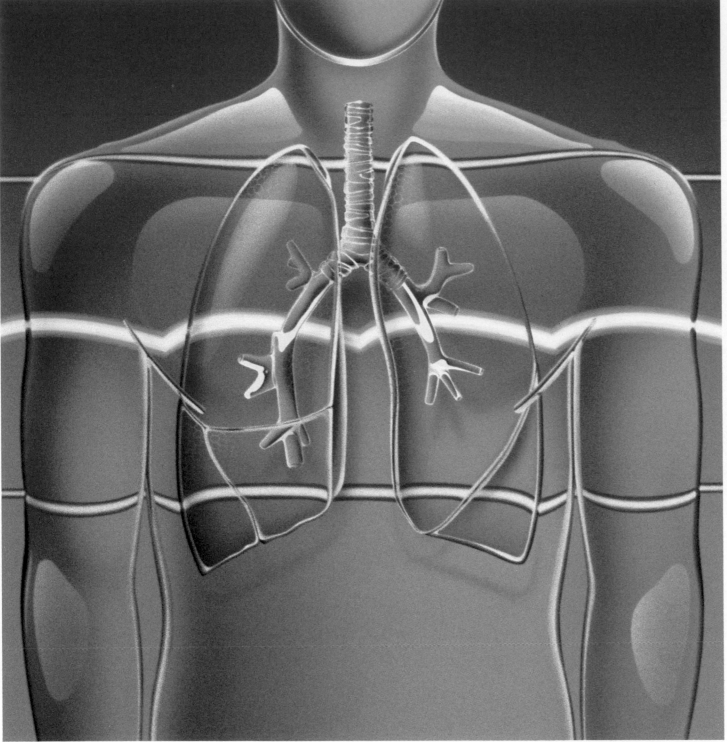

△567

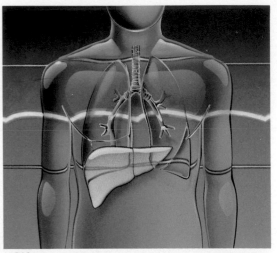

△568

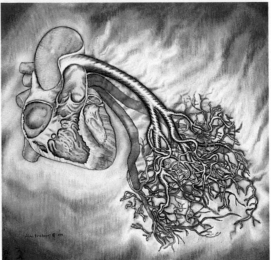

△569

PHILLIP BRIAN EVANS 567,568.

NETHERLANDS 1.
ARCHER ART 2.
DISSECTIONS 3.

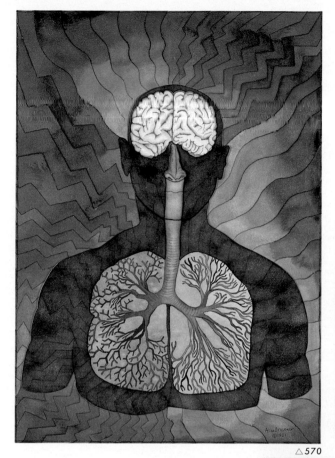

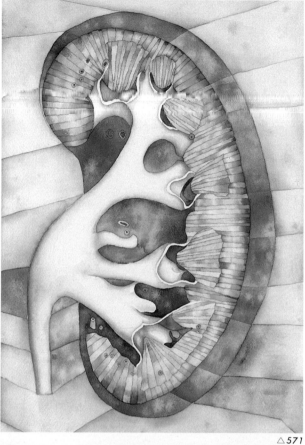

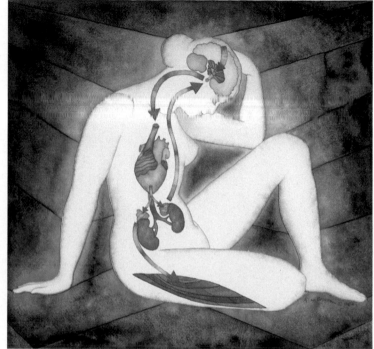

△573

569~574. ALICE BRICKNER

1. U.S.A.
2. DISSECTIONS ; EXPLANATORY GRAPHS
4. POSTGRADUATE MEDICINE, SEPT. 1979 (569)
   HEARST PUBLICATIONS SCIENCE DIGEST, JUNE 1981 (570)
   POSTGRADUATE MEDICINE, NOVEMBER 1978 (571)
   BROCHURE ILLUSTRATING TECHNICAL ASSISTANCE
   (COMPUTER CHIP) (572) MAGAZINE (573)
   DIARRHEAL DISEASES SPRING/1984 (COVER) (574)
5. MCGRAW HILL (569,571)
   SYVA/A SYNTEX CO. (572)
   CONDE NAST PUBLICATIONS (573)
   BURROUGHS WELLCOME CO. (574)

△570   △571

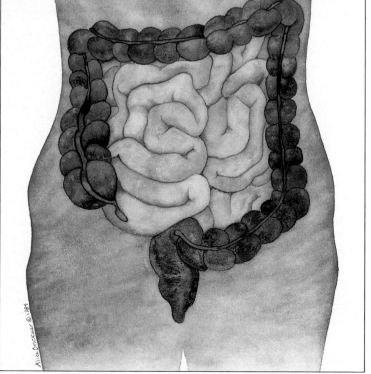

△572   △574

241

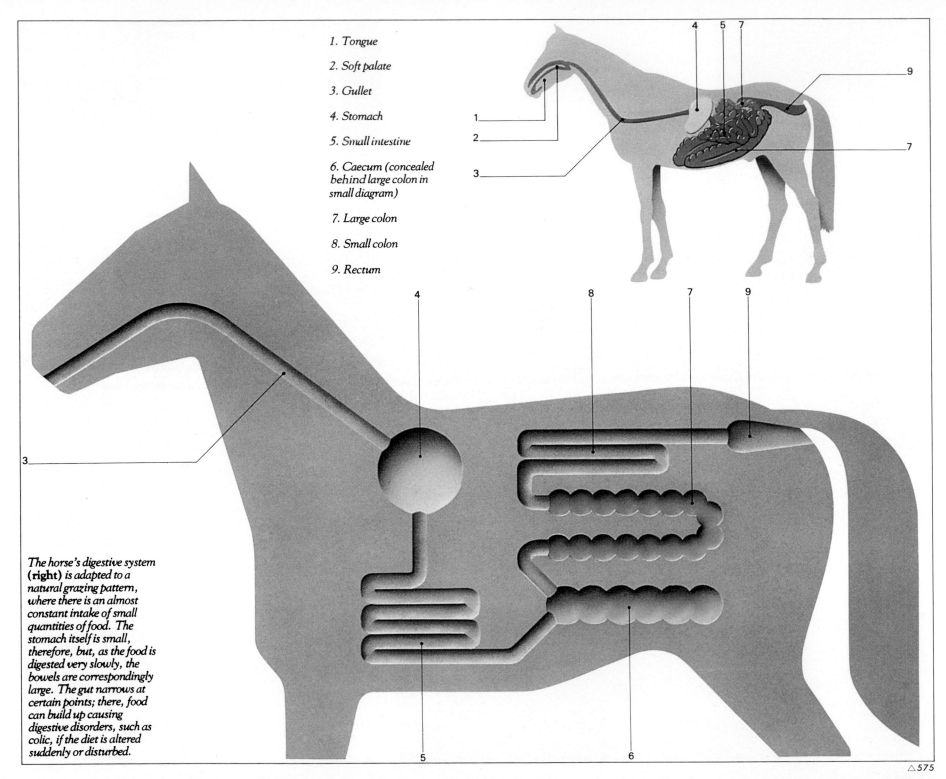

1. Tongue

2. Soft palate

3. Gullet

4. Stomach

5. Small intestine

6. Caecum (concealed behind large colon in small diagram)

7. Large colon

8. Small colon

9. Rectum

The horse's digestive system **(right)** *is adapted to a natural grazing pattern, where there is an almost constant intake of small quantities of food. The stomach itself is small, therefore, but, as the food is digested very slowly, the bowels are correspondingly large. The gut narrows at certain points; there, food can build up causing digestive disorders, such as colic, if the diet is altered suddenly or disturbed.*

△575

The points of the horse

The most striking feature of the horse is that it can perform the many tasks asked of it by man, though its physical make-up is in many ways unsuited to such demands. In the main period of evolution, the horse developed from a four or even five-toed marsh dweller to take the basic form it has today at a relatively early date; and even though it has somewhat changed its shape and improved its performance, the basic working mechanism remains the same.

Such basic physical facts should always colour the rider's attitude to the horse, and what he or she expects of it. With a basic understanding of the so-called points of the horse, it should be possible, for example, to go some way towards lessening the risk of muscular strains. These are all too common and, in extreme cases, can lead to a horse having to rest for weeks, if not months. More important still, knowledge of these points acts as a valuable guide in deciding a suitable or unsuitable horse for the prospective rider. The most vital attribute of any riding horse is depth of girth, which denotes toughness and strength. Tall, leggy horses invariably lack stamina. Short legs and a deep body, with plenty of heart room, are the signs to look for.

The most important points of the horse are its limbs and feet. Both in the wild and in domesticity, the horse depends on its means of locomotion for survival.

Feet and legs require therefore to be as correctly conformed as possible, if the horse is to remain sound and mobile. Correct conformation is, indeed, the most valuable asset any horse can possess.

The hind leg

Experts differ as to whether the most important single asset is a good hind leg or a good foreleg. As the hind leg is the propelling force, it is usually given priority. At the point

Body colours of horses vary. The principal ones are black, brown, bay and chestnut, though Thoroughbreds can be bay/brown, grey and roan as well. Non-Thoroughbred horses and ponies can also be dun, cream, piebald, skewbald, odd-coloured, whole coloured, palomino and Appaloosian. Within all these colours there are variations of shade. If there is any doubt about the colour of a horse, the deciding factor is the colour of its points — that is, the muzzle, tips of the ears, mane, tail and the lower parts of all four legs. Some body colours, correctly pointed, are shown (below).

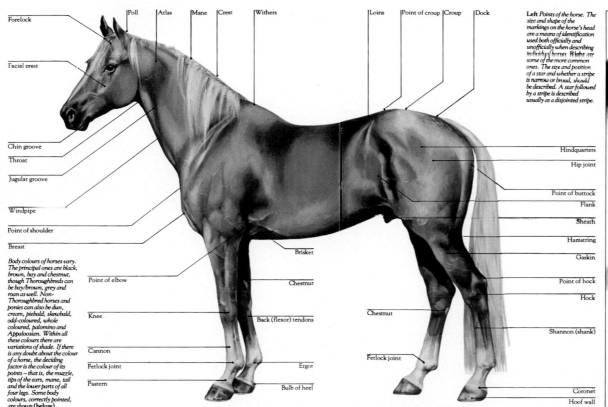

Forelock · Poll · Atlas · Mane · Crest · Withers · Loins · Point of croup · Croup · Dock · Facial crest · Chin groove · Throat · Jugular groove · Windpipe · Point of shoulder · Breast · Point of elbow · Knee · Cannon · Fetlock joint · Pastern · Brisket · Chestnut · Back (flexor) tendons · Ergot · Bulb of heel · Hindquarters · Hip joint · Point of buttock · Flank · Sheath · Hamstring · Gaskin · Point of hock · Hock · Chestnut · Fetlock joint · Shannon (shank) · Coronet · Hoof wall

Left *Points of the horse. The size and shape of the markings on the horse's head are a means of identification used both officially and unofficially when describing individual horses.* **Right** *are some of the more common ones. The size and position of a star and whether a stripe is narrow or broad, should be described. A star followed by a stripe is described usually as a disjointed stripe.*

White face · Stripe · Blaze · Star · Snip

Right *White leg markings are an important means of identification. A sock covers the fetlock and part of the cannon, while a stocking extends to the knee or hock. Other marks take the name of their site.*

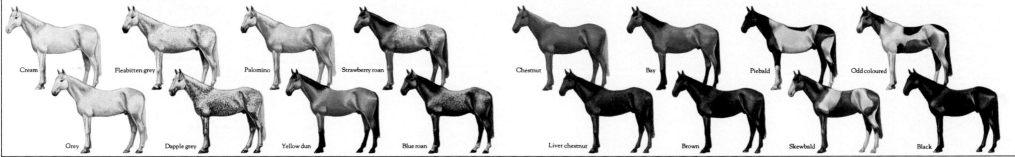

Cream · Grey · Fleabitten grey · Dapple grey · Palomino · Yellow dun · Strawberry roan · Blue roan · Chestnut · Liver chestnut · Bay · Brown · Piebald · Skewbald · Odd coloured · Black

△576

QED PUBLISHING LTD. 575, 576.

ENGLAND 1.
QED PUBLISHING LTD. 2.
DISSECTIONS ; EXPLANATORY GRAPHS 3.
BOOK, "THE BOOK OF THE HORSE" 4.

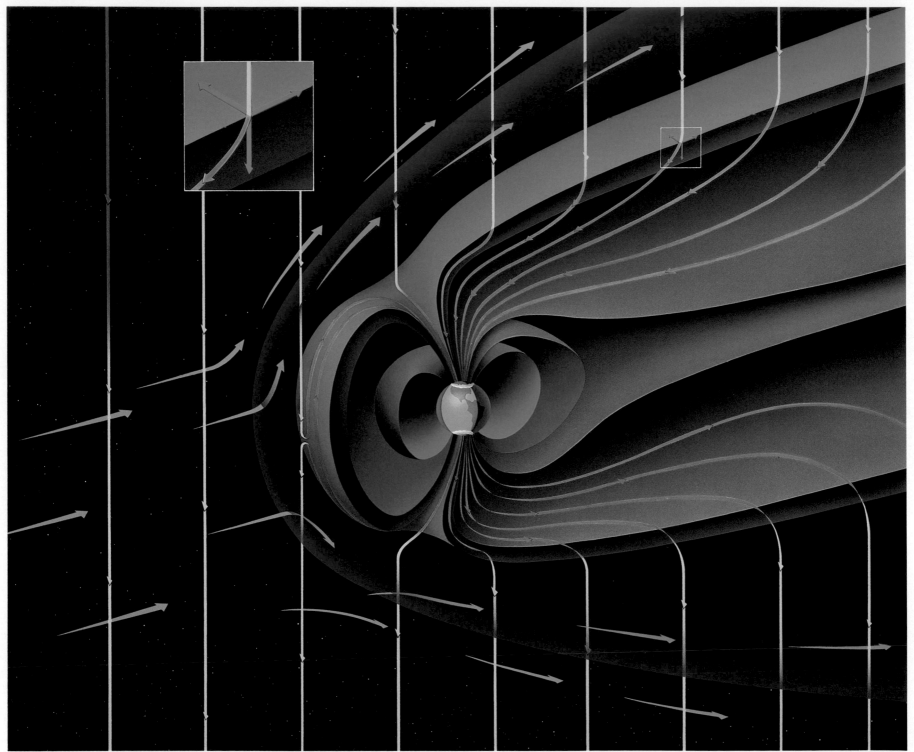

△577

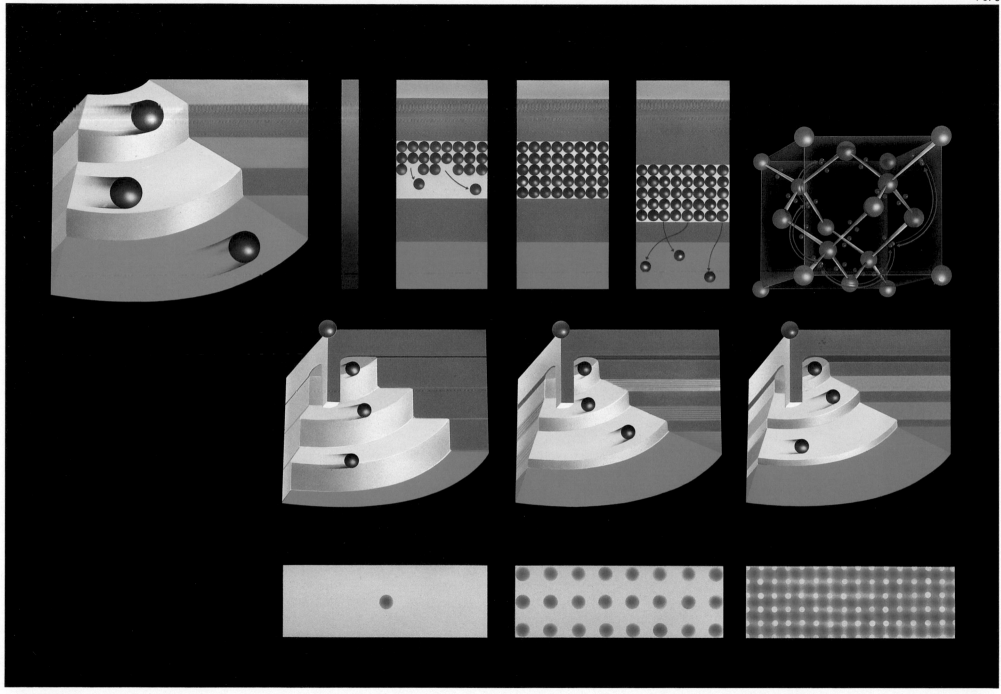

577. NEWTON

1. JAPAN
2. ILLUSTRATOR : MINORU KOBAYASHI
3. FLOW CHARTS
4. NEWTON MAGAZINE
5. ⒸKYOIKUSHA NEWTON
WEATHER FORECASTING SYSTEM BY NUMERICAL VALUES

NEWTON 578.

NEWTON MAGAZINE   4.
ⒸKYOIKUSHA NEWTON 5.   ILLUSTRATOR : RYO OHSHITA   2.
THE TRUE CHARACTER OF SEMICONDUCTOR CLARIPIED BY SOLID ELECTRON THEORY   FLOW CHARTS 3.

JAPAN   1.

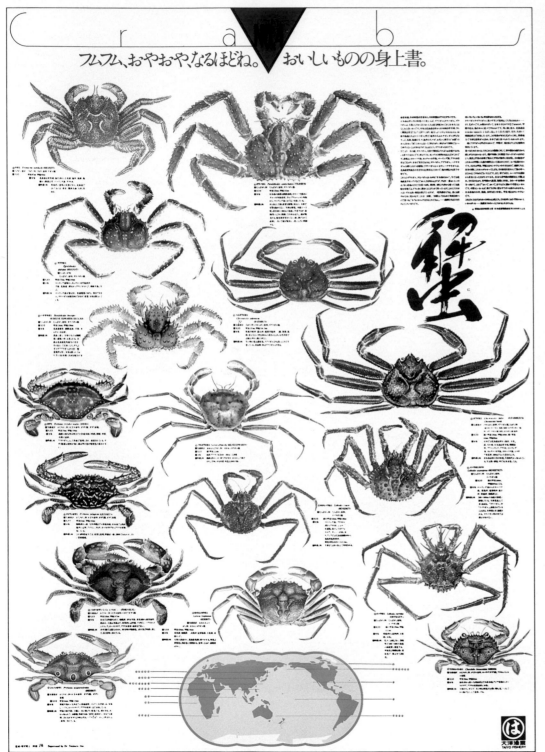

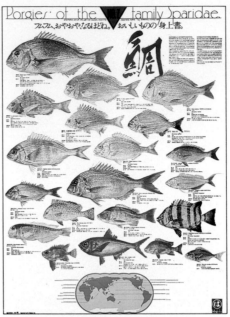

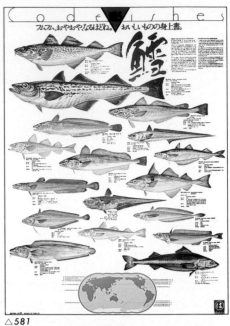

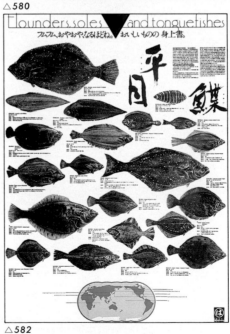

△579

△580

△581

△582

△583

579～583. TAIYO FISHERY CO., LTD.

1. JAPAN
2. TAIYO FISHERY CO., LTD.
   ART DIRECTOR : KUNIHO MISAKA
   ILLUSTRATOR : KATSUHISA SUZUKI
   PRODUCTION SUPERVISOR : TOKIAKI ABE
3. ENCYCLOPEDIA ILLUSTRATIONS
4. POSTER   5. MARINE LIFE

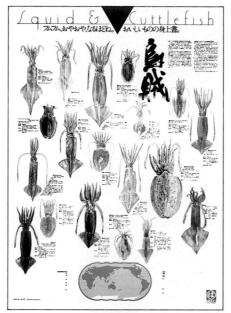

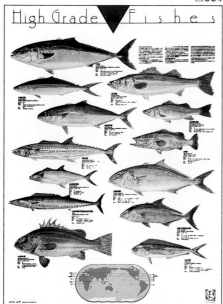

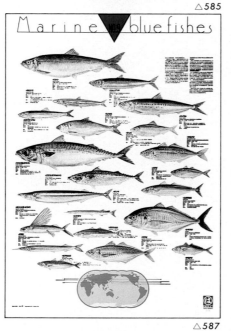

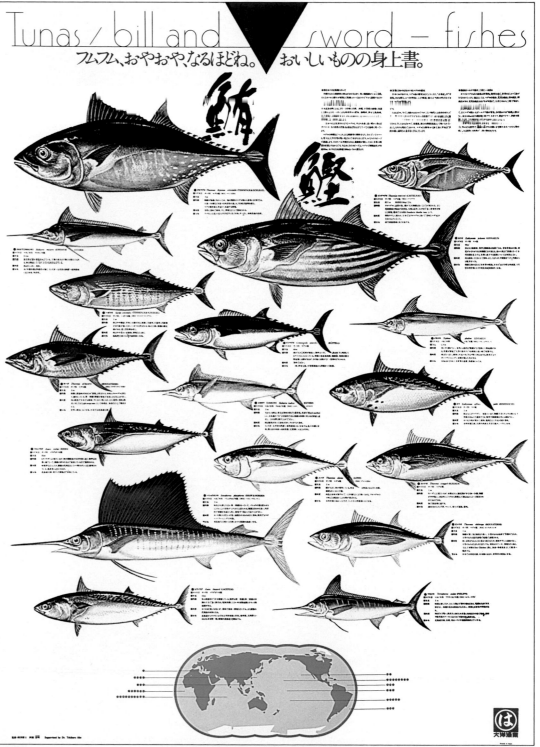

△584

△585

△586

△587

△588

TAIYO FISHERY CO., LTD. 584~588.

JAPAN 1.
TAIYO FISHERY CO., LTD. 2.
ART DIRECTOR : KUNIHO MISAKA
ILLUSTRATOR : KATSUHISA SUZUKI
PRODUCTION SUPERVISOR : TOKIAKI ABE
ENCYCLOPEDIA ILLUSTRATIONS 3.
POSTER 4.
FISH TYPES 5.

ROLF CIGLER/HARALD CIGLER 590~592.

SWITZERLAND 1.
ATELIER CIGLER 2.
ENCYCLOPEDIA ILLUSTRATIONS 3.
RINGIER-PUBLISHER '83 5.
BUTTERFLIES (590)
STUDIES OF OCTOPUS BEHAVIOR, DIPLOMA WORK '82 (591)
PRINTED BY NZZ SCIENCE '85 (592)

Yew

Tutu

Castor oil plant

False acacia

Privet

Horsetail

Deadly
nightshade

Ragwort

Hemlock

Ngaio

Purple
milk-vetch

Avocado

Rangiora

Yellow
star-thistle

Oleander

Buckthorn

St. John's wort

△589

248

QED PUBLISHING LTD. 589.

ENGLAND 1.
QED PUBLISHING LTD. 2.
ENCYCLOPEDIA ILLUSTRATIONS 3.
"THE BOOK OF THE HORSE" 4.
PLANTS EATEN BY HORSES 5.

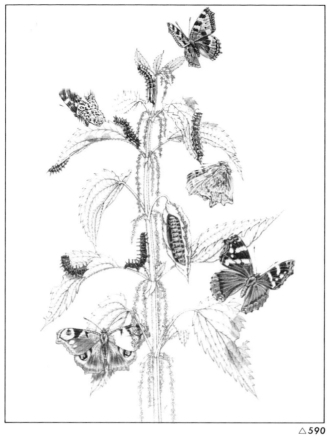

△590

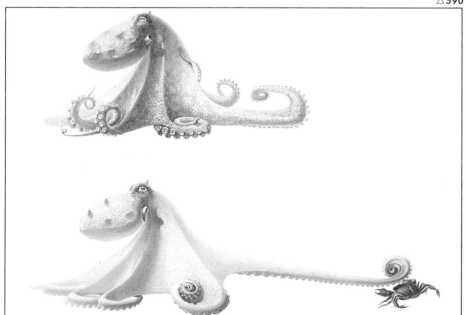

△591 △592

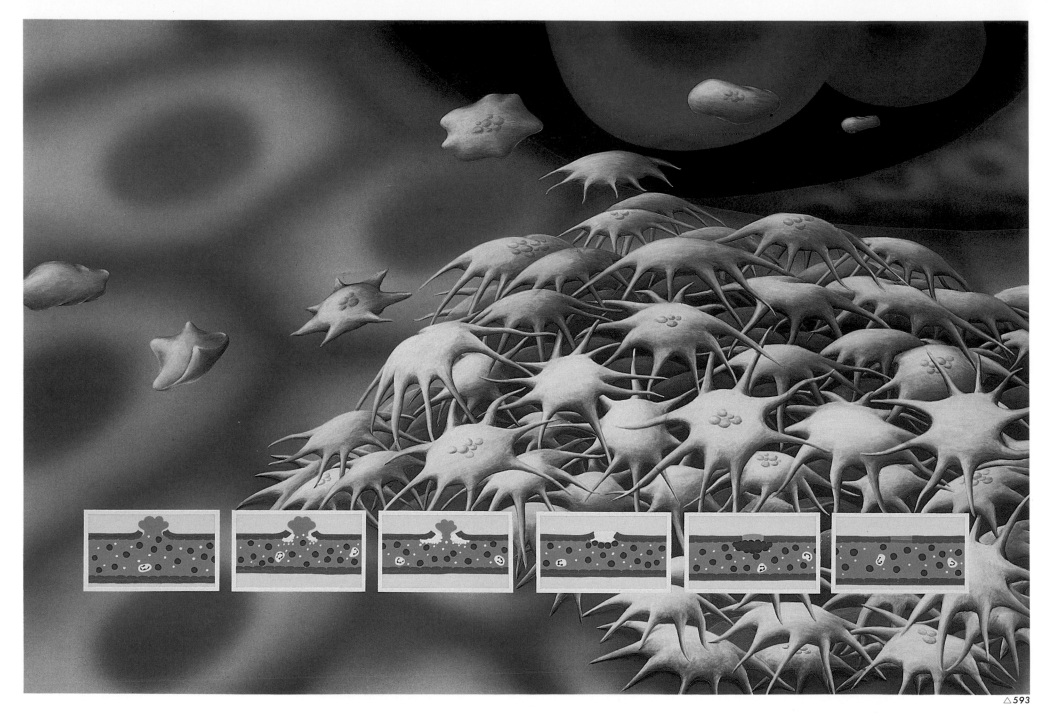

△593

593. NEWTON

1. JAPAN
2. ILLUSTRATOR : ETSUKO TAKAHASHI
3. VISUAL GRAPHS OR FUNCTIONS/PROGRESSIONS

4. NEWTON MAGAZINE
5. ©KYOIKUSHA NEWTON
   BLOOD PLATELETS RESTORE BLOOD VESSELS AND STOP BLEEDING

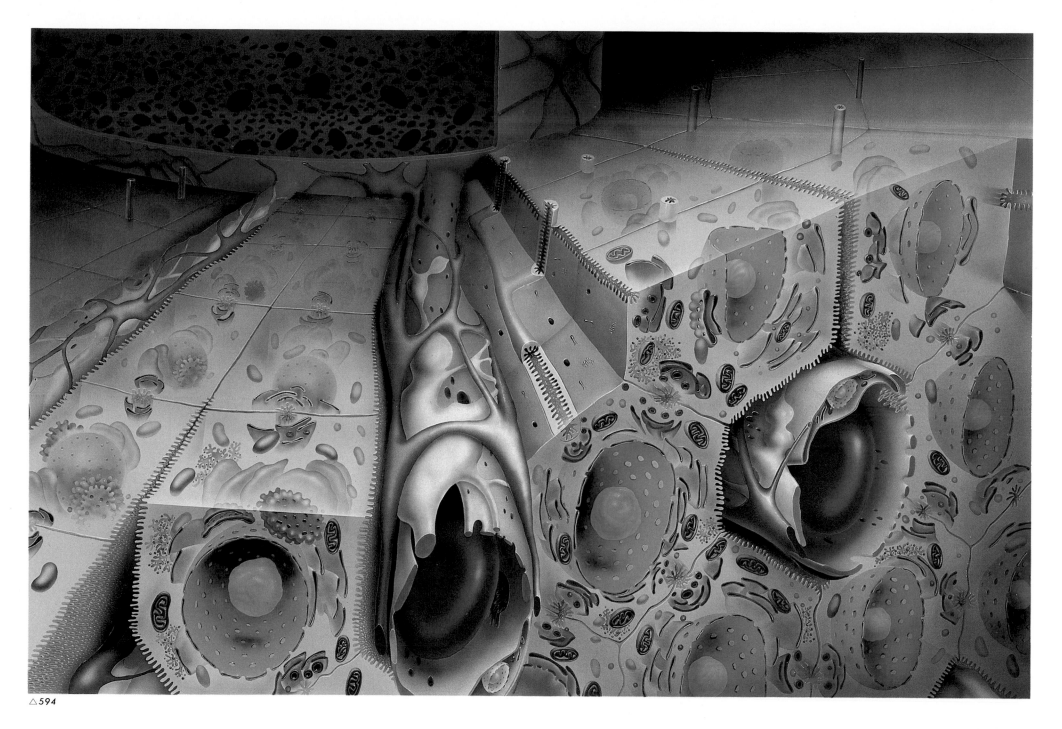

△594

NEWTON 594.

NEWTON MAGAZINE 4.
ⓒKYOIKUSHA NEWTON 5.
FUNCTIONS OF THE LIVER

JAPAN 1.
ILLUSTRATOR : TAKUMI YAMAMOTO 2.
DISSECTIONS ; EXPLANATORY GRAPHS 3.

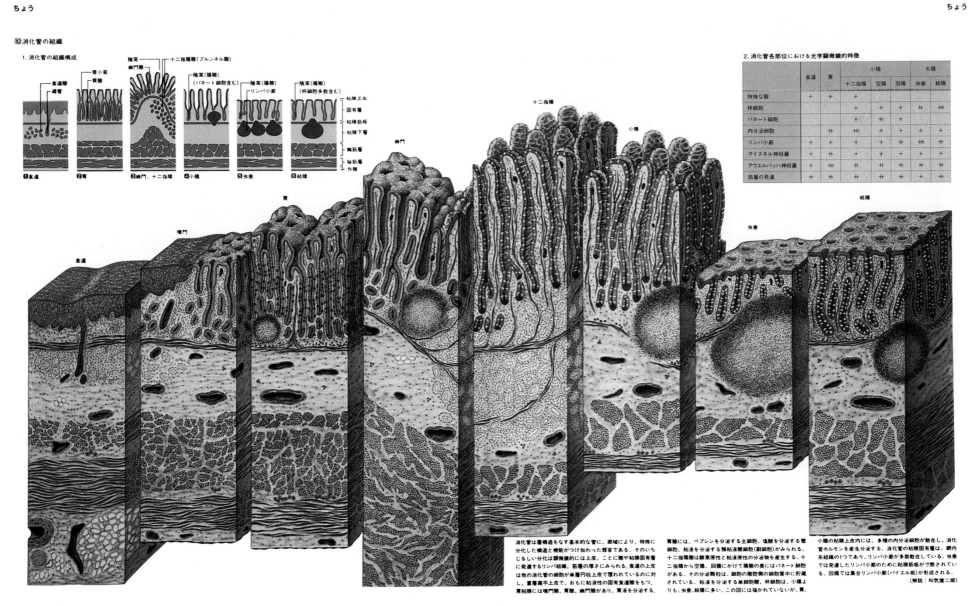

595. TERUYUKI KUNITO

1. JAPAN
2. VISUAL TECHNOLOGY SYSTEMS
   PRODUCE : TOPPAN IDEA CENTER
   ART DIRECTOR : TERUYUKI KUNITO AND 12 OTHERS

DESIGNER : TOSHITSUGU HIRAMATSU AND 55 OTHERS
ILLUSTRATOR : TOMOYUKI NARASHIMA AND 37 OTHERS
3. DISSECTIONS ; EXPLANATORY GRAPHS
4. ENCYCLOPEDIA
5. KODANSHA/STRUCTURE OF THE ALIMENTARY CANAL

△596

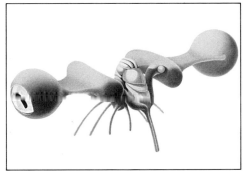

△597

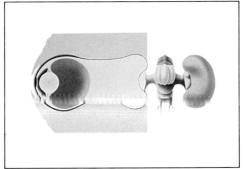

△598

△599

ROLF CIGLER/HARALD CIGLER 596~598.

SWITZERLAND 1.
ATELIER CIGLER 2.
SEGMENT CHARTS (596) 3.
ENCYCLOPEDIA ILLUSTRATIONS (597,598)
THE BRAIN OF AN OCTOPUS 4.
DIPLOMA-WORK '82 (597,598)

NEWTON 599.

JAPAN 1.
ILLUSTRATOR : YUYA KANAI 2.
SEGMENT CHARTS 3.
NEWTON MAGAZINE 4.
©KYOIKUSHA NEWTON 5.
BASIC UNIT OF "LIFE CELL"

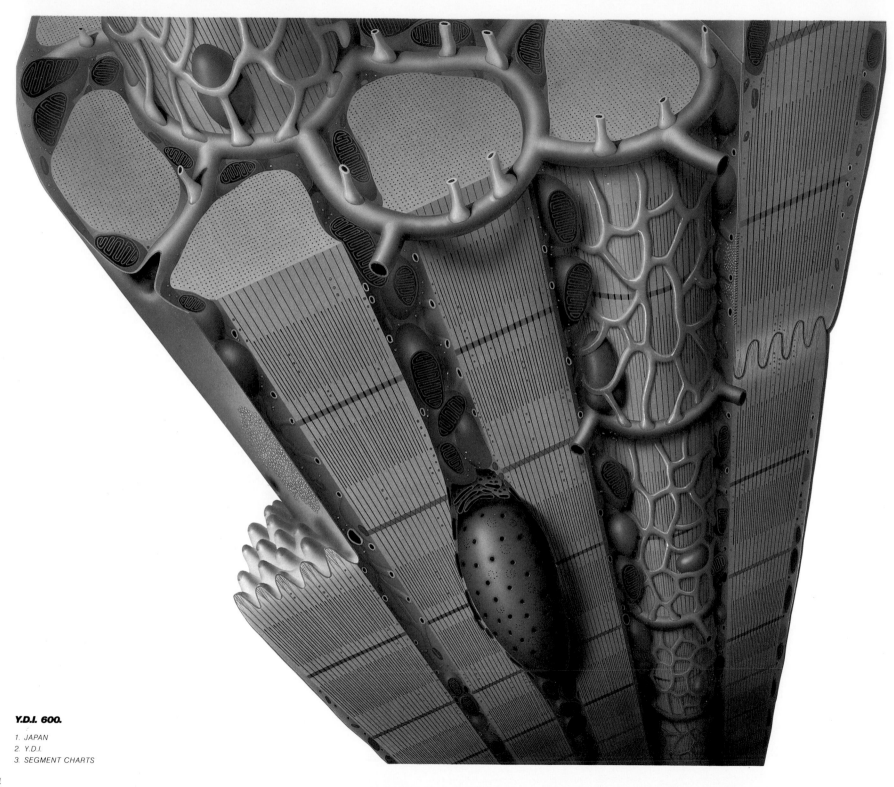

Y.D.I. 600.

1. JAPAN
2. Y.D.I.
3. SEGMENT CHARTS

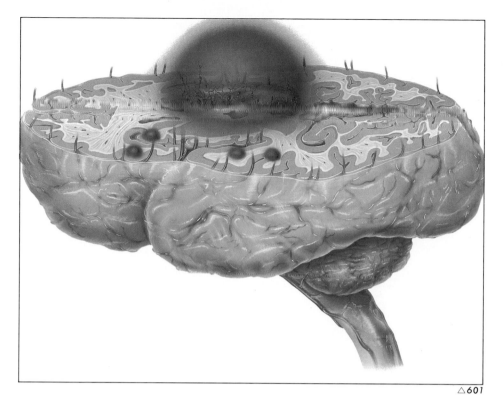

△601

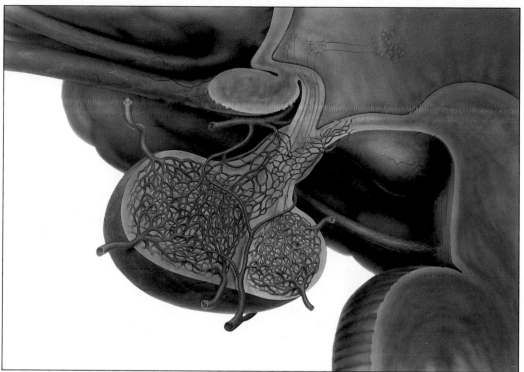

△602 ▽603

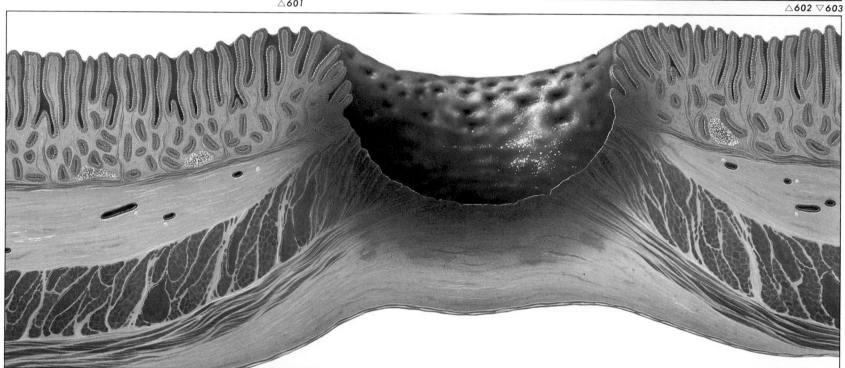

Y.D.I. 601~603.

1. JAPAN
2. Y.D.I.
3. SEGMENT CHARTS

△604

△605

△606

△607

△608

NORIYOSHI ORAI 604～608.

JAPAN 1.
DISSECTIONS ; EXPLANATORY GRAPHS 3.
HOME MEDICAL DICTIONARY 4.
GAKKEN CO., LTD. 5.

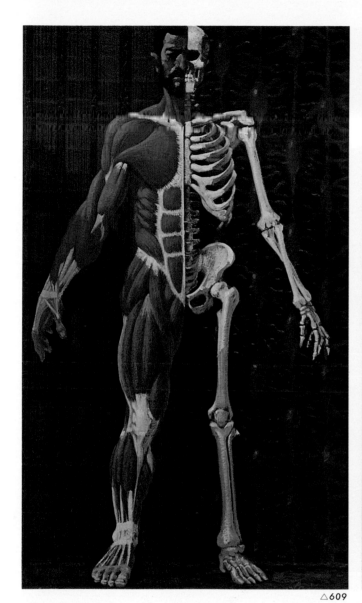

△609

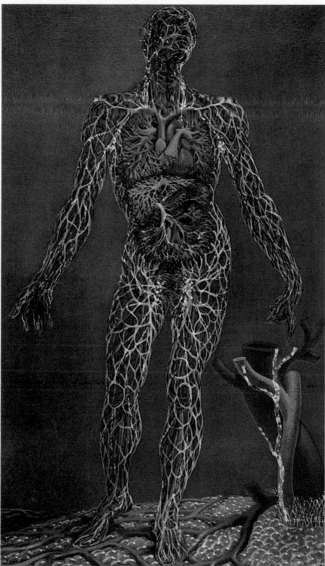

△610

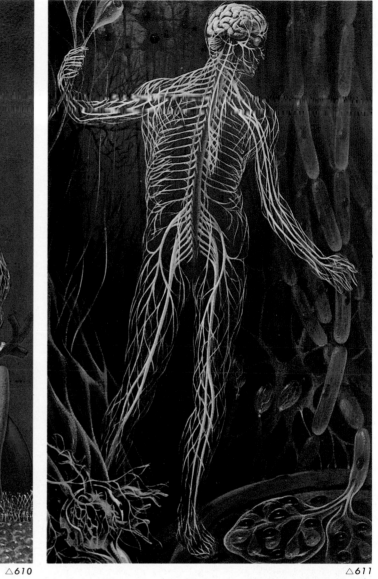

△611

609～611. NORIYOSHI ORAI

1. JAPAN
2. DISSECTIONS ; EXPLANATORY GRAPHS
4. HOME MEDICAL DICTIONARY
5. GAKKEN CO., LTD.

△612

612. KAZUAKI IWASAKI

1. JAPAN
2. COSMOS ORIGIN LTD.
3. SEGMENT CHARTS
4. PICTORIAL BOOK
5. GAKKEN CO., LTD./THE STRUCTURE OF THE GALACTIC SYSTEM

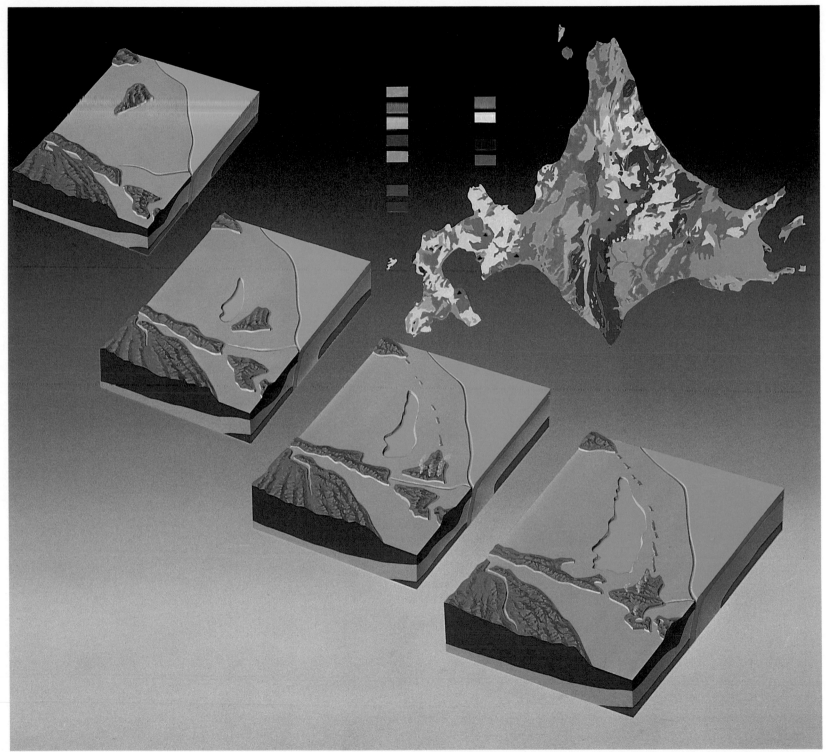

NEWTON 613.

JAPAN 1.
ILLUSTRATOR : SYOICHIRO MASUDA 2.
SEGMENT CHARTS 3.
NEWTON MAGAZINE 4.
ⓒKYOIKUSHA NEWTON 5.
THE ORIGIN OF HOKKAIDO AND ITS
GEOLOGICAL STRUCTURE

△613

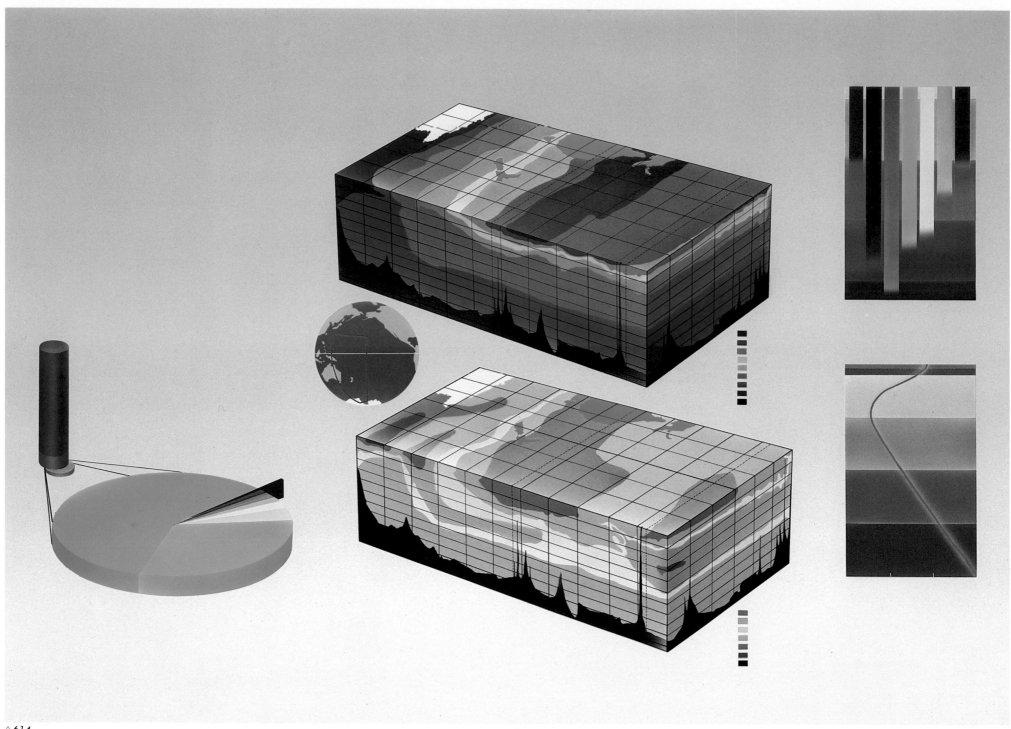

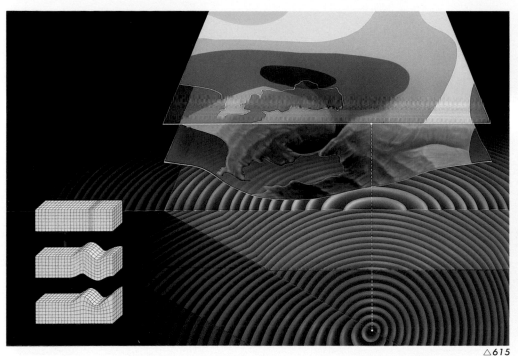

△615

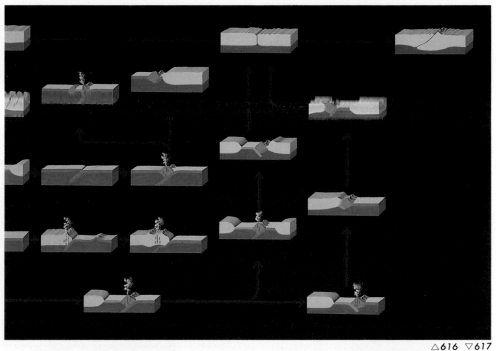

△616 ▽617

614. NEWTON

1. JAPAN
2. ILLUSTRATOR : TAKASHI AOKI
3. SEGMENT CHARTS
4. NEWTON MAGAZINE
5. ©KYOIKUSHA NEWTON
   VARIOUS TYPES OF SEA WATER

615~617. NEWTON

1. JAPAN
2. ILLUSTRATOR : MINORU KOBAYASHI (615)
             ETSUKO TAKAHASHI (616)
             RYUICHI FUTAMI (617)
3. SEGMENT CHARTS
4. NEWTON MAGAZINE
5. ©KYOIKUSHA NEWTON
   THE RELATION BETWEEN THE PROPAGATION OF SEISMIC
   SHOCK WAVES AND DISTRIBUTION
   OF SEISMIC INTENSITY (615)
   CYCLE OF NEW MOUNTAIN-FORMING ACTIVITY (616)
   WEATHER CHART OF HOKKAIDO (617)

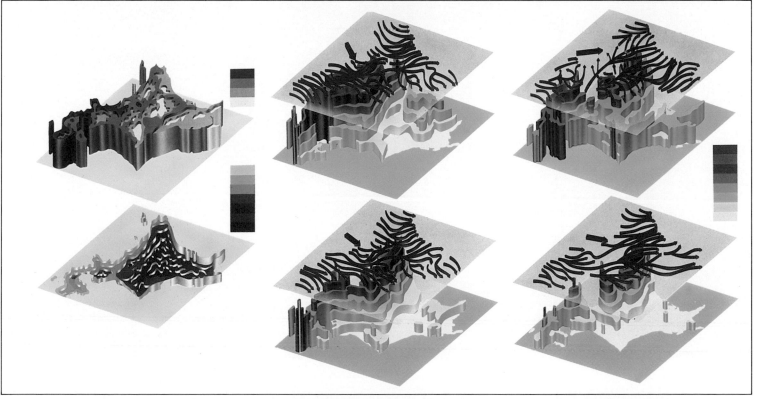

△618

618. NEWTON

1. JAPAN
2. ILLUSTRATOR : SHOICHIRO MASUDA
3. SEGMENT CHARTS
4. NEWTON MAGAZINE
5. ©KYOIKUSHA NEWTON
ORIGIN OF GEOLOGICAL PLATES IN THE CENTRAL DEEP

NEWTON 619.

NEWTON MAGAZINE 4.
©KYOIKUSHA NEWTON 5.
FROM THE EARTH'S BIRTH UNTIL THE APPEARANCE OF ON-LAND CREATURES

JAPAN 1.
ILLUSTRATOR : HIRO DESIGN 2.
SEGMENT CHARTS 3.

△620 ▽621

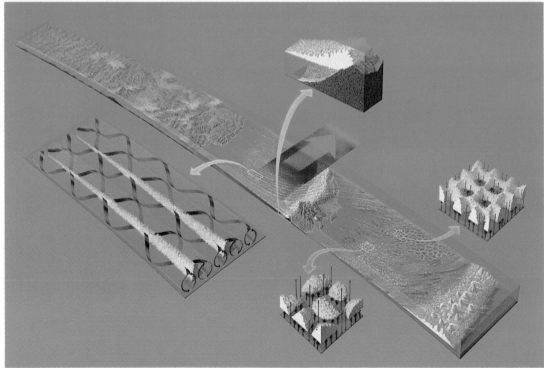

△622

Science

In volcano's shadow, a devastated Spirit Lake; at right, before the deluge

No End Seems to Be in Sight

Until a cap is formed, Mount St. Helens may continue rumbling

When Mount St. Helens finally blew its top after almost two months of rumbling and sputtering, the show was spectacular enough that it hardly required an encore for a century or so. But last week the seemingly inexhaustible volcano gave another lively performance. A second major eruption shook the mountain over the Memorial Day weekend, and steam and ash belched forth in fitful bursts throughout the week. More ominously, seismologists detected tremors originating from deep within the volcano's molten rock core, another sign of restlessness.

To add to the jitters of beleaguered residents, two moderate earthquakes suddenly jolted Mount Margaret, a peak only 13 km (eight miles) northeast of Mount St. Helens. Though scientists emphasized that these seismic disturbances were not hints of an impending eruption, the tremors only added to what might be called a case of tectonic fever on the West Coast. Hundreds of small earthquakes shook the Sierra Nevada in central California, causing landslides and some injuries. At least 100 of the quakes measured above 4.0 on the Richter scale and three reached 6.0 or higher, levels at which there would have been more widespread destruction in populated areas.

None of this earth activity appeared directly related to Mount St. Helens. And, indeed, by midweek Tim Hait, the U.S. Geological Survey's chief spokesman at the scene, was describing Mount St. Helens as "in a relaxed state

of mind." But none of the U.S.G.S. scientists would say how long the calm would last. After Mount St. Helens rose from its slumber in 1831, it erupted 14 times in the next 25 years. Says Hait: "This time it could go on for five years, ten years or 20 years. That's a heck of an answer but there's no way of telling."

The latest round of activity caught scientists by surprise. Though volcanologists have been able to predict almost to the hour when the volcanoes of the Hawaiian Islands will erupt, Mount St. Helens presents a more difficult problem for would-be prognosticators. The molten rock, or magma, underneath the Washington volcano is a thicker, silica-rich material (unlike the less viscous molten basalt of the Hawaiian chain); more pressure must build up before the hot gases trapped within it are released. Thus the mountain erupts infrequently and violently.

No one can tell for sure how soon the mountain will clear itself of these pent-up gases, but U.S.G.S. scientists were saying last week that they would not be surprised if Mount St. Helens continued venting steam, ash and pumice intermittently for another ten or 15 years. The reason, the scientists explained, is that it could take that long for the volcano to complete the internal rebuilding process that will seal it off again.

According to their scenario, some of the molten rock from the subterranean cauldron of magma under the mountain will slowly be forced upward, like toothpaste being squeezed out of a tube. It will push through the vents in the "plug" of debris within the volcano's throat and emerge as lava. When it is finally exposed to the air, the lava will harden rapidly; it will probably not have enough volume or velocity to overflow the volcano's rim. Instead, as it solidifies, it will likely form a dome or cap over the vents. Eventually the dome should become massive enough to plug up the volcano like a cork in a bottle. But the corking process may be interrupted by repeated explosions, as pressure builds up underneath and ruptures the newly formed dome. Admits U.S.G.S. Volcanologist Charles Zablocki: "We are going to school on this one."

The mountain was also providing painful lessons for those who live near it. The prevailing westerly winds suddenly reversed themselves and dropped ash over a huge area from Tacoma, Wash., to Eugene, Ore., including many communities that had so far largely escaped the sooty downpour. Along the coast, thousands of Memorial Day tourists were stranded by the poor visibility and impossible road conditions. In Portland, which likes to call itself the "most livable city," the International Airport was forced to sus-

WHY IT KEEPS RUMBLING
Venting will continue until molten rock working upward through the debris "plug" reaches the air and hardens to form a dome or cap

ORIGINAL PROFILE

3,000 feet
1 mile

PLUG
VENTS
MAGMA (molten rock)

TIME Diagram by Nigel Holmes

TIME, JUNE 9, 1980

620,621. UKEI TOMORI

1. JAPAN
3. SEGMENT CHARTS

NIGEL HOLMES 622.

U.S.A. 1.
SEGMENT CHARTS 2.
TIME MAGAZINE 4.
MOUNT ST. HELENS 5.

264

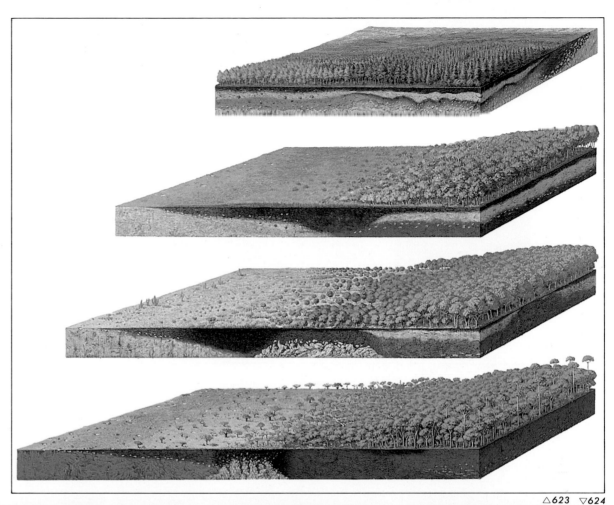

△623 ▽624

265

Simulation of Ground Water Systems With Mathematical Modelling

Dames & Moore

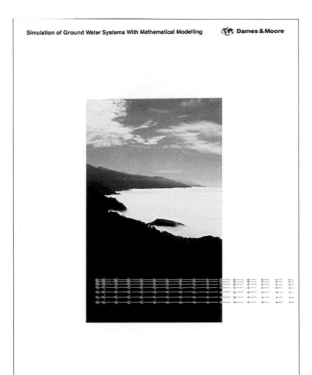

△625 ▽627

Ground Water Modelling
A Versatile Tool for Environmental Planning . . .

Dames & Moore is introducing a growing number of companies to the benefits of using mathematical modeling and computer-assisted analysis to resolve a broad range of industrial and municipal ground water contamination and supply problems. The firm's comprehensive ground water modelling services are effective in simulating all types of ground water regimes and assessing the many variable hydrogeologic factors that affect a ground water system.

Dames & Moore's versatile modeling capabilities have proved successful in the early identification of potential ground water contamination problems as well as the development of remedial programs for contaminated ground water systems. The firm's ground water modeling services can be applied to many aspects of hazardous and nuclear waste facility planning, including facility site selection, conceptual facility design, closure plans, and post-closure monitoring programs.

The advanced modeling capabilities of Dames & Moore combine the speed of the computer with proven analytical techniques that enable the accurate assessment of extensive amounts of variable data both quickly and cost-effectively. Beyond ground water modeling, the firm has extensive modeling capabilities in the areas of soil and rock mechanics, earthquake engineering, heat transfer, hydrology, air quality and meteorology, and coastal and offshore engineering.

An early advocate of modeling, Dames & Moore has developed an extensive in-house library of highly specialized, proprietary computer models. The firm also uses models provided by government agencies and independent research organizations. All programs used by Dames & Moore have been thoroughly tested by the firm's mathematical modeling specialists and validated through the firm's stringent quality assurance program.

Ground Water Modelling Services
- Characterize a ground water regime
- Determine the nature, concentration, gradient, direction and extent of the migration of contaminants
- Evaluate the effectiveness of remedial scenarios
- Support applications for variances from permitting standards
- Assist in conceptual design of hazardous and nuclear waste management facilities
- Evaluate the efficacy of ground water monitoring programs
- Assess the geochemical interaction between ground water and soils

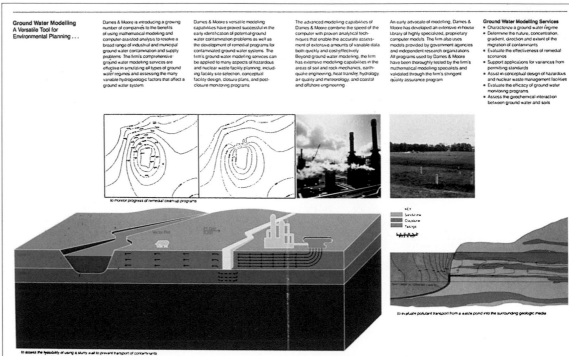

to monitor progress of remedial clean-up programs

to evaluate pollutant transport from a waste pond into the surrounding geologic media

to assess the feasibility of using a slurry wall to prevent transport of contaminants

△626 ▽628

Pollution Control Assessment: A Tool for Loss Control

Dames & Moore

Dames & Moore's Systematic Approach to Environmental Review

For most industries pollution control is one of the most complex, demanding aspects of successful plant management. How a plant manager copes with ever-changing environmental regulations, new control technology and problematic emissions and spills has a significant impact on a plant's bottom line performance.

As a leading environmental and applied earth sciences consulting firm, Dames & Moore has assisted a broad range of industries in minimizing pollution control costs and resolving contamination problems. The firm's experience encompasses all types of pollution control problems — air quality, surface and ground water quality and land contamination as well as hazardous and radioactive waste management.

Dames & Moore's pollution control and waste management specialists are experienced in performing pollution control assessments for a broad range of plant applications, from loss control to plant acquisition, divestiture or closure. The firm's professionals maintain a close working relationship with each client, enabling them to structure a pollution control strategy that is designed to meet the client's exact operating requirements.

The firm's staff has the technical expertise to develop and implement pollution control programs at a single plant or a series of plants, from conceptual design of pollution control strategies through full implementation of a response program governing waste treatment, handling, storage and remedial clean-up programs.

Dames & Moore's staff employs proven techniques, such as decision analysis and computer modeling and mapping, to develop practical recommendations in an efficient and cost effective manner. With a worldwide network of offices, the firm is able to provide consulting services at any plant site promptly and in accordance with local practices and customs.

Pollution Control Assessment Applications
- Loss control and prevention
- Plant divestiture, acquisition and closure
- Project feasibility/risk assessment
- Regulatory compliance
- Long-term management strategies
- Permitting activities

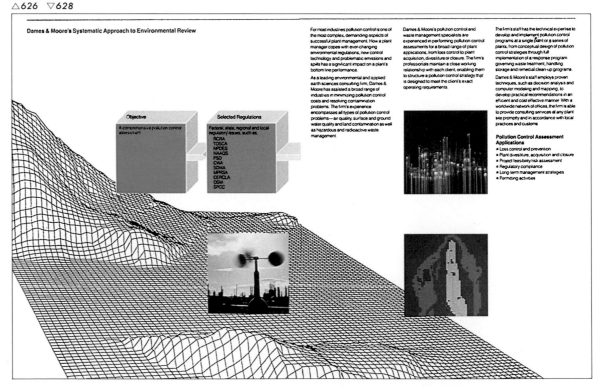

Identification: Penetrating the Waste Problem

Waste problem identification and definition are the first steps to an effective waste management program. While problem recognition is often simple, Dames & Moore stresses the importance of both cause and symptom identification in the belief that accurate definition is the key to a rapid, cost effective solution of a waste management problem.

Defining a waste-related problem requires the accurate, comprehensive testing and characterization of the waste. Among the key questions that must be addressed are:
■ Which waste streams and components are of concern?
■ What physical and chemical characteristics do they exhibit?
■ What quantities are involved?
To answer these questions, Dames & Moore collects all pertinent available data, conducts field sampling and supervises analysis, all in accord with established protocol and quality control procedures.

Along with waste characterization, an analysis of the context in which the waste occurs is vital to problem definition. Such studies, whether conducted in the field or office, are instrumental in assessing the following conditions:
■ Geohydrology
■ Surface-water hydrology
■ Meteorology/air quality
■ Land uses
■ Radiology

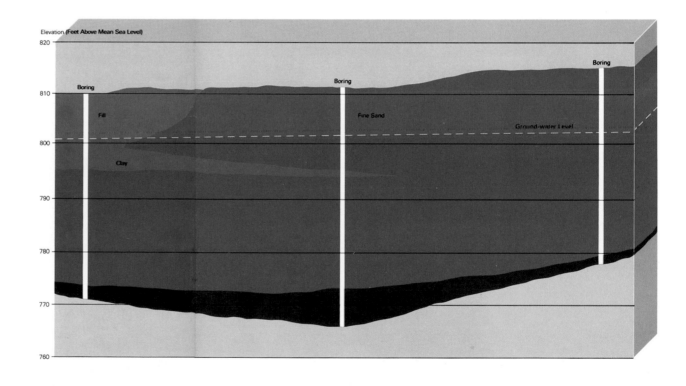

Elevation (Feet Above Mean Sea Level)

Boring   Boring   Boring

Fill   Fine Sand   Ground-water Level

Clay

625~628. BILL BROWN

1. U.S.A.
2. BILL BROWN & ASSOCIATES
   ART DIRECTOR : BILL BROWN
   DESIGNER : SHOJI TERAISHI
3. SEGMENT CHARTS
4. CATALOGUE
5. DAMES & MOORE/ENVIRONMENTAL PLANNING REVIEW

BILL BROWN 629.

U.S.A. 1.
BILL BROWN & ASSOCIATES 2.
ART DIRECTOR : BILL BROWN
DESIGNER : SHOJI TERAISHI
SEGMENT CHARTS 3.
CATALOGUE 4.
DAMES & MOORE/WASTE DISPOSAL STUDY 5.

1. JAPAN
2. SEGMENT CHARTS
5. HOUSING DEVELOPMENT ON THE DESERT

△630

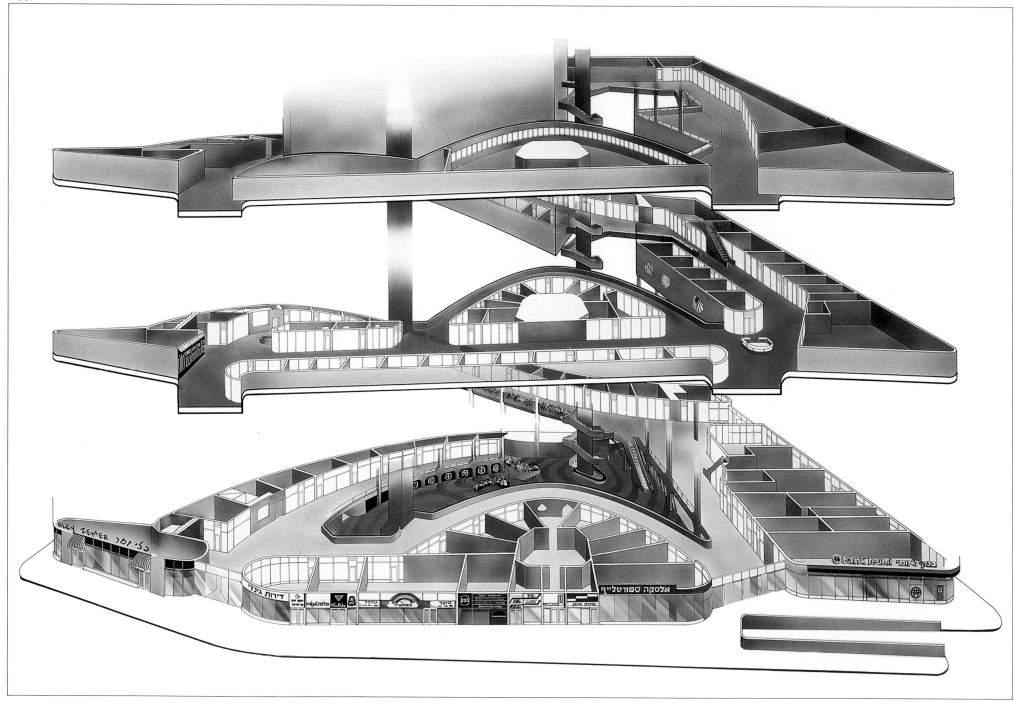

631. SHLOMO COHEN

SHLOMO COHEN/I. AROESTI 632.

1. ISRAEL   COLLABORATOR: I. AROESTI   4. DIZENGOFF CENTER
2. POINTOUT LTD.   3. SEGMENT CHARTS   5. PUBLISHED BY POINTOUT

PUBLISHED BY POINTOUT 5.   SEGMENT CHARTS 3.   ISRAEL 1.
DIZENGOFF CENTER 4.   POINTOUT LTD. 2.

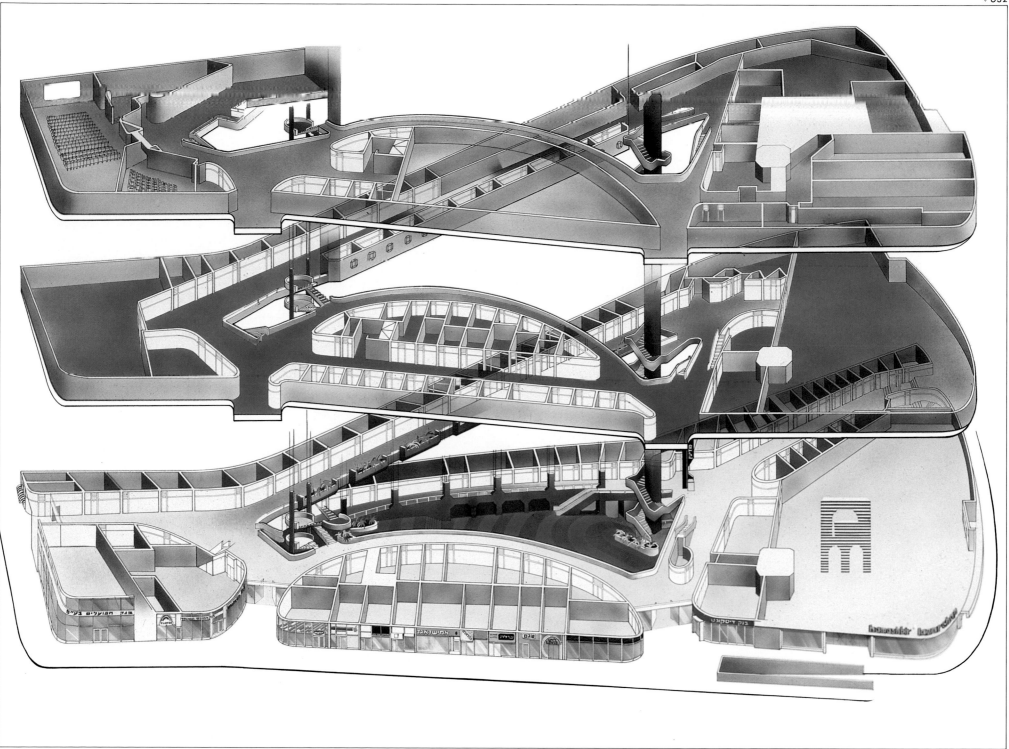

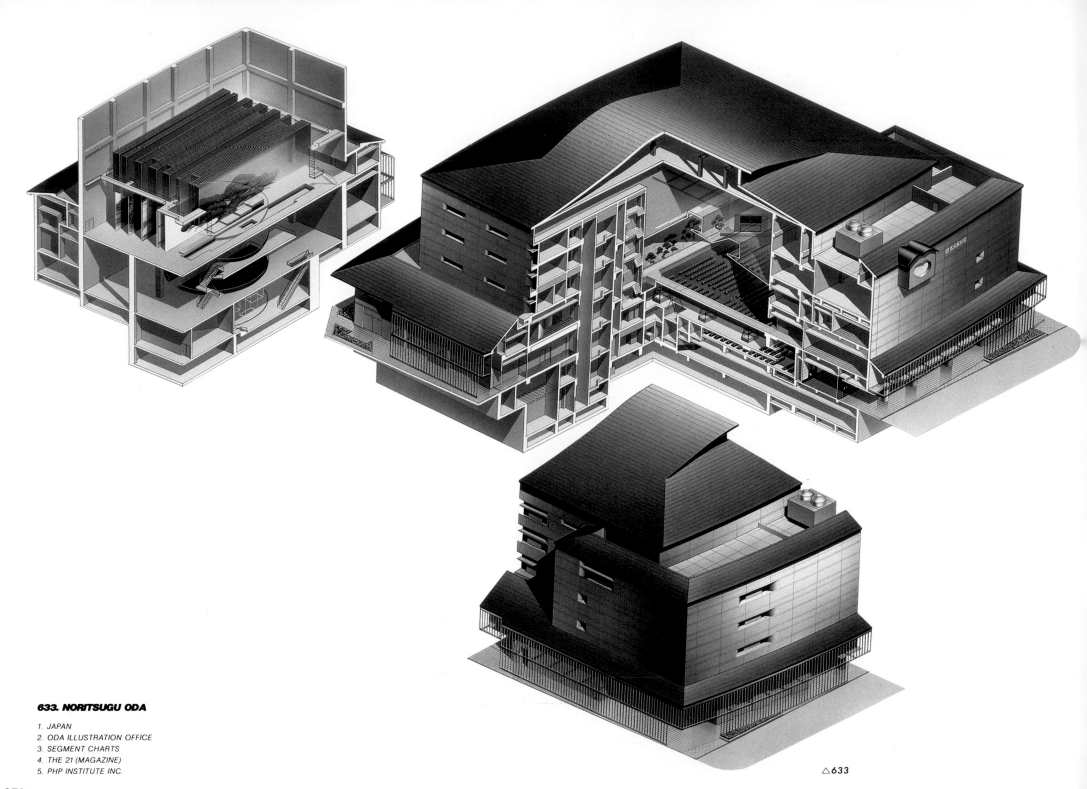

633. NORITSUGU ODA

1. JAPAN
2. ODA ILLUSTRATION OFFICE
3. SEGMENT CHARTS
4. THE 21 (MAGAZINE)
5. PHP INSTITUTE INC.

△633

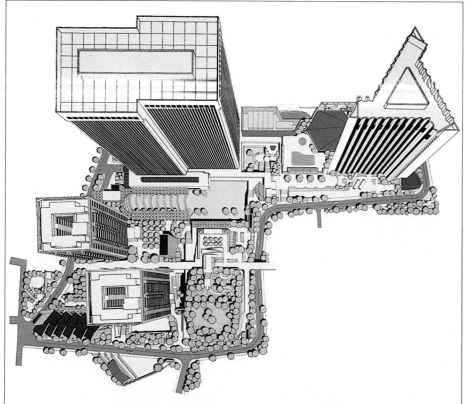

△634

REI INDUSTRIAL DETIGNERS INC. 634.

JAPAN 1.
REI INDUSTRIAL DESIGNERS INC. 2.
SEGMENT CHARTS 3.
RE-DEVELOPMENT AREA SIGN PLANNING. 4.
MORI BUILDING CO., LTD. 5.

635. NORITSUGU ODA

1. JAPAN
2. ODA ILLUSTRATION OFFICE
3. TRANSPARENT DIAGRAMS
4. THE 21 (MAGAZINE)
5. PHP INSTITUTE INC.

636. DAVID PENNEY

1. U.K.
2. SEGMENT CHARTS
4. WALL CHART
5. GERMAN GOVERNMENT
   SOLAR HOUSE

▽636

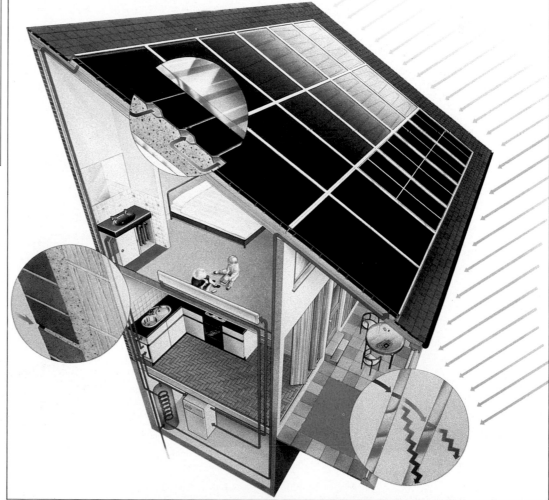

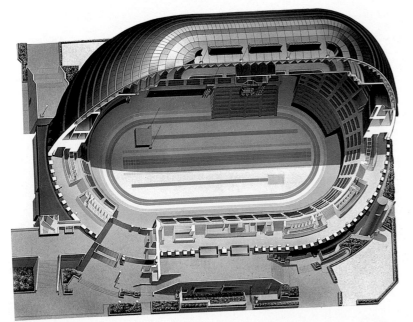

△635

273

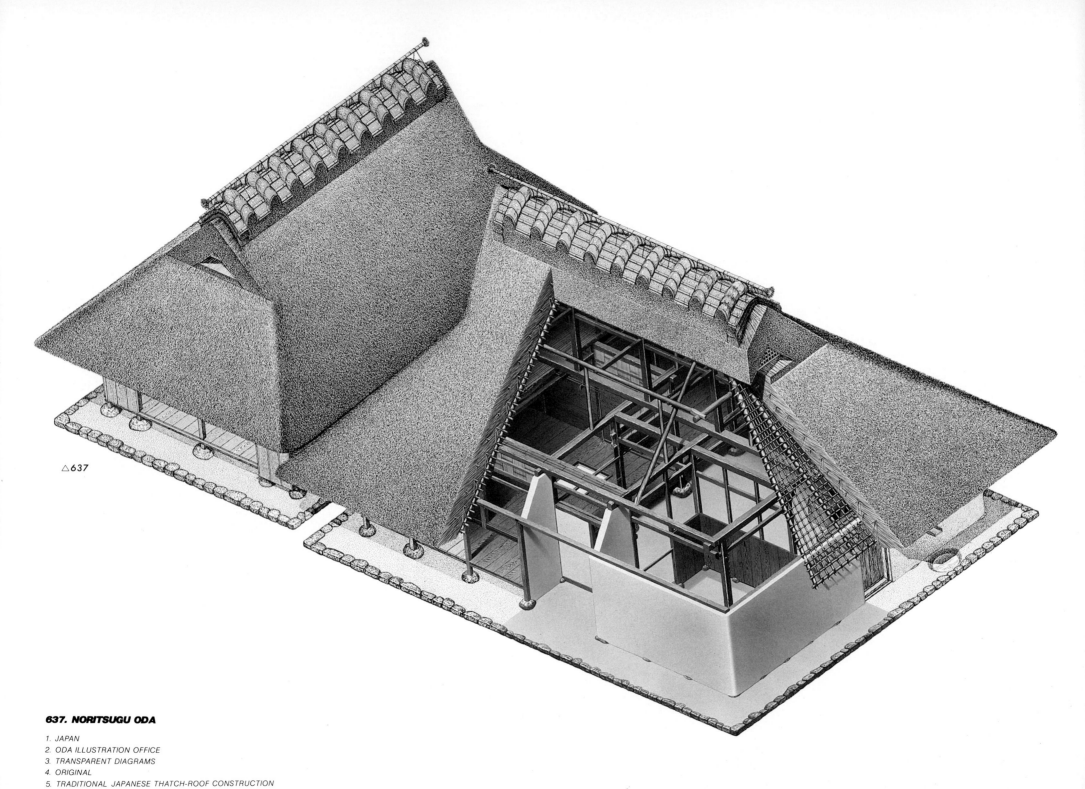

△637

637. NORITSUGU ODA

1. JAPAN
2. ODA ILLUSTRATION OFFICE
3. TRANSPARENT DIAGRAMS
4. ORIGINAL
5. TRADITIONAL JAPANESE THATCH-ROOF CONSTRUCTION

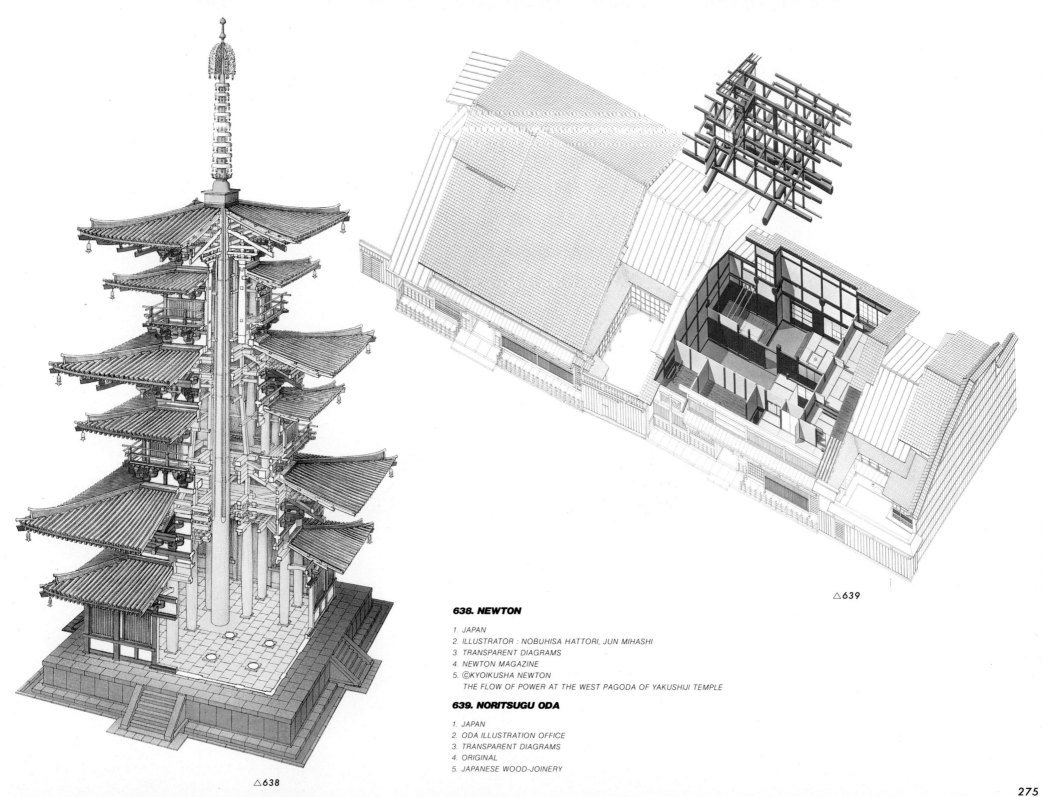

△638

638. NEWTON

1. JAPAN
2. ILLUSTRATOR : NOBUHISA HATTORI, JUN MIHASHI
3. TRANSPARENT DIAGRAMS
4. NEWTON MAGAZINE
5. ©KYOIKUSHA NEWTON
   THE FLOW OF POWER AT THE WEST PAGODA OF YAKUSHIJI TEMPLE

639. NORITSUGU ODA

1. JAPAN
2. ODA ILLUSTRATION OFFICE
3. TRANSPARENT DIAGRAMS
4. ORIGINAL
5. JAPANESE WOOD-JOINERY

△639

△640

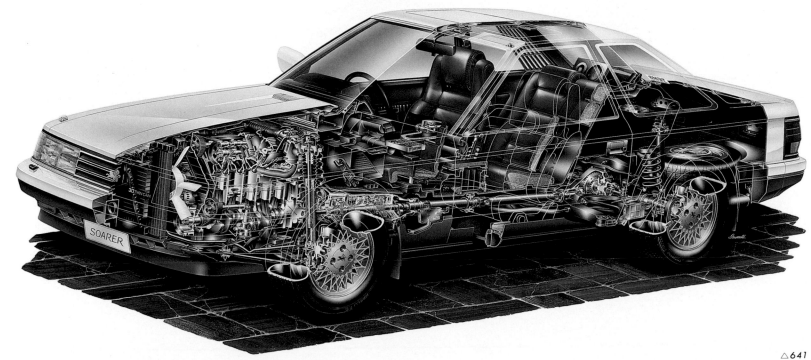

640, 641. TOYOTA MOTOR CORPORATION

1. JAPAN
2. ILLUSTRATION : INOMOTO YOSHIHIRO
3. TRANSPARENT DIAGRAMS
4. PAMPHLET
5. TOYOTA MOTOR CORPORATION
   CAR ENGINE TRANSPARENCIES

△641

△642

△643

△644

HONDA MOTOR CO., LTD. 645.

JAPAN 1.
HONDA MOTOR CO., LTD. 2.
TRANSPARENT DIAGRAMS 3.
PAMPHLET FOR "ACCORD/VIGOR" 4.
HONDA MOTOR CO., LTD. 5.
CAR ENGINE TRANSPARENCIES

644. GORO SHIMAOKA

1. JAPAN
3. TRANSPARENT DIAGRAMS
5. JAPAN AIR LINES
   PASSENGER CAPACITY TRANSPARENCY

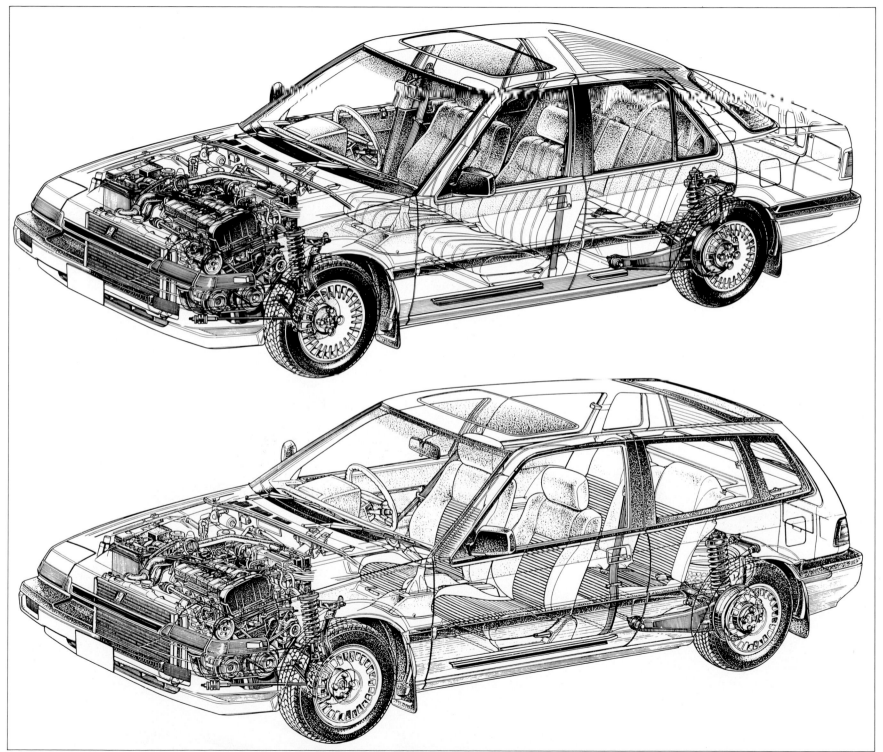

△646

△647   △648   △649

△650

650. MITSUBISHI MOTORS CORPORATION

1. JAPAN
2. MITSUBISHI MOTORS CORPORATION
3. TRANSPARENT DIAGRAMS
4. PAMPHLET/5. TIRE AND ENGINE TRANSPARENCY

651. SHIGEYUKI SAKAGUCHI

1. JAPAN
2. CLARK KENT ILLUSTRATION HOUSE
3. TRANSPARENT DIAGRAMS
4. CATALOGUE FOR FAUCETS
5. TABUCHI MANUFACTURING CO., LTD. /TEMPERATURE CONTROLLED WATER SUPPLY SYSTEM

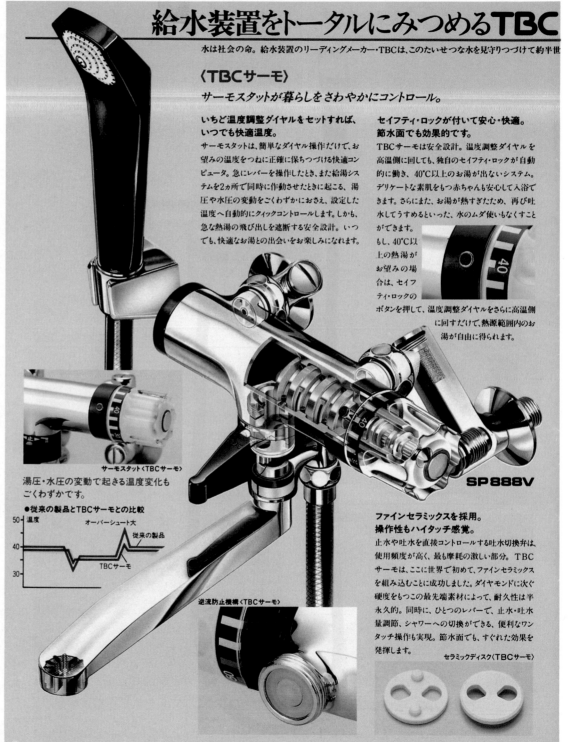

給水装置をトータルにみつめるTBC

水は社会の命。給水装置のリーディングメーカー・TBCは、このたいせつな水を見守りつづけて約半世

〈TBCサーモ〉

サーモスタットが暮らしをさわやかにコントロール。

いちど温度調整ダイヤルをセットすれば、いつでも快適温度。

サーモスタットは、簡単なダイヤル操作だけで、お望みの温度をつねに正確に保ちつづける快適コンピュータ。急にレバーを操作したとき、また給湯システムを2ヵ所で同時に作動させたときに起きる、湯圧や水圧の変動をごくわずかにおさえ、設定した温度へ自動的にクイックコントロールします。しかも、急な熱湯の飛び出しを遮断する安全設計。いつでも、快適なお湯との出会いをお楽しみになれます。

セイフティ・ロックが付いて安心・快適。節水面でも効果的です。

TBCサーモは安全設計。温度調整ダイヤルを高温側に回しても、独自のセイフティ・ロックが自動的に働き、40℃以上のお湯が出ないシステム。デリケートな素肌をもつ赤ちゃんも安心して入浴できます。さらにまた、お湯が熱すぎるため、再び吐水してうすめるといった、水のムダ使いもなくすことができます。

もし、40℃以上の熱湯がお望みの場合は、セイフティ・ロックのボタンを押して、温度調整ダイヤルをさらに高温側に回すだけで、熱源範囲内のお湯が自由に得られます。

サーモスタット〈TBCサーモ〉

湯圧・水圧の変動で起きる温度変化もごくわずかです。

●従来の製品とTBCサーモとの比較

SP888V

ファインセラミックスを採用。操作性もハイタッチ感覚。

止水や吐水を直接コントロールする吐水切換弁は、使用頻度が高く、最も摩耗の激しい部分。TBCサーモは、ここに世界で初めて、ファインセラミックスを組み込むことに成功しました。ダイヤモンドに次ぐ硬度をもつこの最先端素材によって、耐久性は半永久的。同時に、ひとつのレバーで、止水・吐水量調節、シャワーへの切換ができる、便利なワンタッチ操作も実現。節水面でも、すぐれた効果を発揮します。

逆流防止機構〈TBCサーモ〉

セラミックディスク〈TBCサーモ〉

△651

281

652,653.
HUBERT MAGNIER

FRANCE 1.
TRANSPARENT DIAGRAMS (652) 3.
ANALYSIS (653)
CATALOGUE 4.
WASHING MACHINE 5.
TRANSPARENCY (652)
EUROPHANE (653)

△652 △653

△655

△657

△656

△658

△659

△660

△661

△662

660. HONDA MOTOR CO., LTD.

1. JAPAN
2. HONDA MOTOR CO., LTD.
3. TRANSPARENT DIAGRAMS
4. CATALOGUE
5. MOTORCYCLE TRANSPARENCY

661. MAKOTO OUCHI

1. JAPAN
2. ELLIPSE GUIDE
3. TRANSPARENT DIAGRAMS
5. YAMAHA MOTOR LTD.
   MOTORCYCLE TRANSPARENCY

662. HIDEO HATSUGAI

1. JAPAN
2. TRANSPARENT DIAGRAMS
4. CATALOGUE FOR A VIDEO CASSETTE TAPE
5. VIDEO CASSETTE TRANSPARENCY

△663

△664

NORITSUGU ODA 663,664.

JAPAN 1.
ODA ILLUSTRATION OFFICE 2.
TRANSPARENT DIAGRAMS 3.
MATSUSHITA ELECTRIC INDUSTRIAL CO., LTD. 5.
PORTABLE CD PLAYER

△665

△666

△667　▽668

MINOLTA CAMERA CO., LTD. 666,667.

JAPAN 1.
MINOLTA CAMERA CO., LTD. 2.
TRANSPARENT DIAGRAMS 3.
CATALOGUE 4.
MINOLTA CAMERA STRUCTURE TRANSPARENCIES 5.

665. SHIGEYUKI SAKAGUCHI

1. JAPAN
2. CLARK KENT ILLUSTRATION HOUSE
3. TRANSPARENT DIAGRAMS
4. CATALOGUE FOR OVERSEAS MARKET
5. DAIHATSU MOTOR CO., LTD.
   DAIHATSU "ROCKY" MODEL ENGINE

GORO SHIMAOKA 668.

JAPAN 1.
TRANSPARENT DIAGRAMS 3.
COPY MACHINE TRANSPARENCY 5.

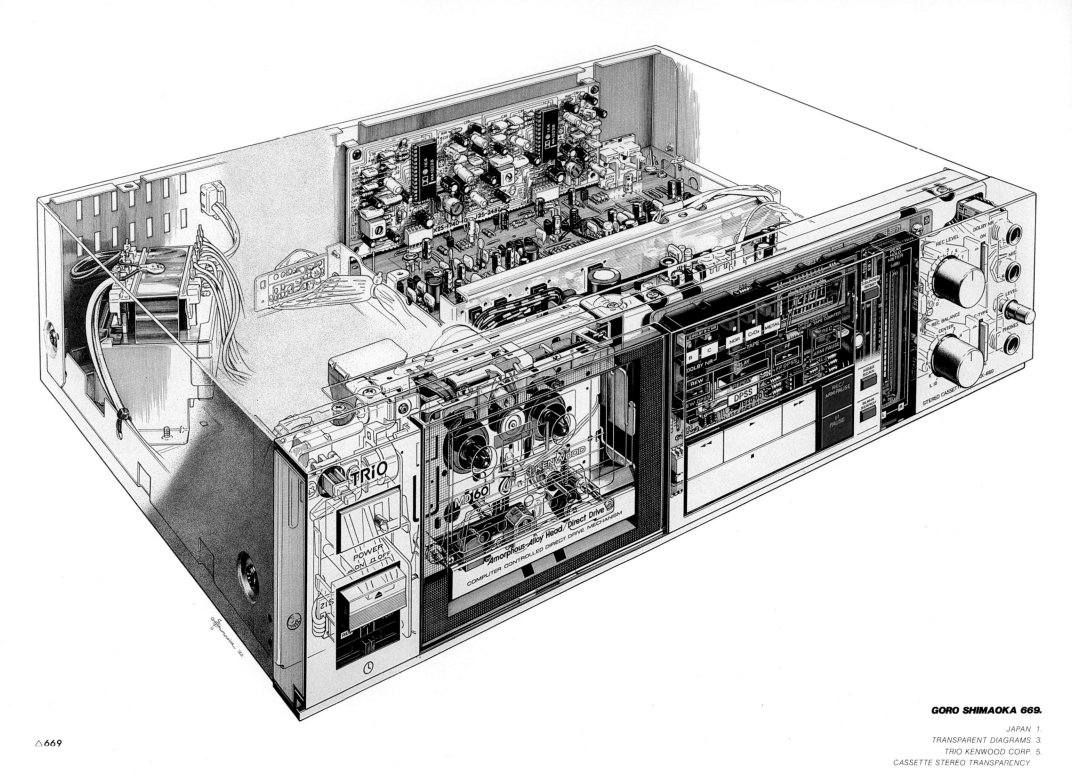

GORO SHIMAOKA 669.

JAPAN 1.
TRANSPARENT DIAGRAMS 3.
TRIO KENWOOD CORP. 5.
CASSETTE STEREO TRANSPARENCY

△669

290

670. HIDEO HATSUGAI

1. JAPAN
2. TRANSPARENT DIAGRAMS
4. CATALOGUE
5. VICTOR COMPANY OF JAPAN, LTD. CD PLAYER TRANSPARENCY

△670

グラフィック表示機構

グラフィック専用LSI（μPD7220A）

グラフィックVRAM
グラフィック専用LSI、大容量グラフィックVRAMの搭載で、1,120×780ドットの高精彩グラフィックを高速に処理。また拡張グラフィック処理機構（オプション）により、4,096色から16色を選んで表示できる高速カラーグラフィック処理が可能です。

セパレートタイプの本体
①5インチ1MバイトFDD2台内蔵型、②5インチFDD＋3.5インチ20Mバイトハードディスク内蔵型、③8インチFDD2台接続型、④8インチFDD接続＋20Mバイトハードディスク内蔵型の4タイプから選べる本体。自由度の高いセパレートタイプです。

カスタムVLSI
多数のカスタムVLSIの採用で、高性能ハードウェアをコンパクトに実現しました。

CPUにスーパーマイクロプロセッサ"80286"を搭載
本体の心臓部に16ビットCPUの最高峰"80286(8MHz)"を搭載。高速・強力な処理を実現します。

数値演算プロセッサ"80287"
"80287"を実装することにより、科学技術計算などが高速に処理できます。（オプション）

内蔵3.5インチ20Mバイトハードディスク

05mkⅡカード
N5200モデル05mkⅡで開発したアプリケーションソフトや多彩な流通ソフトが、N5200モデル07で活用できます。（オプション）

大容量1Mバイトメインメモリ
標準1Mバイトのメインメモリを実装しました。最大8Mバイトまで拡張可能。大容量・高速処理を可能にします。

立ち上げデバイス切換スイッチ

14インチ超高精彩ディスプレイ
大型で見やすい14インチの超高精彩タイプ。高精彩グラフィックをはじめ24×24ドットの美しい・明朝体日本語表示を実現しました。視線に合わせて見やすい方向・角度に向けられるチルト・スィーベル機構を採用。使用目的によって、カラー・グリーン・ペーパーホワイトの3タイプから選べます。

豊富なインタフェース
コミュニケーションインタフェース、プリンタインタフェースを実装しました。さらに4オプションでRS-232C、GP IBインタフェース、高速シリアルインタフェースなどさまざまなインタフェースをサポート。多彩なシステム構成を可能とします。

拡張スロット（最大4スロット）

超高速RAMファイル
本体の拡張スロットに1MバイトのRAMファイルを2つまで実装可能です。超高速アクセスが可能なファイルとして活用できます。（オプション）

最大160Mバイトのハードディスクシステム
増設用ハードディスクの接続により、最大160Mバイトの大規模ハードディスクシステムを実現しました。大量データの高速処理が可能となります。

多彩なプリンタ・周辺機器
日本語OAプリンタ、日本語カラーシリアルプリンタなど選べる11種のプリンタ。多機能電話機、イメージリーダ、OCRをはじめとする多彩な周辺機器が接続できます。

内蔵5インチ1Mバイトフロッピィディスク

JIS第1・第2水準日本語大容量ROM
高度な日本語処理を実現する日本語大容量ROMを内蔵しました。JIS第2水準までの漢字を含む約8,000種の文字表示が可能です。

JIS配列薄型キーボード
JIS配列薄型キーボードをはじめ、標準薄型キーボード、ワンタッチで項目入力ができるインテリジェントキーボードの中から用途に合わせて自由に選べます。

△671

671. SHIGEYUKI SAKAGUCHI

1. JAPAN
2. CLARK KENT TECHNICAL ILLUSTRATION HOUSE
3. SEGMENT CHARTS
4. ADVERTISEMENT IN NEWSPAPER
5. NEC CORP.
PERSONAL COMPUTER TRANSPARENCY

PHILLIP BRIAN EVANS 672.

NETHERLANDS 1.
ARCHER ART 2.
ANALYSIS 3.
RUNNING SHOE/SOLE TRANSPARENCY 5.

△672

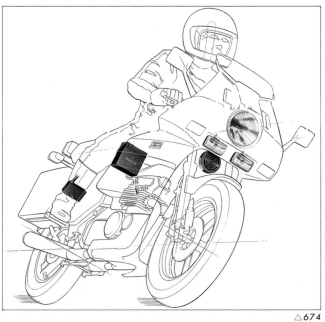

△673

△674

△676

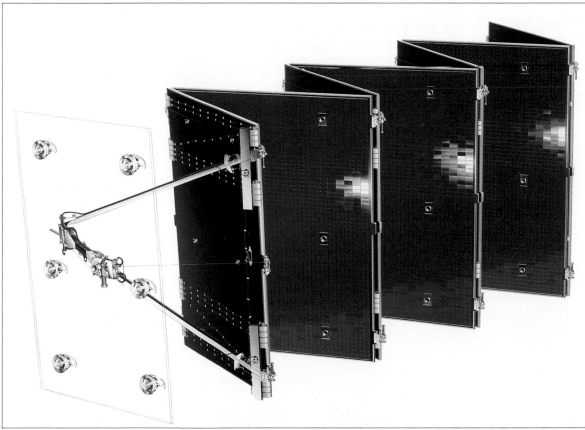

△675

COUNTOURIADIS-ORESTIS 673.

SPAIN 1.
ORESTIS-ESTUDIO 2.
ANALYSIS 3.
VIDEO CASSETTE TRANSPARENCY 5.

PHILLIP BRIAN EVANS 674, 675.

NETHERLANDS 1.
ARCHER ART 2.
TRANSPARENT DIAGRAMS (614) 3.
ANALYSIS (675)
BOSCH (674) 5.
SPACE SATELLITE (675)

FUJINE YANO 676.

JAPAN 1.
TRANSPARENT DIAGRAMS 3.
ISEKI 5.
TRACTOR ENGINE TRANSPARENCY

NIGEL HOLMES 677.

U.S.A. 1.
SEGMENT CHARTS 3.
NEW YORK TIMES (NEWSPAPER-USA) 5.
STEEL RADIAL TIRE STRUCTURE

SHIONOGI & CO., LTD. 678.

JAPAN 1.
SHIONOGI & CO., LTD. 2.
SEGMENT CHARTS 3.
MAGAZINE AND NEWSPAPER 4.
VITAMIN TABLET CONTENT BREAKDOWN 5.

Battle Rages Over Recall of Firestone 500's

By REGINALD STUART

DETROIT — "I think they have to bite the bullet or there's going to be a slow bloodletting."

Representative John E. Moss, Democrat of California, was talking about officials of the Firestone Tire and Rubber Company, which is embroiled in a hydra-headed controversy over the safety of its Firestone 500 steel-belted radial tires.

Tomorrow company representatives are scheduled to appear before the Department of Transportation in Washington to argue once again that the 23.6 million "500" radials produced since 1971 are safe and that the 13 million or so "500s" still on the road should not be recalled. The agency urged a total recall earlier this year in the wake of reports of more than 14,000 tire failures, 29 deaths, more than 50 injuries and hundreds of property-damage accidents involving the tires.

Two Federal agencies and a Congressional subcommittee chaired by Mr. Moss are investigating the alleged defects of the radials, and dozens of consumers are suing Firestone for millions of dollars.

The case is being watched closely by businessmen and analysts. The outcome could determine Firestone's financial future. It could bring to light what some believe are industry-wide safety and performance problems with radial tires. And it raises broader issues about the manner and extent of Government regulation of private corporations.

Firestone officials declined requests for interviews last week to discuss the controversy, explaining that they would have nothing to say prior to tomorrow's hearings. But the company has retained Washington attorney Clark Clifford, whose capacity as a negotiator was most recently tested when he represented former Office of Management and Budget Director Bert Lance before

Continued on Page 7

Reginald Stuart is a reporter based in Detroit for The New York Times.

More than 14,000 auto accidents have been reported involving the 500. One cause: adhesion problems between the steel belts and the tread above and the body ply below. Drawing shows separation, belts shredding.

Tread shoulder
Sidewall
Steel belts
Body ply

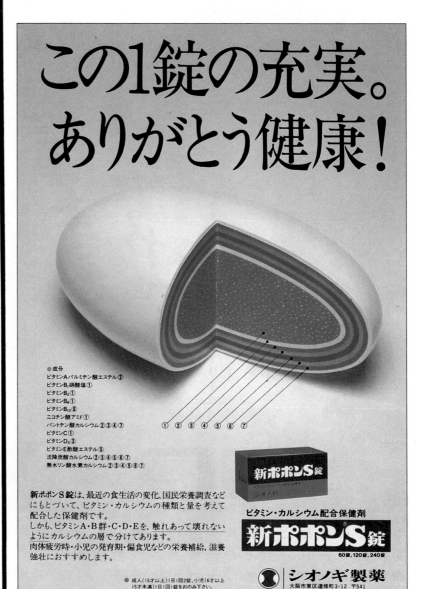

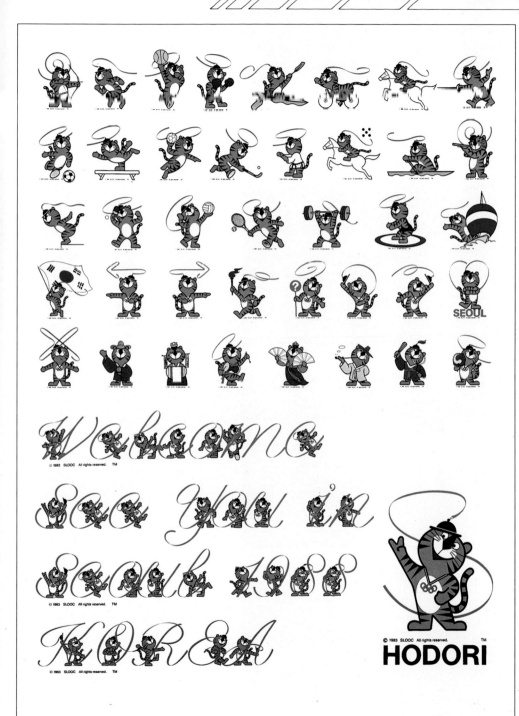

HODORI

△679

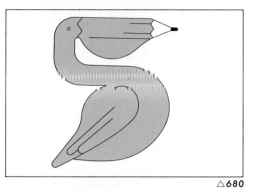

△680

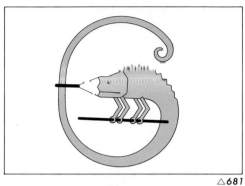

△681

△682

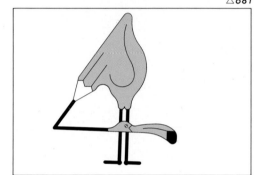

△683

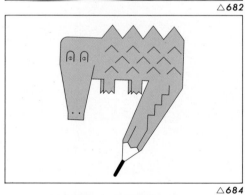

△684

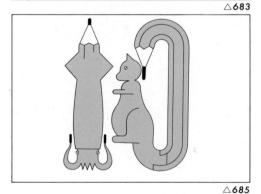

△685

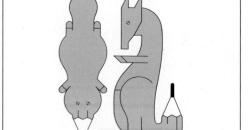

△686

HYUN KIM 679.

KOREA 1.
DESIGN PARK 2.
CREATIVE DIAGRAMS 3.
'88 SEOUL OLYMPIC MASCOT 4.
SEOUL OLYMPIC ORGANIZING COMMITTEE 5.

MAMORU BABA 680~686.

JAPAN 1.
CREATIVE DESIGN STUDIO GALLOP 2.
CREATIVE DIAGRAMS 3.

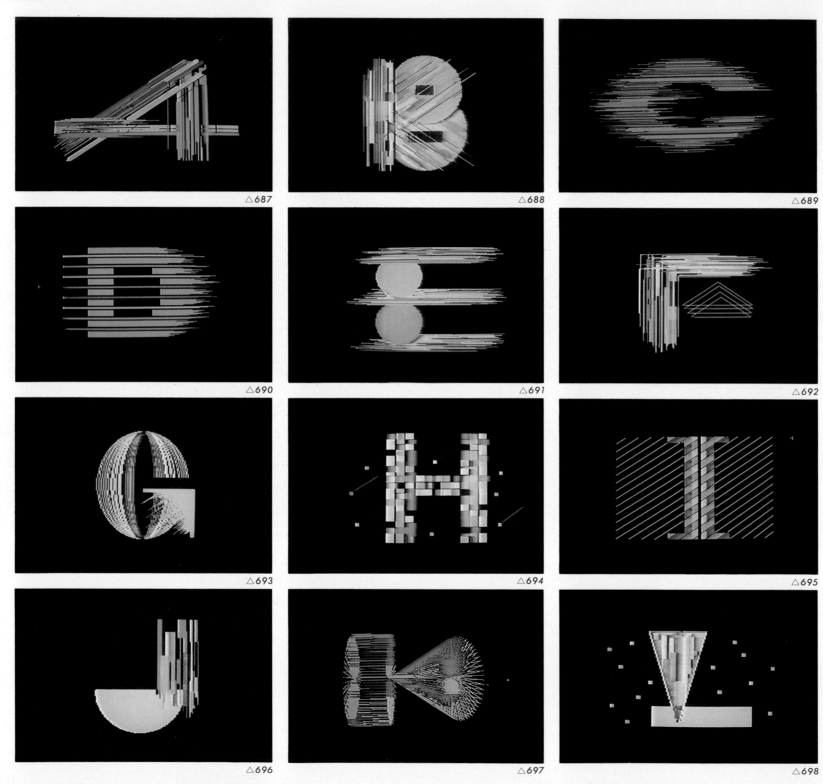

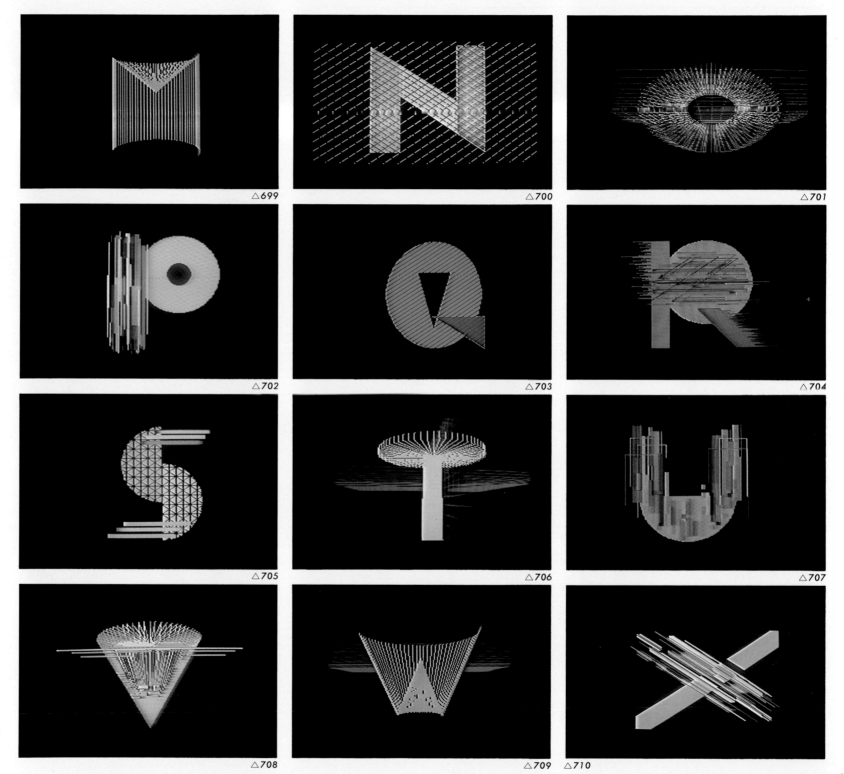

△699
△700
△701
△702
△703
△704
△705
△706
△707
△708
△709 △710

687～710 TADASHI SATO

1. JAPAN
2. NIPPON DESIGN CENTER
3. COMPUTER GRAPHICS-CREATIVE DIAGRAMS
4. EXHIBITION
5. ALPHABET

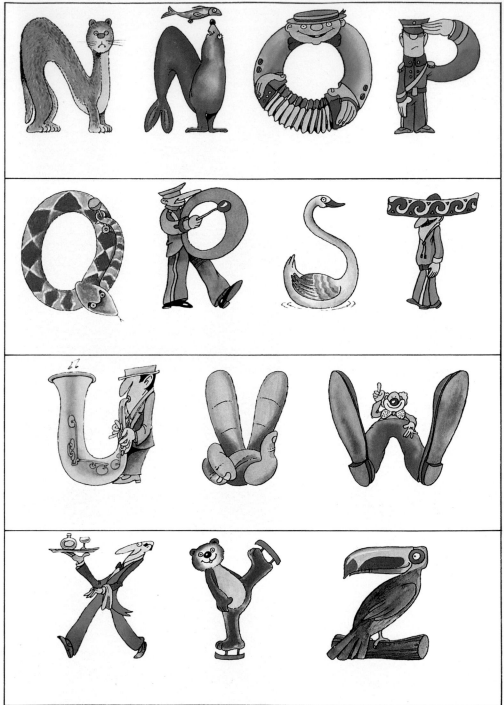

711,712 JORGE SALAS

1. SPAIN

2. SALAS & GRAF

3. CREATIVE DIAGRAMS

4. TEACHING AIO-READING

5. EDITORIAL ESPASA-CALPE, BOOK

△711

△712

713~716. JOZEF SUMICHRAST

1. U.S.A.
2. CREATIVE DIAGRAMS
4. POSTER
5. HEBREW ALPHABET

▽714   ▽715   ▽716   △713

Jozef Sumichrast

△717

△718

△719

△720 △721

JEFFREY A. SPEAR 717～721.

U.S.A. 1.
CREATIVE DIAGRAMS 3.
LOGOS 5.

722~725. FATTAL, VAHE

1. U.S.A.
2. FATTAL & COLLINS
3. CREATIVE DIAGRAMS
4. "AMERICAN LANGUAGE CENTER" LOGOMARK (722)
   POSTER FOR "MARKET INTEREST ACCOUNT" CAMPAIGN (725)
   LEAFLET (723 724)
5. UCLA EXTENSION (722)
   FIRST INTERSTATE BANK CORP. (723 725)

AMERICAN LANGUAGE CENTER

△722

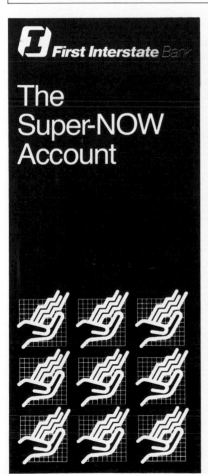

△723

△724

△725

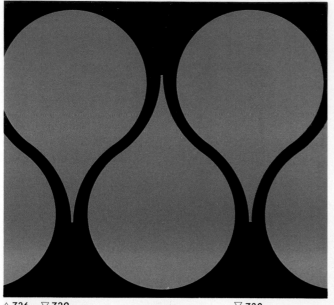

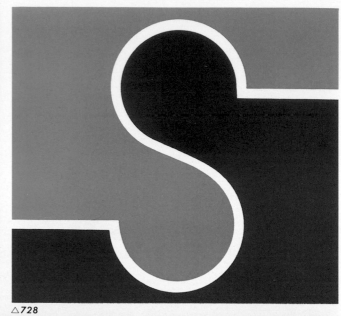

△726　▽729　　　　　　　　▽730　　△727　　　　　　　　　　　　　△728

TYPOGRAFIA
996　5　1985

△731

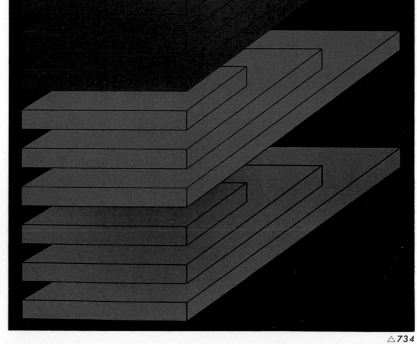

△732

726～728,734. FELIX BELTRAN

1. MEXICO
2. FELIX BELTRAN & ASSOCIADOS
3. CREATIVE DIAGRAMS
4. POSTERS
5. UNIVERSIDAD AUTONOMA METROPOLITANA, MEXICO (726～728)
   APPLE COMPLITERS, MEXICO (734)
   USE AND SAVE OIL (726)
   INDUSTRIAL UPKEEP (727)
   SYMBOLS COURSE (728)
   APPLE EDUCATIONAL PROGRAM (734)

729～733. VIADISLAV ROSTOKA

1. CZECHOSLOVAKIA
3. CREATIVE DIAGRAMS
4. TYPOGRAFIA/MAGAZINE COVER (729,730)
   DESIGN AROUND US / EXHIBITION SYMBOL (731)
   –RD– RAILWAY SYMBOL (733)
   COCK SYMBOL (732)
5. CZECHOSLOVAK PRINTING SOCIETY (729,730)
   SLOVAK NATIONAL GALLERY (731)
   NATIONAL RAILWAYS (733)
   INSTITUTE FOR POULTRY RESEARCH (732)

△733

△734

PREESCOLAR
santillana

CURSO 83-84

△735

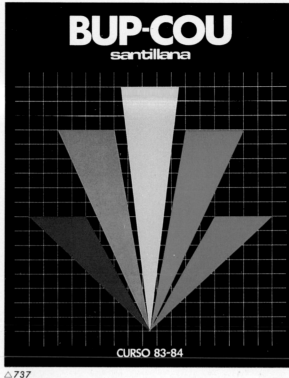

EGB
santillana

CURSO 83-84

△736

BUP-COU
santillana

CURSO 83-84

△737

**735~737.
ANTONIO DIAZ
ASOCIADOS S.A.**

1. SPAIN
2. ANTONIO DIAZ
   ASSOCIADOS S.A.
3. CREATIVE DIAGRAMS
4. FRONT PAGE OF
   CATALOGUE FOR
   PRESCHOOL
   (CHILDREN AGE 4-6)
   (735)
   FRONT PAGE OF
   CATALOGUE FOR
   MIDDLE SCHOOL
   (CHILDREN AGE 6-14)
   (736)
   FRONT PAGE OF
   CATALOGUE FOR
   HIGH SCHOOL
   (CHILDREN AGE 14-18)
   (737)
5. SANTILLANA, S.A.
   (SANTILIANA, S.A.,
   EDITORS SPECIALIZING
   IN SCHOOLBOOKS)

L

Creations

eight

Armstrong TYPOGRAPHY

STARFIRE

Baseball

BICYCLE

REVOLVER

SCHIZOPHRENIC   compulsive   INFERIORITY

GRANDIOSE DELUSIONS   introvert   MANIC DEPRESSIVE

△738

Touch

eight

THUNDER & LIGHTNING

STARSHIP

VICTORIA

interview

UP DATE

DUCA
FRANK DUCA PRESS

MOTOR CYCLE MANIA

BEELZEBUBS

NEW YORK FASHION INDUSTRY

THE GREAT BANK GOES BERSERK SWEEPSTAKES

△739

MAY ALLOW OR REQUIRE LOOKING AT IDEAS FROM BOTH SIDES.

© JOHN LANGDON 1985

Philosophy

IS A SCIENCE DEFINED AS THE PURSUIT, STUDY & LOVE OF WISDOM.

△740

**738~740 JOHN
WILBUR LANGDON**

1. U.S.A.
2. JOHN LANGDON
   DESIGN
3. CREATIVE DIAGRAMS
5. LOGOS

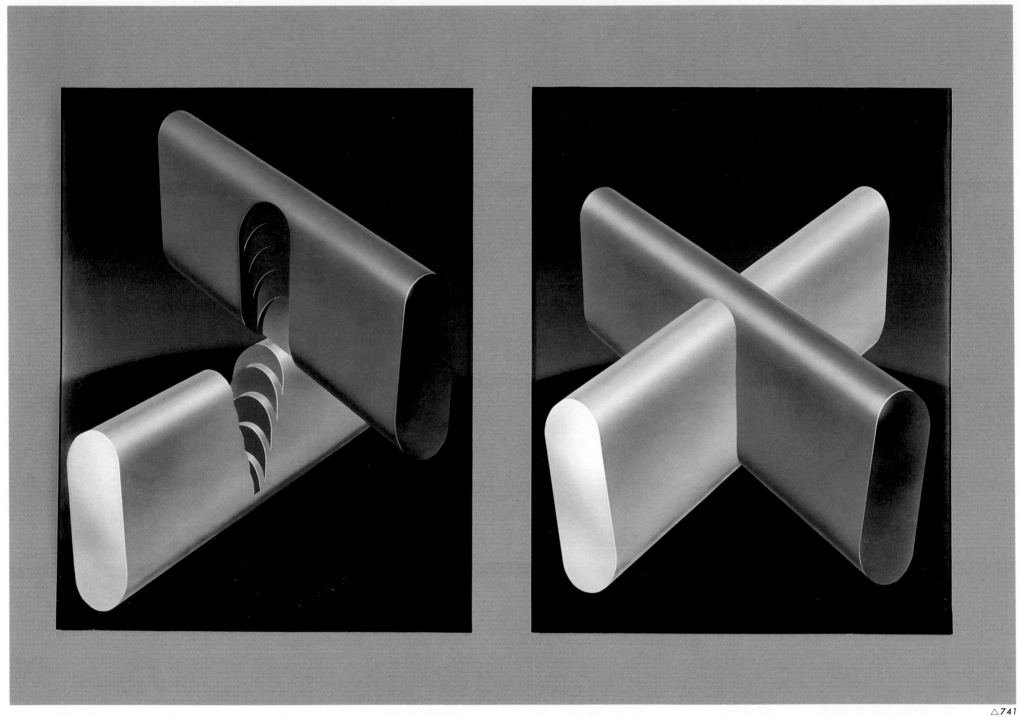

△741

741. DOUGLAS BOYD

1. U.S.A.   2. DOUGLAS BOYD DESIGN AND MARKETING   3. PICTORIAL DIAGRAMS   4. BROCHURE   5. XEROX COMPUTER SERVICES

INDEX

DIAGRAPHIC

INDEX

I Inagaki, Koichiro

Inagaki Associates
Suzuki Bldg.
2-12-14 Minamiaoyama
Minato-ku, Tokyo
Japan
P.37, 93
#89, 90, 223

Ishihara, Show

P.152–155
#329–332

Isokawa, Hiroshi

Dentsu Incorporated
1-11, Tsukiji
Chuo-ku, Tokyo 104
Japan
P.190, 191
#421, 422

Iwamoto, Yasunori

Nippon Univac Information
Systems Kaisha, Ltd.
Akasaka Twin Tower Main Bldg.
17-22 Akasaka 2-chome
Minato-ku, Tokyo
Japan
P.207
#468

Iwasaki, Kazuaki

Cosomos Origin Limited
4-20-26 Seiiku, Joto-ku
Osaka-shi, Osaka
Japan
P.104–107, 258
#237–242, 612

J Japan Air Lines Co., Ltd.

8F Tokyo Bldg.
2-7-3 Marunouchi, Chiyoda-ku
Tokyo, Japan
P.188, 189
#418–420

Japan Radio Co.

11-9-3 Yuraku-cho, Chiyoda-ku
Tokyo, Japan
P.232
#540, 541, 544

K Kardinata, Han

PT Citra Indonesia
JL Cibeber IV/1 Block Q-3
Kebayoran Baru
Jakarta 12180
Indonesia
P.16, 17
#32–34

Kawakita, Hideya

Japan Belier Art Center Inc.
1-16-3 Ginza
Chuo-ku, Tokyo
Japan
P.164, 165
#352, 353

Kim, Hyun

Design Park
501 LSY Bldg.
28-18 Phildong-3ka
Chung-ku, Seoul
Korea
P.295
#679

K Kingder, Hwong

2f No. 1 Lane 790-24 Sec 5
Chung Shaug E. Rd.
Taiwan, R.O.C.
P.142, 143
#311–315

Kojitani, Hiroshi

Kojitani-Irie Inc.
3F Dai-ni Seihou Bldg.
3-5-2 Kitaaoyama
Minato-ku, Tokyo
Japan
P.58, 179
#159, 400

Kovacevic, Nino

61000 Ljublijana
Ob Zici 13
Yugoslavia
P.14, 15, 53, 71, 130, 131
#28–31, 148–150, 185, 288–298

Kunito, Teruyuki

V.T.A
5-13-14 Koishikawa
Bunkyo-ku, Tokyo
Japan
P.126, 238, 239, 252
#279, 561–566, 595

L Langdon, John Wilbur

John Langdon Design
106 S. Marion Avenue
Wenonah, New Jersey 08090
USA
P.303
#738–740

L Lertola, Joe

c/o Inagaki Associates
Suzuki Bldg.
2-12-14 Minamiaoyama
Minato-ku, Tokyo
Japan
P.127
#281

Lopez, Roberto

Circuito Diplomaticos 15-A
Ciudad Satelite
Naucalpan Edo. de Mexico
53100 Mexico
P.128
#283, 284

M MINOLTA Camera Co., Ltd.

Sekaiboueki-centar Bldg.
2-4-1 Hamamatsu-cho
Minato-ku, Tokyo
Japan
P.289
#666, 667

Magnier, Hubert

11 Avenue Danielle Casanova
93360 Neuilly-Plaisance
France
P.282, 283
#652–654

Mitsubishi Motors Corporation

5-33-8 Shiba
Minato-ku, Tokyo
Japan
P.280, 281
#647–650

The Diagram Group

Diagram Visual Information Ltd.
195 Kentish Town Road
London NW5
England
P.22–27, 37, 68, 186, 187, 412, 417
#46–64, 91–93, 179–181, 412, 417

Thomas, Gregory

CBS Television Network
6255 Sunset Blvd. Suite 2206
Los Angeles, California 90028
USA
P.200, 210, 211
#449, 477–479, 480, 481, 483

Tomoda, Minoru

Tomoda Minoru Illustration Off
Nakagin B1.
8-11-9 Ginza
Chuoku, Tokyo
Japan
P.134, 137
#302, 305, 306

Tomori, Ukei

2-36-5 Bessho
Urawa-shi, Saitama
Japan
P.132, 133, 136, 264, 265, 268, 269
#299–301, 304, 620, 621, 623, 630

J Unno, Yukihiro/Okada,

Takehiko/Konaka, Isao
c/o Chic et Choc
308 Daikanyama Mansion
4-1 Daikanyama
Shibuya-ku, Tokyo
Japan
P.138
#307

V VU S.R.L.

Via Manzoni 39
20121 Milano
Italy
P.59
#162

Varela, Marcelo

Lazzeretti, Laura
Estudio Hache S.R.L.
Arcos 2672
1428 Buenos Aires
Republica Argentina
P.129
#287

W Wissing, Benno/Stegmeyer, John

The Wissing Gengler Group, Inc.
40 Hay St.
Providence, Rhode Island 02903
USA
P.4, 8, 21, 140, 141
#4, 14, 15, 45, 309, 310

Wright, Marjo R.

88c Road 20, Bahay Toro
Project 8, Quezon City
Philippines
P.21
#44

Y Y.D.I.

204 Vip Shinjuku-gyoen
31 Daikyo-cho
Shinjuku-ku, Tokyo
Japan
P.108, 236, 237, 254, 255
#244, 555–560, 600–603

Y Yano, Fujine

9-7-20 Higashikaigan Kita
Chigasaki-shi, Kanagawa
Japan
P.277, 280, 293
#642, 643, 646, 649, 676

JCA ANNUAL 6

All Good Things Must Come to an End ...
JCA illustration annuals will never be the same again. For 10 years JCA annuals have set an unmatchable standard of excellence and have become the directory of international talent. That was a good century for JCA, but we're putting an end to it ... with JCA-6, WHERE THE GREAT THINGS START!
Our next annual will surpass any annual you've seen before, even previous JCA publications. Larger pages and more frequent issues will help JCA-6 and its successors end the time and distance barriers in the international art market. JCA-6 will be the ultimate directory of international talent, making all other sources obsolete. You can't afford to miss it!

長い間皆様に親しんで頂いたJCA ANNUALが、昨年迎えた10周年を皮切りに更にワイドな年鑑として、ビッグなスケールで編算・紹介されています。作品の厳選など、内容の充実を計ると共に、更に拡がるクライアンツニーズに敏速にお応えする為に発刊サイクルも縮少されました。JCAが自身をもってお届けするJCA ANNUAL第6弾を、是非あなたのアイデアソースとして、又、作品選定のディレクトリーとしてお使い下さい。

JCA年鑑6仕様内容：
- ●総作品数：1400点
- ●総ページ数：528頁
- ●色：フルカラー
- ●230㎜×300㎜
- ●上製本、ハードカバー付。
- ●総重量：3.0kg内外

INTERNATIONAL PHOTOGRAPHY EXPOSED 2

When the first edition of Commercial Photography Exposed was released to the world in 1983, the praise was universally approving. CPE's triumph has generated nothing but the highest expectations for its successor, International Photography Exposed. Today those expectations have been met and surpassed! The powerful ICO network has again gathered the world's finest commercial photography. IPE-II, with improved binding and layouts, is the ultimate showcase for these outstanding works.

Let this guide to the world's premier photographic talent be your inspiration to new levels of excellence in commercial art!

"CPE"の第1巻が初めて皆さまの前に登場したのは2年前の1983年。発刊当初より各方面で絶賛を博し、大きな反響を呼ぶと共に、早くから"IPE-2"発刊への期待が数多く寄せられました。そしていま、ICOネットワークの総力を結集し前号にも勝る充実した内容と、装丁、レイアウト、など装いも新たにお届けいたします。タイトルも一新し、"IPE"と改めました。

この"IPE-2"に収録された世界のトップコマーシャル・フォトグラファーの作品1つ、1つが大きな刺戟となって、あなたの創造性が触発されたとき、より素晴らしいコマーシャルアートが生まれることでしょう。

● IPE2 仕様内容　　● サイズ：303㎜×230㎜　　● 色：フルカラー
● 総頁数：464頁　　● 総重量：3kg内外　　● 上製本・ハードカバー付

THE GOLDEN IPE

The Golden International Photography Exposed

A special commemorative edition of IPE is going to be published in Spring 1987. It has been named The GOLDEN IPE as it commemorates ICO members numbering over 4,000 this year.

Only those International Photographers who meet the selection requirements will be entitled to be included in this specially packaged, metallic-gold, boxed edition. We are eagerly waiting to see who will rise in the field of worldwide, Commercial Photography to be acclaimed in International circles next Spring.

So let us all look forward to The GOLDEN IPE from JCA which will be compiled with the worldwide co-operation of the ICO bureaus and the JCA bureaus in 32 cities in Japan.

「ゴールデンIPE」発刊決定

ICOメンバー総勢4000名突破記念として来春1987年度お目見えします。

その名も特別発刊記念にふさわしく「ゴールデンIPE」と命名されました。

世界の本当に選び抜かれたフォトグラファーだけが、ボックス型のこの金の箱の中に収録される権利を勝ち取ることができます。

さて来春、世界中のコマーシャルマーケットにはばたくインターナショナルップフォトグラファーは誰でしょう。

全ICOビュロー、32地点に及ぶ日本国内JCAビューローが総力を結集したこの「ゴールデンIPE」に是非ご期待下さい。

なお詳しいお問い合わせは㈱JCA出版へ。

LES PACKAGINGS DU MONDE
FEATURING CORPORATE & BRAND IDENTITY

noAH

DIRECTORY OF INTERNATIONAL PACKAGE DESIGN

I

The long awaited package design annual "noAH", featuring works by the world's top packaging creators, is now complete!
This special edition is a full-color display of the latest works of designers from over twenty-four countries. In addition, top design studios' work concepts, flow charts, corporate identities, and other valuable information items have been included in our newest edition "noAH" is truly the world's most unique and effective international package design publication.

Number of pages: 464 pages　　*Color: Full-color*
Size: 230mm × 300mm　　*Weight: Approx. 2.8kg*
Hard-covered binding with vinyl cover　*Price: ¥20,000, $84.00 (US)*

待望の世界のトップパッケージデザインアーティスト達によるパッケージデザイン年鑑"noAH"が完成しました。本書は、24ヵ国を越える国々の近代的パッケージデザインスタジオとそのデザイナー達の最新作を一堂に網羅し、ワークフローやCI技法を取り入れた彼ら一流のワークコンセプトを集録致しました。皆様のご期待を裏切る事なく、本書が世界中で珍重されるパッケージデザイン業界へのインターナショナルスーパーエディションとしてふさわしい年鑑だと確信しております。

noAH パッケージデザイン年鑑の仕様内容.
● 総ページ数：496頁　　　　　● 色：フルカラー
● サイズ：230㎜×300㎜　　　● 総重量：2.8kg　内外
● 上製本：ビニールカバー付　● 定価：20,000円 US $ 84.00

EPILOGUE

We now come to the end of our trip through the world of DIA-GRAPHICS. We hope our publication has been an interesting as well as useful collection of communication media for both clients and designers.

At JCA PRESS Inc., we have a firm commitment; to produce the highest quality annuals, to promote effective communication between our creators and clients, and to discover and expose new talent. It is our wish to thank all those who were instrumental in the achievement of this book; the ICO bureaus and business affiliates, the artists, and all the people who in some way contributed to this annual.

Special thanks goes to the following:
Edward Archer (Holland), Hildegard Kron, Bill Brown, Howard Goldstein (USA), Vladislav Stransky (Switzerland), Johanna Bradshaw (England), Giorgio Tavacchi (Italy), Gordon Tani (USA), Gonzalez Teja (Spain), Marjo Wright, Desiree Wright (Philippines), Eiko Sekine (France), Nura Aiden Silver (Canada), Ric Noyle, Koichi Yanagizawa (USA), Tsugihiko Hayakawa, Haruhiko Suzaki, Toru Hirayoshi, Haruyoshi Nagumo, Ukei Tomori, Kazuhiro Anzai, Sin Yamazaki, Tadashi Masuda, Yuji Takeda (Japan).

The companies which cooperated:
OMNI Publications, International Ltd. (NY), Dentsu Inc., Nippon Graphic Map, Chic et choc, YDI Inc., Tokyo Designers Institute, Kyoiku-sha, Gakken, NHK.

Diagraphics

July 30, 1986

JCA Press Inc.

Planning & Editorial Staff
Kou Takeishi, Takaaki Mamiya, Koichi Nakazawa, Takamichi Homma, Masaki Matsuura, Kenichiro Sakurai, Yuka Yamaguchi

Translation Staff
Micky H. Sakhrani, Lynley Ogilvie, Ikue Sekido, Sanae Tokura, Susie Wells, Osamu Watanabe

Front Cover Photo
Benno Vissing, John Stegmever, Yasushi Okita, Eitetsu Nozawa, Peter Skalar, Ukei Tomori, Newton, Etsuko Takahashi, Art Kobo, Kazuho Ito

Title Page Calligraphy
Koson Mochizuki (deceased)

Production Assistance
International Creators' Organization (ICO) Bureaus, JCA Bureaus, Sun Press Co., Ltd., Shun Koubou & Aspect Design Space

JCA Headquarters
Japan Creators' Association (JCA)
Umehara Bldg. 4th Floor, 3-1-29 Roppongi, Minato-ku, Tokyo, Japan
Tel: (03) 582-4201　Fax: (03) 586-4018

Publisher: JCA Press Inc.
5-12-3 Higashikaigan Kita, Chigasaki, Kanagawa, Japan
Tel: 0467-85-2725　Fax: 0467-86-1501
President: Norio Mochizuki

Printer: Mitsumura Printing Co.

わたくしどもは、ダイヤグラム的表現法という名の世界旅行を終えてその帰途につきました。

ユーザーとデザイナーとの間のコミュニケーションを発展させた媒体である当年鑑が、しかるべき成果を収めたものと期待しております。

わたくしどもの目標は、当初のものと何ら変わっておりません。つまり、選び抜かれたアーチスト、及びクライアンツに対し、最高の年鑑をお届けすること、また、アーチスト、クライアンツ間の効果的コミュニケーションの促進をはかること、そして、新しい才能の発見、普及に努めることです。

当年鑑の出版にあたり、ご協力下さいました皆様方に、心より感謝申し上げます。

ICOビューロー及びICOビジネス提携者、アーチスト、そして各方面においてご協力いただいた方々、これらすべての皆様の貢献によって〝ダイヤグラフィックス〟が完成したのです。

チーフディレクター　武石　幸

下記の皆様には、多大なるご協力を承わりました。ここに私共の心からの感謝の意を表しますと共に、そのご芳名を記し、お礼のことばに変えさせていただきます。

エドワード・アーチャー様（オランダ）ヒルディガード・クローン様、ビル・ブラウン様、ハワード・ゴールドステイン様（USA）、ブラディスラ・ストランスキー様（スイス）ジョアンナ・ブラッドショー様（イギリス）ジョージオ・タバッチ様（イタリア）ゴードン・谷様（USA）テジャー・ゴンザレス様（スペイン）マージョ・ライト、デジレ・ライト様（フィリッピン）関根英子様（フランス）ヌラ・アイディーン様（カナダ）リック・ノエル様（USA）柳沢弘一様（USA）早川次彦様、州嵩晴彦様、平良徹様、南雲治喜様、友利宇景様、安斉和博様、山崎晨様、増田正様、武田雄二様、（日本）　（順不同）

ご協力いただいた企業

オムニ・パブリケーション インターナショナル㈱（NY）、㈱電通、日本グラフィックマップ㈱、シック・エ・ショック、東京デザイナー学院、㈱教育社、㈱YDI、㈱学研、NHK、

DIAGRAPHICS

発刊年月日／1986年7月30日
発行所／JCA出版
企画・編集・制作スタッフ／
武石　幸・間宮　敬明・中沢　浩一・本間　隆道・松浦　正貴・桜井謙一郎・山口　由香
翻訳スタッフ／
ミッキー　サカラニ・リンリー オギルビー・関戸　郁恵・戸倉　早苗・スージー・ウェルズ・渡辺　修
表紙作品／
ベンノウィッシング・ジョンステグメバー・ヤシオキタ・エイテツノザワ・ピーター　スカラル・友利　宇景・ニュートン・高橋　悦子・アート工房・伊藤　一穂
扉の書／望月　香邨（故人）
制作協力／インターナショナル　クリエイターズ機構（ICO）ビューローズ、JCAビューローズ、㈱サンプレス、瞬工房＆アスペクトデザインスペース
JCA本部／日本クリエイターズ協会〈JCA〉東京都港区六本木3-1-29（梅原ビル4F）
Tel：（0467）85-2725　Fax：（0467）86-1501
発行人／望月　紀男
印刷・製版／㈱光村原色版印刷所